I may have entered my middle years, but my head is still full of thoughts... Like, if I go over this hill, a mysterious village will greet my eyes, or if I walk along a street with strong sunlight casting dark shadows, it'll be the year 1945. Or if I follow this street, it will lead to another world. That's why I like to go to new towns. My imagination really takes off early in the afternoon on a bright day. Some may consider that escaping reality——and maybe it is——but it builds my enthusiasm. Now on to the layouts I'm working on today!

—HIROSHI SHIIBASHI,
2011

HIROSHI SHIIBASHI debuted in BUSINESS JUMP magazine with *Aratama*. NURA: RISE OF THE YOKAI CLAN is his breakout hit. He was an assistant to manga artist Hirohiko Araki, the creator of *Jojo's Bizarre Adventure*. *Steel Ball Run* by Araki is one of his favorite manga.

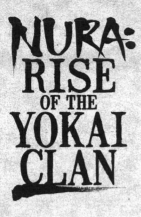

NURA: RISE OF THE YOKAI CLAN
VOLUME 19
SHONEN JUMP Manga Edition

Story and Art by HIROSHI SHIIBASHI

Translation – John Werry
Touch-up Art and Lettering – Annaliese Christman
Graphics and Cover Design – Fawn Lau
Editor – Megan Bates

Printed in Canada

Published by VIZ Media, LLC
P.O. Box 77010
San Francisco, CA 94107

10 9 8 7 6 5 4 3 2 1
First printing, February 2014

WITHDRAWN

www.viz.com   www.shonenjump.com

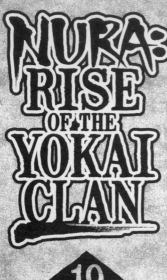

NURA: RISE OF THE YOKAI CLAN

19

GHOST STORY: KUDAN

STORY AND ART BY
HIROSHI SHIIBASHI

CHARACTERS

RIHAN NURA

Rikuo's father. Under his leadership as Second Heir, the Nura clan flourished. He was killed by his ex-wife Yamabuki-Otome, who was under Nue's control. Rikuo was just a young child at the time.

RIKUO NURA

Though he appears to be a human boy, he's actually the grandson of Nurarihyon, a yokai. His grandfather's blood makes him one-quarter yokai, and he transforms into a yokai at times.

KIYOTSUGU

Rikuo's classmate. He has adored yokai ever since he was saved by Rikuo in his yokai form, leading him to form the Kiyojuji Paranormal Patrol.

KANA IENAGA

Rikuo's classmate and a childhood friend. Even though she hates scary things, she's a member of the Kiyojuji Paranormal Patrol for some reason.

KUROTABO

A Nura clan yokai, also known as the Father of Destruction. One of the clan's best warriors, he hides a healthy arsenal of lethal weapons under his priest's robe. He teaches Rikuo an Equip technique called Meld.

YUKI-ONNA

A yokai of the Nura clan who is in charge of looking after Rikuo. She disguises herself as a human and attends the same school as Rikuo to protect him from danger. When in human form, she goes by the name Tsurara Oikawa. Her mother is Setsura.

OTOME YAMABUKI

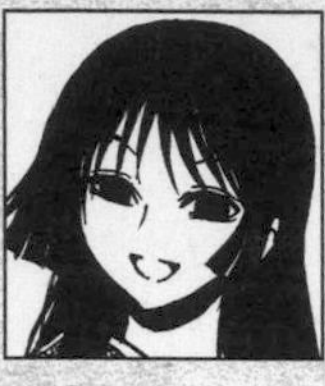

A kindhearted yokai who is Rihan's first wife. After learning that she could not bear children, she left the Nura clan and died. However, Nura used a spell to resurrect her and she became a vessel for Hagoromo-Gitsune.

NURARIHYON

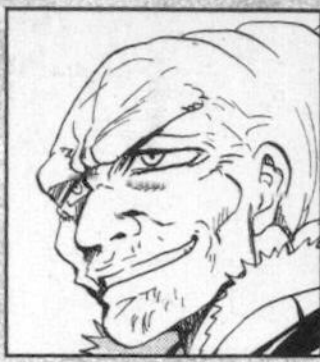

Rikuo's grandfather and the Lord of Pandemonium. To prepare for all-out war with Nue, he intends to pass leadership of the Nura clan—a powerful yokai consortium—to Rikuo. He's a mischievous sort.

YANAGIDA

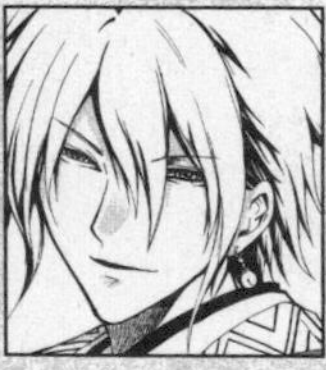

A yokai of the Hundred Stories clan who collects strange experiences from various places to include as part of the Hundred Stories. He kidnaps Torii and attempts to incorporate her into a story, but Kurotabo stops it.

GOROZAEMON SANMOTO

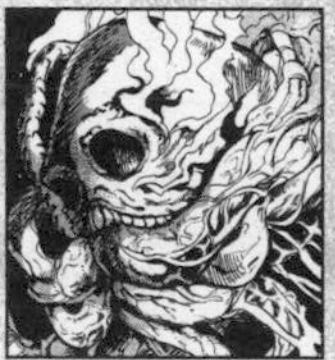

Has a history with Rihan and holds a grudge against the Nura clan. In order to take revenge against Rihan, he manipulates Nue into using Yamabuki-Otome. He leads the Hundred Stories clan.

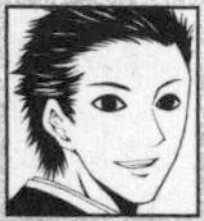

ENCHO

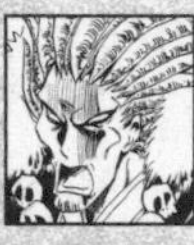

AOTABO

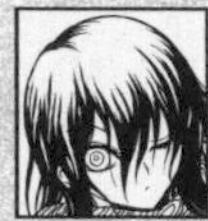

SETSURA

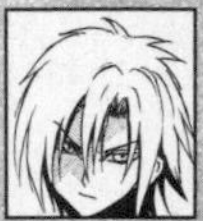

KUBINASHI

STORY SO FAR

Rikuo Nura is a seventh-grader at Ukiyoe Middle School. At a glance, he appears to be just another average, normal boy. But he's actually the grandson of the yokai Overlord Nurarihyon. He's also the Third Heir of the powerful Nura clan. He spends his days in hopes that he will someday become a great yakuza boss who leads a Hundred Demons.

During the Edo Period, an ayakashi created by someone was attacking people, and Rihan, the Second Heir of the Nura clan, was in pursuit. One night, he was attacked by an assassin named Kurotabo who was sent by his opponent, but he easily defeated him. When more assassins appeared, however, he ran into trouble and plunged into the river...

Deceiving his enemies, Rihan secretly investigated them and determined the location of Sanmoto, the overlord of the Hundred Stories clan who was pulling the strings. Rihan launched an attack, finally bringing him face to face with Sanmoto! Rihan was furious as he led the Nura clan, and the Hundred Stories clan crumbled before them. In a tight spot, Sanmoto elected to become a yokai, thereby completing the Hundred Stories clan.

As an ayakashi, Sanmoto has split into separate entities representing his various body parts, and now he attacks the people of the city. The Nura clan tries to address the situation, but they cannot handle the multiplying ayakashi generated by Sanmoto, and the city's children fall into danger. Then Kurotabo appears!

TABLE OF CONTENTS

NURA:RISE OF THE YOKAI CLAN

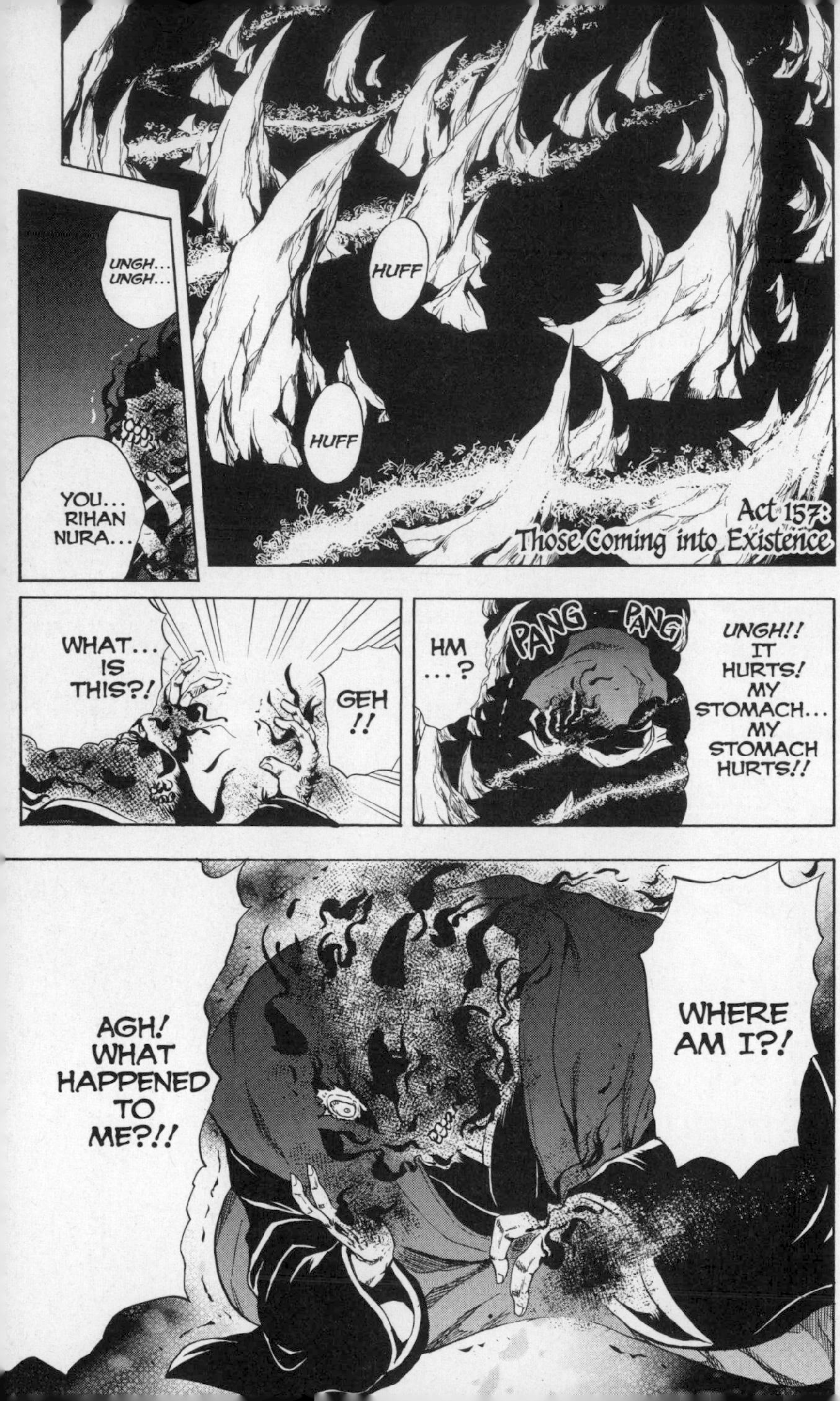
HUFF
HUFF
Act 157: Those Coming into Existence
UNGH... UNGH...
YOU... RIHAN NURA...
UNGH!! IT HURTS! MY STOMACH... MY STOMACH HURTS!!
PANG PANG
HM ...?
GEH !!
WHAT... IS THIS?!
WHERE AM I?!
AGH! WHAT HAPPENED TO ME?!!

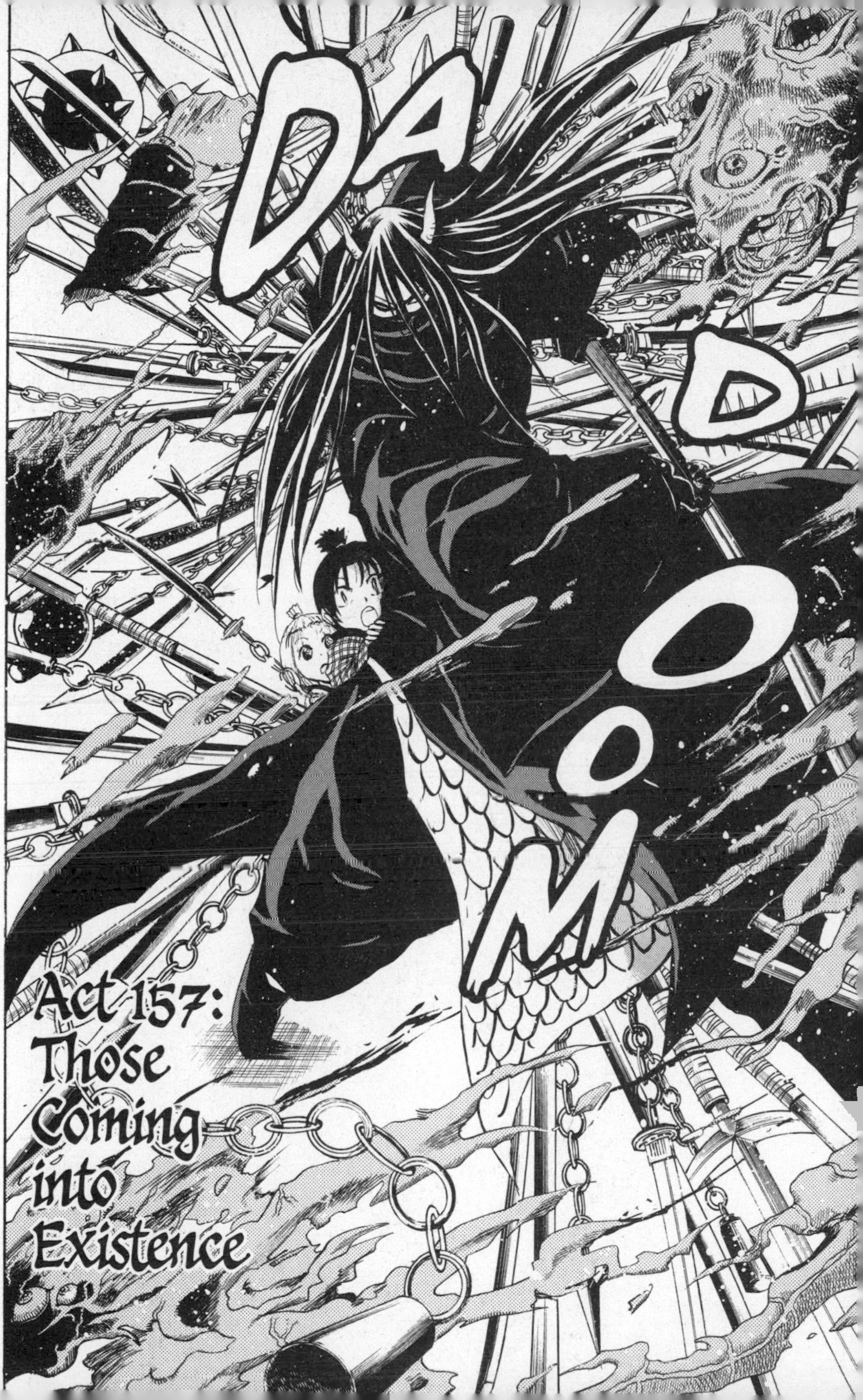
DA
DOOM
Act 157: Those Coming into Existence

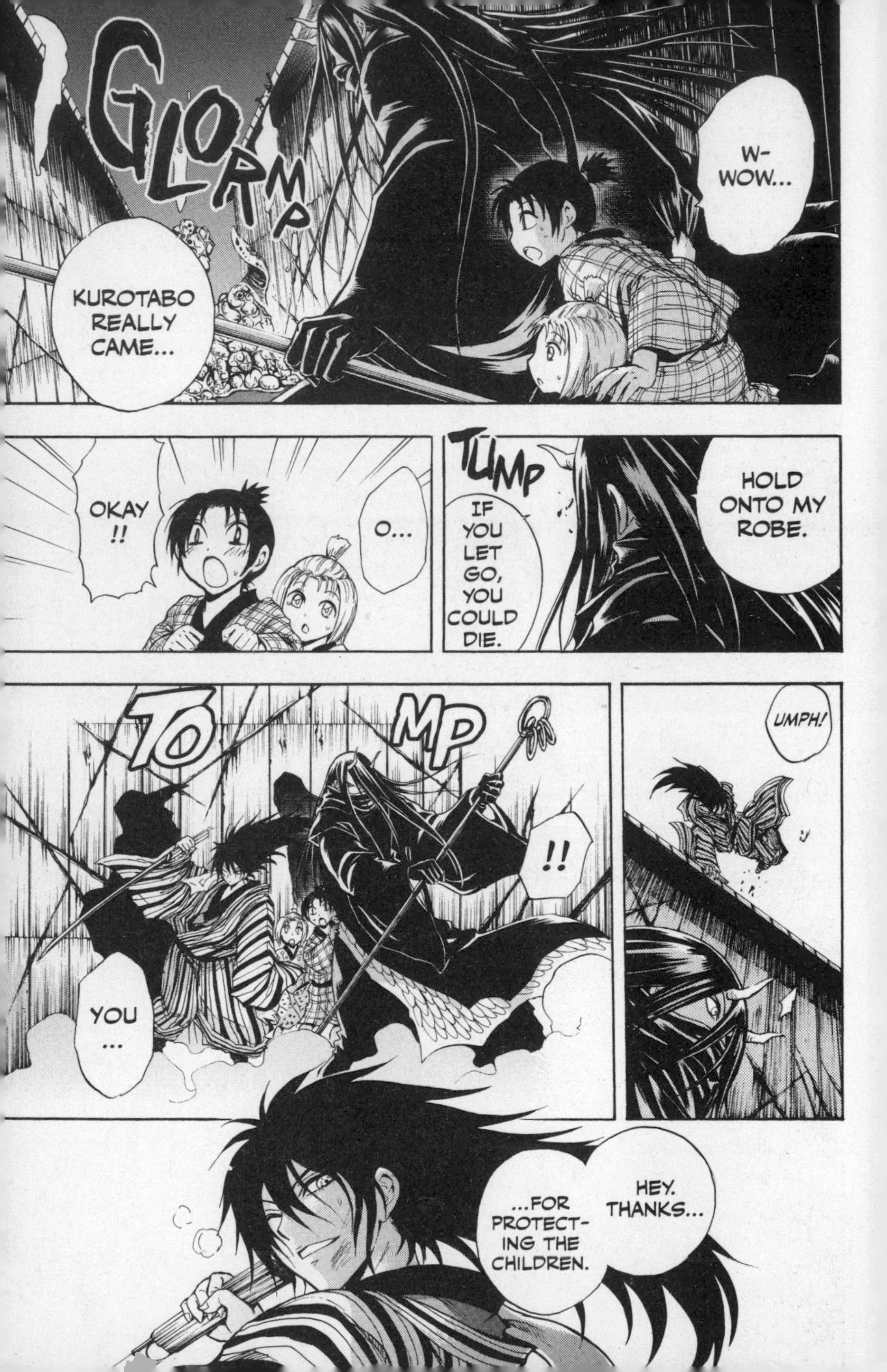
W-
WOW...
GLORMP
KUROTABO REALLY CAME...
HOLD ONTO MY ROBE.
TUMP
IF YOU LET GO, YOU COULD DIE.
O...
OKAY !!
UMPH!
TOMP
!!
YOU ...
HEY. THANKS...
...FOR PROTECT-ING THE CHILDREN.

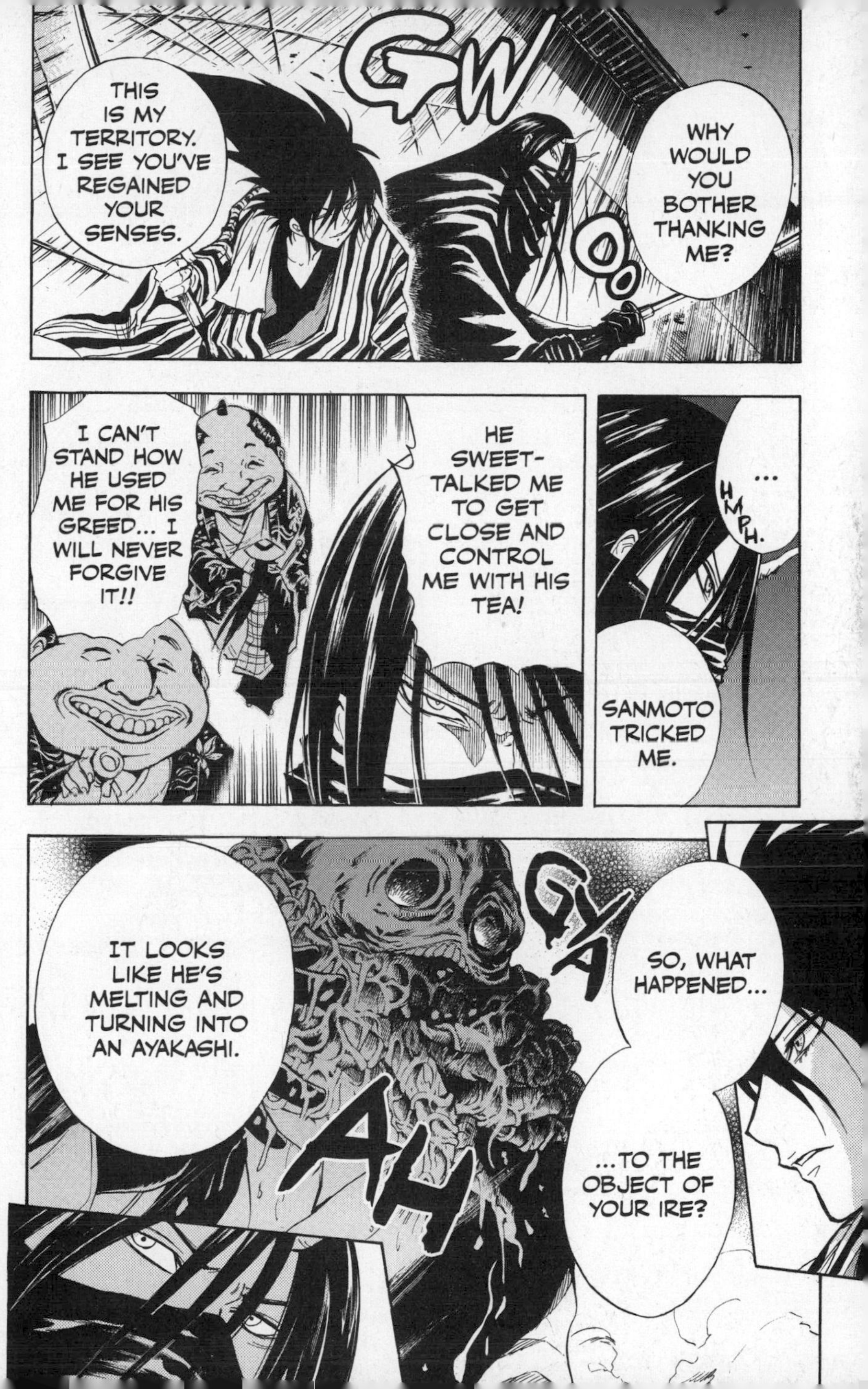
WHY WOULD YOU BOTHER THANKING ME?
GW
OOO
THIS IS MY TERRITORY. I SEE YOU'VE REGAINED YOUR SENSES.
... HMPH.
SANMOTO TRICKED ME.
HE SWEET-TALKED ME TO GET CLOSE AND CONTROL ME WITH HIS TEA!
I CAN'T STAND HOW HE USED ME FOR HIS GREED... I WILL NEVER FORGIVE IT!!
SO, WHAT HAPPENED...
...TO THE OBJECT OF YOUR IRE?
GYA
AH
IT LOOKS LIKE HE'S MELTING AND TURNING INTO AN AYAKASHI.

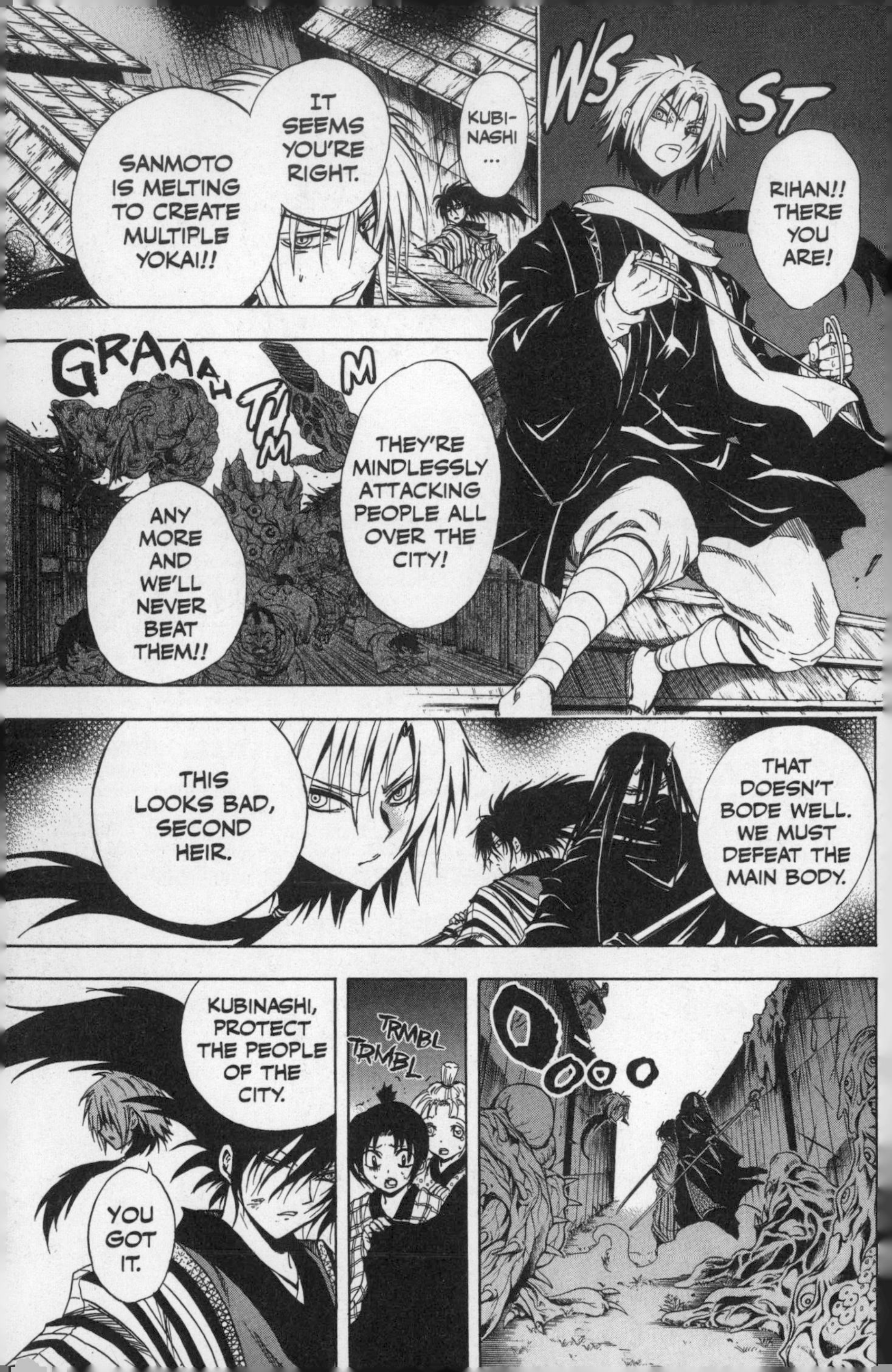
WS
ST
RIHAN!! THERE YOU ARE!
KUBI-NASHI...
IT SEEMS YOU'RE RIGHT.
SANMOTO IS MELTING TO CREATE MULTIPLE YOKAI!!
M
THMM
GRAAAAH
THEY'RE MINDLESSLY ATTACKING PEOPLE ALL OVER THE CITY!
ANY MORE AND WE'LL NEVER BEAT THEM!!
THAT DOESN'T BODE WELL. WE MUST DEFEAT THE MAIN BODY.
THIS LOOKS BAD, SECOND HEIR.
OOOOO
TRMBL TRMBL
KUBINASHI, PROTECT THE PEOPLE OF THE CITY.
YOU GOT IT.

WHUP

YOU HANG IN THERE, TOO.

SLOSH

SWIP

FWOOOSH

MEIKYOSHISUI!!

...SAKURA!!

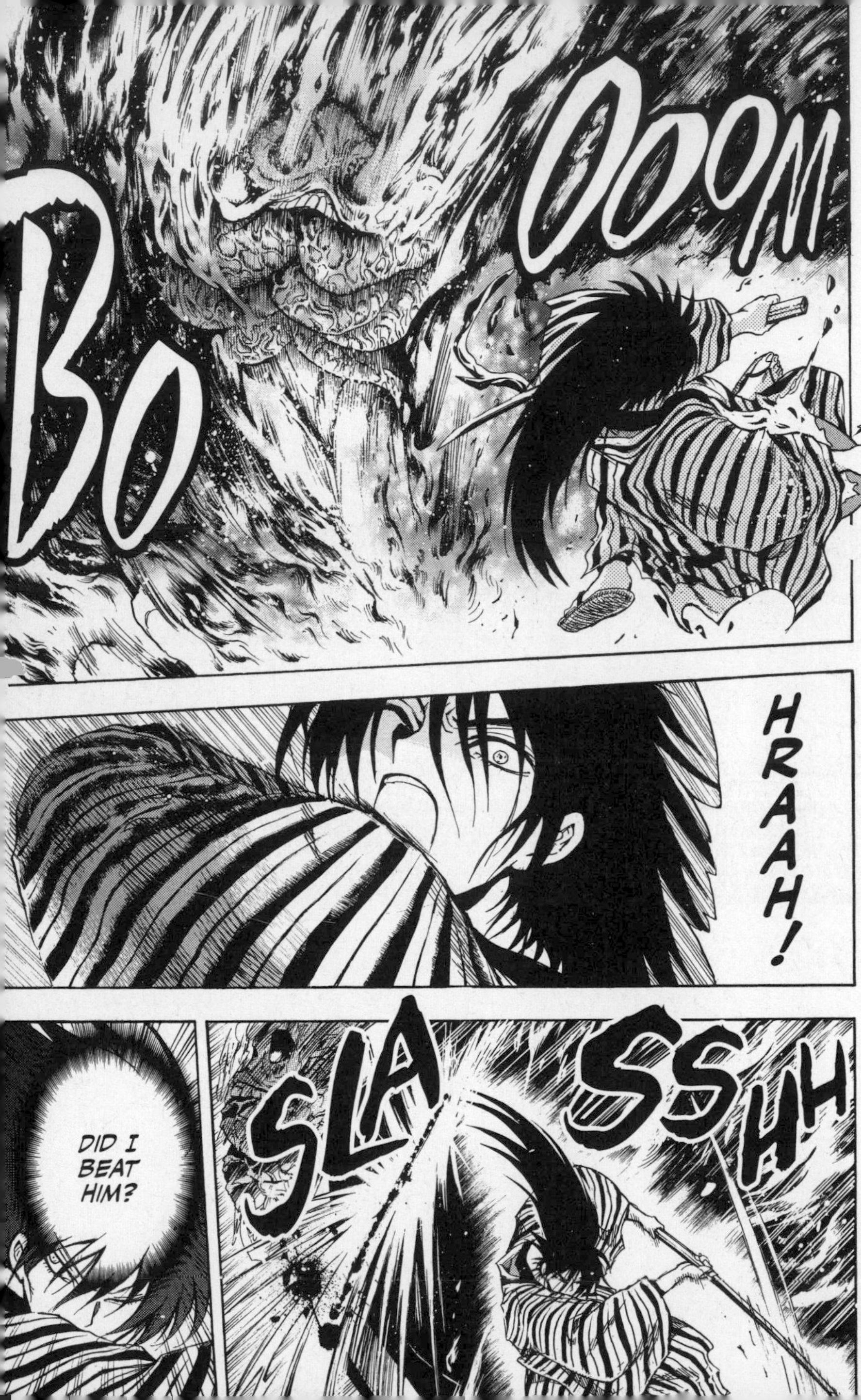
BOOOOM
HRAAAH!
SLASSHH
DID I BEAT HIM?

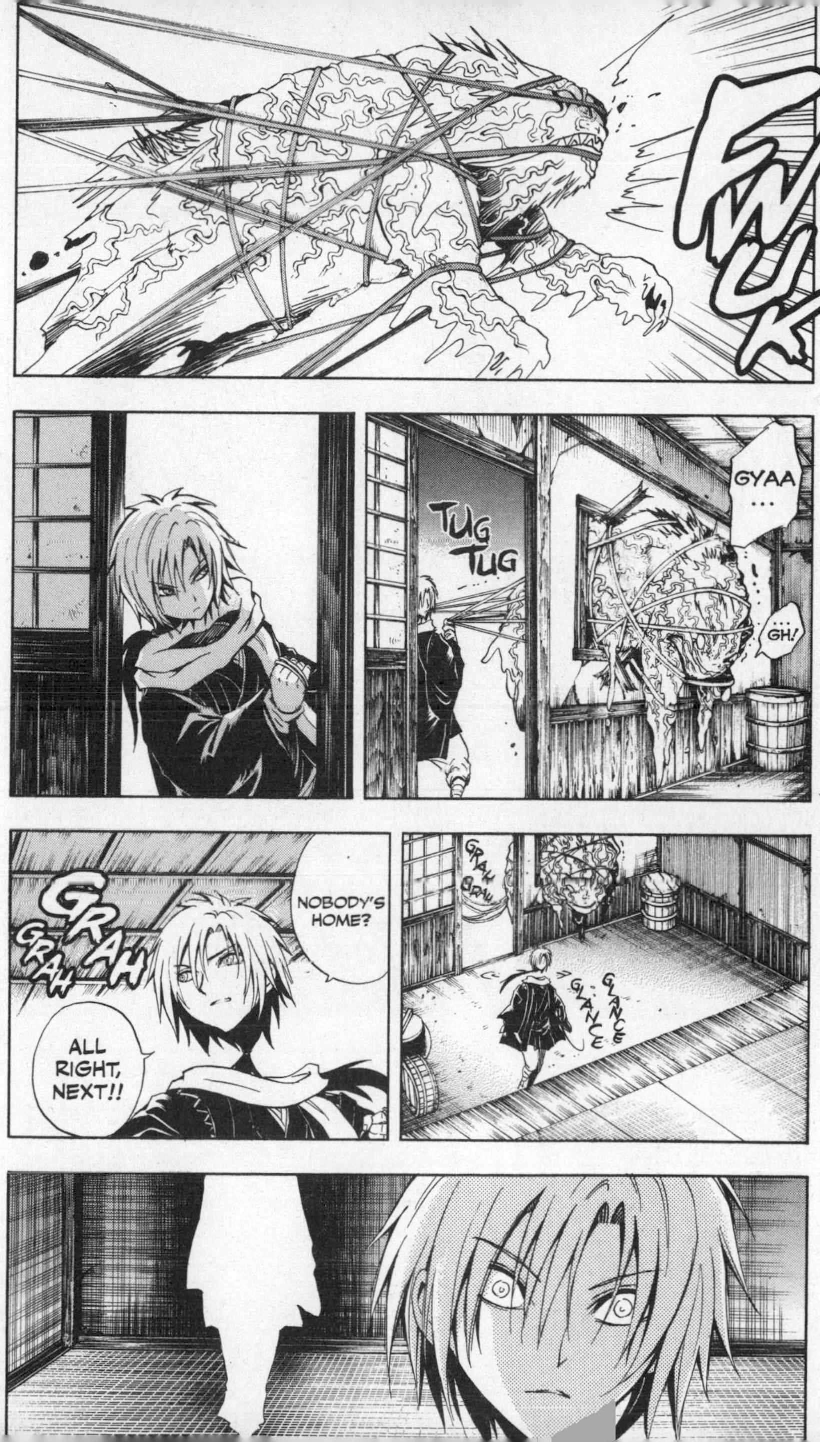
FWUK
GYAA...
!
...GH!
TUG TUG
GRAH GRAH
GLANCE GLANCE
GRAH GRAH
NOBODY'S HOME?
ALL RIGHT, NEXT!!

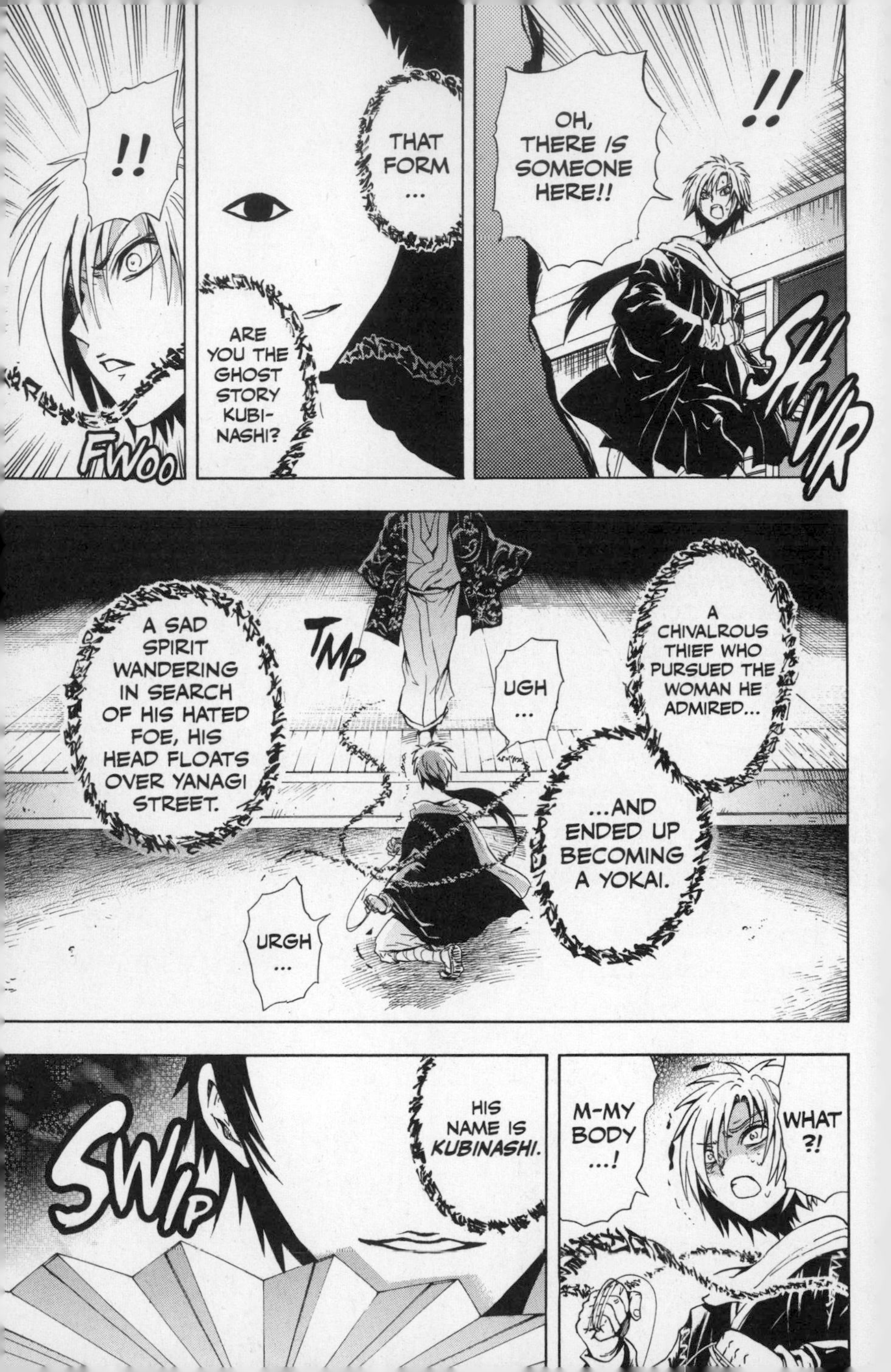
!!
OH, THERE IS SOMEONE HERE!!
SHVIR
THAT FORM ...
ARE YOU THE GHOST STORY KUBI-NASHI?
!!
FWOO
A CHIVALROUS THIEF WHO PURSUED THE WOMAN HE ADMIRED...
UGH ...
TMP
...AND ENDED UP BECOMING A YOKAI.
A SAD SPIRIT WANDERING IN SEARCH OF HIS HATED FOE, HIS HEAD FLOATS OVER YANAGI STREET.
URGH ...
WHAT?!
M-MY BODY ...!
HIS NAME IS *KUBINASHI*.
SWIP

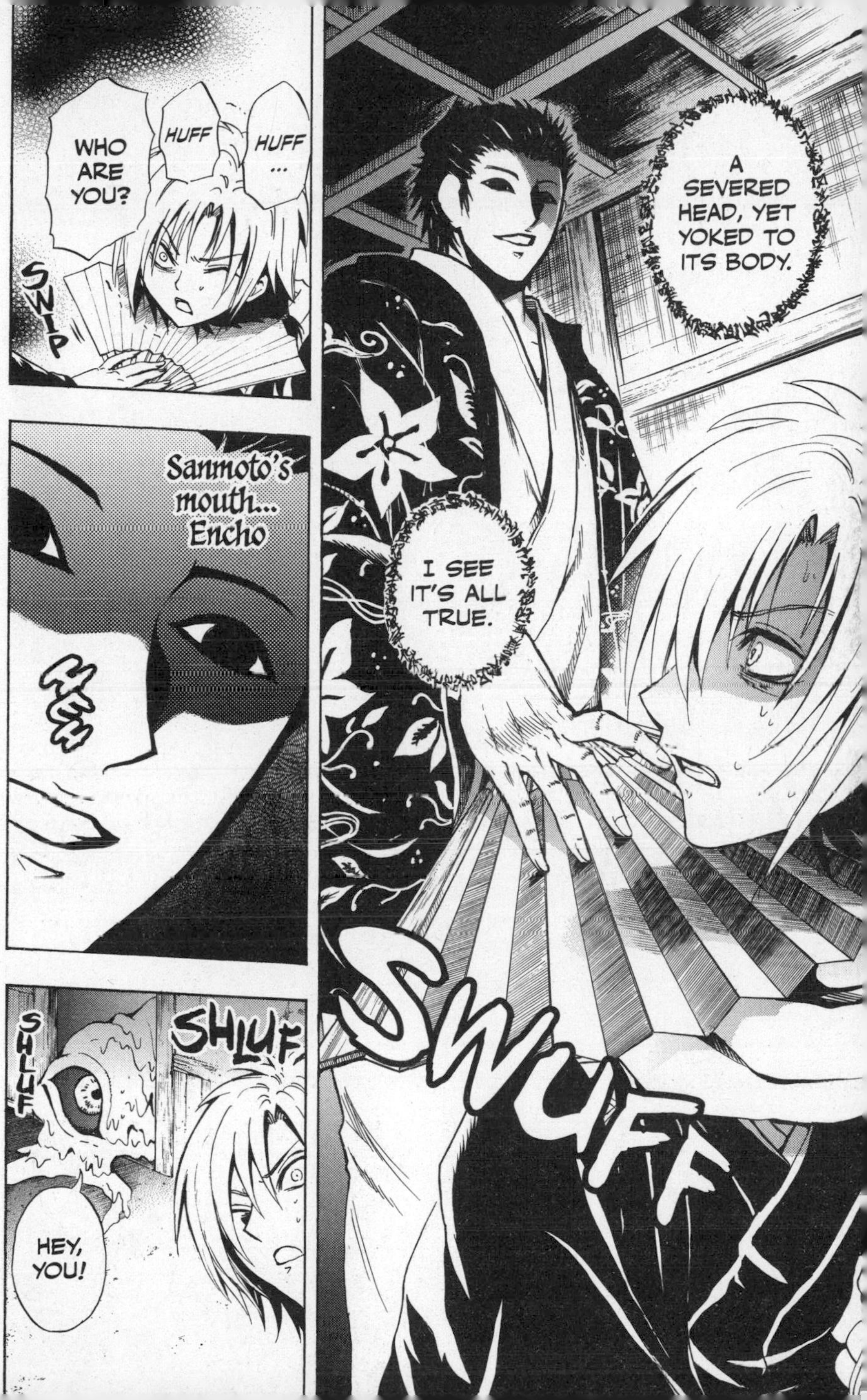
A SEVERED HEAD, YET YOKED TO ITS BODY.
I SEE IT'S ALL TRUE.
SWUFF
HUFF ...
HUFF
WHO ARE YOU?
SWIP
Sanmoto's mouth... Encho
HEH
SHLUF
SHLUF
HEY, YOU!

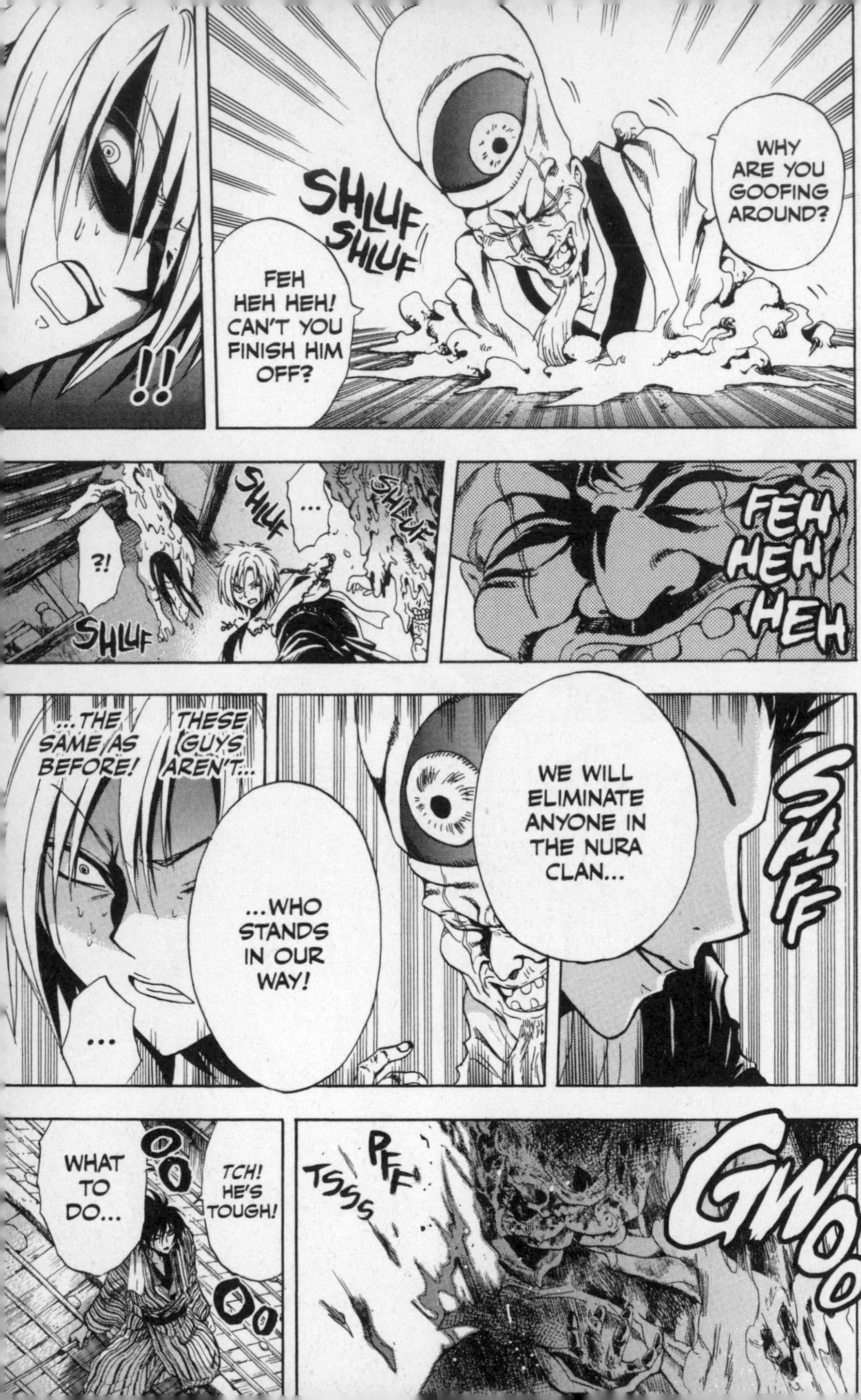
WHY ARE YOU GOOFING AROUND?
SHLUF SHLUF
FEH HEH HEH! CAN'T YOU FINISH HIM OFF?
!!
FEH HEH HEH
SHLUF
...
SHLUF
?!
SHLUF
SHFF
WE WILL ELIMINATE ANYONE IN THE NURA CLAN...
...WHO STANDS IN OUR WAY!
THESE GUYS AREN'T...
...THE SAME AS BEFORE!
...
GWOOO
PFFF
TSSS
TCH! HE'S TOUGH!
WHAT TO DO...

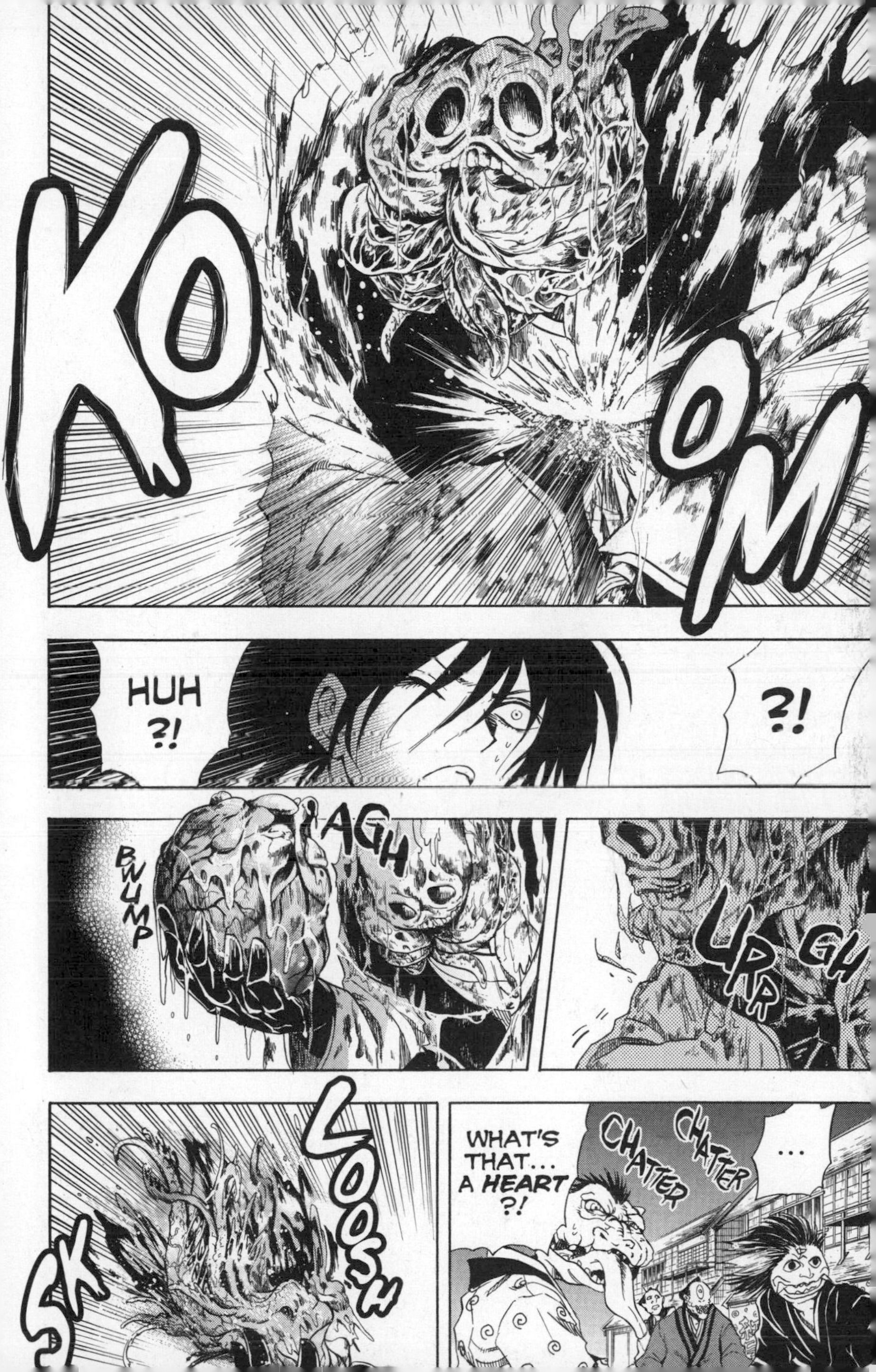
KOOM
?!
HUH ?!
URRGH
AGH
BWUMP
CHATTER
CHATTER
...
WHAT'S THAT... A HEART ?!
LOOOSH
SK

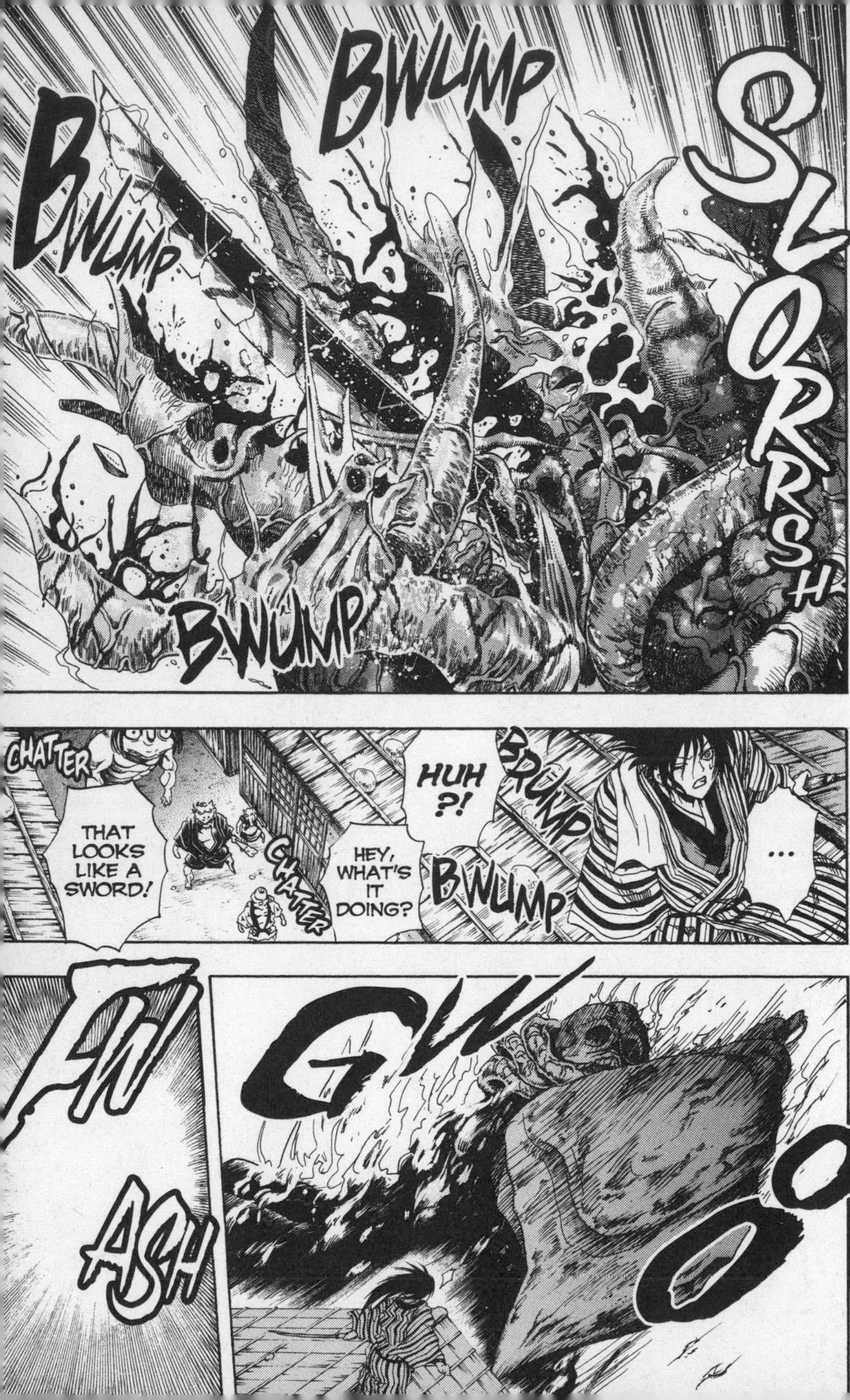
SLORRSH
BWUMP
BWUMP
BWUMP
...
BRUMP
BWUMP
HUH?!
HEY, WHAT'S IT DOING?
CHATTER
THAT LOOKS LIKE A SWORD!
CHATTER
GWOOO
FWASH

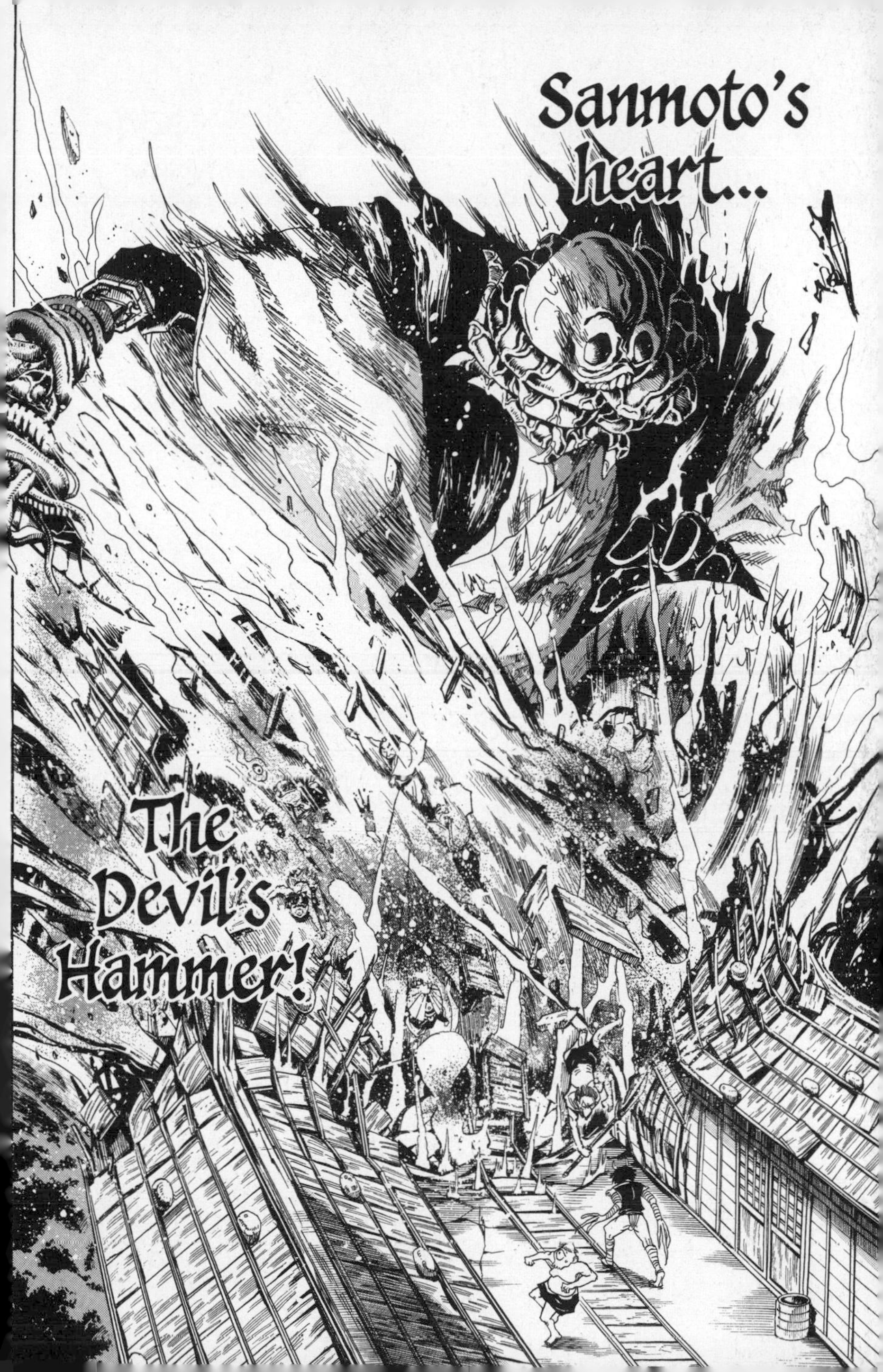
Sanmoto's heart...
The Devil's Hammer!

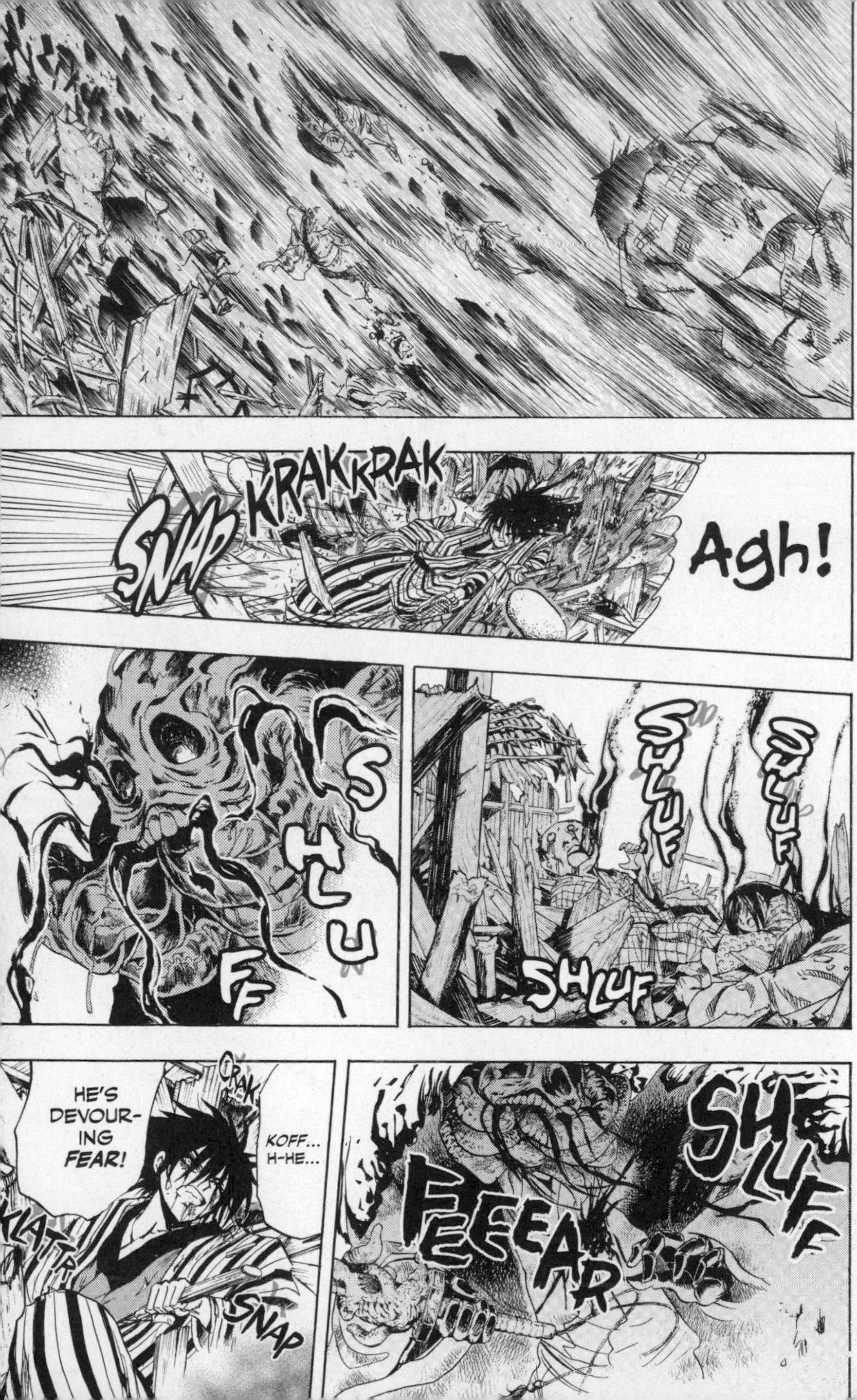
Agh!
KRAKKRAK
SNAP
SHLUF
SHLUF
SHLUF
SHLUFF
SHLUFF
FEEEAR
CRAK
KOFF... H-HE...
HE'S DEVOURING FEAR!
KLATTR
SNAP

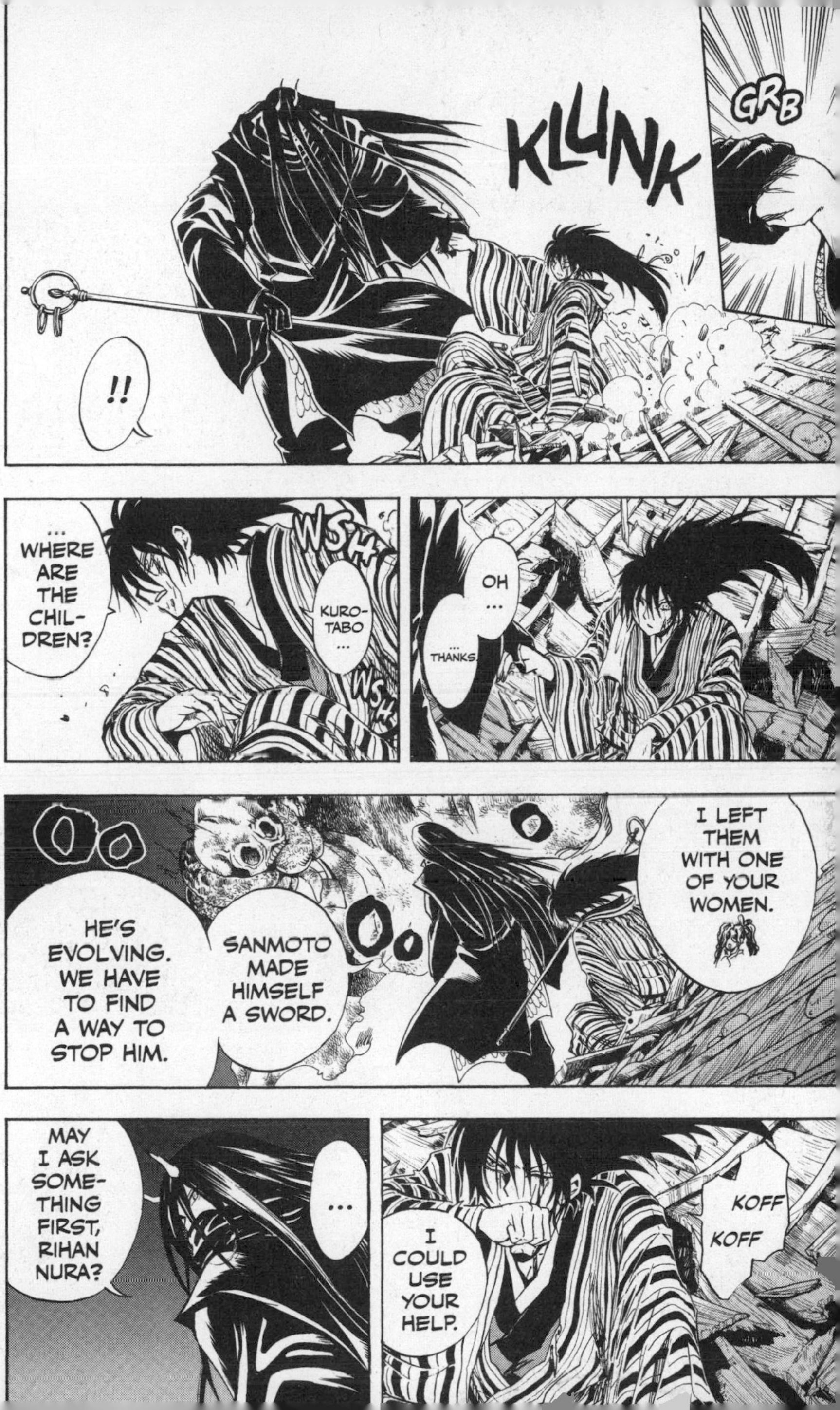
GRB
KLUNK
!!
OH ...
... THANKS.
WSH
KURO-TABO ...
WSH
... WHERE ARE THE CHIL-DREN?
I LEFT THEM WITH ONE OF YOUR WOMEN.
SANMOTO MADE HIMSELF A SWORD.
HE'S EVOLVING. WE HAVE TO FIND A WAY TO STOP HIM.
KOFF
KOFF
I COULD USE YOUR HELP.
...
MAY I ASK SOME-THING FIRST, RIHAN NURA?

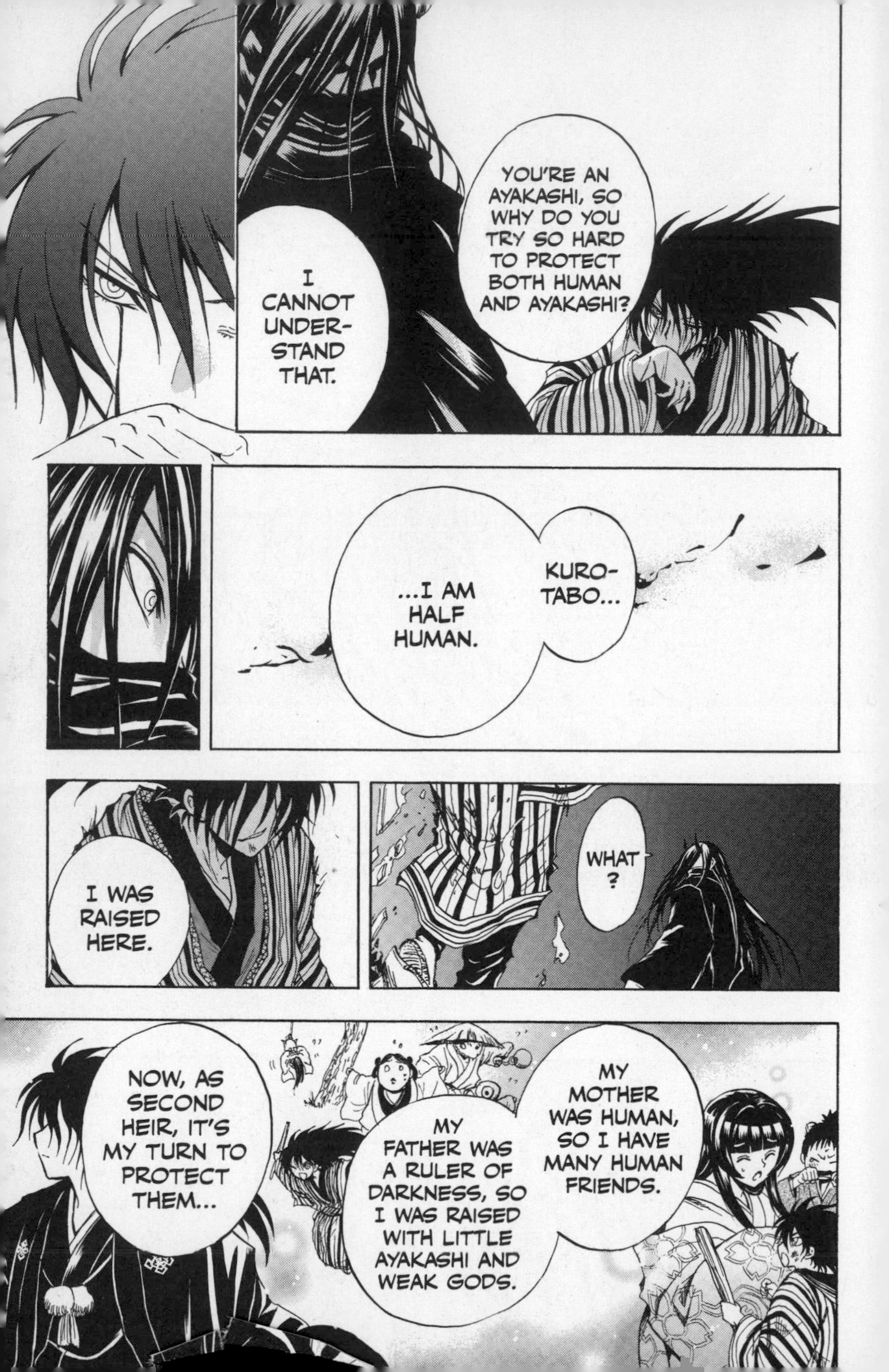
YOU'RE AN AYAKASHI, SO WHY DO YOU TRY SO HARD TO PROTECT BOTH HUMAN AND AYAKASHI?
I CANNOT UNDER-STAND THAT.
KURO-TABO...
...I AM HALF HUMAN.
WHAT?
I WAS RAISED HERE.
MY MOTHER WAS HUMAN, SO I HAVE MANY HUMAN FRIENDS.
MY FATHER WAS A RULER OF DARKNESS, SO I WAS RAISED WITH LITTLE AYAKASHI AND WEAK GODS.
NOW, AS SECOND HEIR, IT'S MY TURN TO PROTECT THEM...

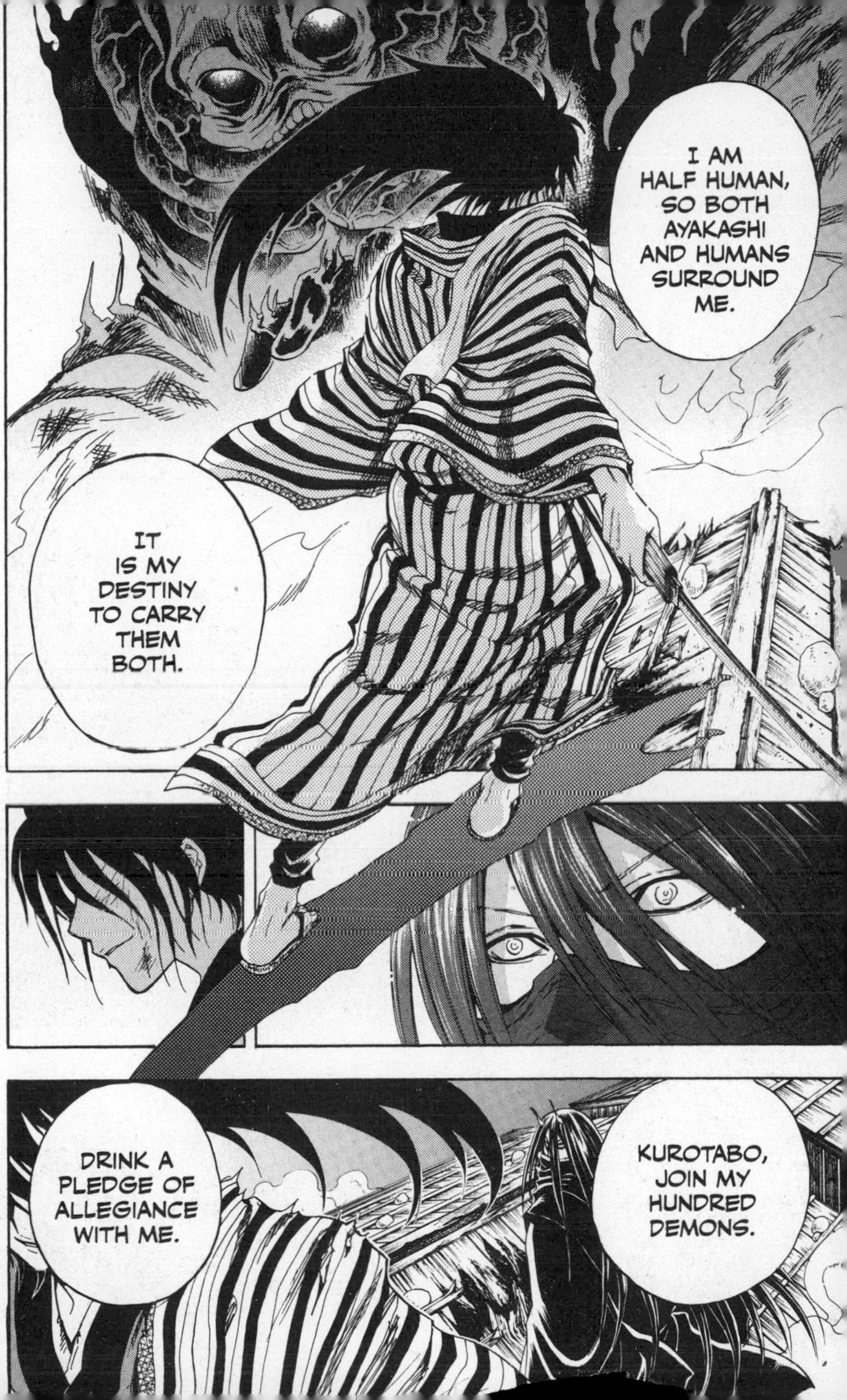
I AM HALF HUMAN, SO BOTH AYAKASHI AND HUMANS SURROUND ME.
IT IS MY DESTINY TO CARRY THEM BOTH.
KUROTABO, JOIN MY HUNDRED DEMONS.
DRINK A PLEDGE OF ALLEGIANCE WITH ME.

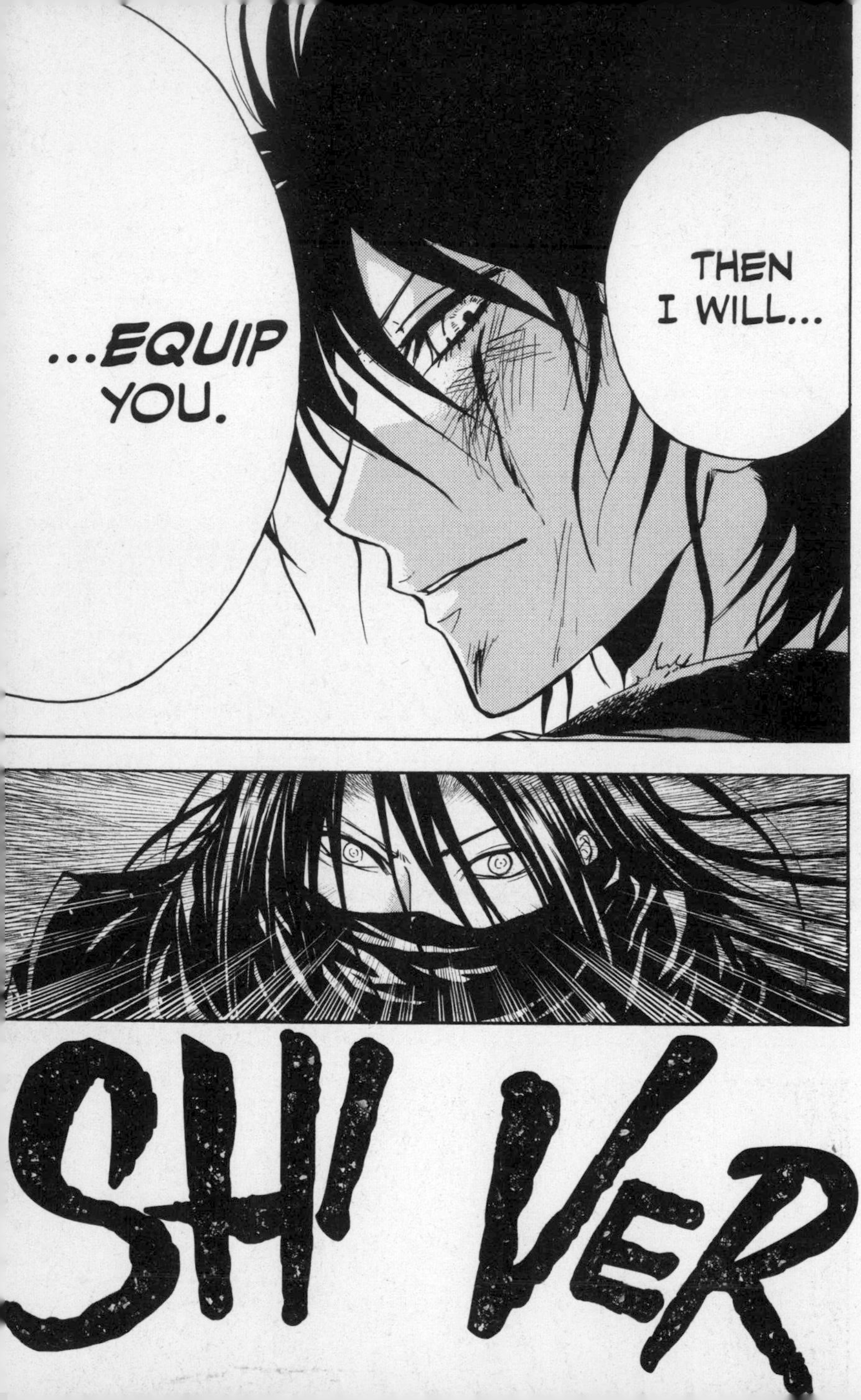
THEN I WILL...
...EQUIP YOU.
SHIVER

NURA: RISE OF THE YOKAI CLAN

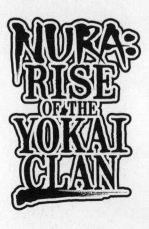

Act 158: A Pledge at the Edge of a Strange Land

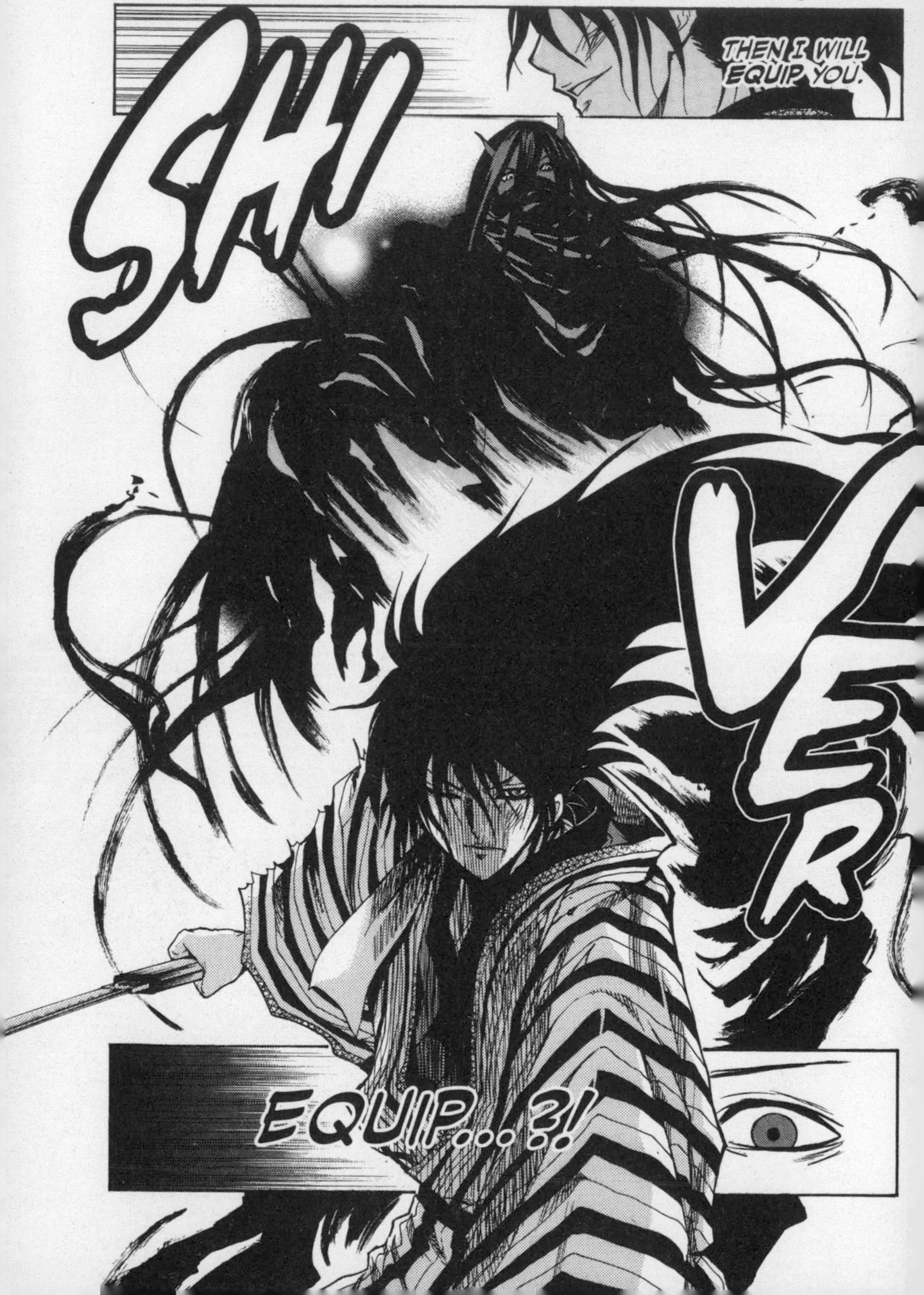
THEN I WILL EQUIP YOU.
EQUIP...?!

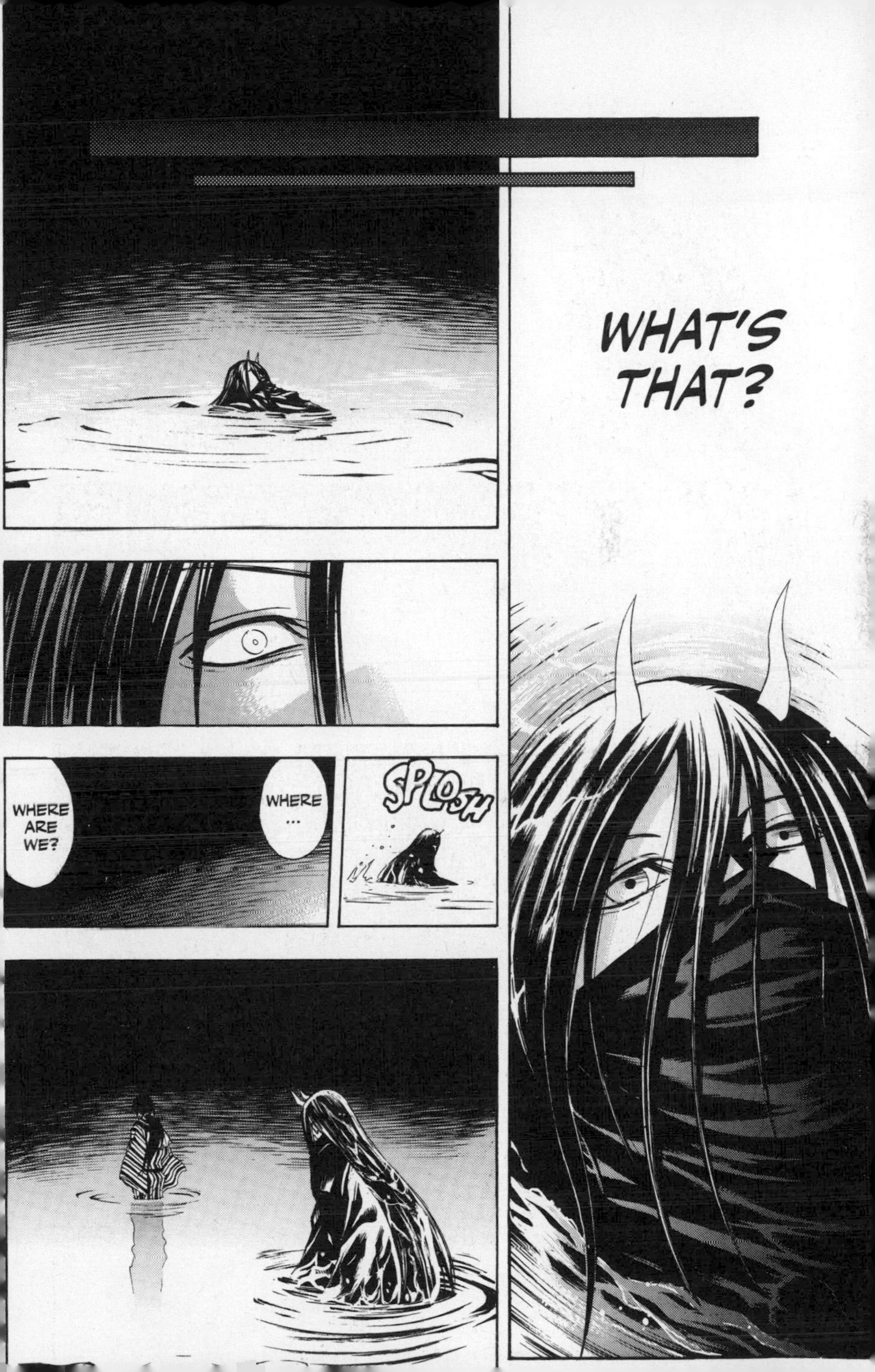
WHAT'S THAT?
SPLOSH
WHERE ...
WHERE ARE WE?

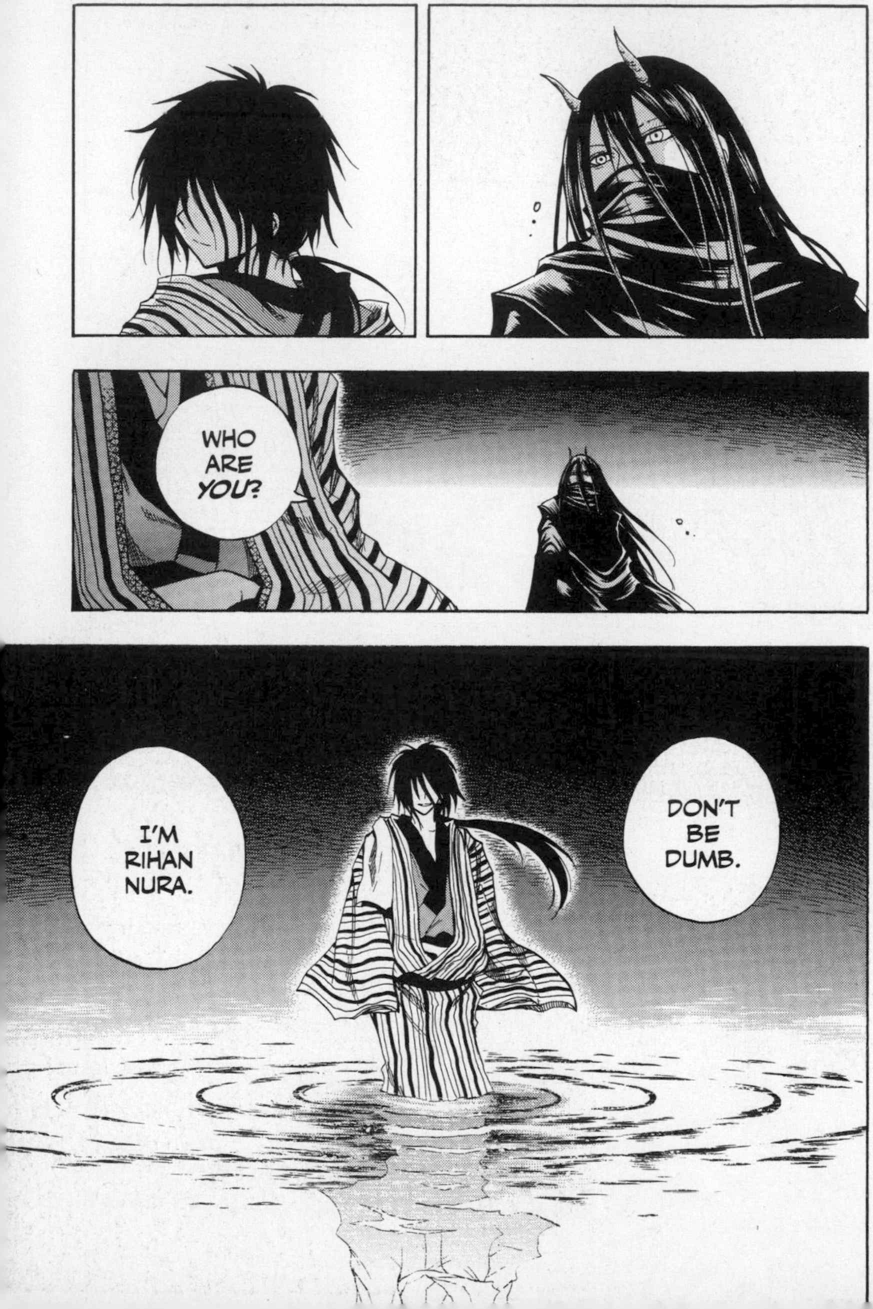
WHO ARE YOU?
DON'T BE DUMB.
I'M RIHAN NURA.

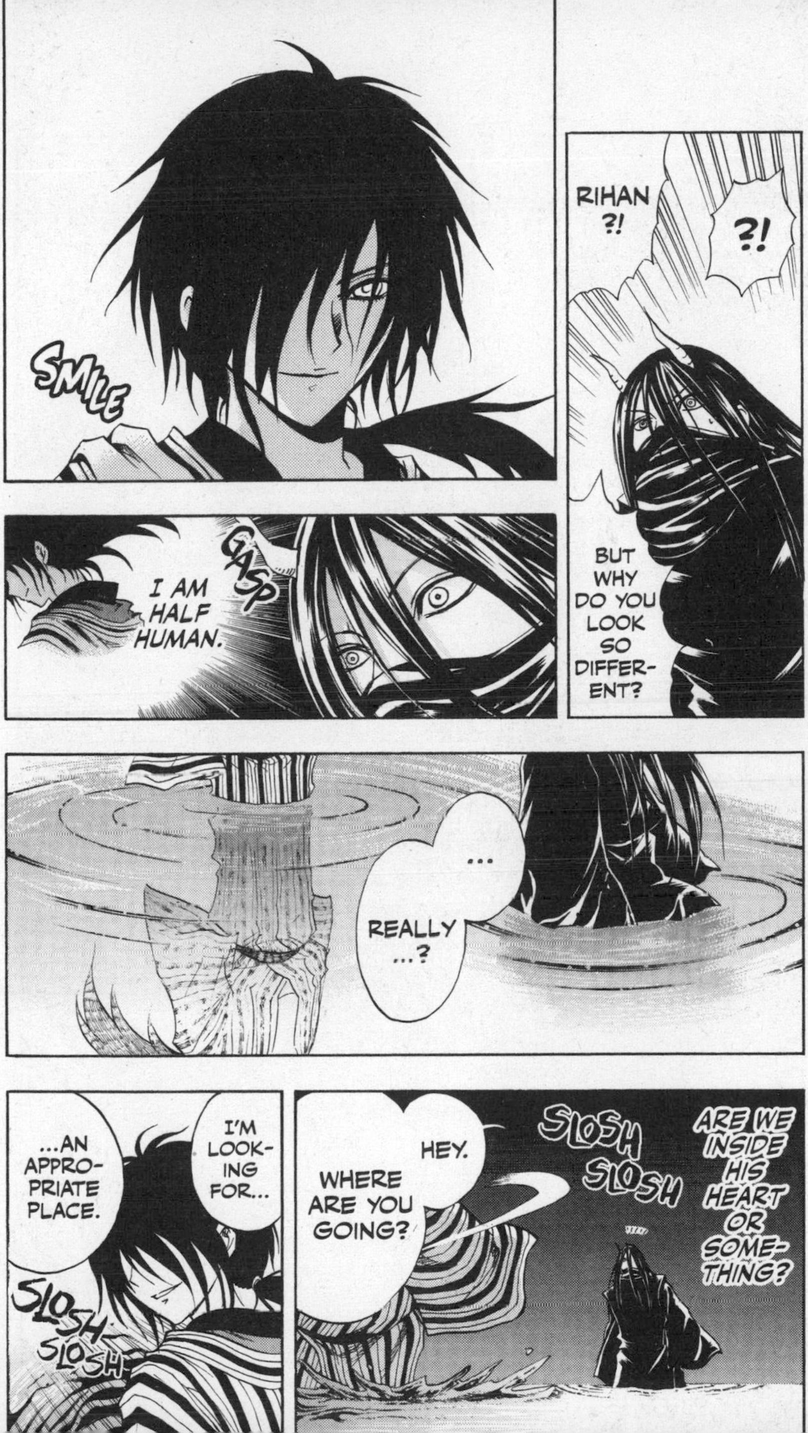
?!
RIHAN ?!
BUT WHY DO YOU LOOK SO DIFFERENT?
SMILE
GASP
I AM HALF HUMAN.
...
REALLY ...?
ARE WE INSIDE HIS HEART OR SOMETHING?
SLOSH SLOSH
HEY.
WHERE ARE YOU GOING?
I'M LOOKING FOR...
...AN APPROPRIATE PLACE.
SLOSH SLOSH

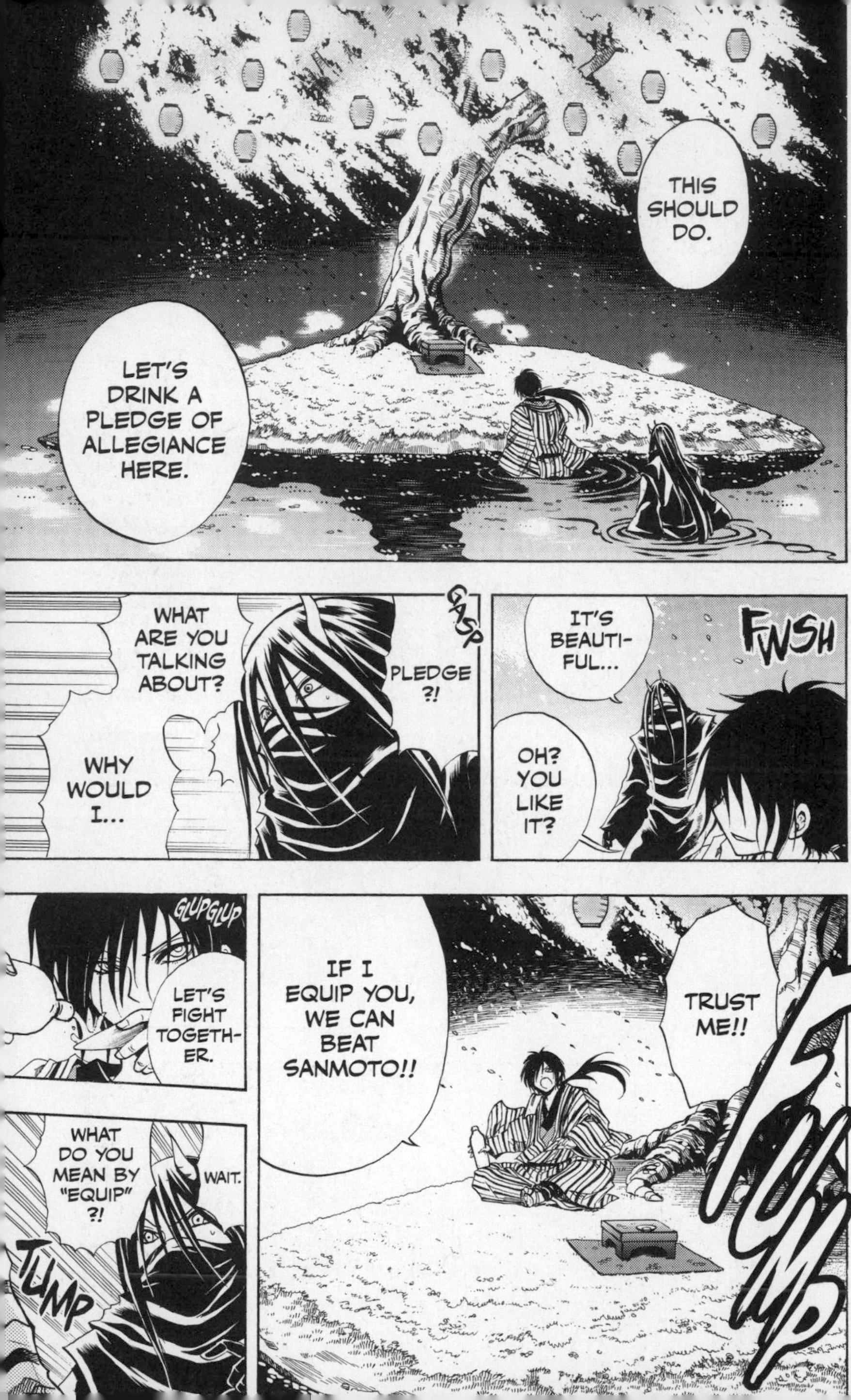
THIS SHOULD DO.
LET'S DRINK A PLEDGE OF ALLEGIANCE HERE.
FWSH
IT'S BEAUTIFUL...
OH? YOU LIKE IT?
GASP
PLEDGE?!
WHAT ARE YOU TALKING ABOUT?
WHY WOULD I...
TRUST ME!!
IF I EQUIP YOU, WE CAN BEAT SANMOTO!!
GLUPGLUP
LET'S FIGHT TOGETHER.
WAIT.
WHAT DO YOU MEAN BY "EQUIP"?!
TUMP

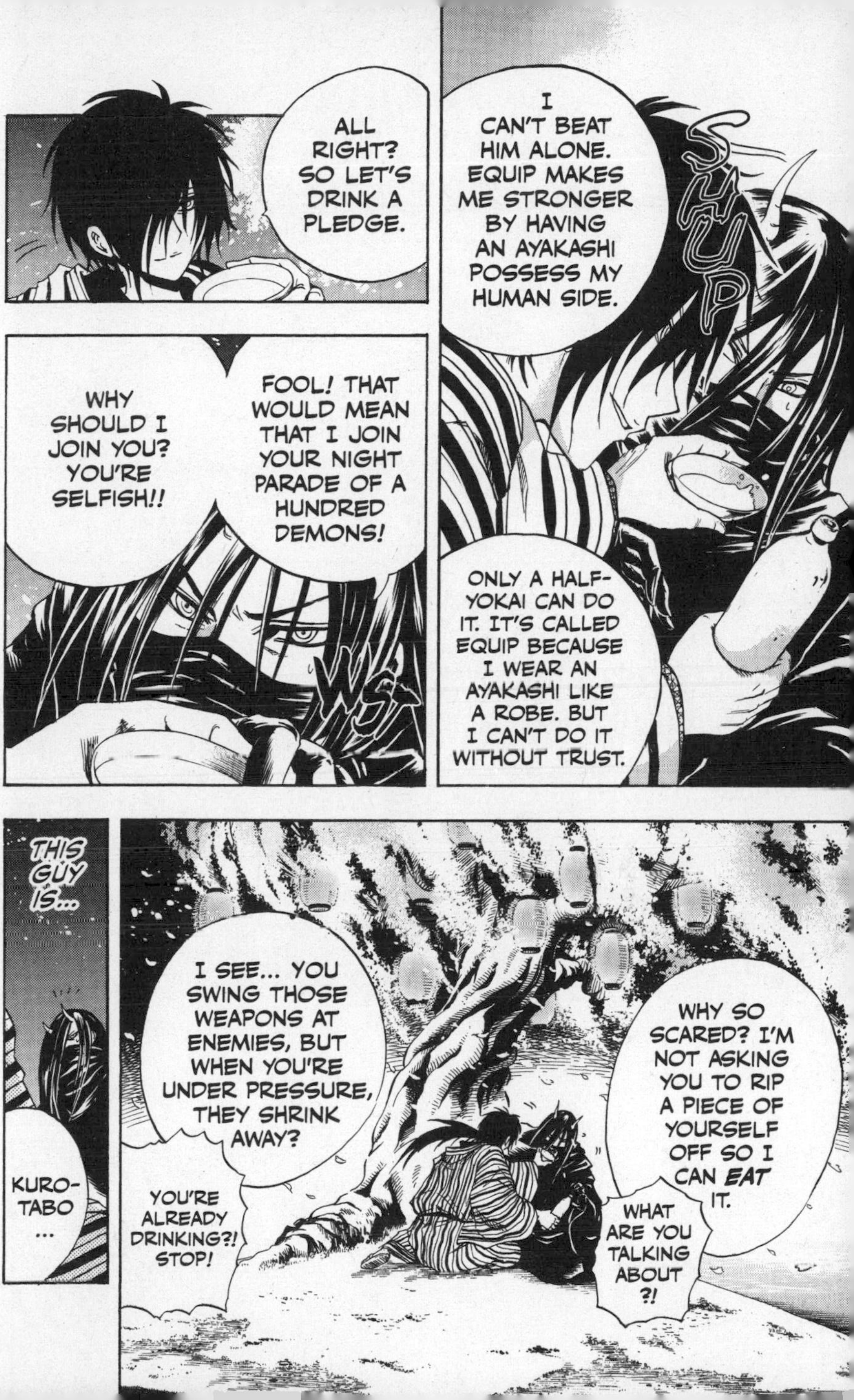
I CAN'T BEAT HIM ALONE. EQUIP MAKES ME STRONGER BY HAVING AN AYAKASHI POSSESS MY HUMAN SIDE.
SHUP
ONLY A HALF-YOKAI CAN DO IT. IT'S CALLED EQUIP BECAUSE I WEAR AN AYAKASHI LIKE A ROBE. BUT I CAN'T DO IT WITHOUT TRUST.
ALL RIGHT? SO LET'S DRINK A PLEDGE.
FOOL! THAT WOULD MEAN THAT I JOIN YOUR NIGHT PARADE OF A HUNDRED DEMONS!
WHY SHOULD I JOIN YOU? YOU'RE SELFISH!!
WS
WHY SO SCARED? I'M NOT ASKING YOU TO RIP A PIECE OF YOURSELF OFF SO I CAN *EAT* IT.
I SEE... YOU SWING THOSE WEAPONS AT ENEMIES, BUT WHEN YOU'RE UNDER PRESSURE, THEY SHRINK AWAY?
WHAT ARE YOU TALKING ABOUT ?!
YOU'RE ALREADY DRINKING?! STOP!
THIS GUY IS...
KURO-TABO ...

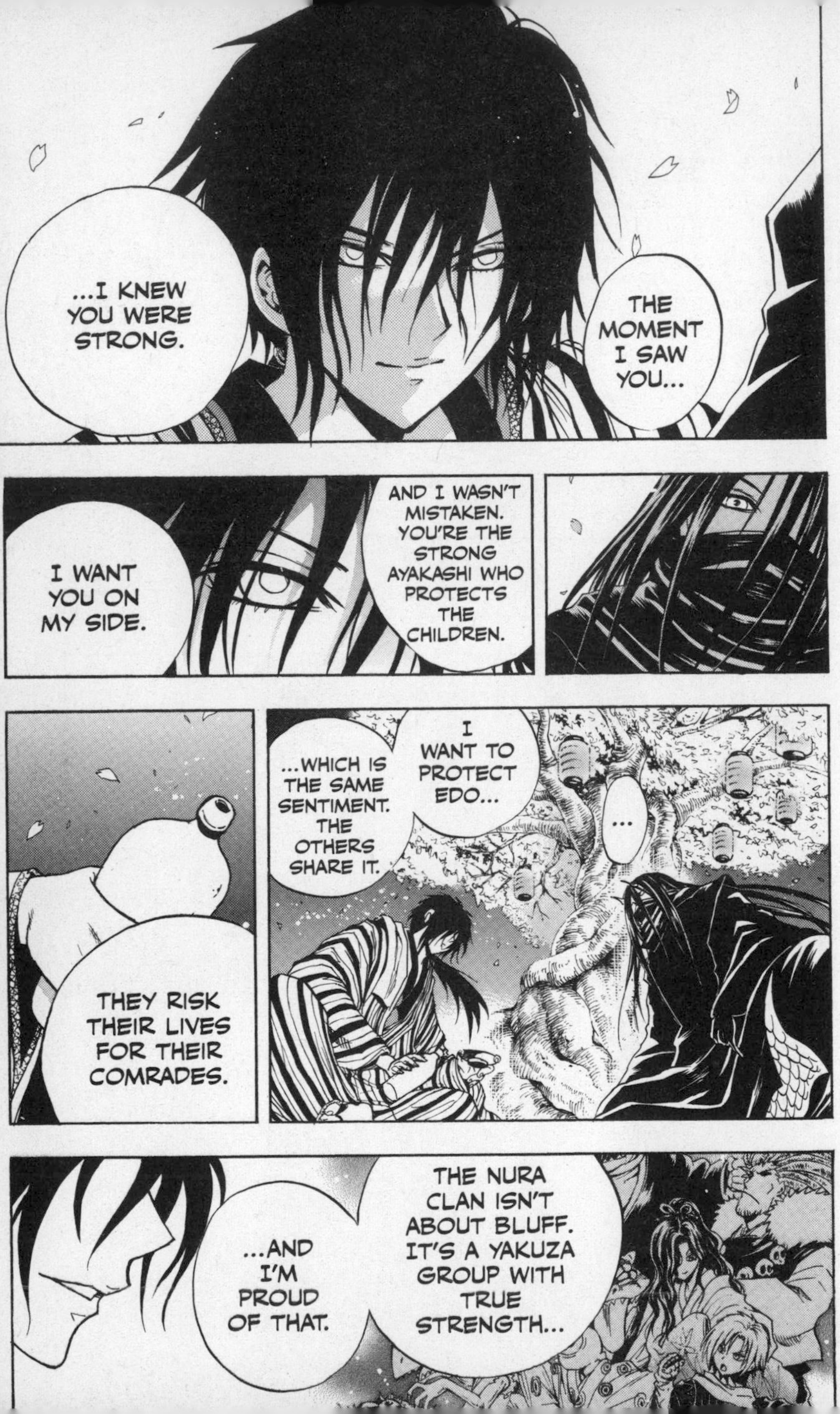
THE MOMENT I SAW YOU...
...I KNEW YOU WERE STRONG.
AND I WASN'T MISTAKEN. YOU'RE THE STRONG AYAKASHI WHO PROTECTS THE CHILDREN.
I WANT YOU ON MY SIDE.
...
I WANT TO PROTECT EDO...
...WHICH IS THE SAME SENTIMENT. THE OTHERS SHARE IT.
THEY RISK THEIR LIVES FOR THEIR COMRADES.
THE NURA CLAN ISN'T ABOUT BLUFF. IT'S A YAKUZA GROUP WITH TRUE STRENGTH...
...AND I'M PROUD OF THAT.

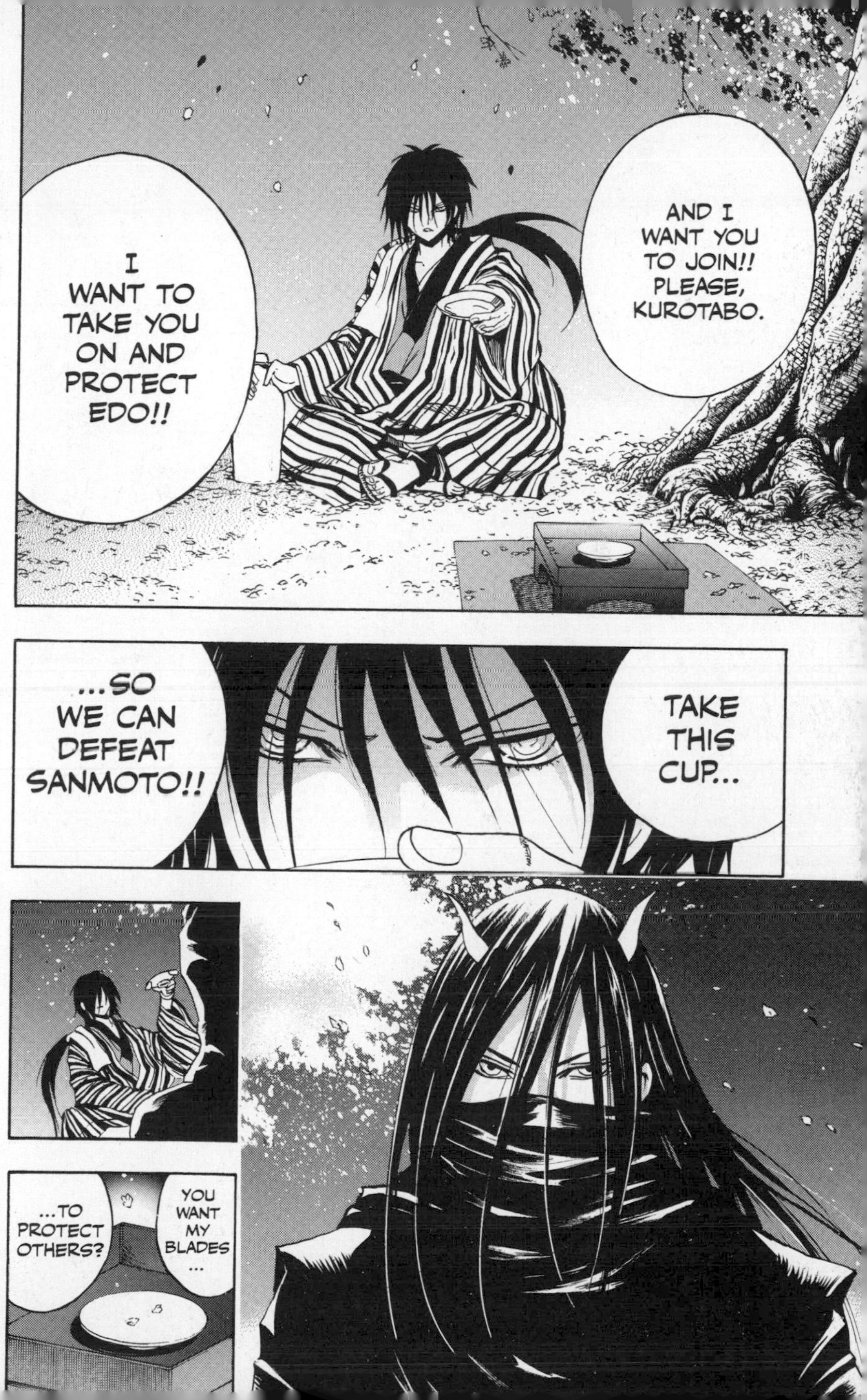
AND I WANT YOU TO JOIN!! PLEASE, KUROTABO.
I WANT TO TAKE YOU ON AND PROTECT EDO!!
TAKE THIS CUP...
...SO WE CAN DEFEAT SANMOTO!!
YOU WANT MY BLADES ...
...TO PROTECT OTHERS?

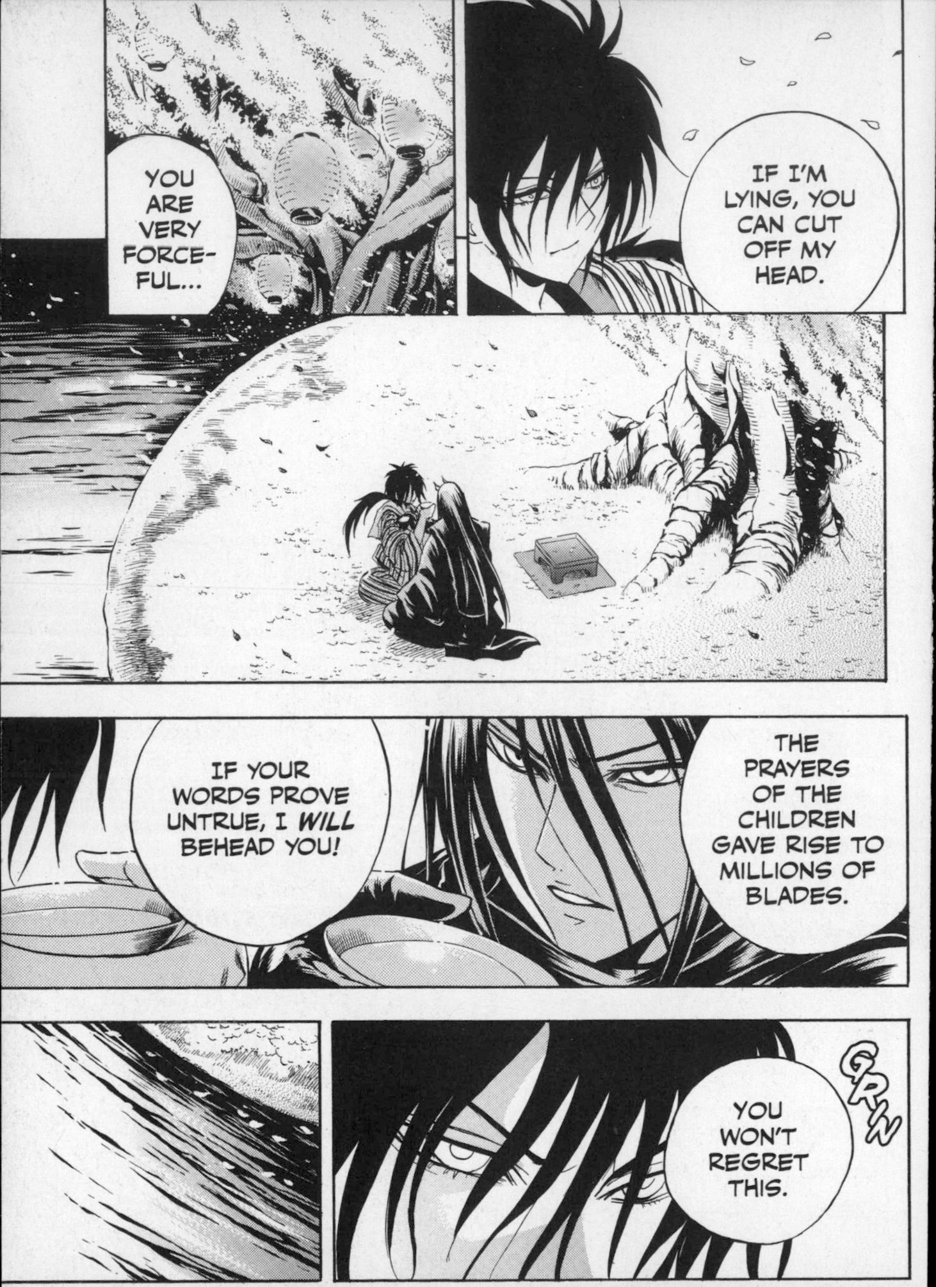
IF I'M LYING, YOU CAN CUT OFF MY HEAD.
YOU ARE VERY FORCE-FUL...
THE PRAYERS OF THE CHILDREN GAVE RISE TO MILLIONS OF BLADES.
IF YOUR WORDS PROVE UNTRUE, I *WILL* BEHEAD YOU!
GRIN
YOU WON'T REGRET THIS.

Act 158: A Pledge at the Edge of a Strange Land

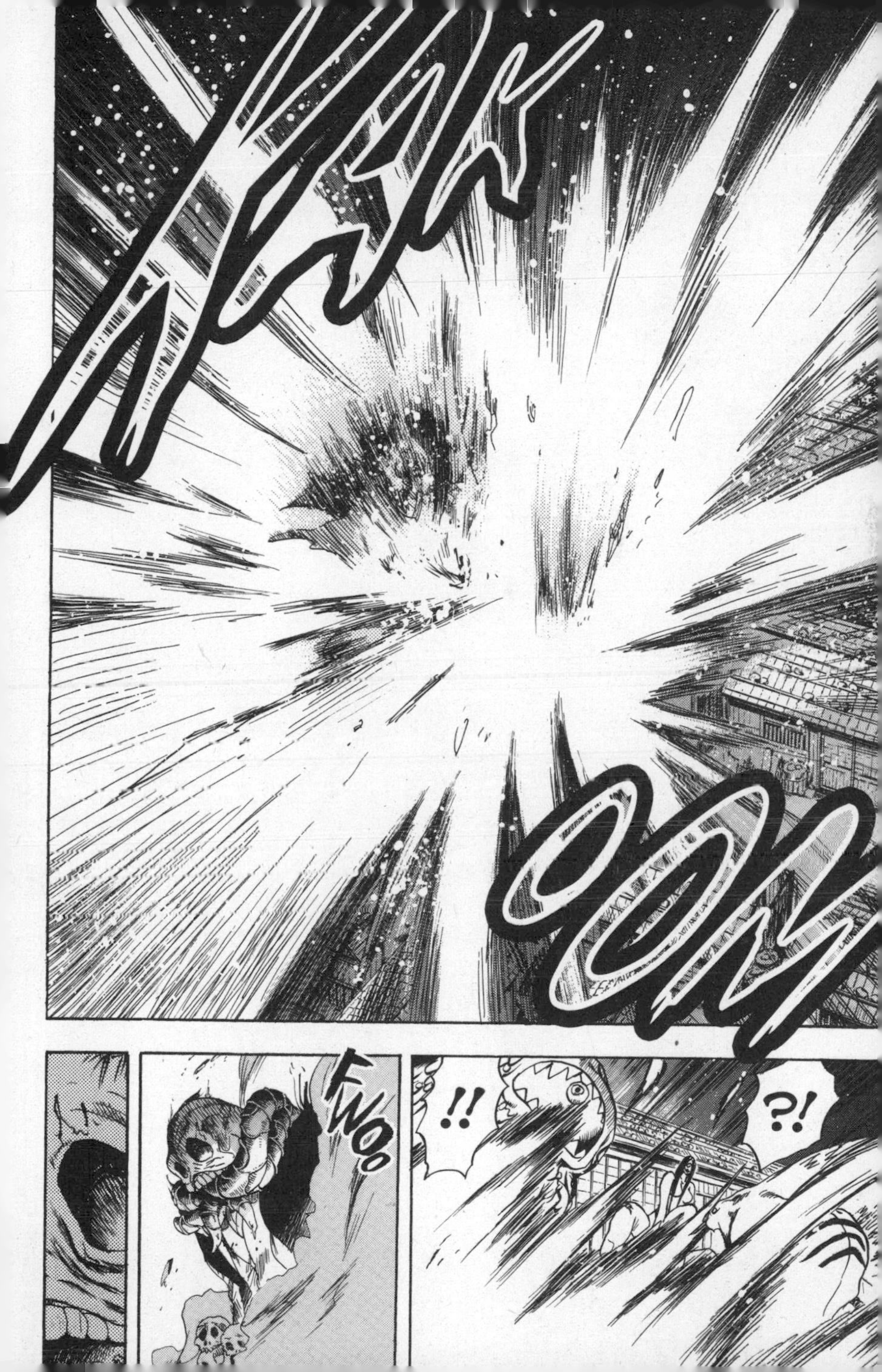
OOM
?!
!!
FWOO

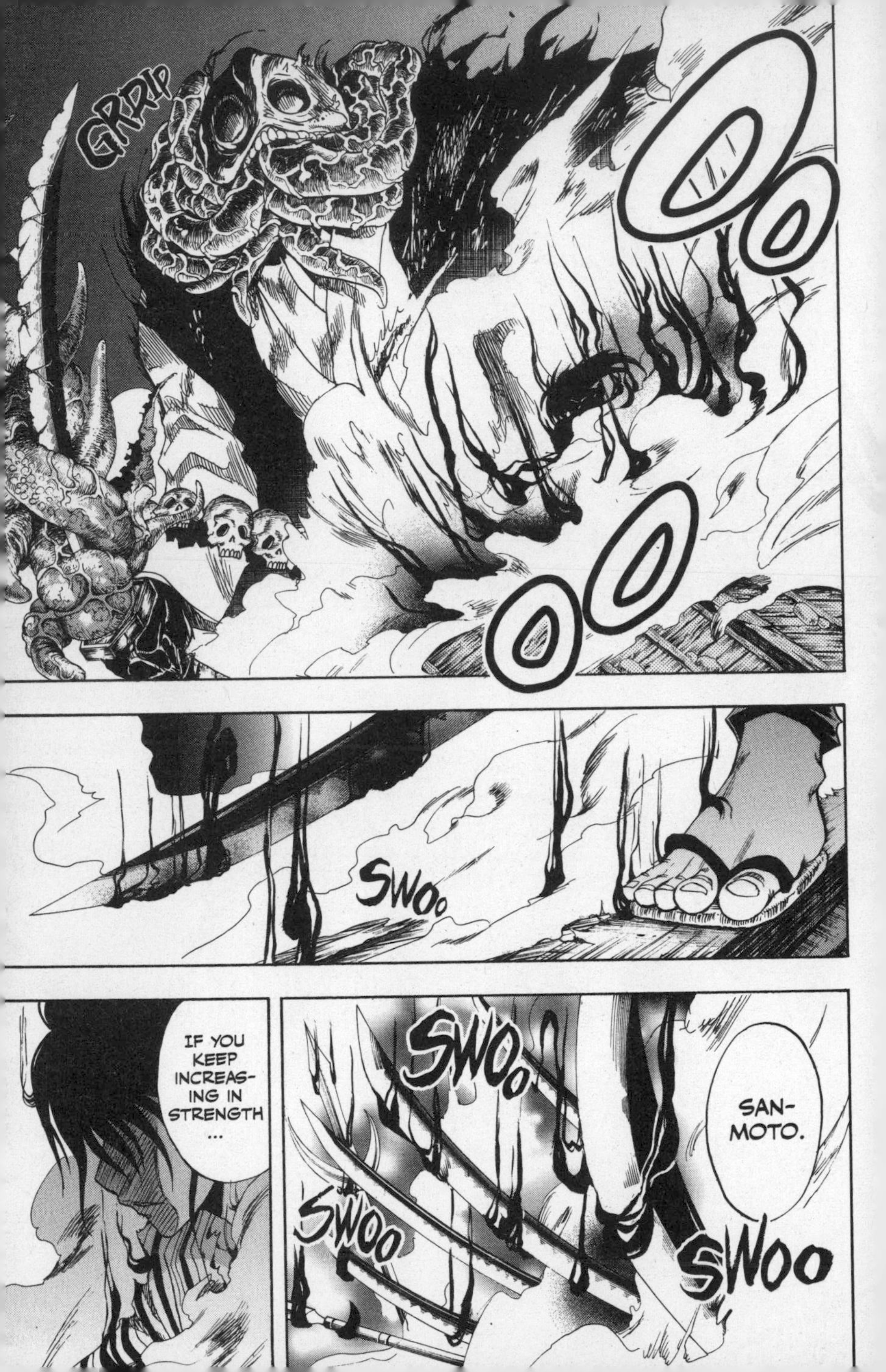
OOOOO
GRRIP
SWOo
SAN-MOTO.
SWOo
SWOO
SWOO
IF YOU KEEP INCREASING IN STRENGTH ...

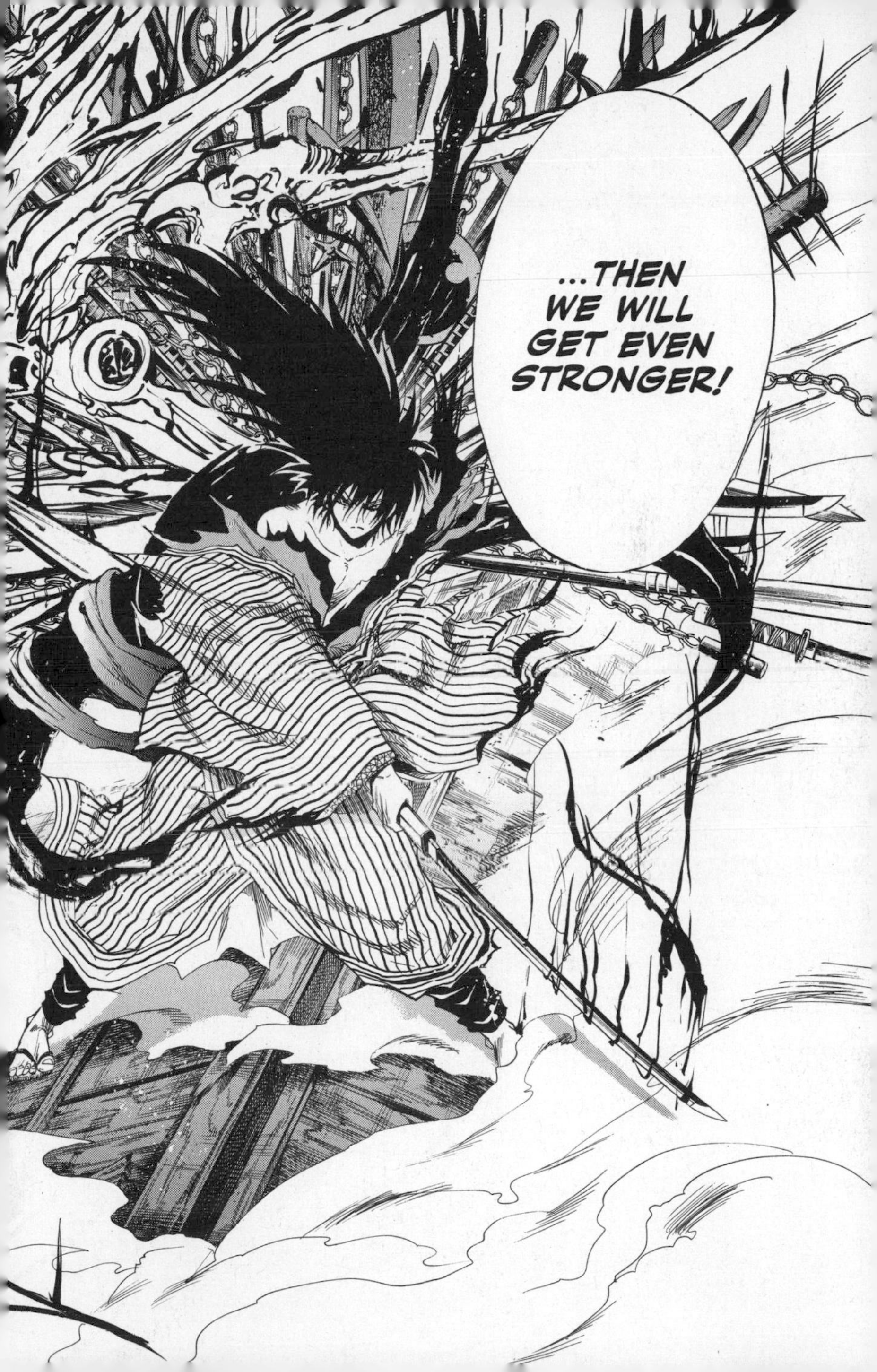
...THEN WE WILL GET EVEN STRONGER!

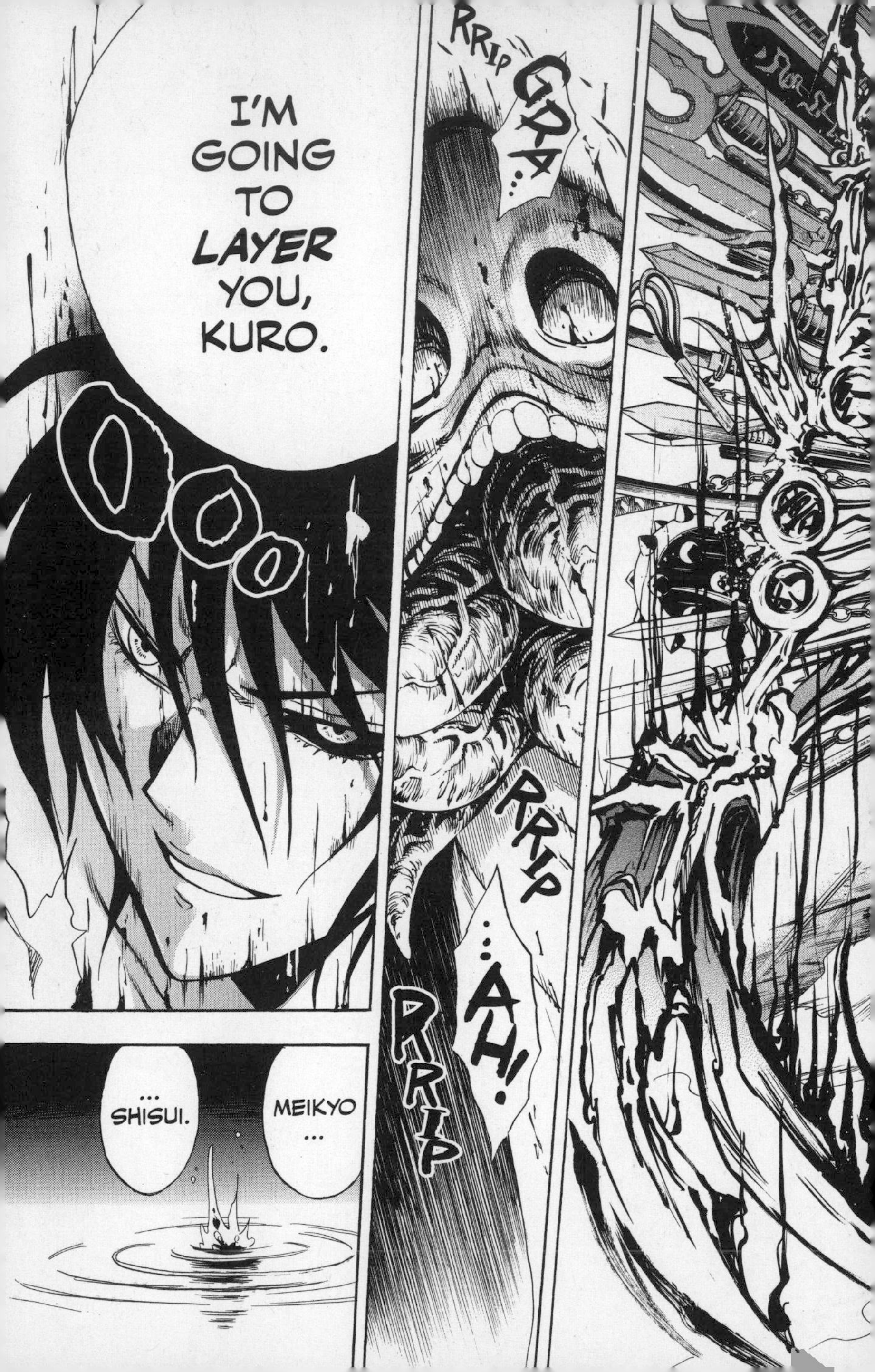
RRIP
GRA...
RRIP
...AH!
RRIP
I'M GOING TO LAYER YOU, KURO.
MEIKYO ...
... SHISUI.

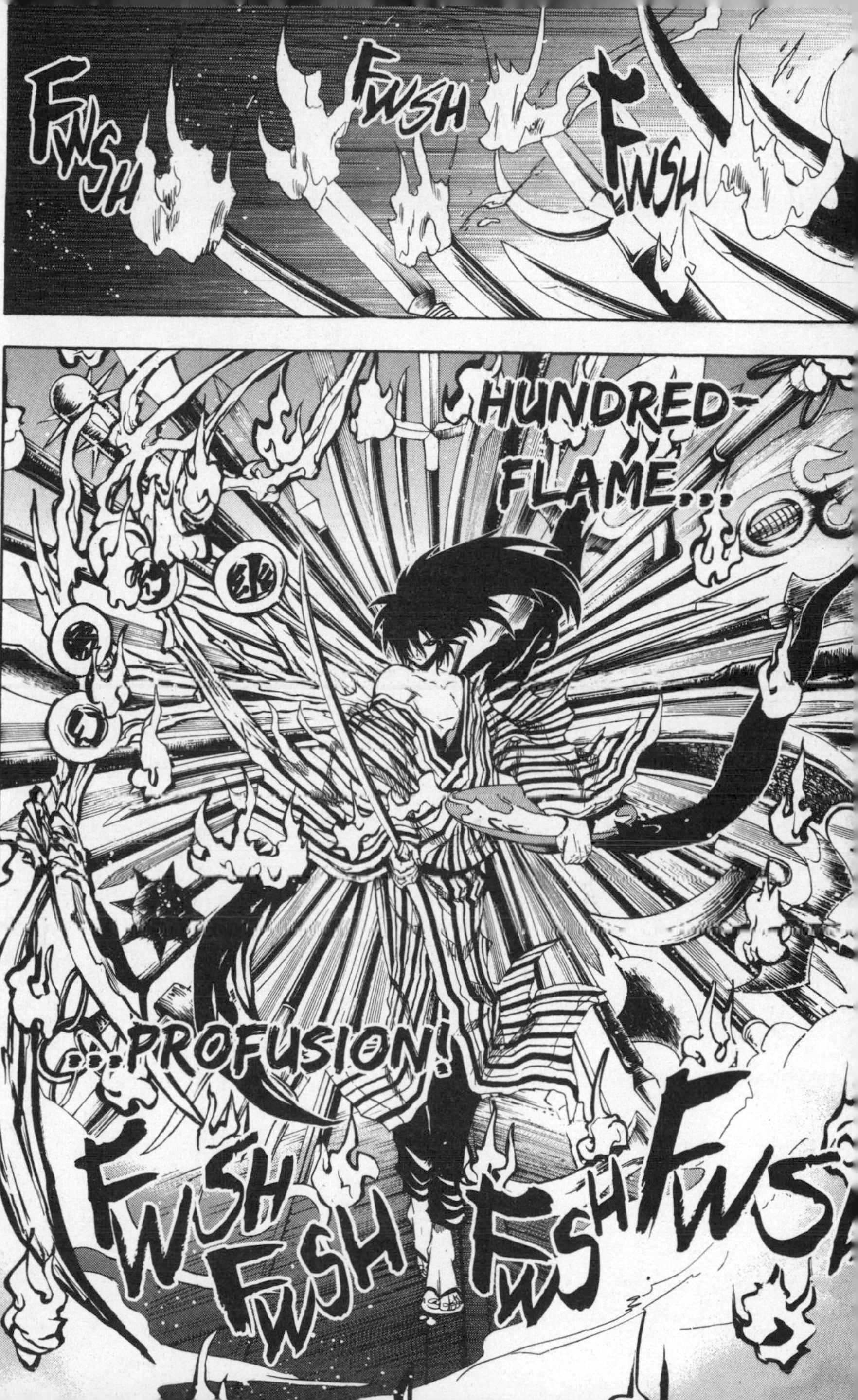
FWSH
FWSH
FWSH
HUNDRED-FLAME...
...PROFUSION!
FWSH
FWSH
FWSH
FWSH
FWSH

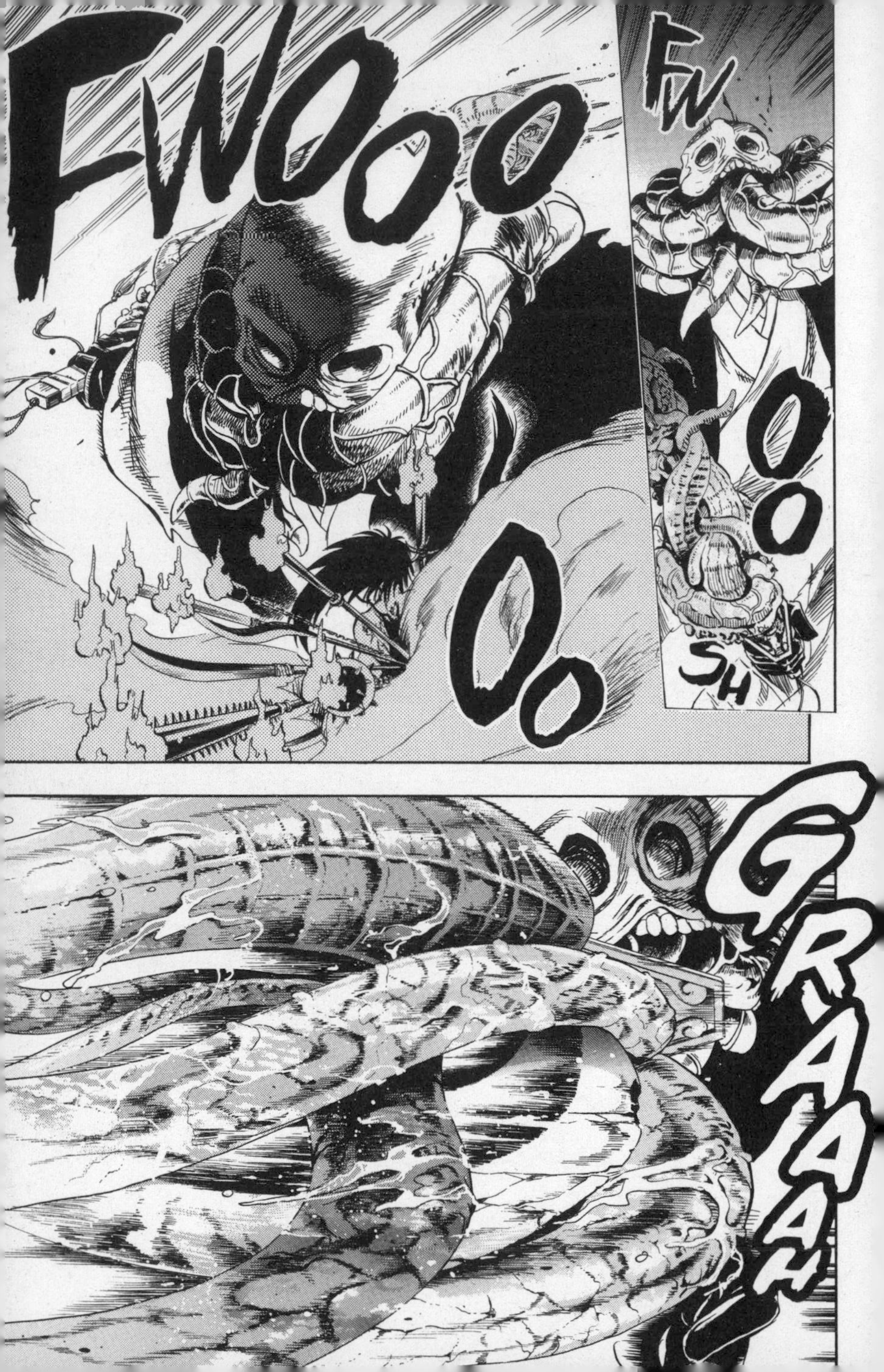
FWOOO
SH
FWOOOOO
GRAAAH

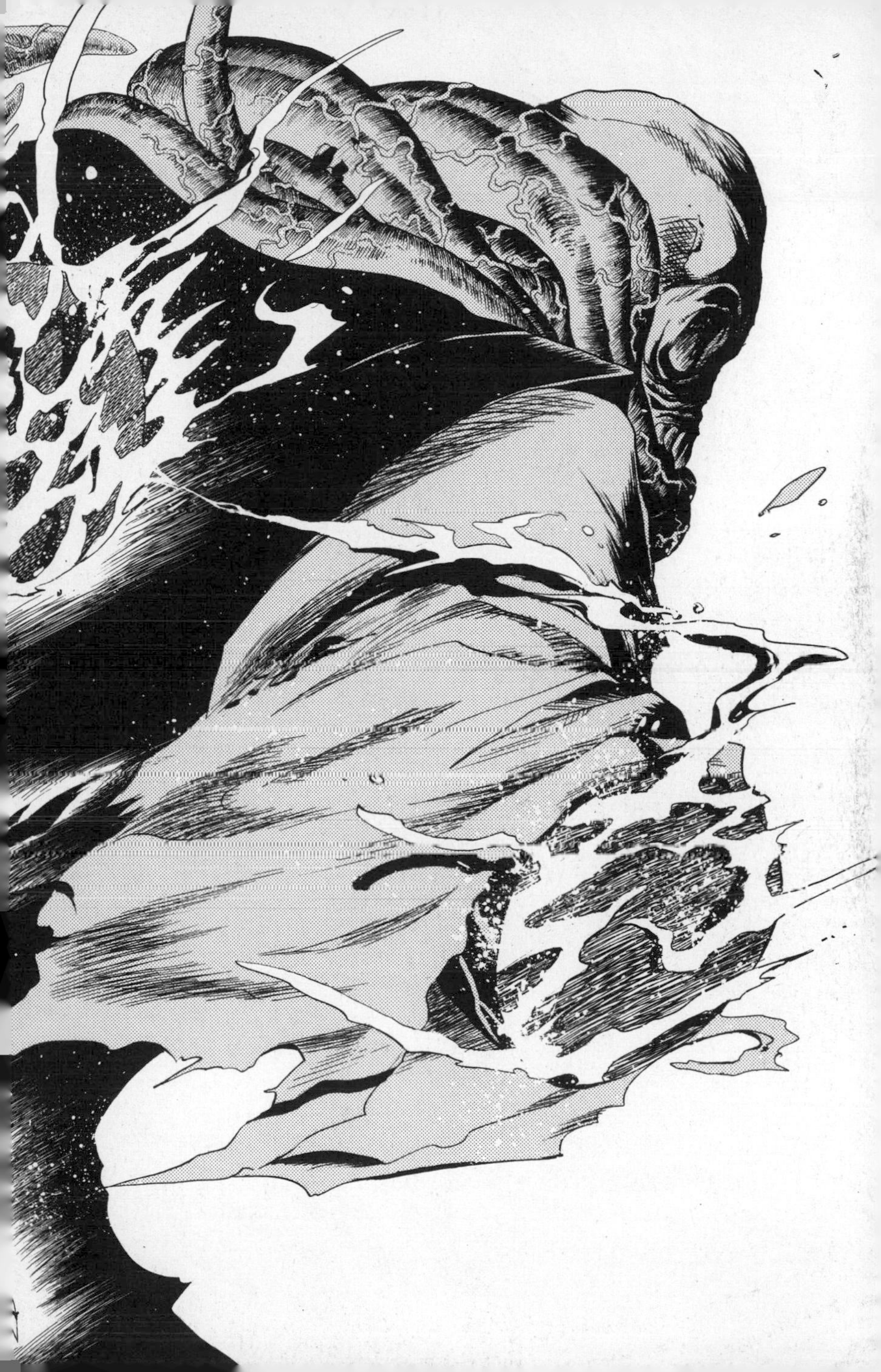

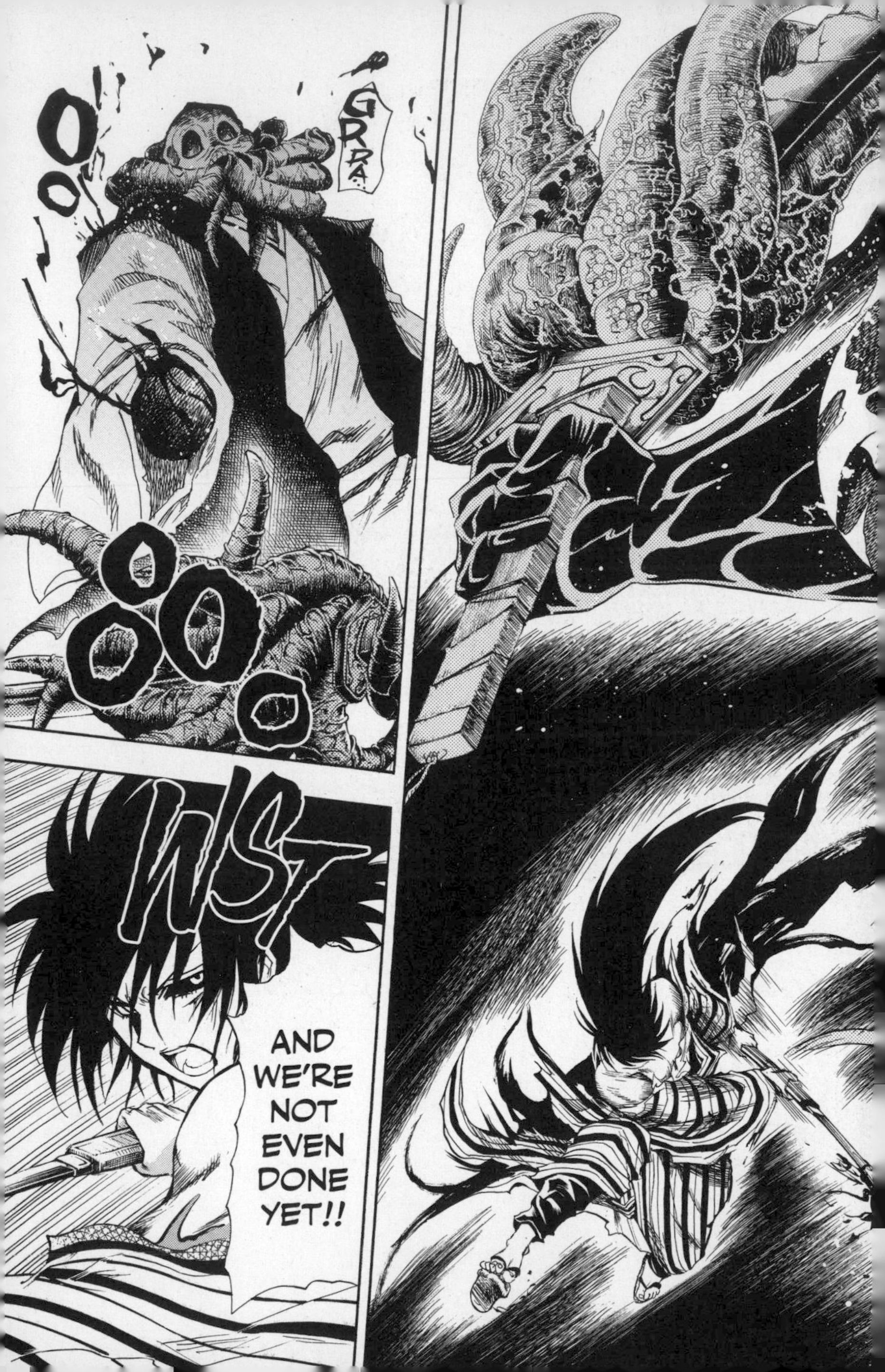
GRDA...
OO!!
OOOO
WST
AND WE'RE NOT EVEN DONE YET!!

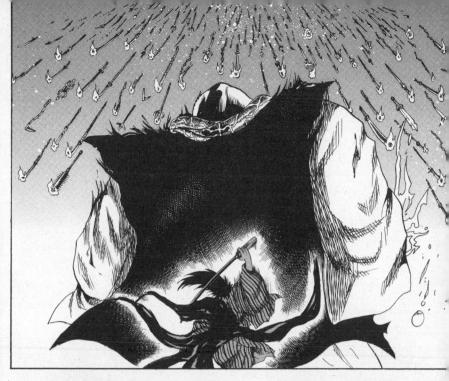

OÖOAR...

GRRR

WSST

DO IT!!

KURO...

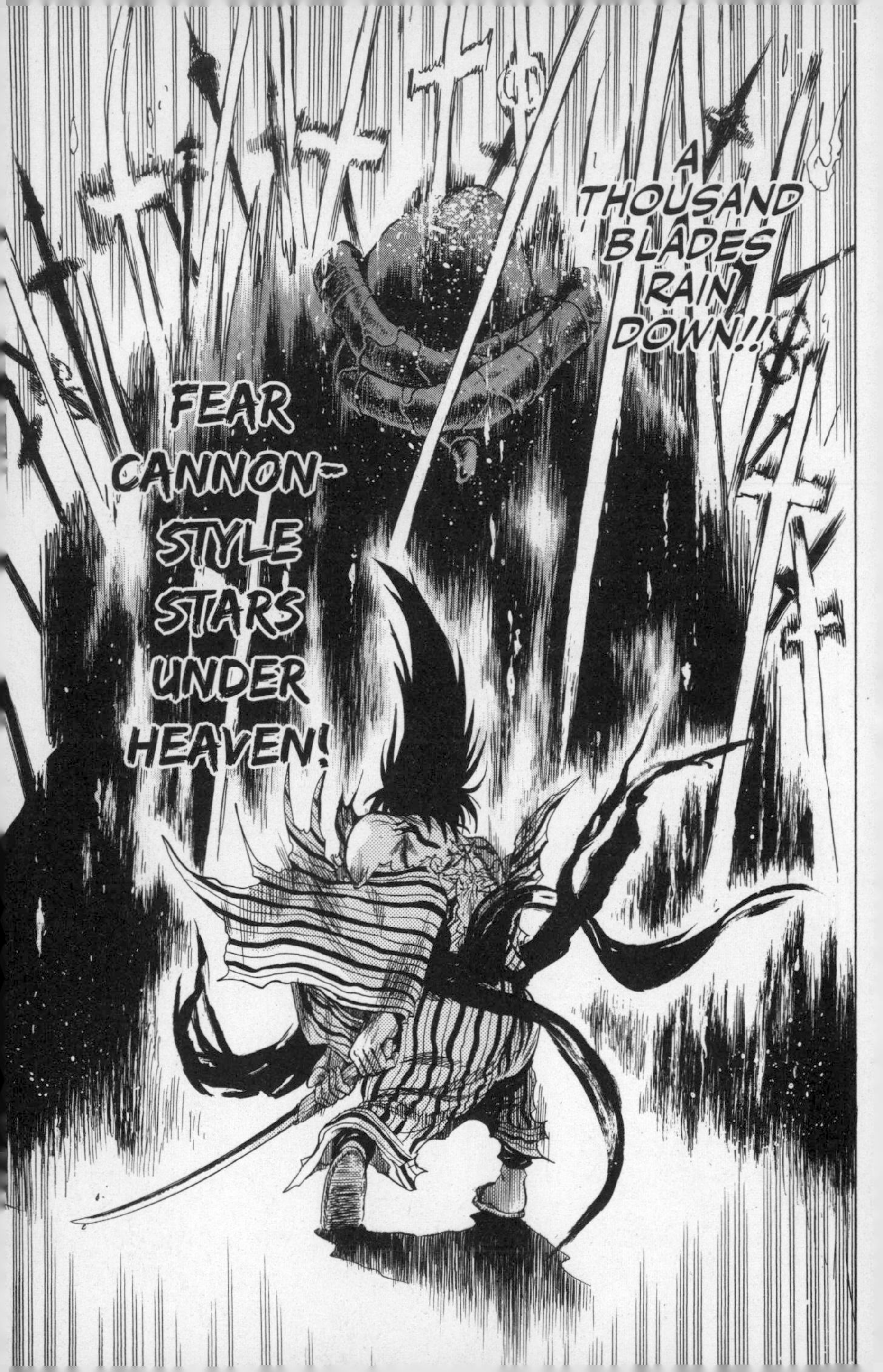
A THOUSAND BLADES RAIN DOWN!!
FEAR CANNON-STYLE STARS UNDER HEAVEN!

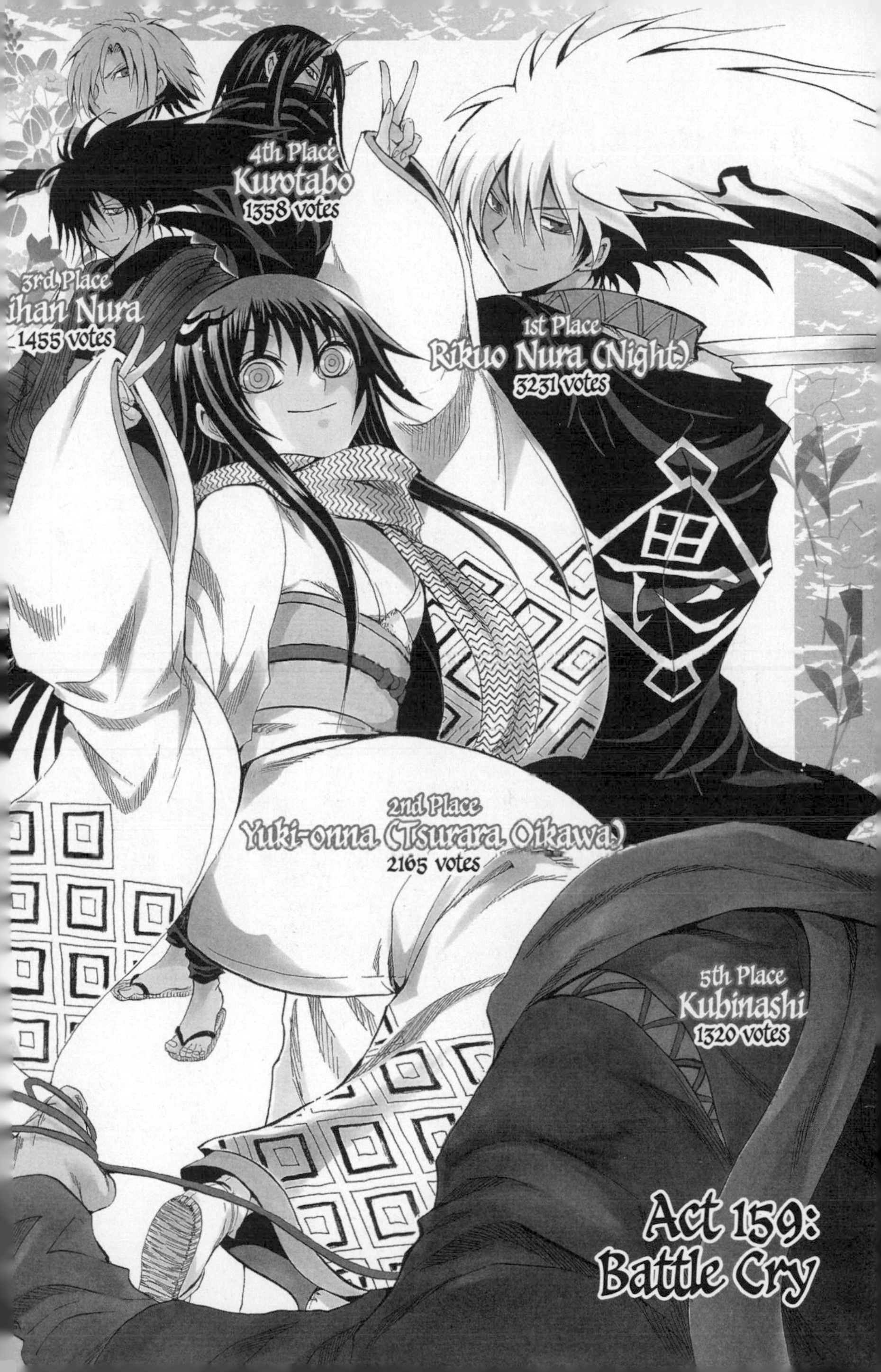
4th Place
Kurotabo
1358 votes
1st Place
Rikuo Nura (Night)
3231 votes
3rd Place
ihan Nura
1455 votes
2nd Place
Yuki-onna (Tsurara Oikawa)
2165 votes
5th Place
Kubinashi
1320 votes
Act 159:
Battle Cry

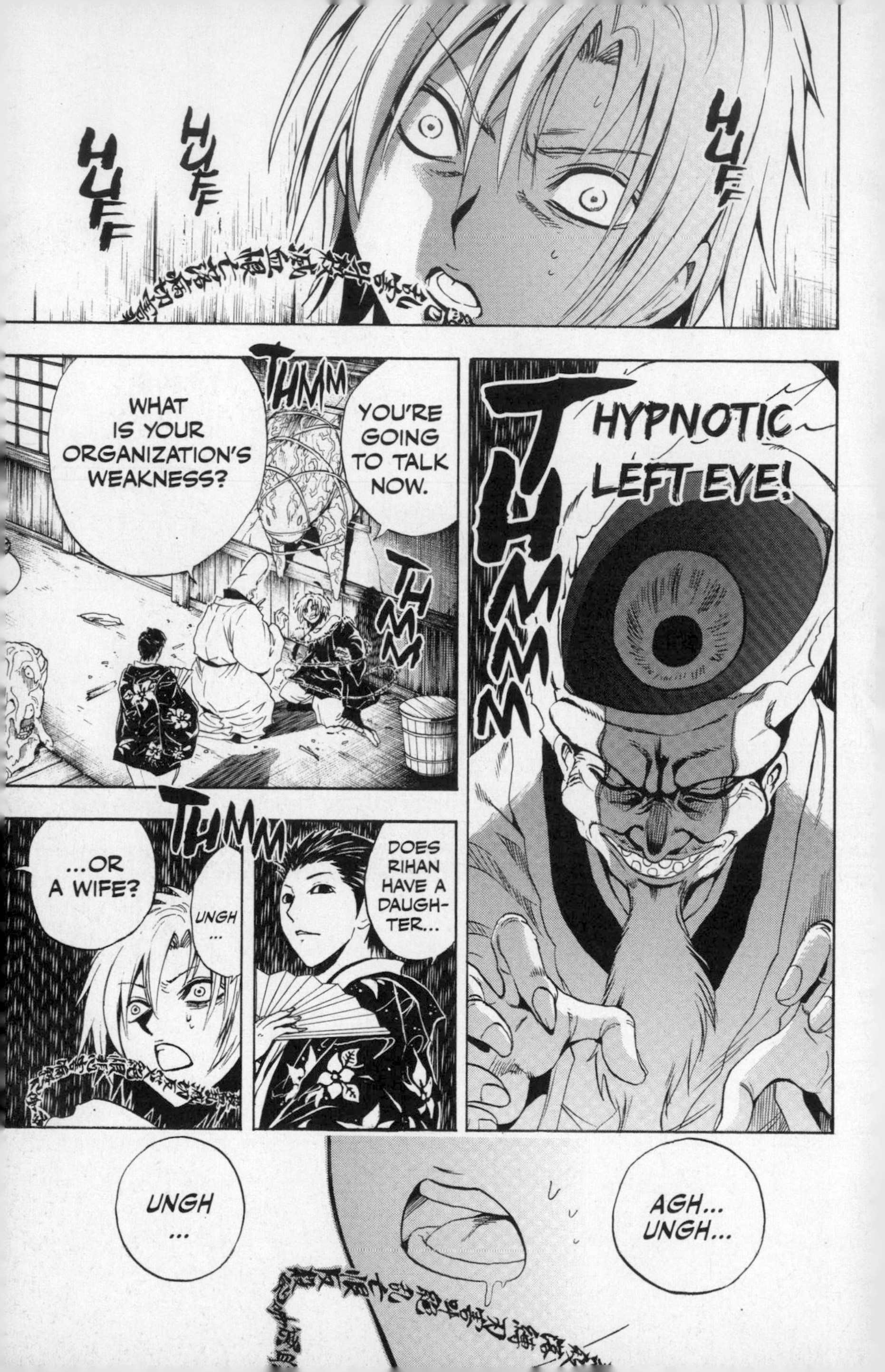
HUFF
HUFF
HUFF
THMMMM
HYPNOTIC LEFT EYE!
THMM
YOU'RE GOING TO TALK NOW.
THMM
WHAT IS YOUR ORGANIZATION'S WEAKNESS?
THMM
DOES RIHAN HAVE A DAUGH-TER...
UNGH ...
...OR A WIFE?
AGH... UNGH...
UNGH ...

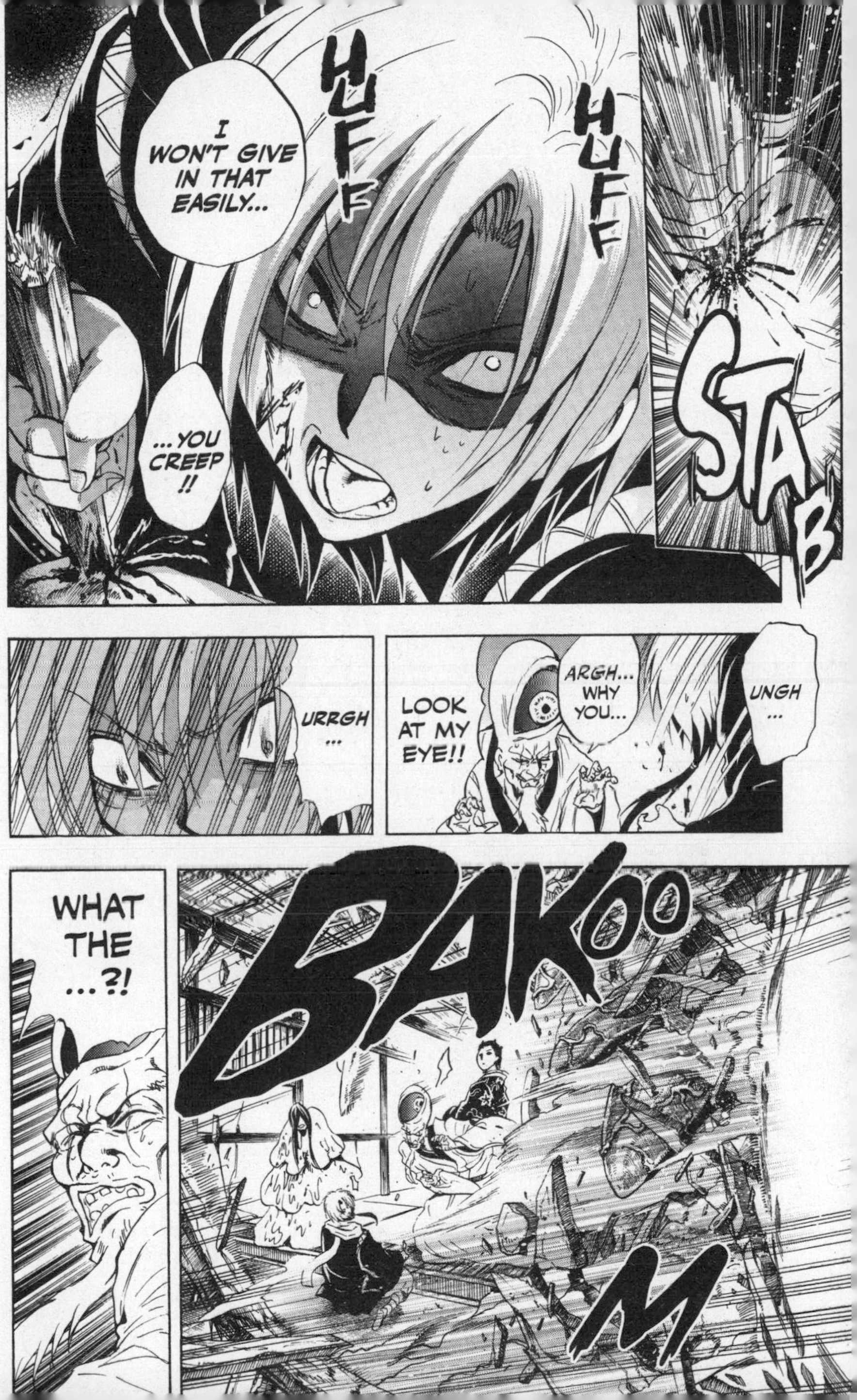
STAB
HUFF
HUFF
I WON'T GIVE IN THAT EASILY...
...YOU CREEP!!
UNGH...
ARGH... WHY YOU...
LOOK AT MY EYE!!
URRGH...
BAKOOOM
WHAT THE...?!

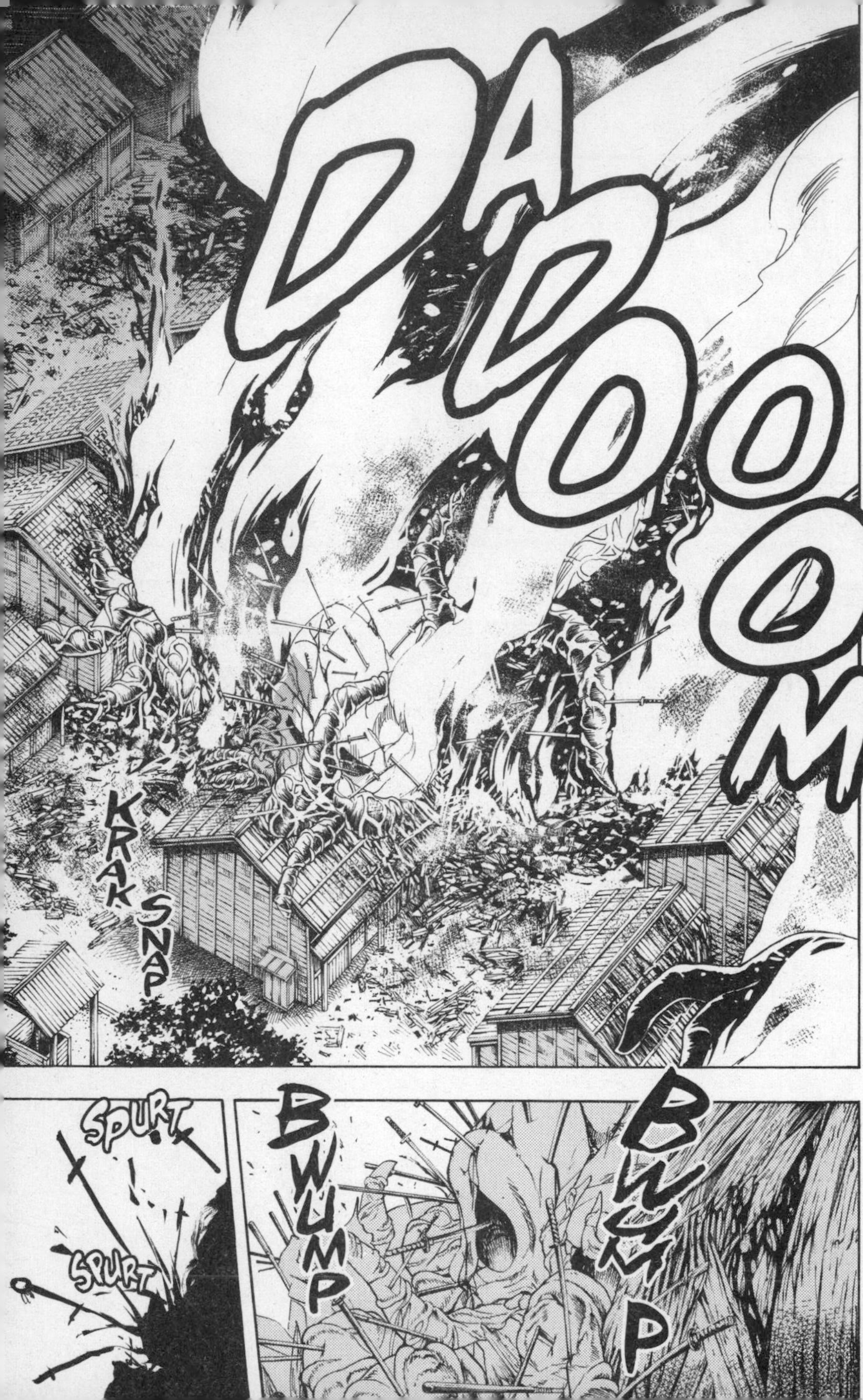
DADOOOOM
KRAK
SNAP
BWUMP
BWUMP
SPURT
SPURT

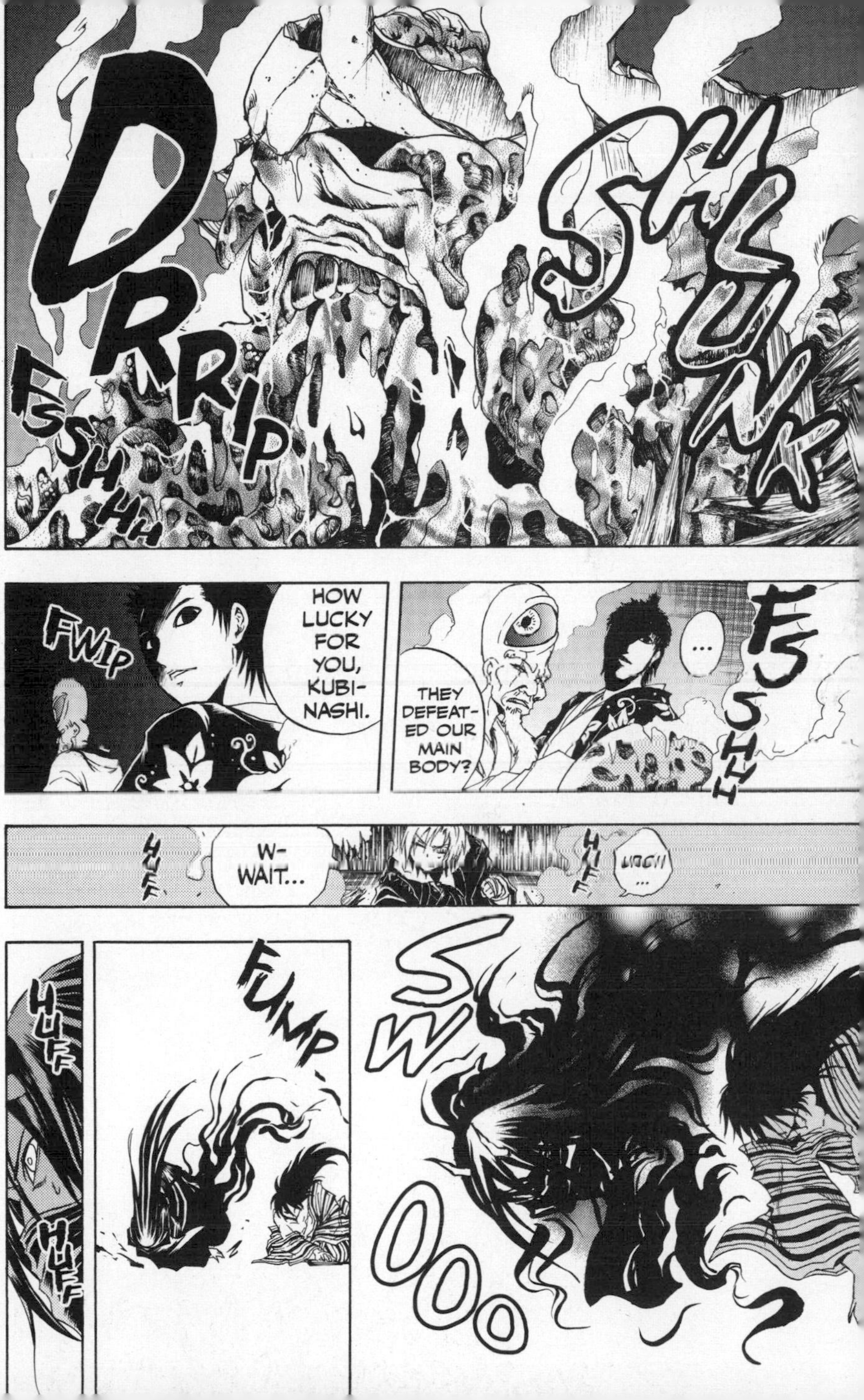
SHUNK
DRRIP
FSSHHH
FSSHHH
...
THEY DEFEATED OUR MAIN BODY?
HOW LUCKY FOR YOU, KUBINASHI.
FWIP
HUFF
W-WAIT...
HUFF
SWOOO
FUMP
HUFF
HUFF

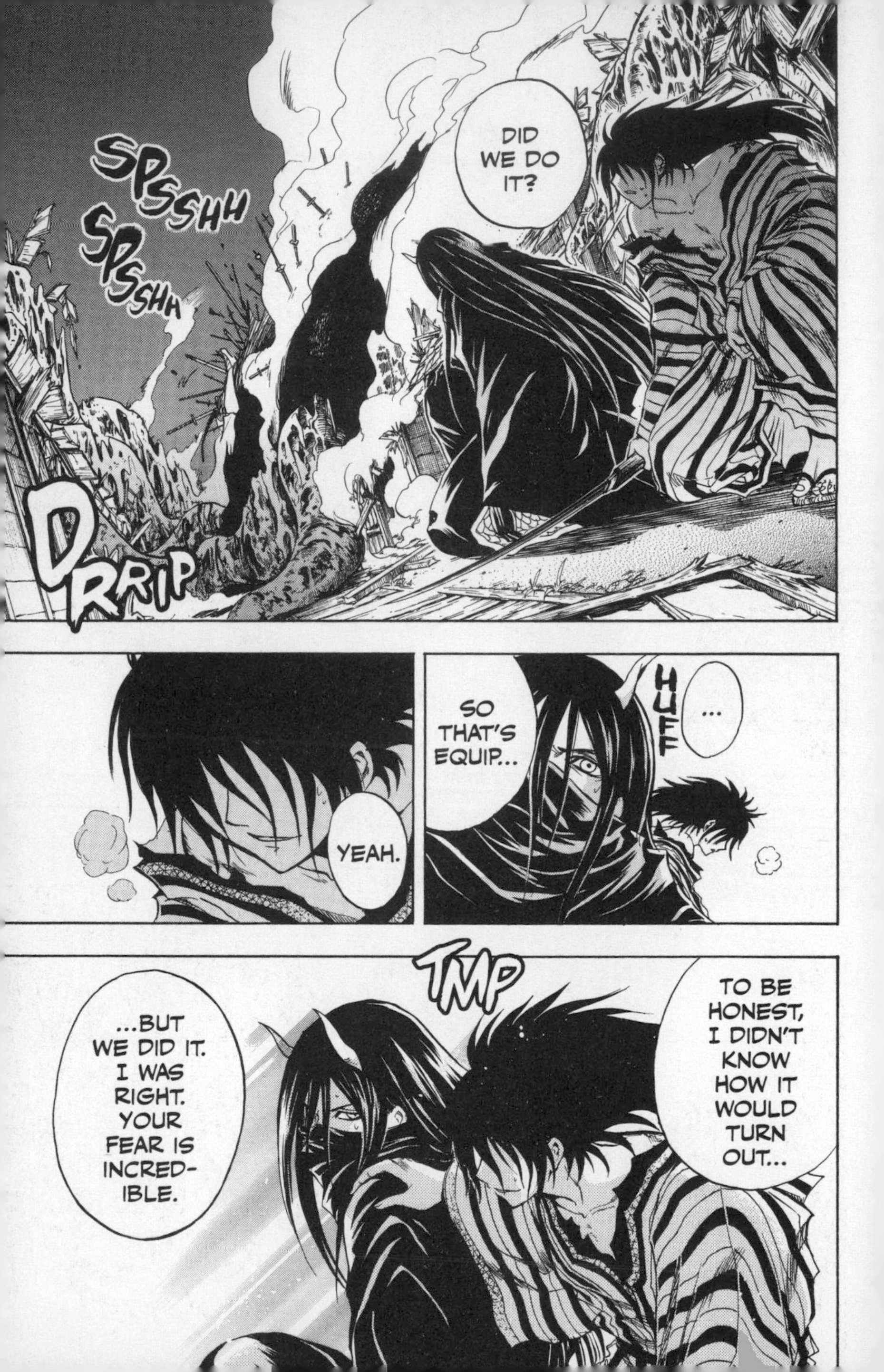
DID WE DO IT?
SPSSHH
SPSSHH
DRRIP
...
HUFF
SO THAT'S EQUIP...
YEAH.
TMP
TO BE HONEST, I DIDN'T KNOW HOW IT WOULD TURN OUT...
...BUT WE DID IT. I WAS RIGHT. YOUR FEAR IS INCRED-IBLE.

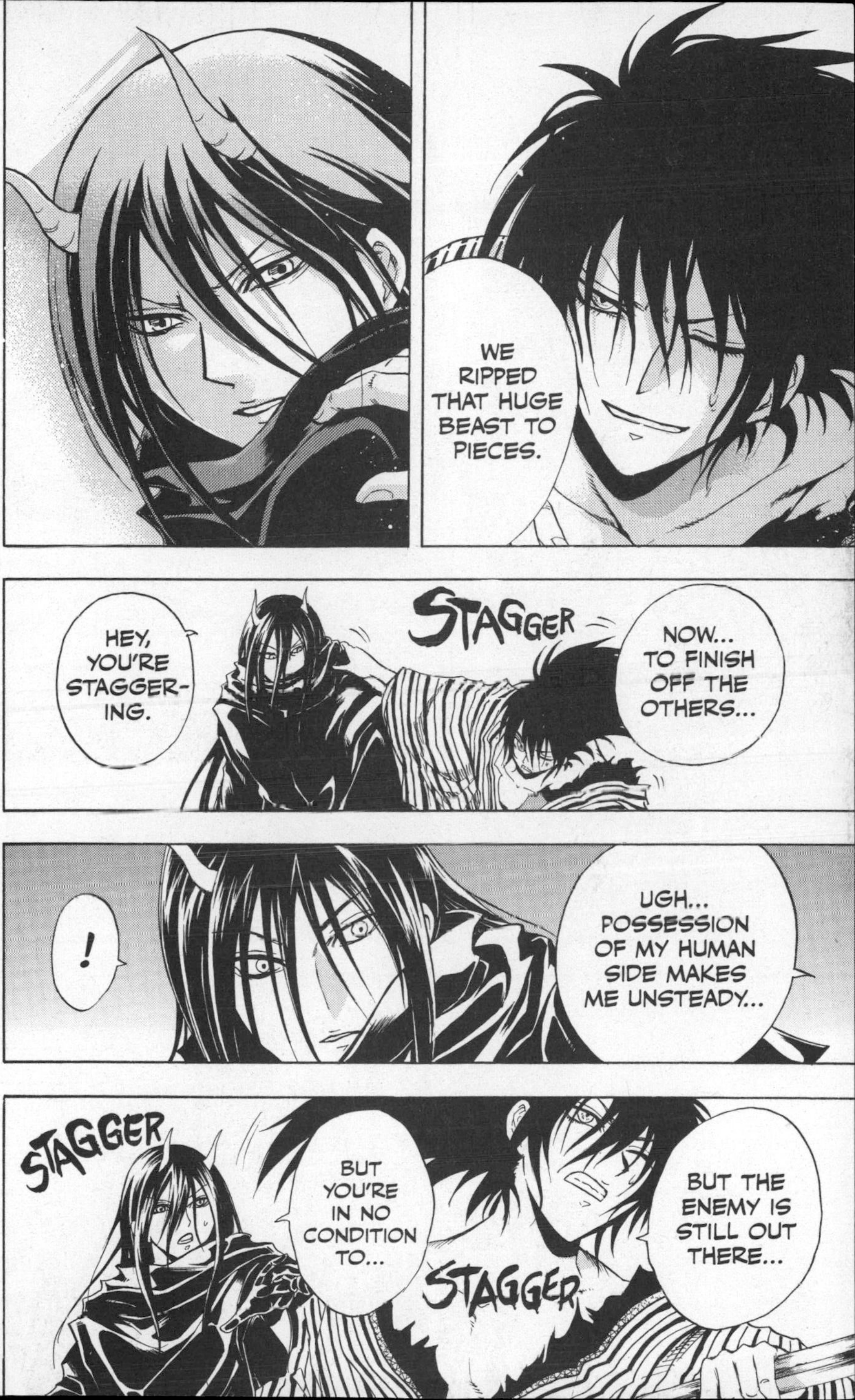
WE RIPPED THAT HUGE BEAST TO PIECES.
NOW... TO FINISH OFF THE OTHERS...
STAGGER
HEY, YOU'RE STAGGER-ING.
UGH... POSSESSION OF MY HUMAN SIDE MAKES ME UNSTEADY...
!
BUT THE ENEMY IS STILL OUT THERE...
STAGGER
BUT YOU'RE IN NO CONDITION TO...
STAGGER

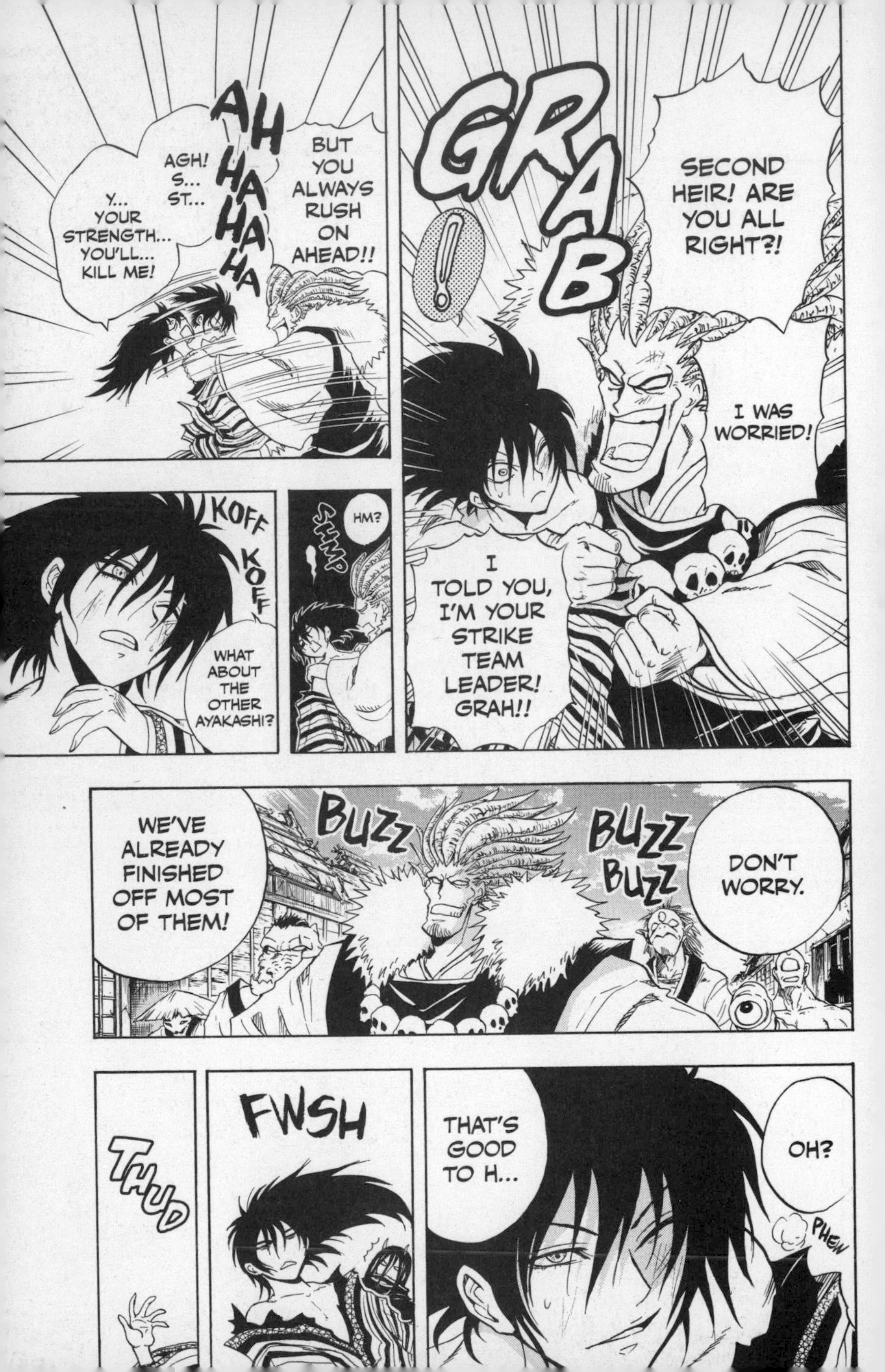
GRAB
!
SECOND HEIR! ARE YOU ALL RIGHT?!
I WAS WORRIED!
I TOLD YOU, I'M YOUR STRIKE TEAM LEADER! GRAH!!
BUT YOU ALWAYS RUSH ON AHEAD!!
AHHAHAHAHA
AGH! S... ST...
Y... YOUR STRENGTH... YOU'LL... KILL ME!
HM?
SHMP
KOFF KOFF
WHAT ABOUT THE OTHER AYAKASHI?
DON'T WORRY.
BUZZ BUZZ
BUZZ
WE'VE ALREADY FINISHED OFF MOST OF THEM!
OH?
PHEW
THAT'S GOOD TO H...
FWSH
THUD

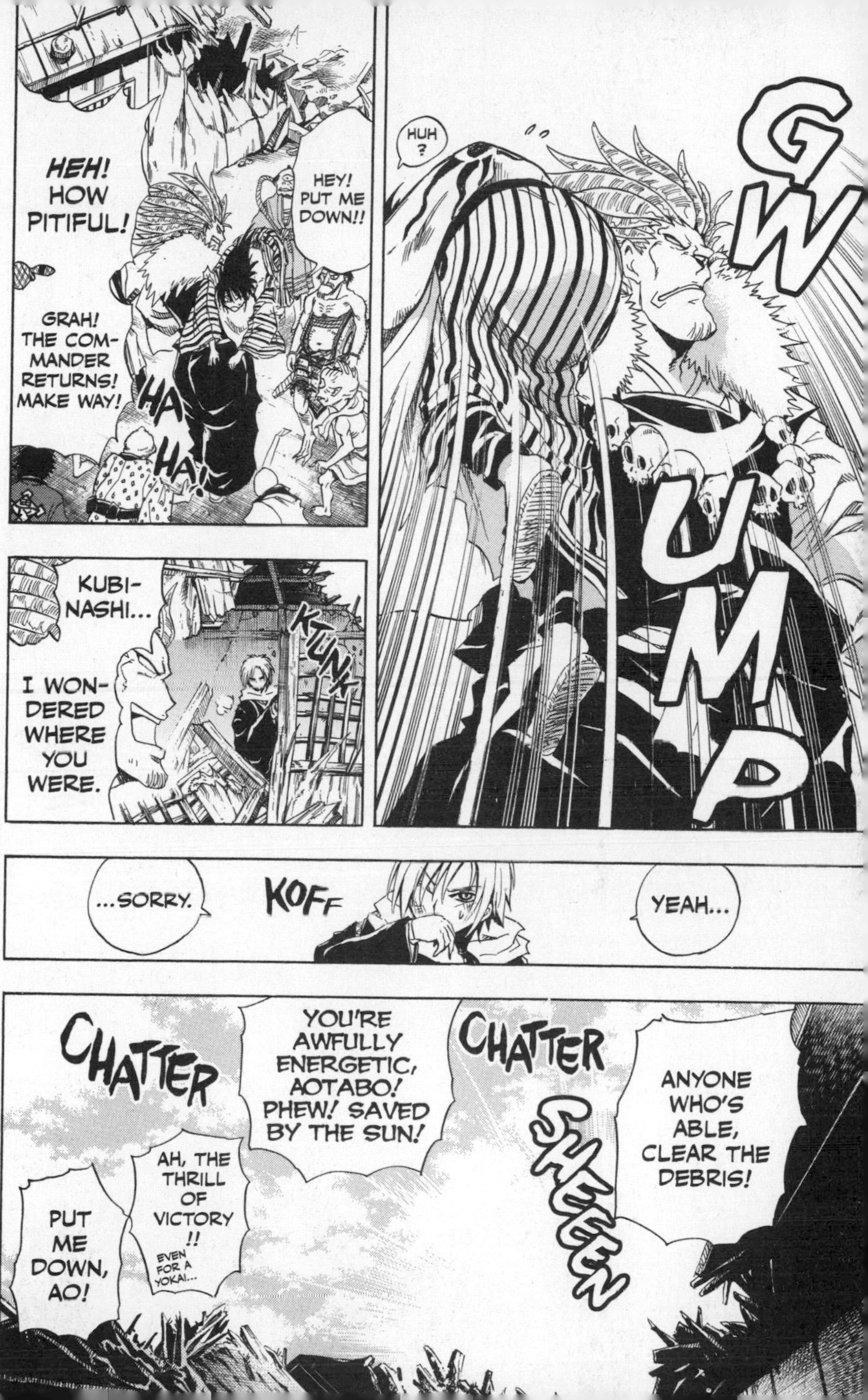
HUH?
GWUMP
HEY! PUT ME DOWN!!
HEH! HOW PITIFUL!
GRAH! THE COMMANDER RETURNS! MAKE WAY!
HA HA!
KUBINASHI...
KLUNK
I WONDERED WHERE YOU WERE.
YEAH...
KOFF
...SORRY.
ANYONE WHO'S ABLE, CLEAR THE DEBRIS!
CHATTER
SHEEEN
YOU'RE AWFULLY ENERGETIC, AOTABO! PHEW! SAVED BY THE SUN!
CHATTER
AH, THE THRILL OF VICTORY!! EVEN FOR A YOKAI...
PUT ME DOWN, AO!

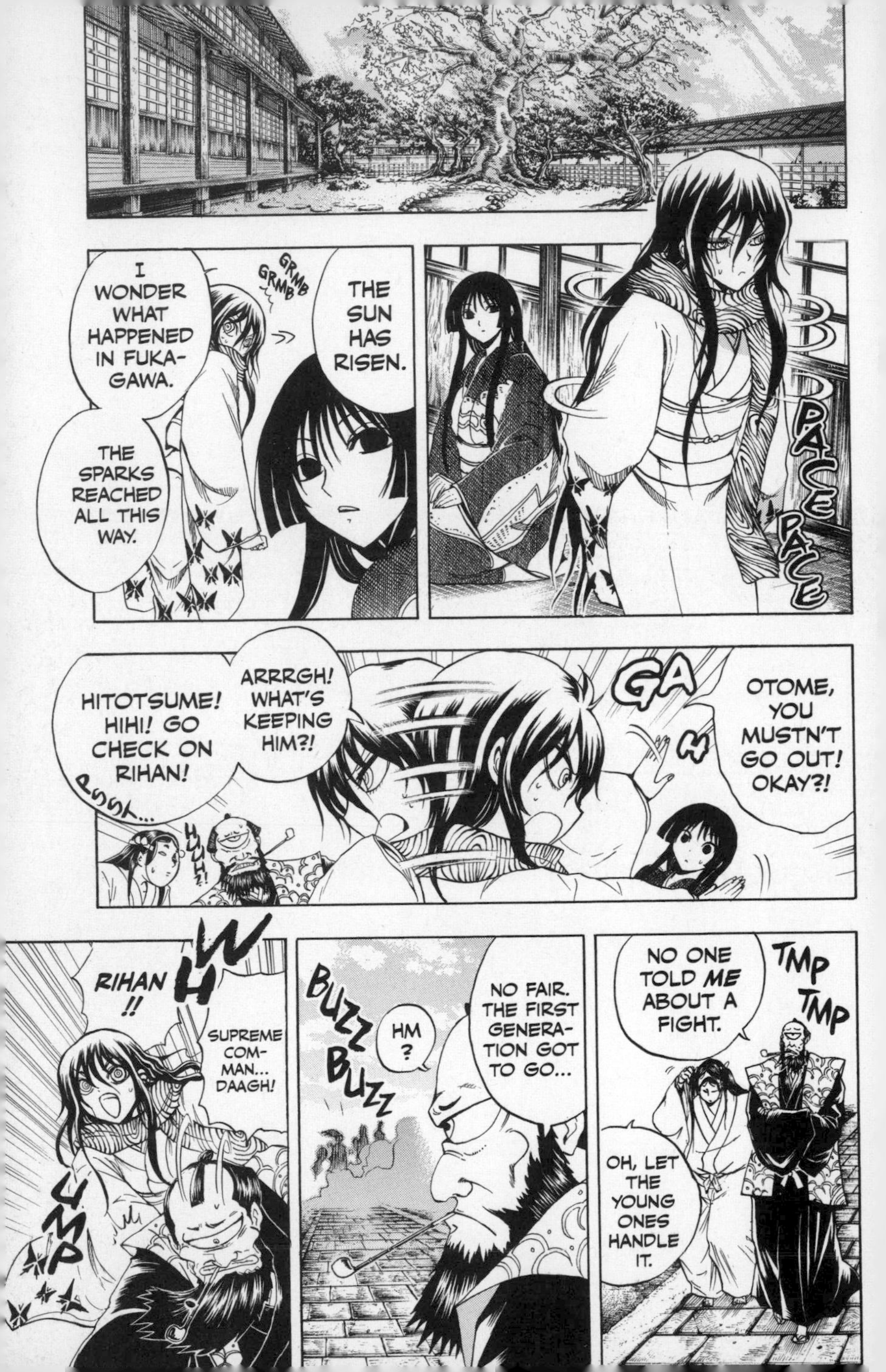
PACE PACE
THE SUN HAS RISEN.
GRMB GRMB
I WONDER WHAT HAPPENED IN FUKA-GAWA.
THE SPARKS REACHED ALL THIS WAY.
OTOME, YOU MUSTN'T GO OUT! OKAY?!
GA H
ARRRGH! WHAT'S KEEPING HIM?!
HITOTSUME! HIHI! GO CHECK ON RIHAN!
TMP TMP
NO ONE TOLD *ME* ABOUT A FIGHT.
OH, LET THE YOUNG ONES HANDLE IT.
NO FAIR. THE FIRST GENERA-TION GOT TO GO...
HM?
BUZZ BUZZ
WHH
RIHAN!!
SUPREME COM-MAN... DAAGH!
UMP

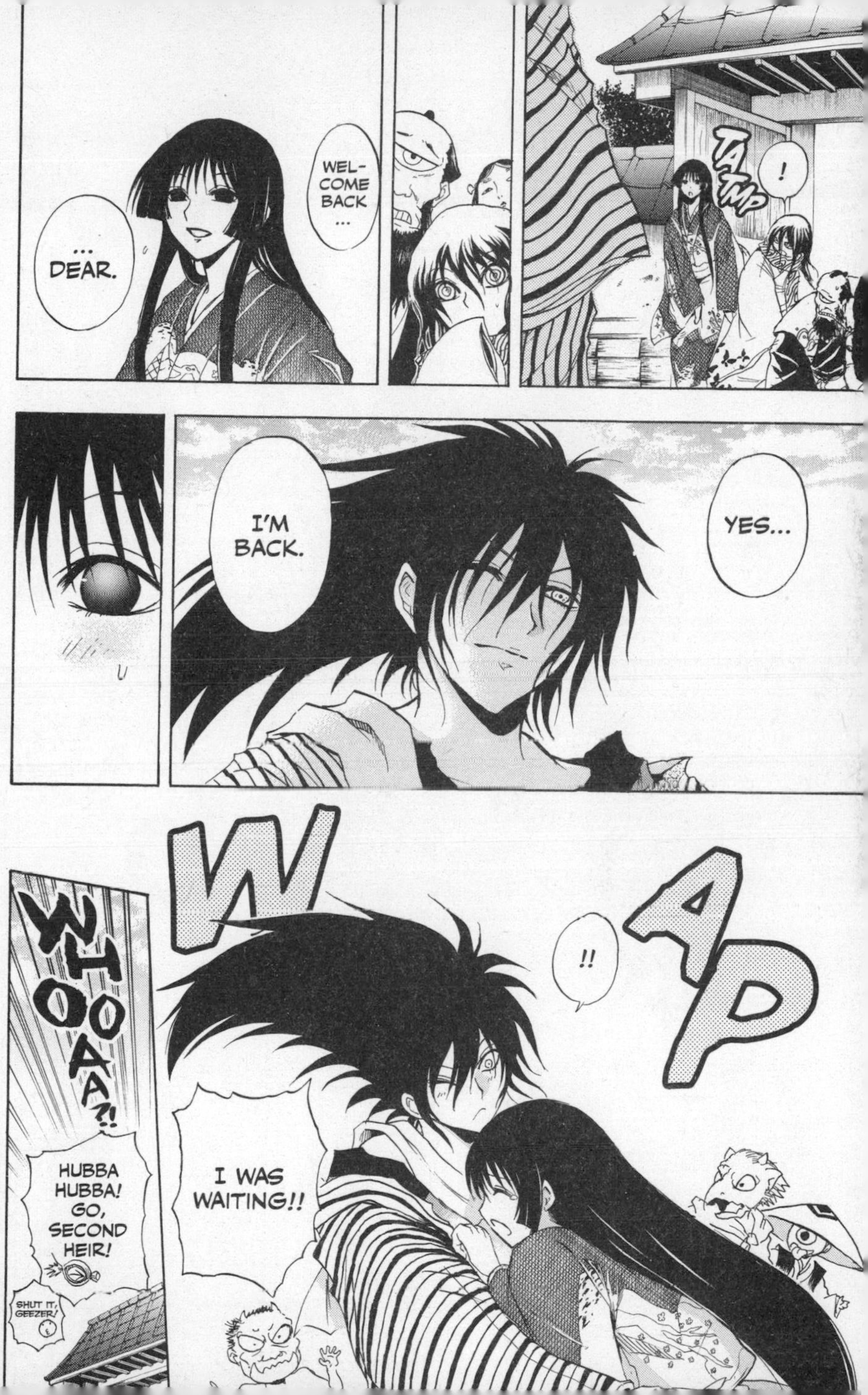
!
TA TMP
WEL-COME BACK ...
... DEAR.
YES...
I'M BACK.
WAP
!!
I WAS WAITING!!
WHOOAA?!
HUBBA HUBBA! GO, SECOND HEIR!
SHUT IT, GEEZER!

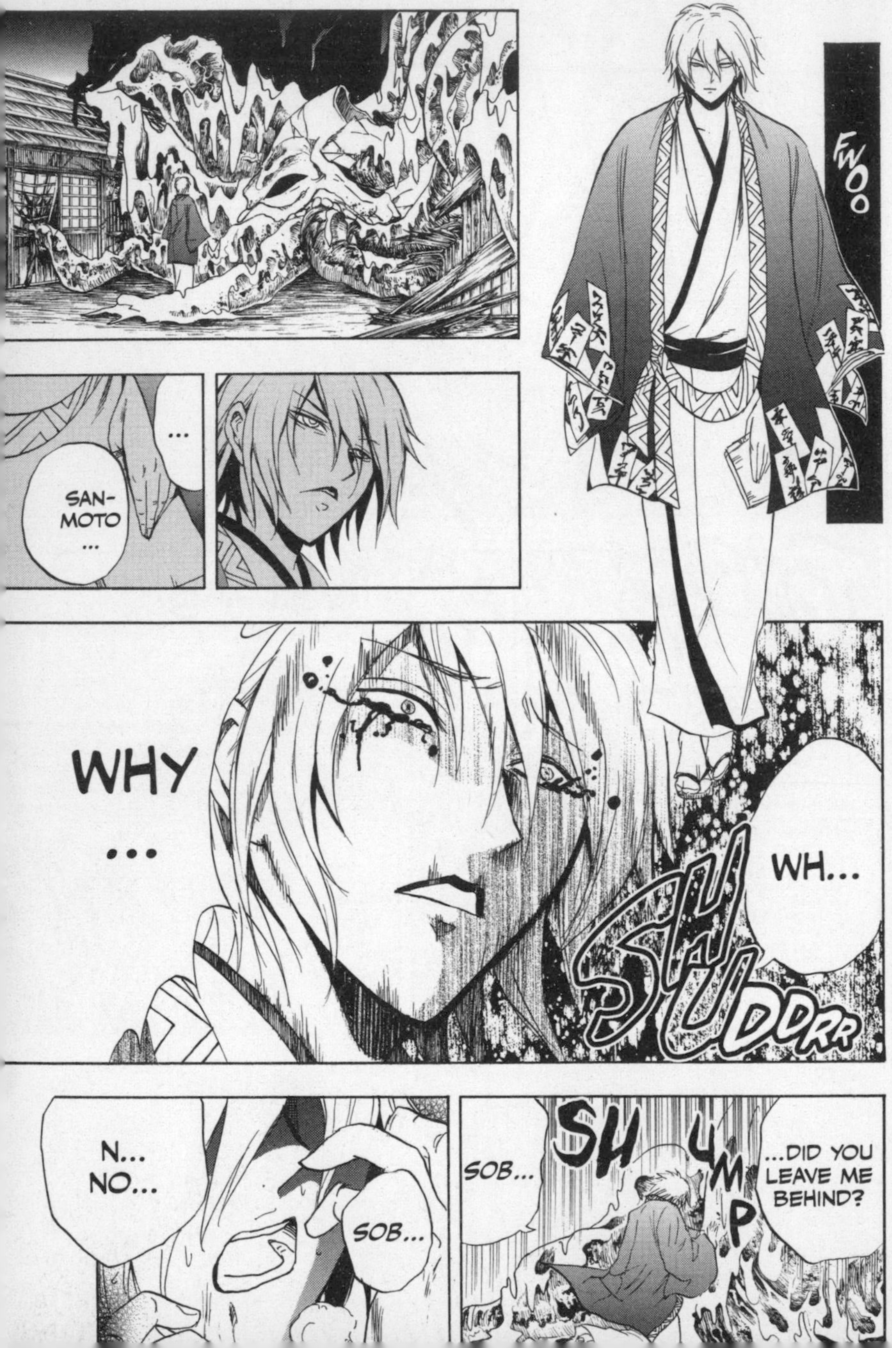

FWOO
...
SAN-MOTO ...
WH...
SHUDDRR
WHY ...
...DID YOU LEAVE ME BEHIND?
SHUMP
SOB...
N... NO...
SOB...

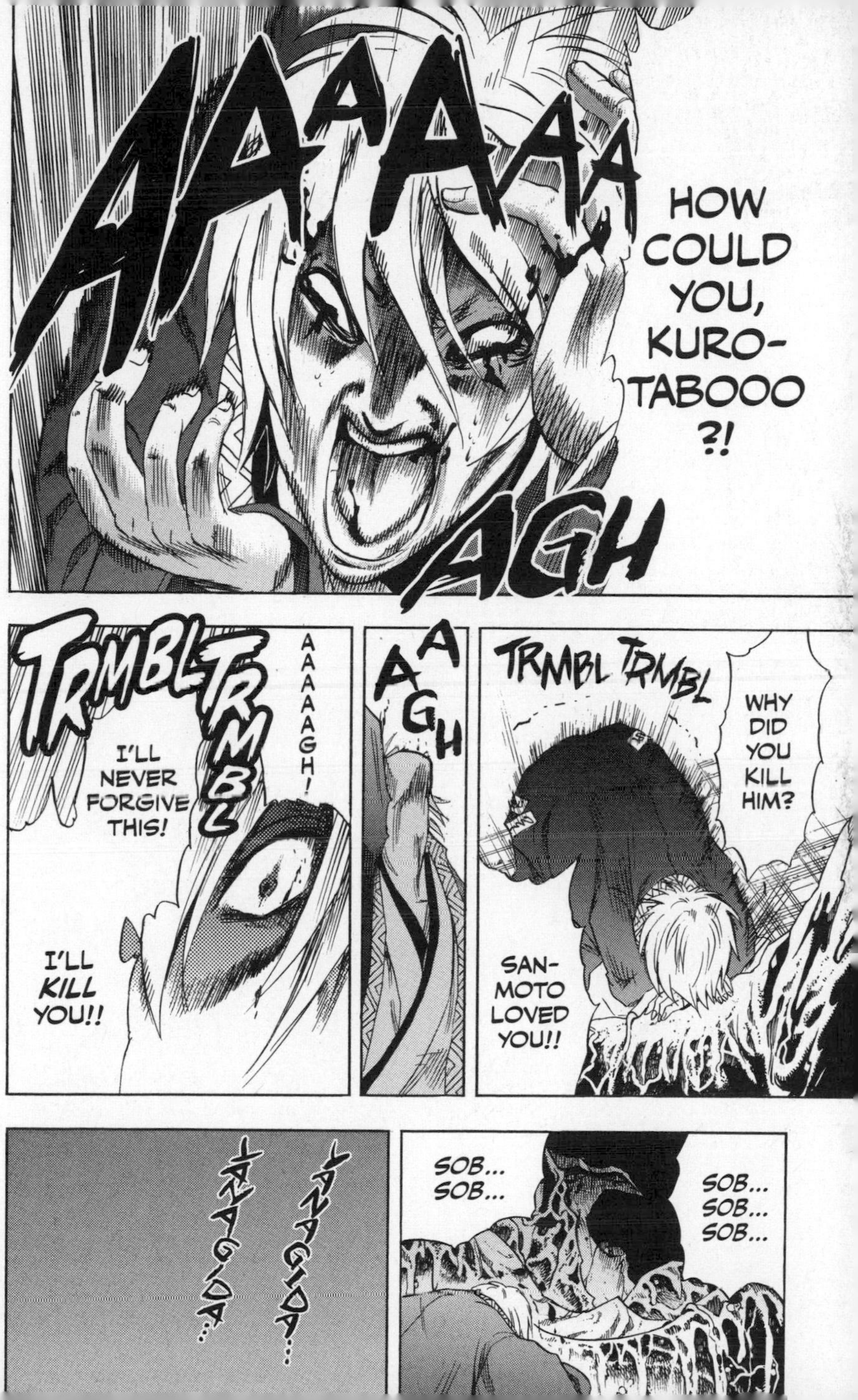
AAAAAA
HOW COULD YOU, KURO-TABOOO ?!
AGH
TRMBL TRMBL
WHY DID YOU KILL HIM?
SAN-MOTO LOVED YOU!!
AAGH
AAAAAAGH!
TRMBL TRMBL
I'LL NEVER FORGIVE THIS!
I'LL KILL YOU!!
SOB... SOB... SOB...
SOB... SOB...
YANAGIDA...
YANAGIDA...

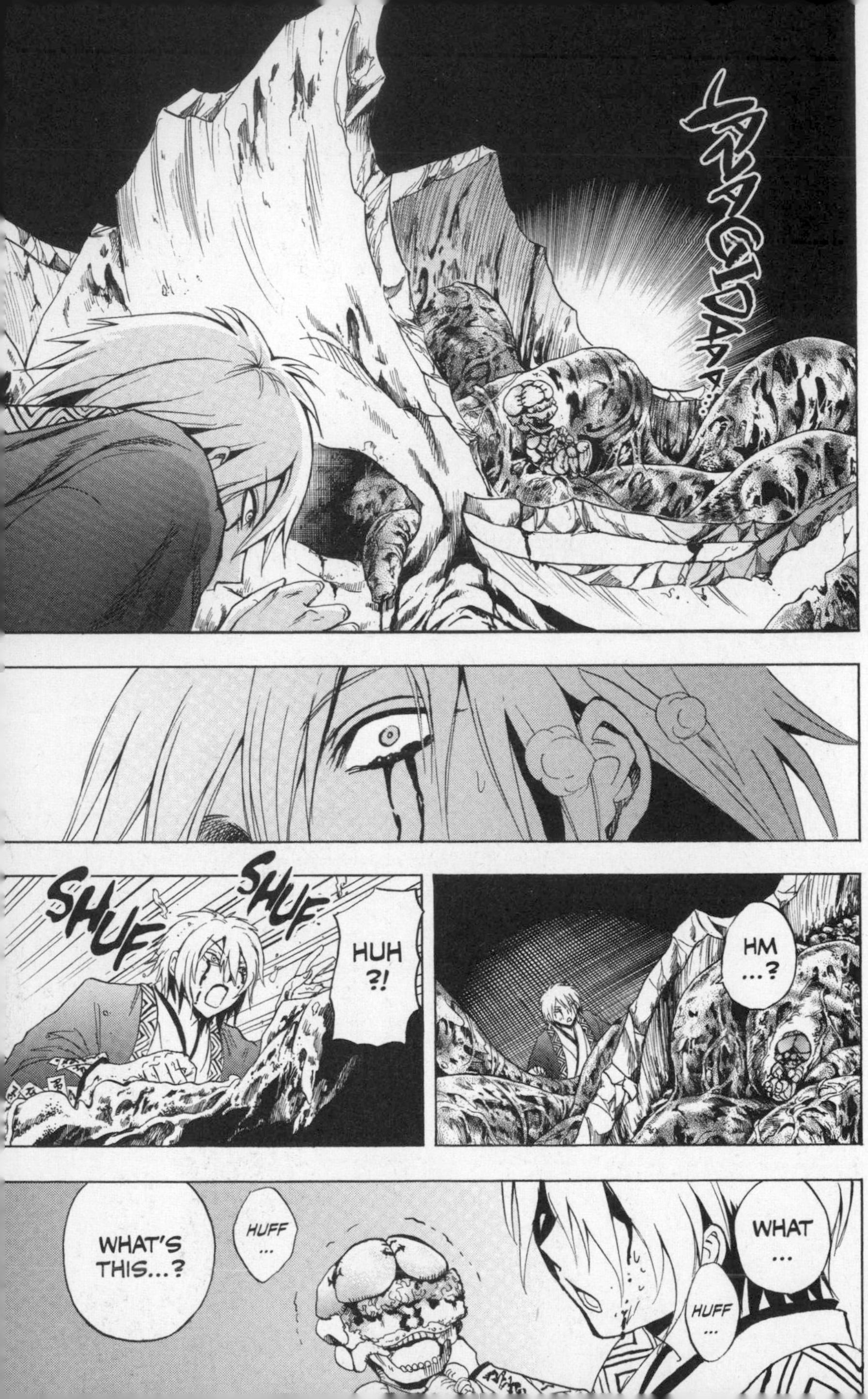
YANAGIDAAA...
HM ...?
SHUF
SHUF
HUH ?!
WHAT ...
HUFF ...
HUFF ...
WHAT'S THIS...?

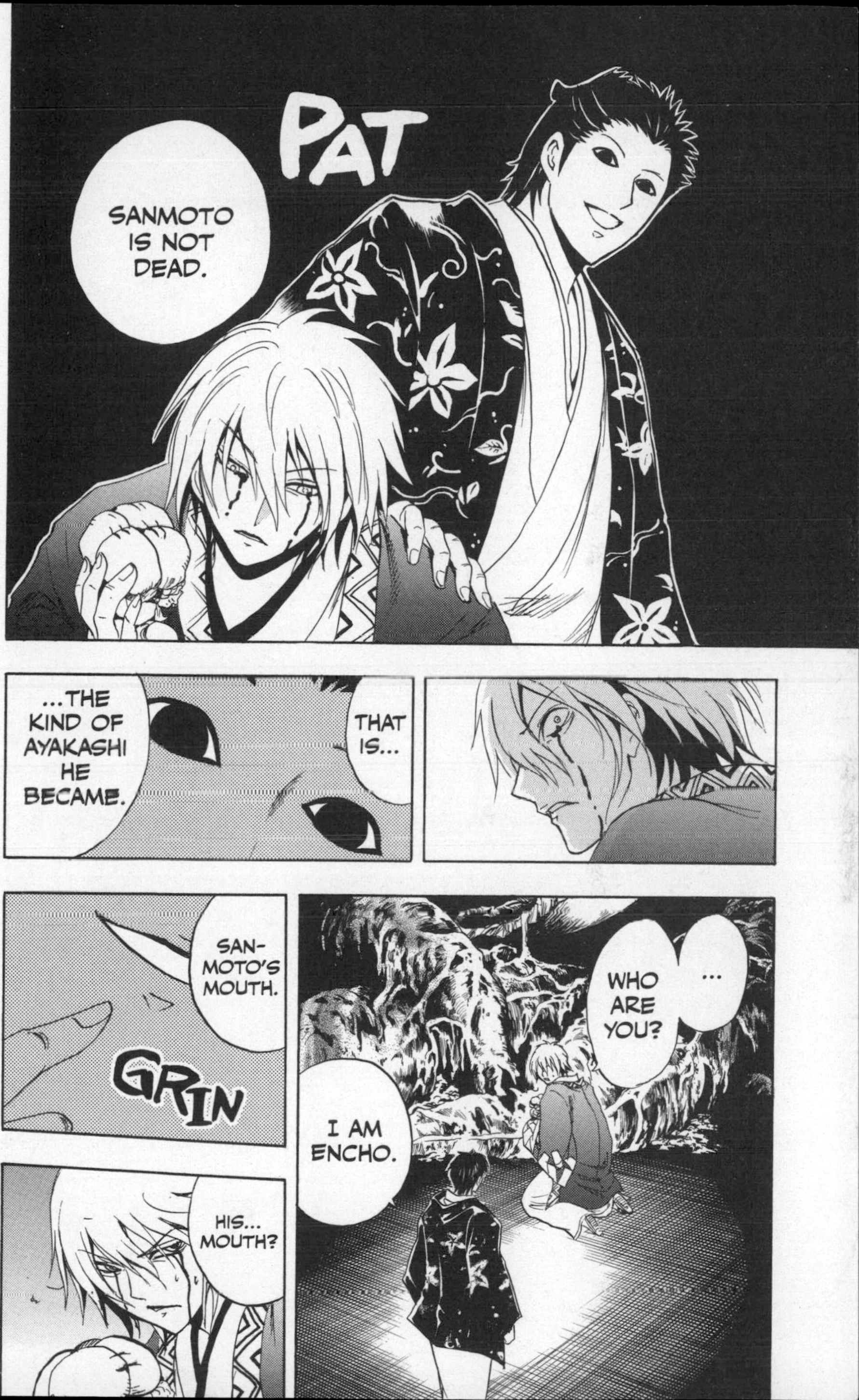
PAT
SANMOTO IS NOT DEAD.
THAT IS...
...THE KIND OF AYAKASHI HE BECAME.
...
WHO ARE YOU?
I AM ENCHO.
SAN-MOTO'S MOUTH.
GRIN
HIS... MOUTH?

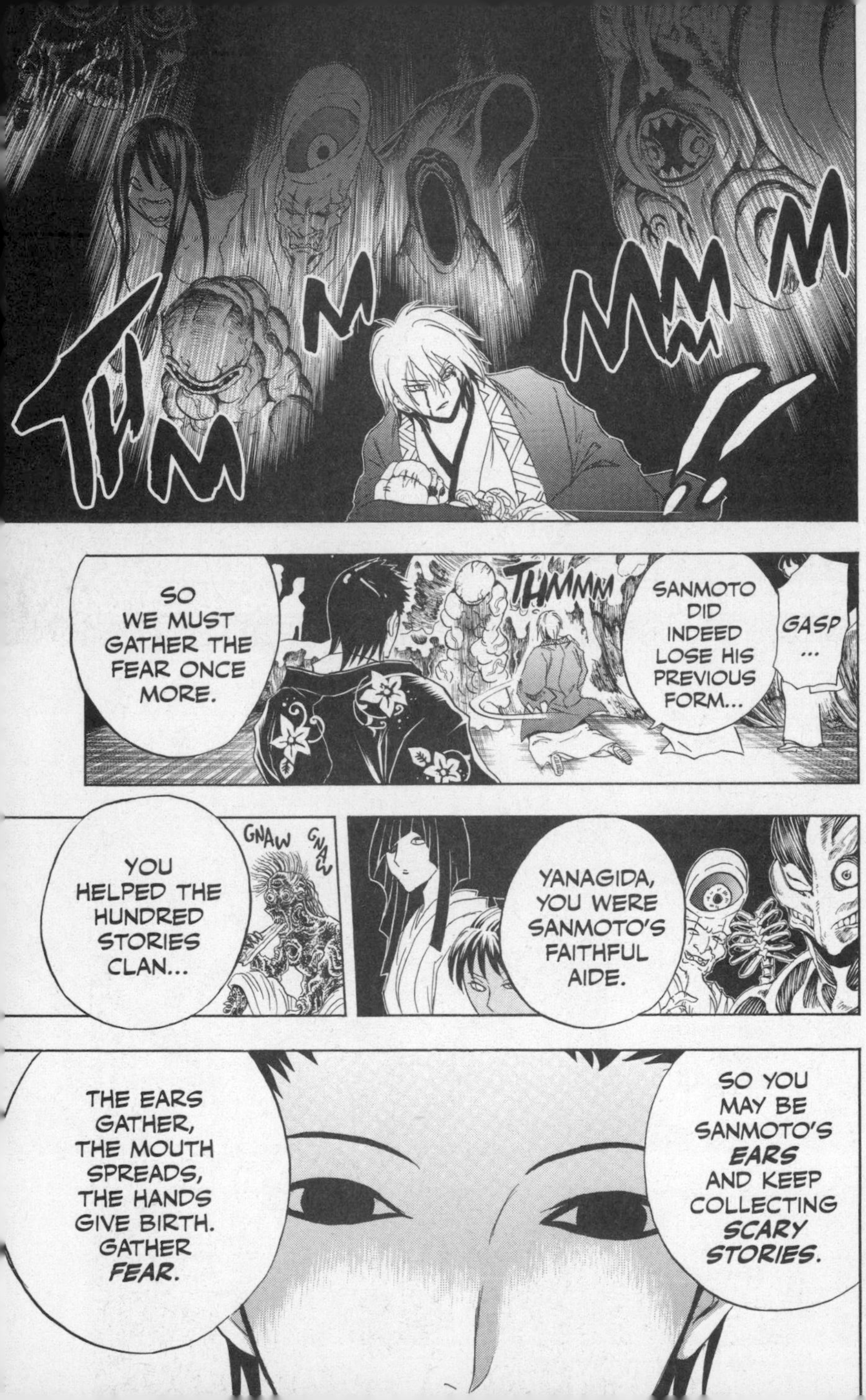
THMMMMMMM
GASP...
SANMOTO DID INDEED LOSE HIS PREVIOUS FORM...
THMMM
SO WE MUST GATHER THE FEAR ONCE MORE.
YANAGIDA, YOU WERE SANMOTO'S FAITHFUL AIDE.
GNAW GNAW
YOU HELPED THE HUNDRED STORIES CLAN...
SO YOU MAY BE SANMOTO'S *EARS* AND KEEP COLLECTING *SCARY STORIES*.
THE EARS GATHER, THE MOUTH SPREADS, THE HANDS GIVE BIRTH. GATHER *FEAR*.

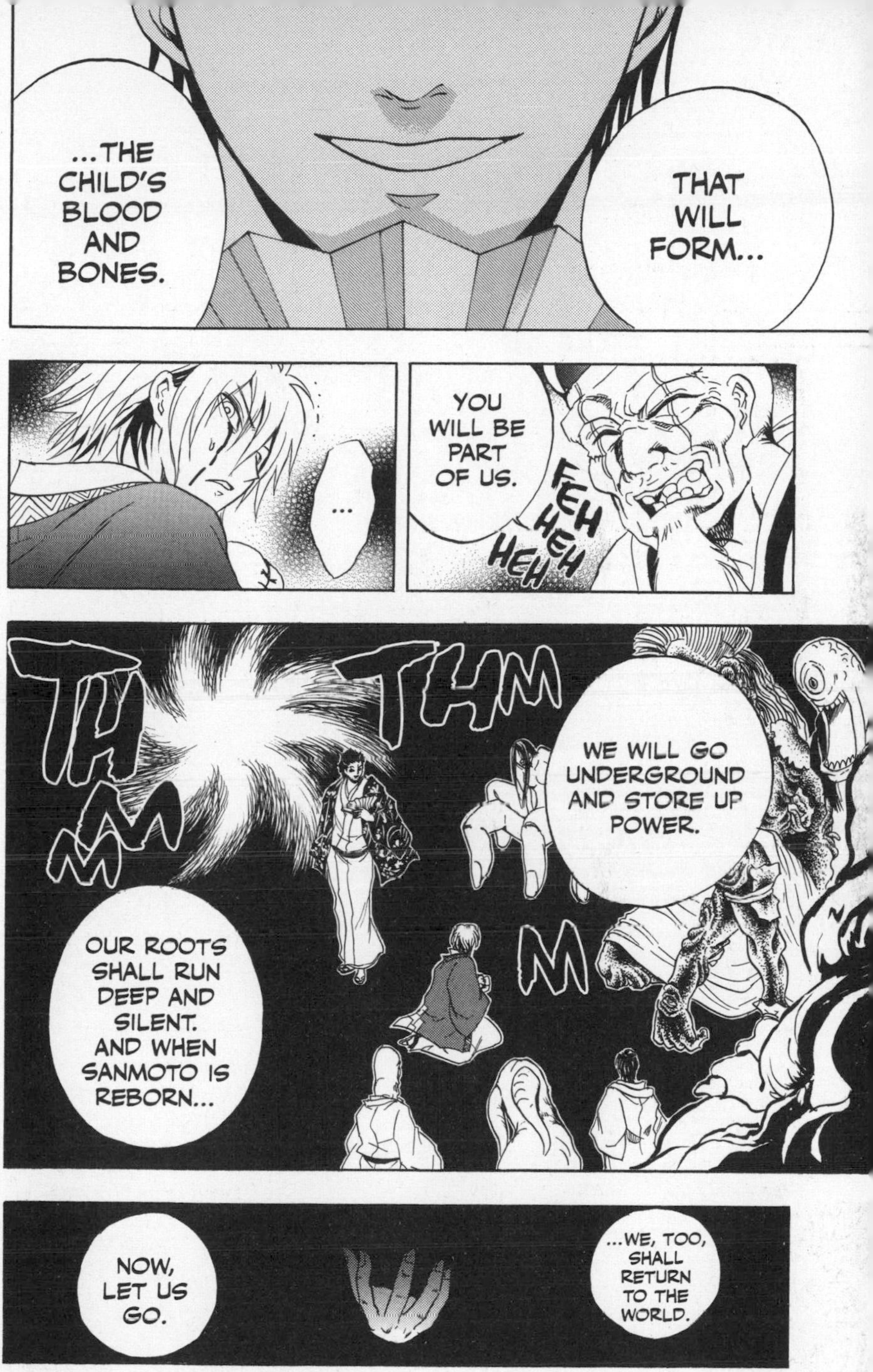
THAT WILL FORM...
...THE CHILD'S BLOOD AND BONES.
YOU WILL BE PART OF US.
FEH HEH HEH
...
WE WILL GO UNDERGROUND AND STORE UP POWER.
THM M
THMM
OUR ROOTS SHALL RUN DEEP AND SILENT. AND WHEN SANMOTO IS REBORN...
...WE, TOO, SHALL RETURN TO THE WORLD.
NOW, LET US GO.

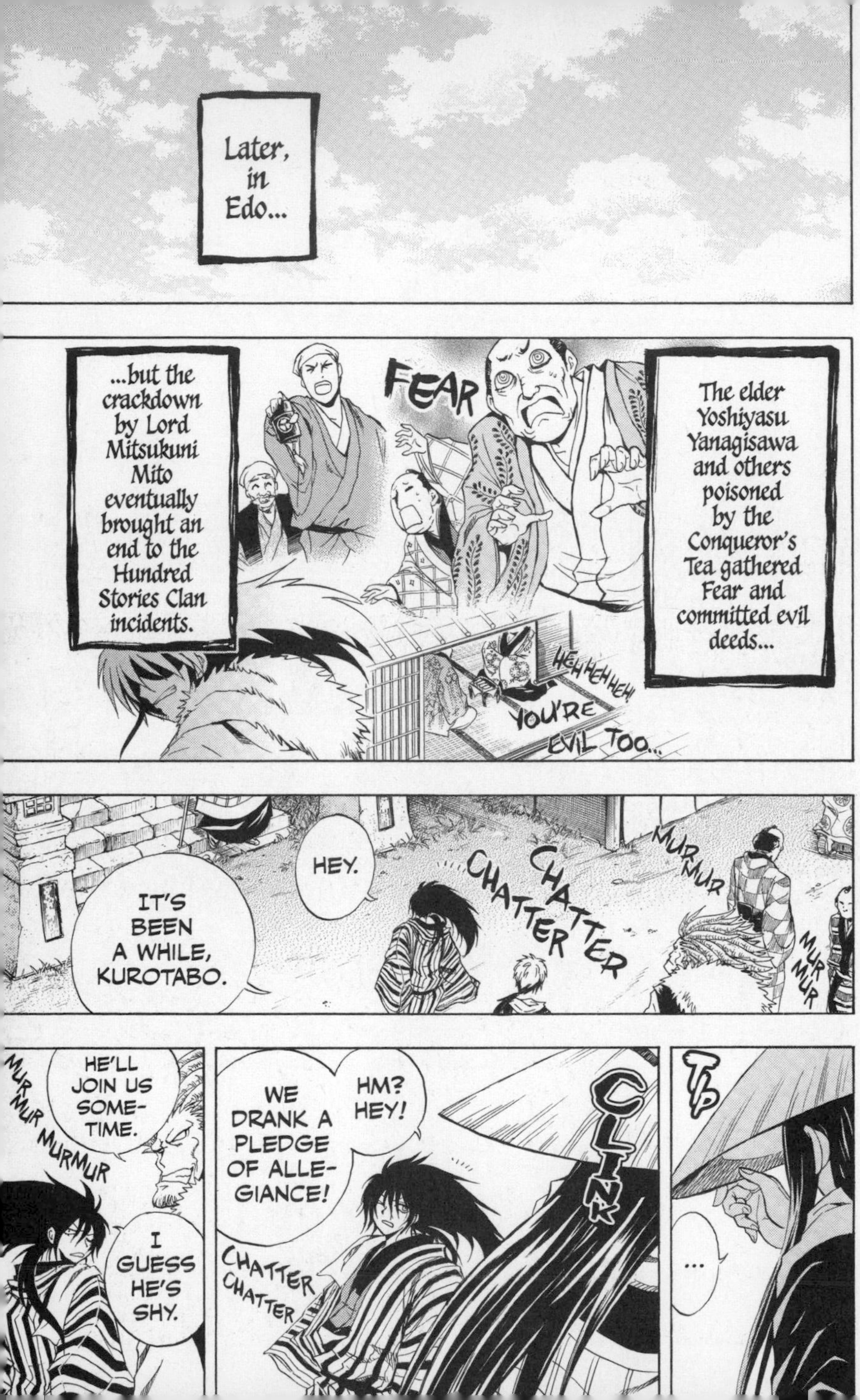
Later, in Edo...
The elder Yoshiyasu Yanagisawa and others poisoned by the Conqueror's Tea gathered Fear and committed evil deeds...
FEAR
...but the crackdown by Lord Mitsukuni Mito eventually brought an end to the Hundred Stories Clan incidents.
HEH HEH HEH!
YOU'RE EVIL TOO...
MURMUR
MURMUR
CHATTER CHATTER
HEY.
IT'S BEEN A WHILE, KUROTABO.
TP
...
CLINK
HM? HEY!
WE DRANK A PLEDGE OF ALLE-GIANCE!
CHATTER CHATTER
HE'LL JOIN US SOME-TIME.
MUR MUR MURMUR
I GUESS HE'S SHY.

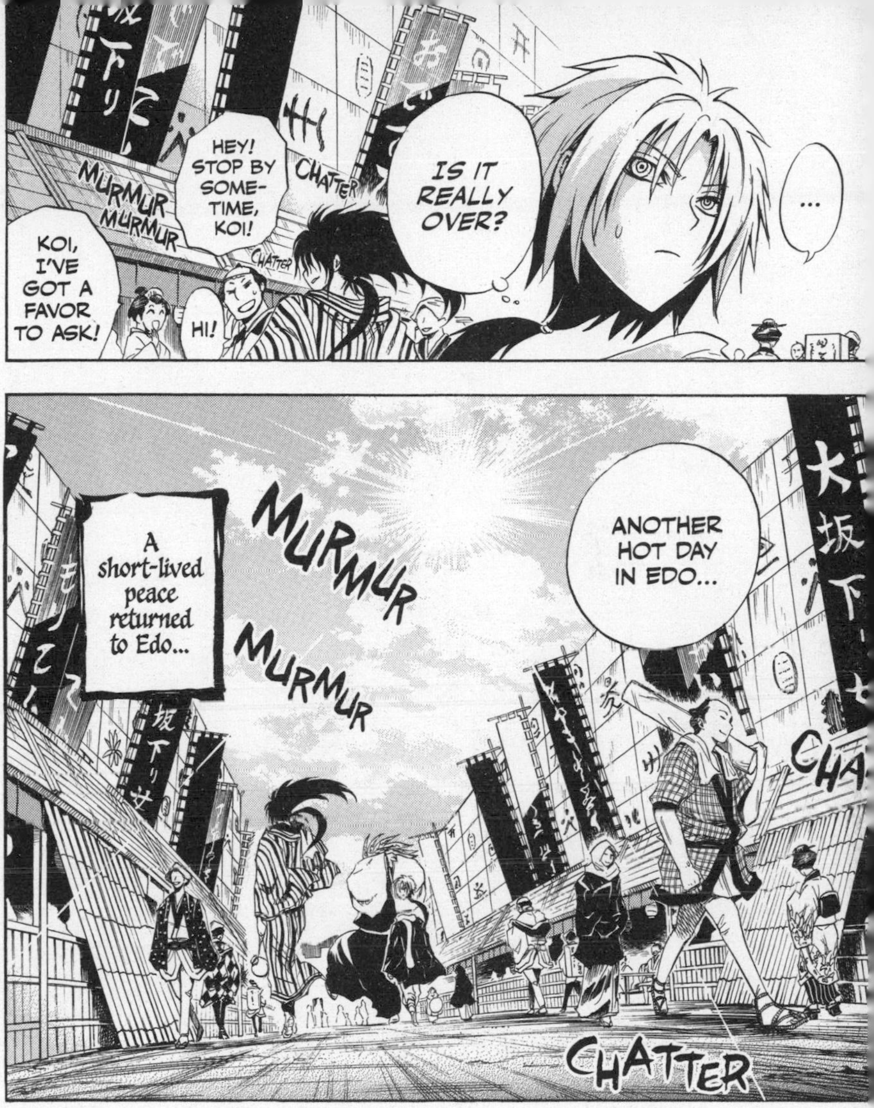
...
IS IT REALLY OVER?
CHATTER
HEY! STOP BY SOME-TIME, KOI!
MURMUR MURMUR
CHATTER
KOI, I'VE GOT A FAVOR TO ASK!
HI!
ANOTHER HOT DAY IN EDO...
CHA
MURMUR MURMUR
A short-lived peace returned to Edo...
CHATTER

...but that was just the beginning of a 300-year battle...

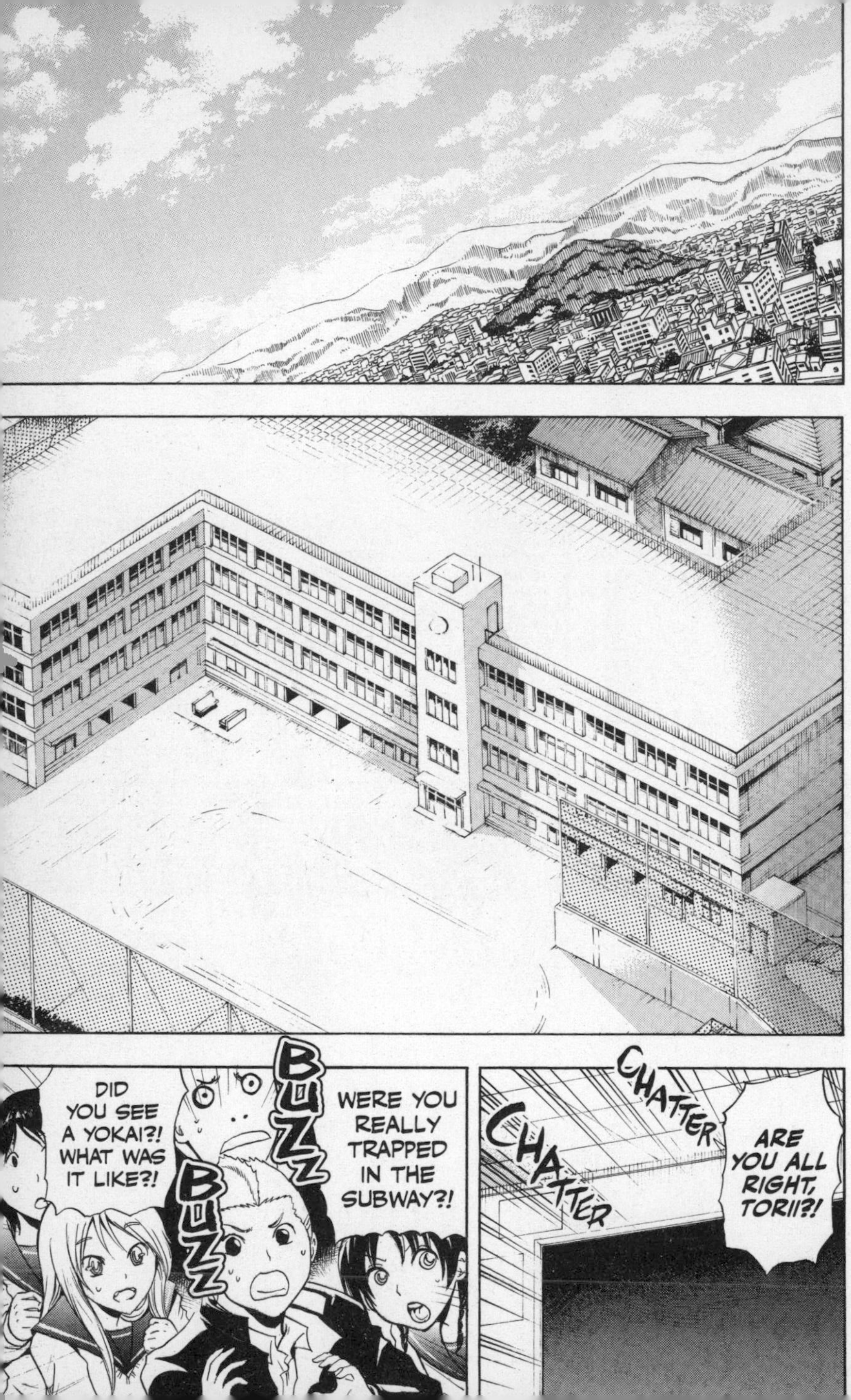
ARE YOU ALL RIGHT, TORII?!
CHATTER
CHATTER
WERE YOU REALLY TRAPPED IN THE SUBWAY?!
BUZZ
BUZZ
DID YOU SEE A YOKAI?! WHAT WAS IT LIKE?!

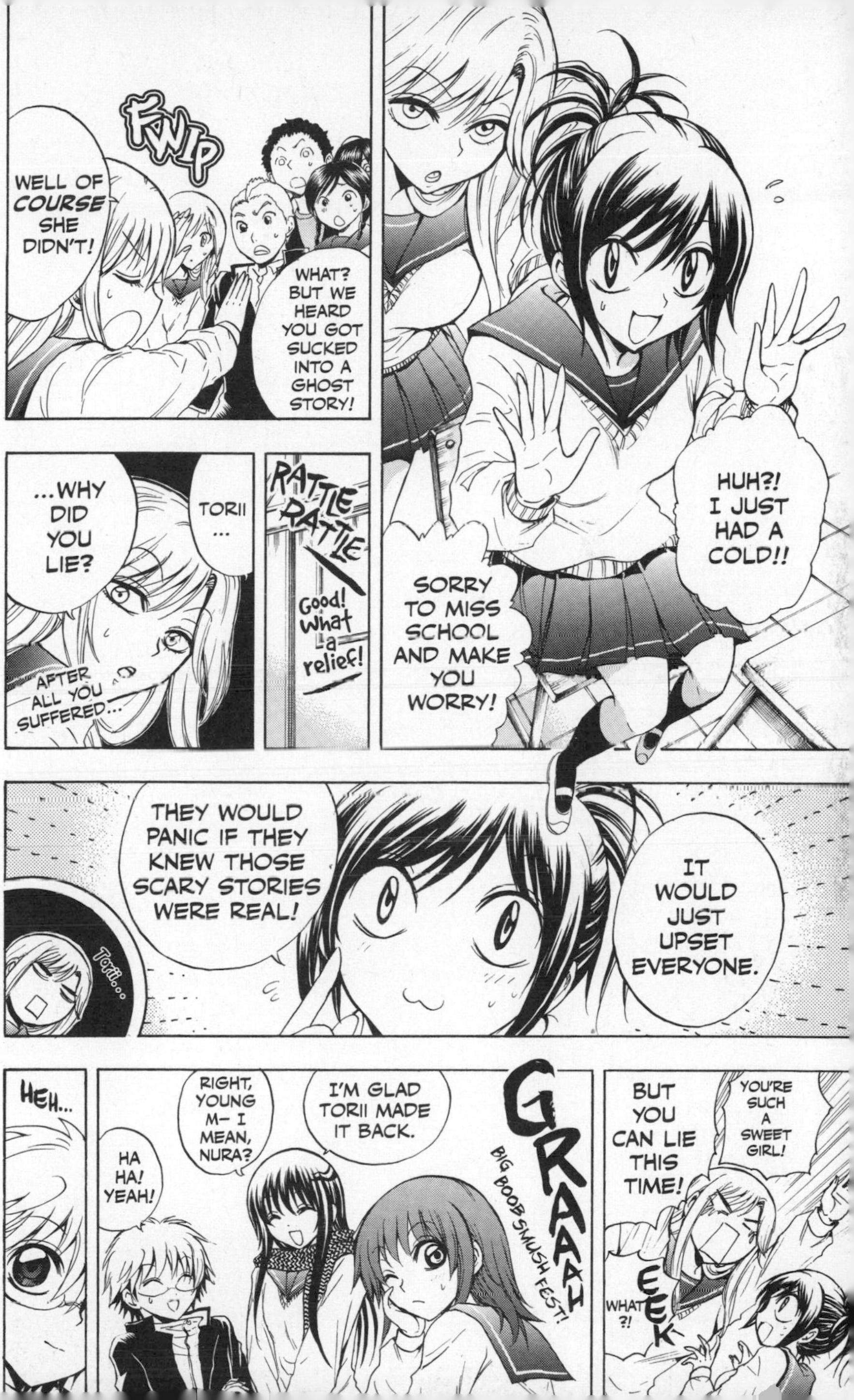
HUH?! I JUST HAD A COLD!!
SORRY TO MISS SCHOOL AND MAKE YOU WORRY!
FWIP
WHAT? BUT WE HEARD YOU GOT SUCKED INTO A GHOST STORY!
WELL OF COURSE SHE DIDN'T!
RATTLE RATTLE
Good! What a relief!
TORII ...
...WHY DID YOU LIE?
AFTER ALL YOU SUFFERED...
IT WOULD JUST UPSET EVERYONE.
THEY WOULD PANIC IF THEY KNEW THOSE SCARY STORIES WERE REAL!
Torii...
YOU'RE SUCH A SWEET GIRL!
BUT YOU CAN LIE THIS TIME!
EEK
WHAT?!
GRAAAH
BIG BOOB SMUSH FEST!
I'M GLAD TORII MADE IT BACK.
RIGHT, YOUNG M— I MEAN, NURA?
HA HA! YEAH!
HEH...

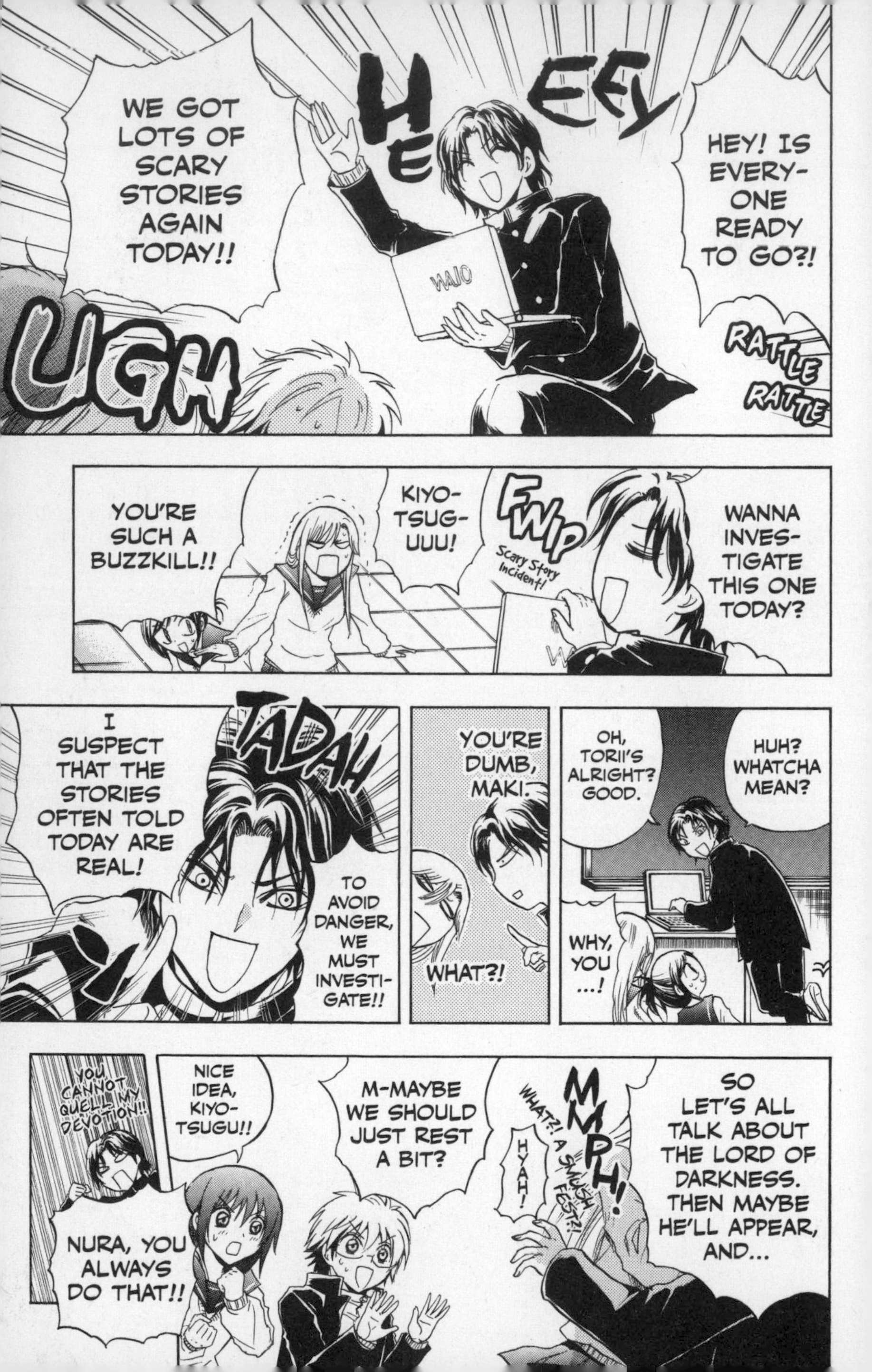

HEEEY
HEY! IS EVERYONE READY TO GO?!
RATTLE RATTLE
WE GOT LOTS OF SCARY STORIES AGAIN TODAY!!
UGH
WANNA INVESTIGATE THIS ONE TODAY?
FWIP
Scary Story Incident!
KIYOTSUGUUU!
YOU'RE SUCH A BUZZKILL!!
HUH? WHATCHA MEAN?
OH, TORII'S ALRIGHT? GOOD.
WHY, YOU ...!
YOU'RE DUMB, MAKI.
WHAT?!
TADAH
I SUSPECT THAT THE STORIES OFTEN TOLD TODAY ARE REAL!
TO AVOID DANGER, WE MUST INVESTIGATE!!
SO LET'S ALL TALK ABOUT THE LORD OF DARKNESS. THEN MAYBE HE'LL APPEAR, AND...
MMMPH!
WHAT?! A SMUSH FEST?!
HYAH!
M-MAYBE WE SHOULD JUST REST A BIT?
NICE IDEA, KIYOTSUGU!!
NURA, YOU ALWAYS DO THAT!!
YOU CANNOT QUELL MY DEVOTION!!

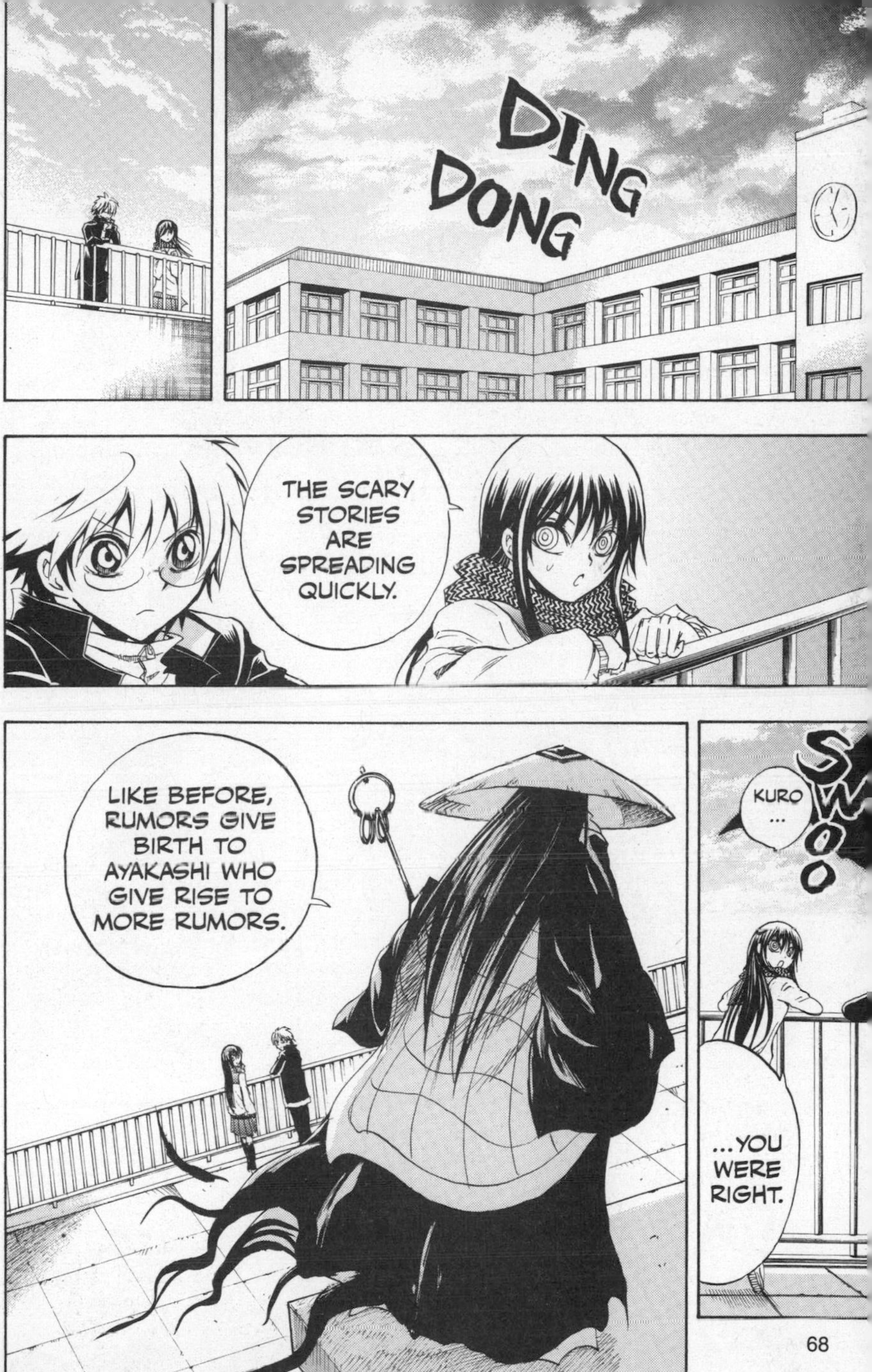
DING DONG
THE SCARY STORIES ARE SPREADING QUICKLY.
SWOO
KURO ...
...YOU WERE RIGHT.
LIKE BEFORE, RUMORS GIVE BIRTH TO AYAKASHI WHO GIVE RISE TO MORE RUMORS.

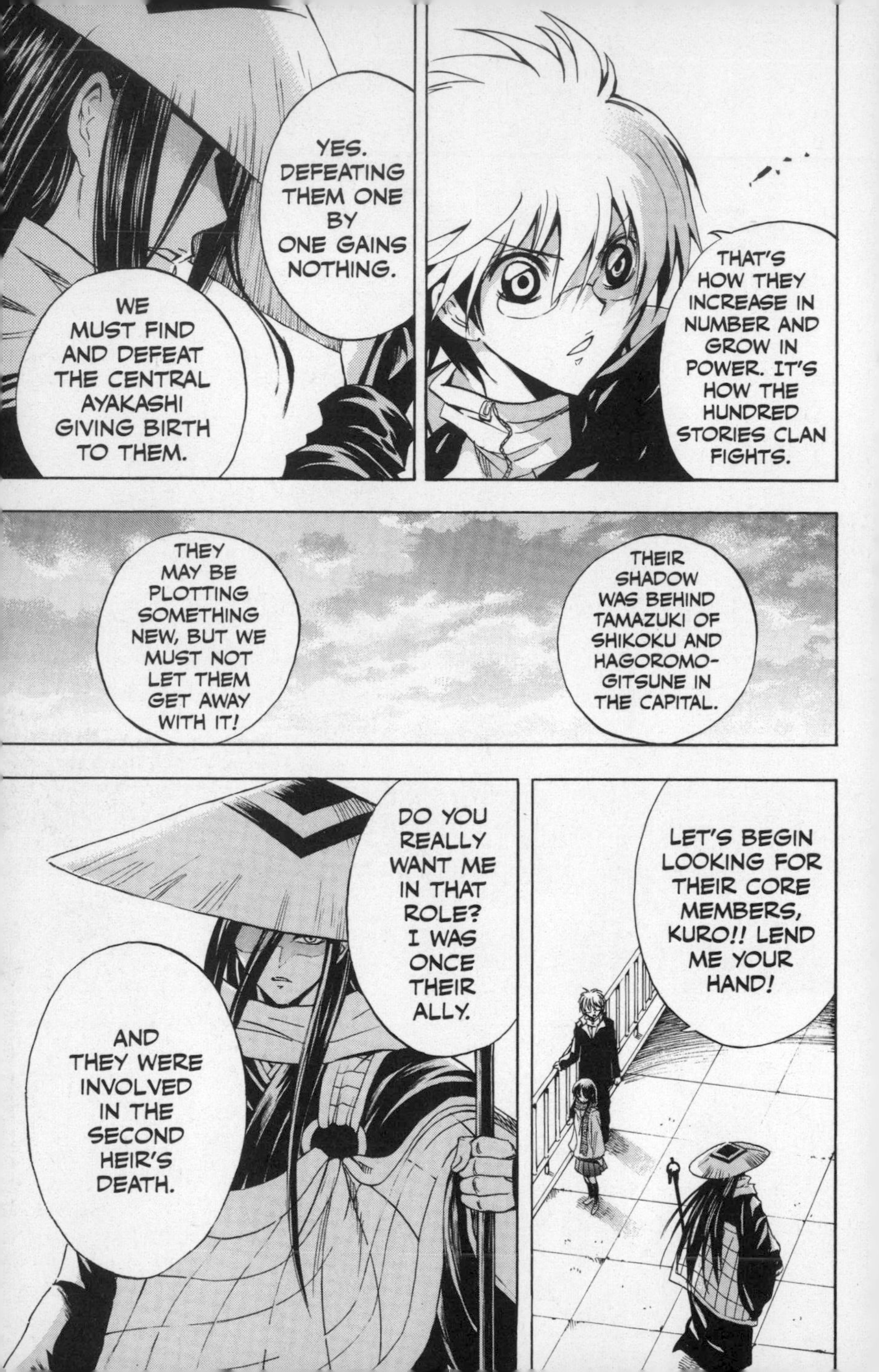
THAT'S HOW THEY INCREASE IN NUMBER AND GROW IN POWER. IT'S HOW THE HUNDRED STORIES CLAN FIGHTS.
YES. DEFEATING THEM ONE BY ONE GAINS NOTHING.
WE MUST FIND AND DEFEAT THE CENTRAL AYAKASHI GIVING BIRTH TO THEM.
THEIR SHADOW WAS BEHIND TAMAZUKI OF SHIKOKU AND HAGOROMO-GITSUNE IN THE CAPITAL.
THEY MAY BE PLOTTING SOMETHING NEW, BUT WE MUST NOT LET THEM GET AWAY WITH IT!
LET'S BEGIN LOOKING FOR THEIR CORE MEMBERS, KURO!! LEND ME YOUR HAND!
DO YOU REALLY WANT ME IN THAT ROLE? I WAS ONCE THEIR ALLY.
AND THEY WERE INVOLVED IN THE SECOND HEIR'S DEATH.

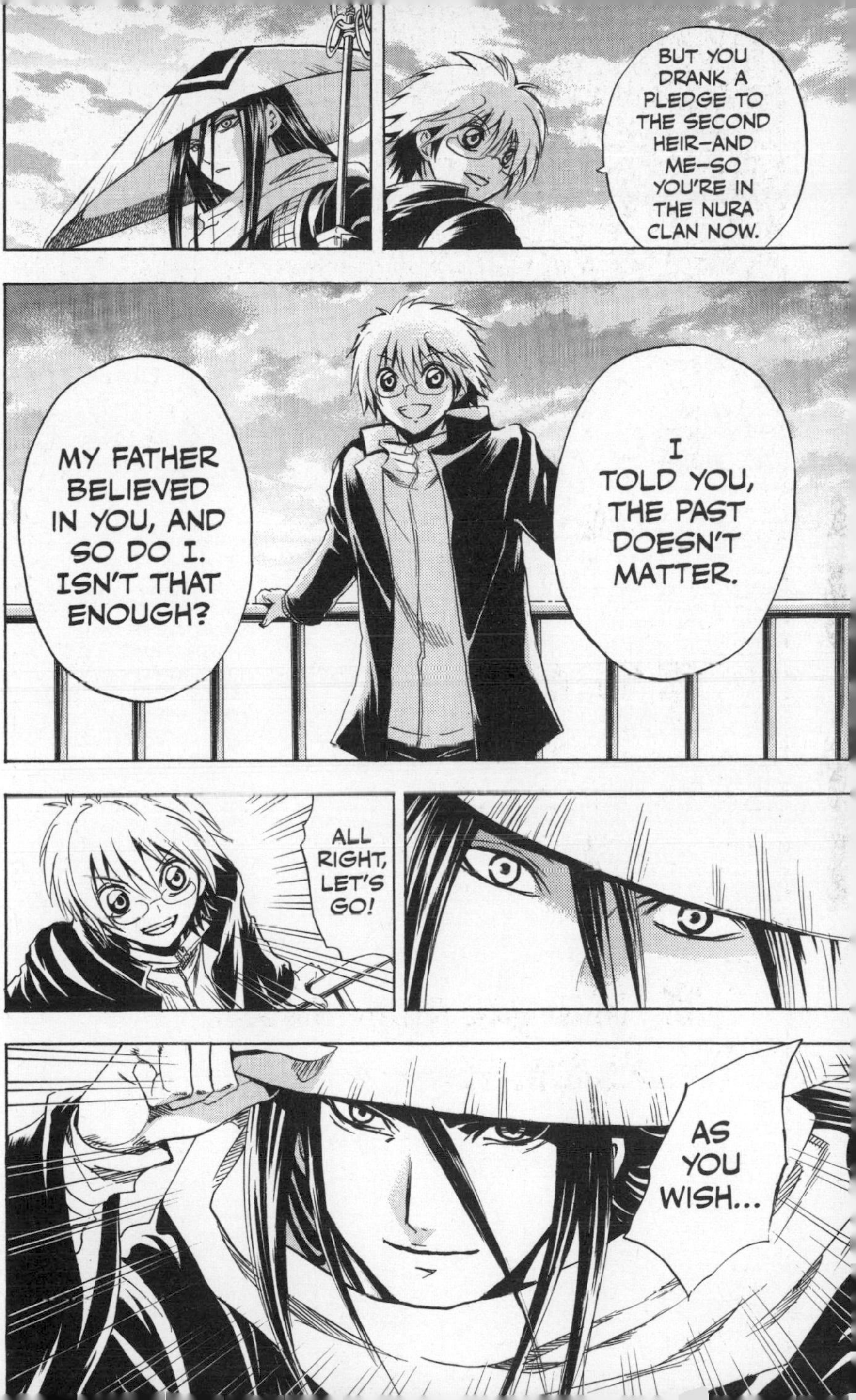
BUT YOU DRANK A PLEDGE TO THE SECOND HEIR—AND ME—SO YOU'RE IN THE NURA CLAN NOW.
I TOLD YOU, THE PAST DOESN'T MATTER.
MY FATHER BELIEVED IN YOU, AND SO DO I. ISN'T THAT ENOUGH?
ALL RIGHT, LET'S GO!
AS YOU WISH...

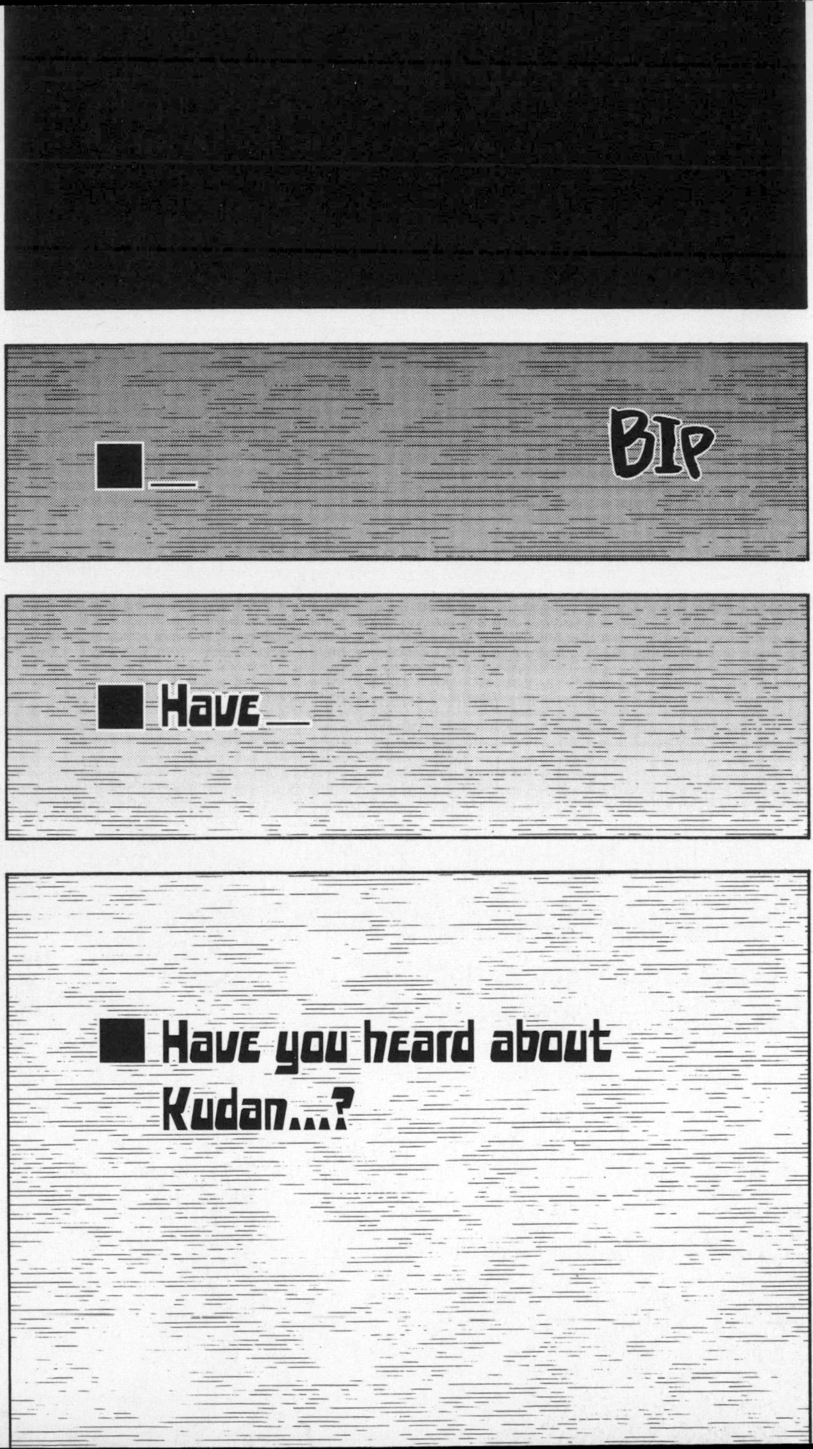
BIP
Have_
Have you heard about Kudan...?

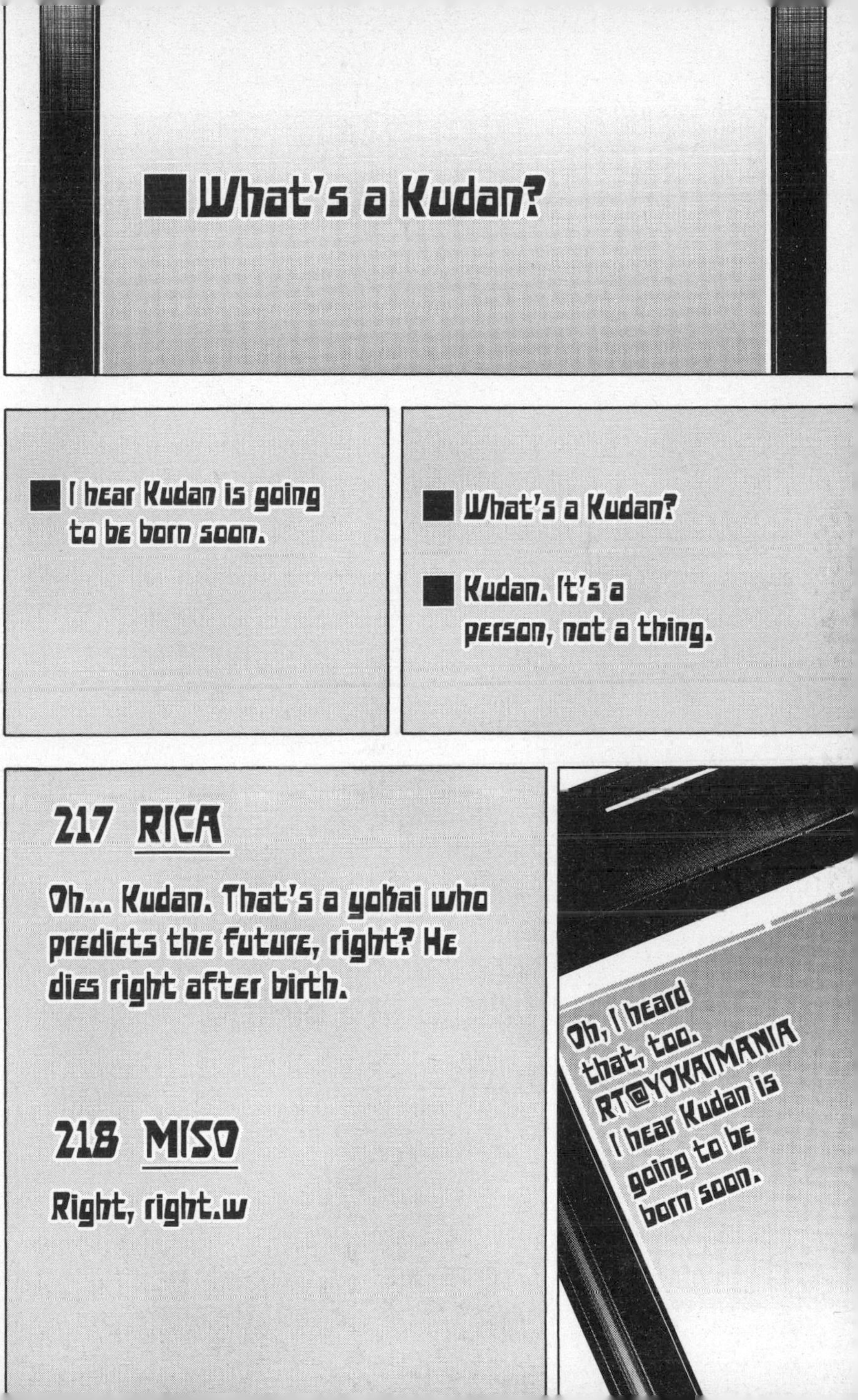
■What's a Kudan?
■What's a Kudan?
■Kudan. It's a person, not a thing.
■I hear Kudan is going to be born soon.
Oh, I heard that, too. RT@YOKAIMANIA I hear Kudan is going to be born soon.
217 RICA
Oh... Kudan. That's a yokai who predicts the future, right? He dies right after birth.
218 MISO
Right, right.w

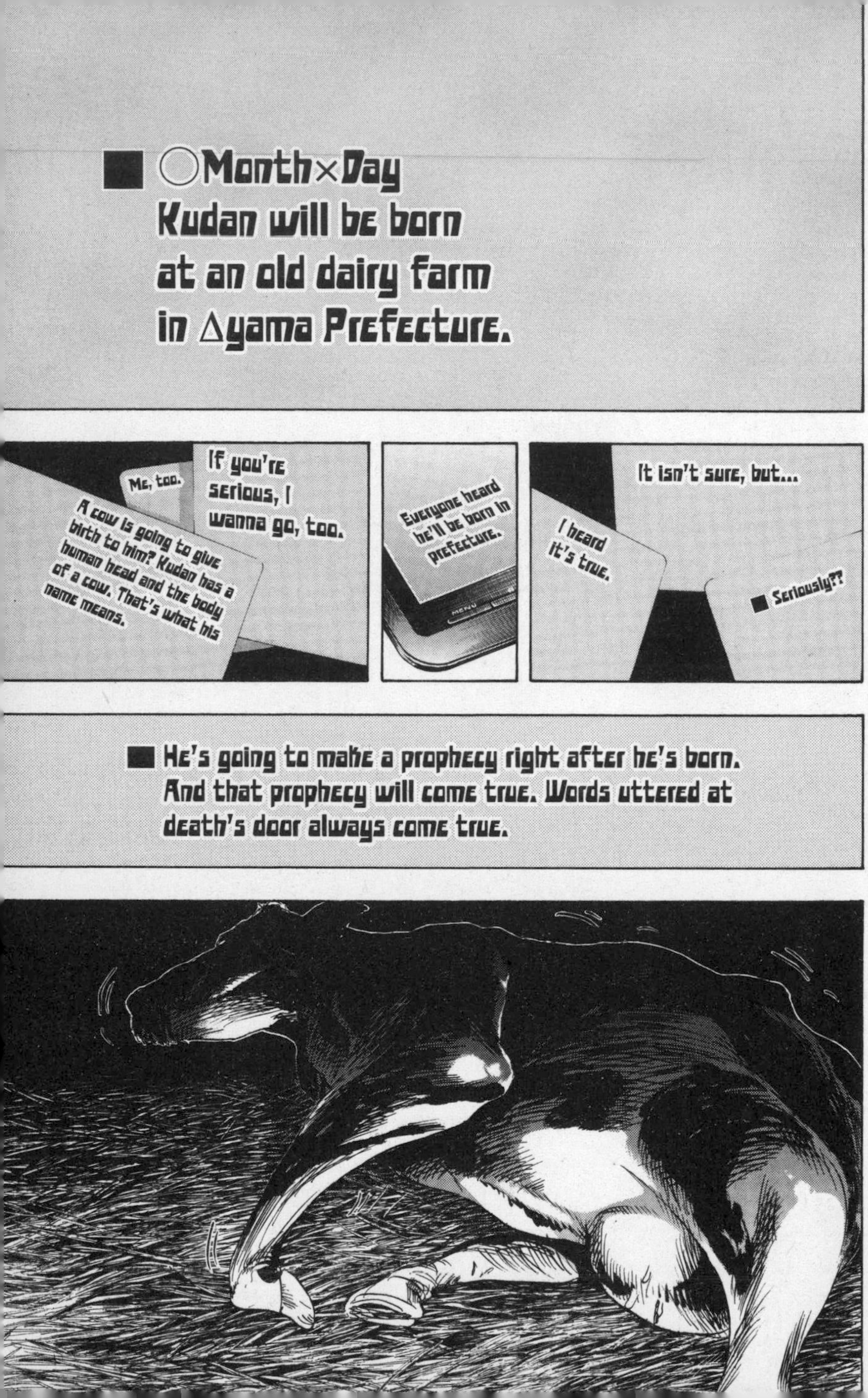
■ ○Month×Day Kudan will be born at an old dairy farm in △yama Prefecture.
It isn't sure, but...
I heard it's true.
■ Seriously??
Everyone heard he'll be born in prefecture.
If you're serious, I wanna go, too.
Me, too.
A cow is going to give birth to him? Kudan has a human head and the body of a cow. That's what his name means.
■ He's going to make a prophecy right after he's born. And that prophecy will come true. Words uttered at death's door always come true.

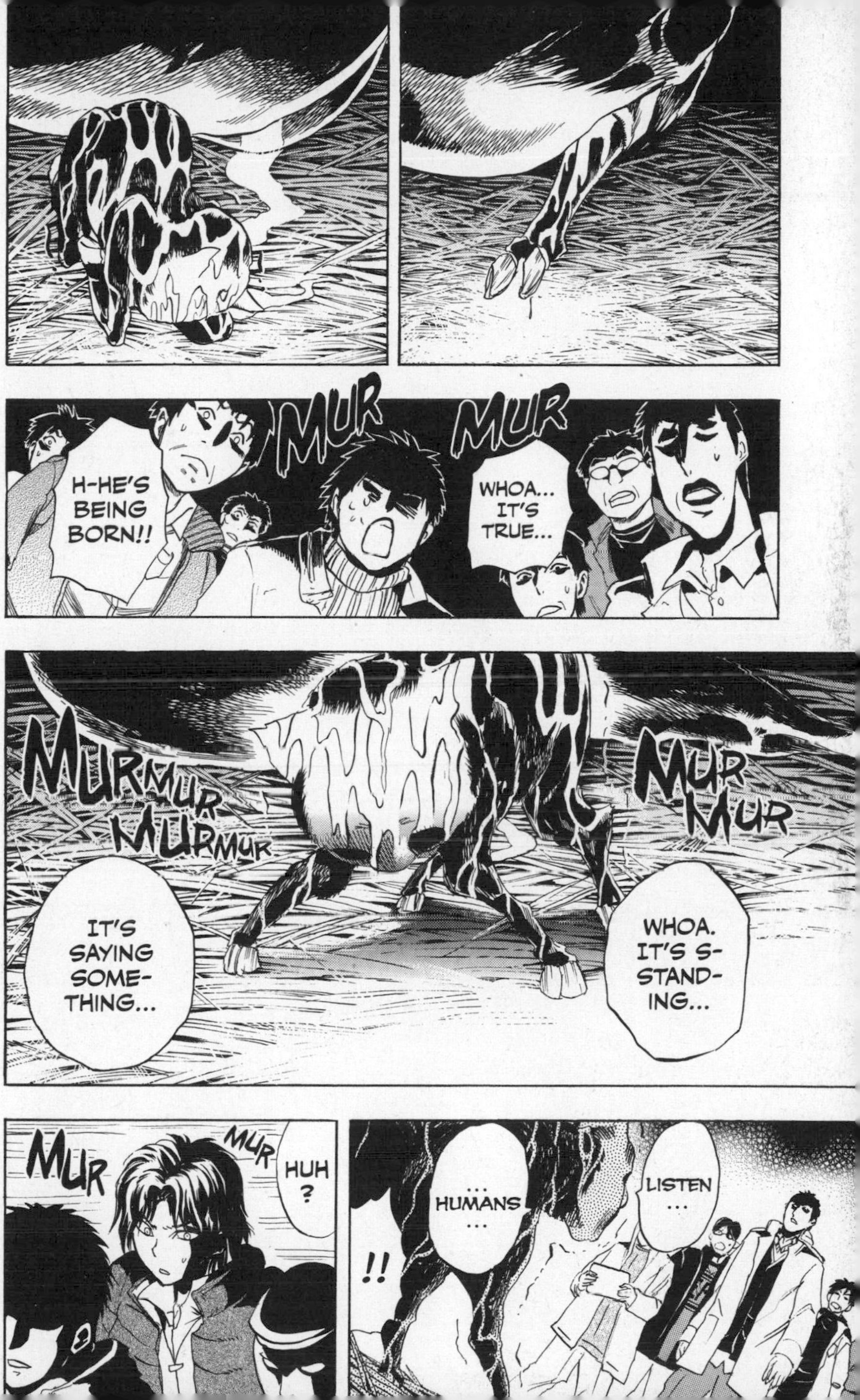
MUR
WHOA... IT'S TRUE...
MUR
H-HE'S BEING BORN!!
MUR MUR
WHOA. IT'S S-STANDING...
MURMUR MURMUR
IT'S SAYING SOMETHING...
LISTEN...
...HUMANS...
!!
HUH?
MUR
MUR

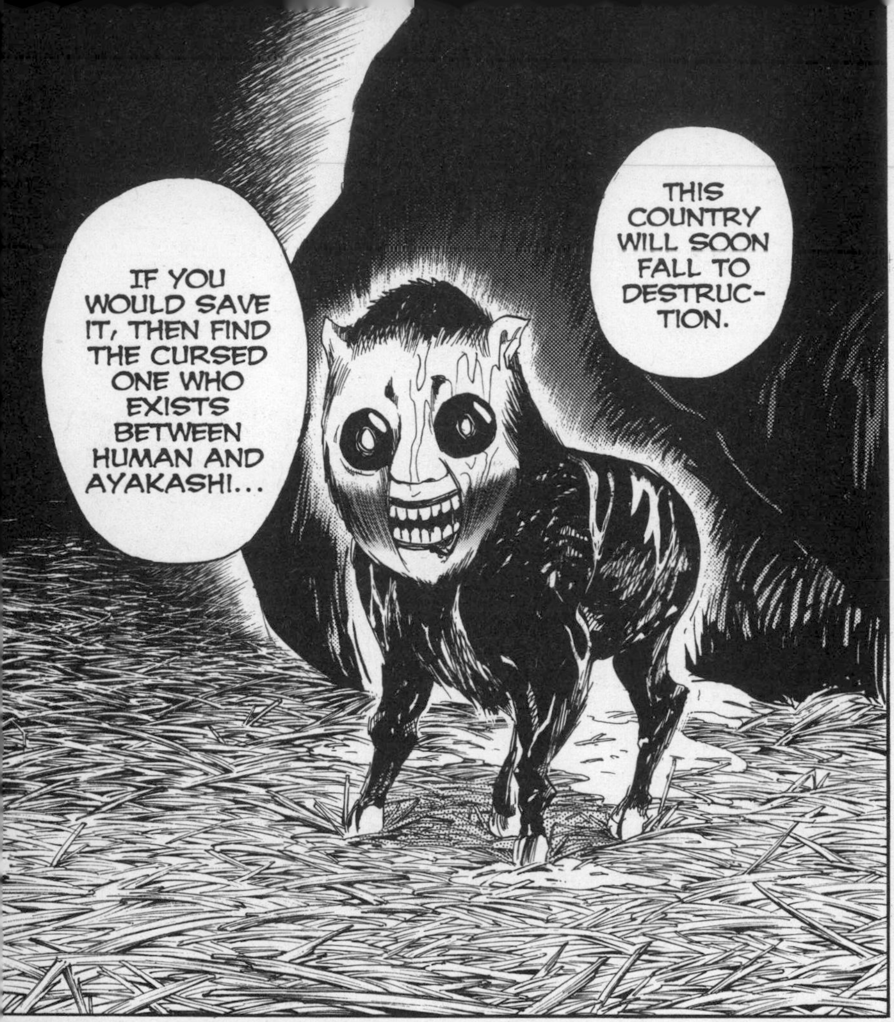
THIS COUNTRY WILL SOON FALL TO DESTRUCTION.
IF YOU WOULD SAVE IT, THEN FIND THE CURSED ONE WHO EXISTS BETWEEN HUMAN AND AYAKASHI...
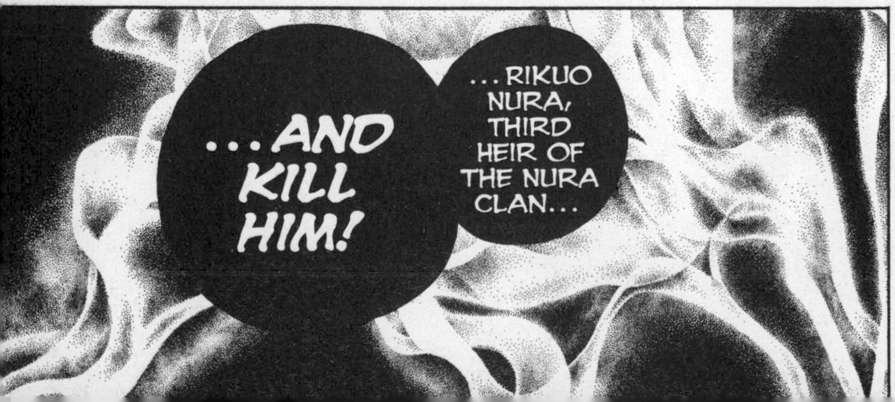
...RIKUO NURA, THIRD HEIR OF THE NURA CLAN...
...AND KILL HIM!

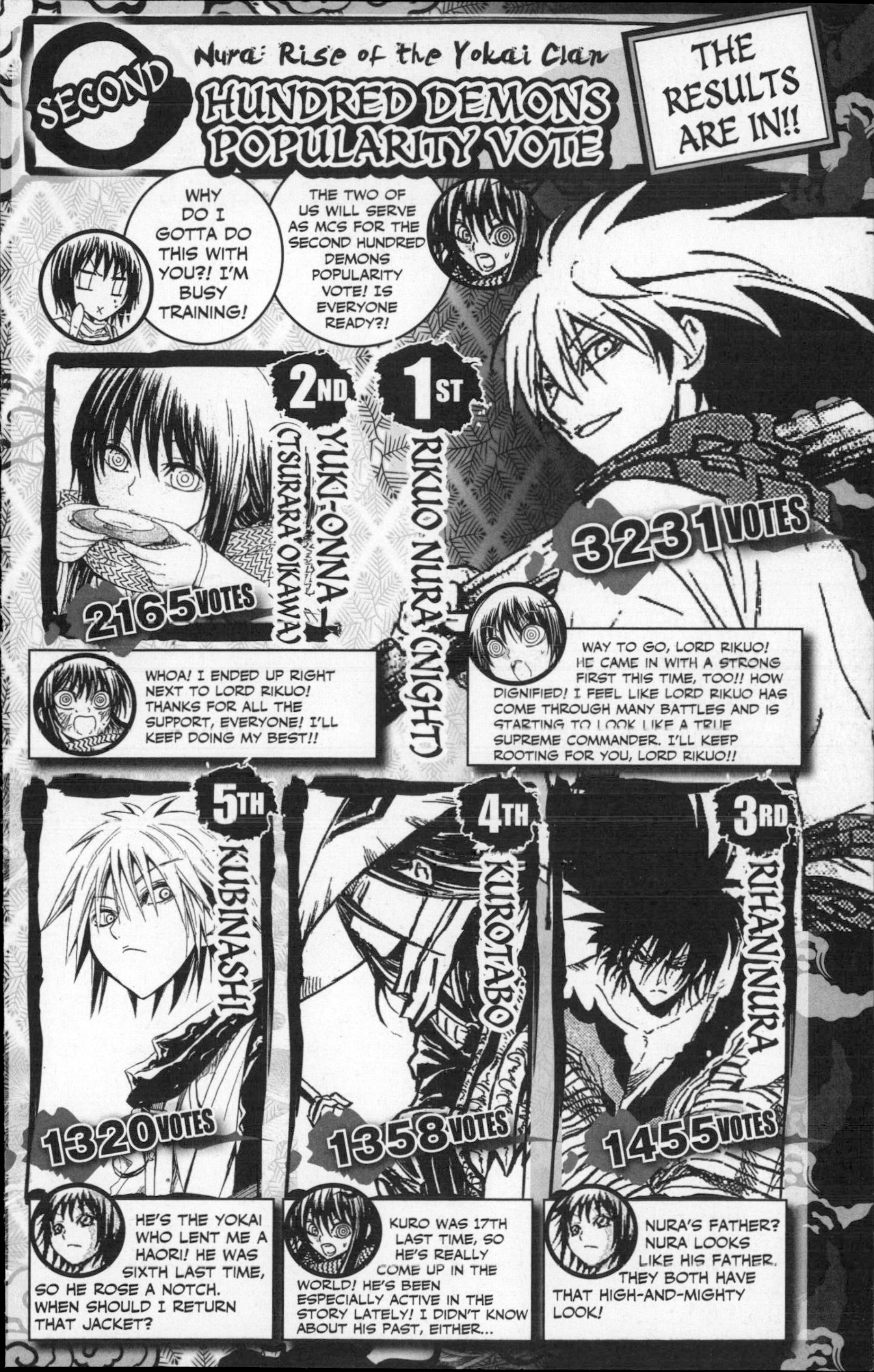
SECOND
Nura: Rise of the Yokai Clan
HUNDRED DEMONS POPULARITY VOTE
THE RESULTS ARE IN!!
THE TWO OF US WILL SERVE AS MCS FOR THE SECOND HUNDRED DEMONS POPULARITY VOTE! IS EVERYONE READY?!
WHY DO I GOTTA DO THIS WITH YOU?! I'M BUSY TRAINING!
1ST
RIKUO NURA (NIGHT)
3231 VOTES
WAY TO GO, LORD RIKUO! HE CAME IN WITH A STRONG FIRST THIS TIME, TOO!! HOW DIGNIFIED! I FEEL LIKE LORD RIKUO HAS COME THROUGH MANY BATTLES AND IS STARTING TO LOOK LIKE A TRUE SUPREME COMMANDER. I'LL KEEP ROOTING FOR YOU, LORD RIKUO!!
2ND
YUKI-ONNA (TSURARA OIKAWA)
2165 VOTES
WHOA! I ENDED UP RIGHT NEXT TO LORD RIKUO! THANKS FOR ALL THE SUPPORT, EVERYONE! I'LL KEEP DOING MY BEST!!
3RD
RIHAN NURA
1455 VOTES
NURA'S FATHER? NURA LOOKS LIKE HIS FATHER. THEY BOTH HAVE THAT HIGH-AND-MIGHTY LOOK!
4TH
KUROTABO
1358 VOTES
KURO WAS 17TH LAST TIME, SO HE'S REALLY COME UP IN THE WORLD! HE'S BEEN ESPECIALLY ACTIVE IN THE STORY LATELY! I DIDN'T KNOW ABOUT HIS PAST, EITHER...
5TH
KUBINASHI
1320 VOTES
HE'S THE YOKAI WHO LENT ME A HAORI! HE WAS SIXTH LAST TIME, SO HE ROSE A NOTCH. WHEN SHOULD I RETURN THAT JACKET?

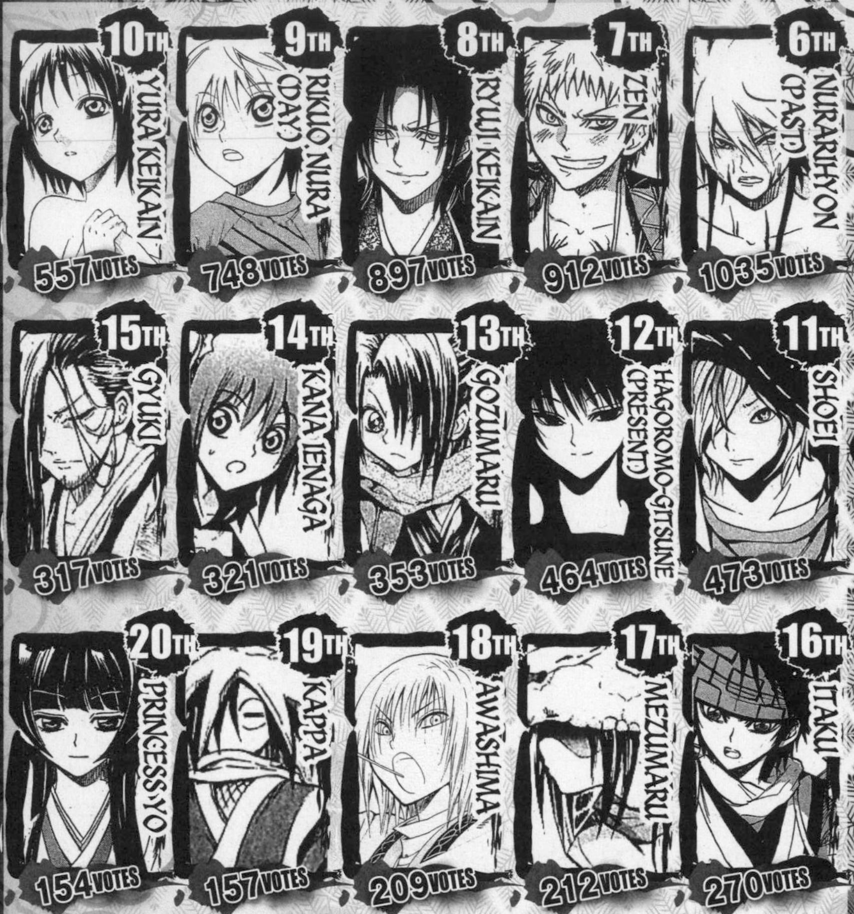
6TH
NURARIHYON (PAST)
1035 VOTES
7TH
ZEN
912 VOTES
8TH
RYUJI KEIKAIN
897 VOTES
9TH
RIKUO NURA (DAY)
748 VOTES
10TH
YURA KEIKAIN
557 VOTES
11TH
SHOEI
473 VOTES
12TH
HAGOROMO-GITSUNE (PRESENT)
464 VOTES
13TH
GOZUMARU
353 VOTES
14TH
KANA IENAGA
321 VOTES
15TH
GYUKI
317 VOTES
16TH
ITAKU
270 VOTES
17TH
MEZUMARU
212 VOTES
18TH
AWASHIMA
209 VOTES
19TH
KAPPA
157 VOTES
20TH
PRINCESS YO
154 VOTES

Results for 21st through 59th place!!

21 Kuromaru / 135 votes
21 Otome Yamabuki / 135 votes
23 Tamazuki / 131 votes
23 Setsura / 131 votes
25 Wakana Nura / 128 votes
26 Hidemoto Keikain the Thirteenth / 125 votes
27 Yanagida / 119 votes
28 Ibaraki-Doji / 114 votes
28 Kejoro / 115 votes
30 Ryota-Neko / 113 votes
31 Nurarihyon (present) / 112 votes
32 Inugami / 110 votes
32 Yosuzume / 110 votes
34 Aotabo / 107 votes
35 Shokera / 77 votes
35 Hihi / 77 votes
35 Rinko / 77 votes
38 Natsumi Torii / 74 votes
39 Mamiru Keikain / 73 votes
40 Karasu-Tengu / 71 votes
41 Saori Maki / 66 votes
42 Kyokotsu (daughter) / 65 votes
43 Masatsugu Keikain / 60 votes
43 Tsuchigumo / 60 votes
45 Sannokuchi / 47 votes
45 Akifusa Keikain / 47 votes
45 Reira / 47 votes
48 Hitotsume / 45 votes
49 Shiibashi-sensei / 44 votes
49 Natto-Kozo / 44 votes
51 Sasami / 43 votes
51 Senba / 43 votes
53 Kidomaru / 41 votes
53 Kokehime / 41 votes
55 Amezo / 40 votes
56 Abe no Seimei / 39 votes
56 Zashikiwarashi / 39 votes
56 Nure-Garasu / 39 votes
59 Gashadokuro / 38 votes
59 Shinako Suganuma / 38 votes
59 Tosakamaru / 38 votes

FROM THE ARTICLE PUBLISHED IN WEEKLY JUMP VOL. 29, 2011.

Act 160: Prophecy

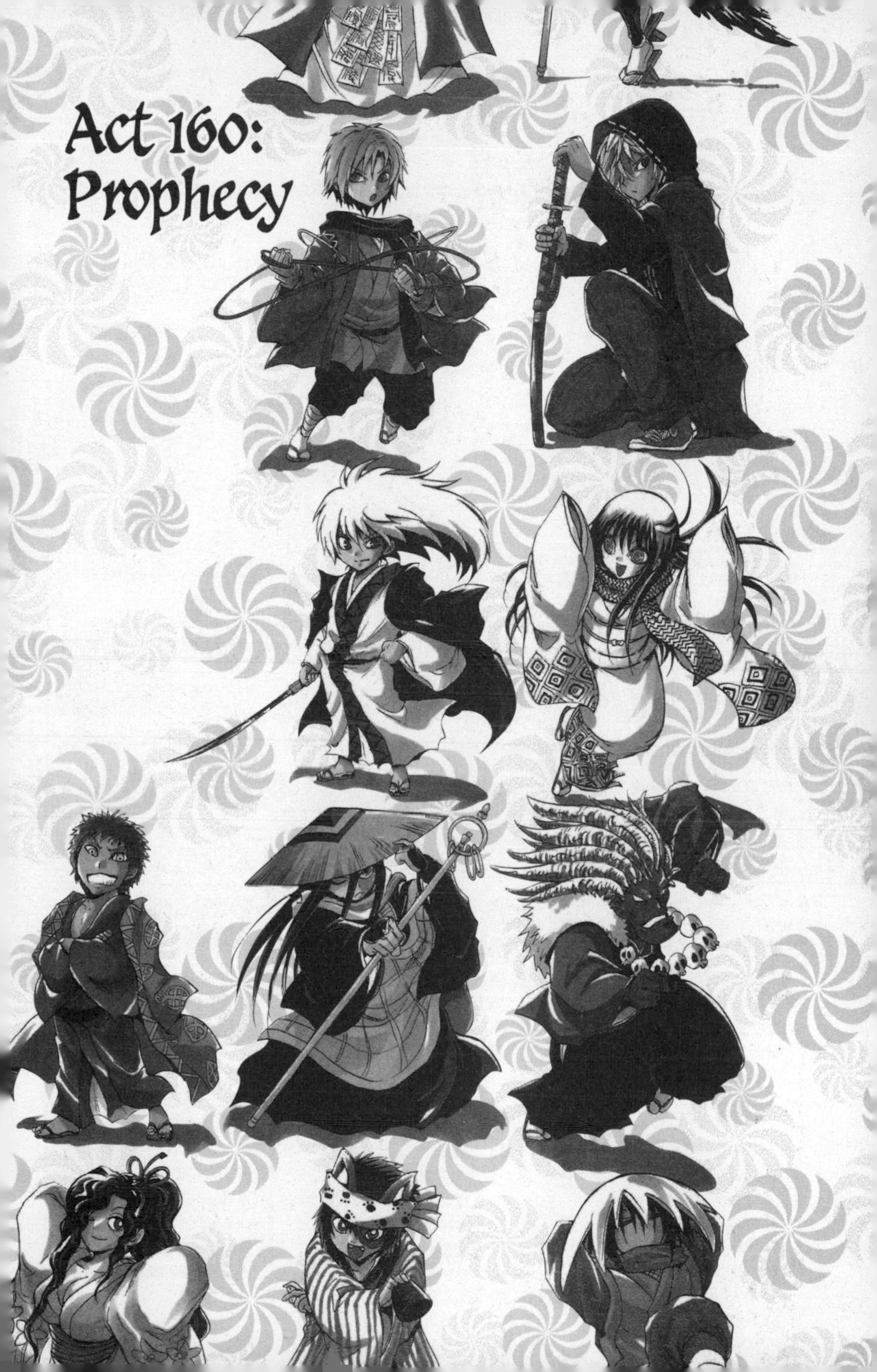

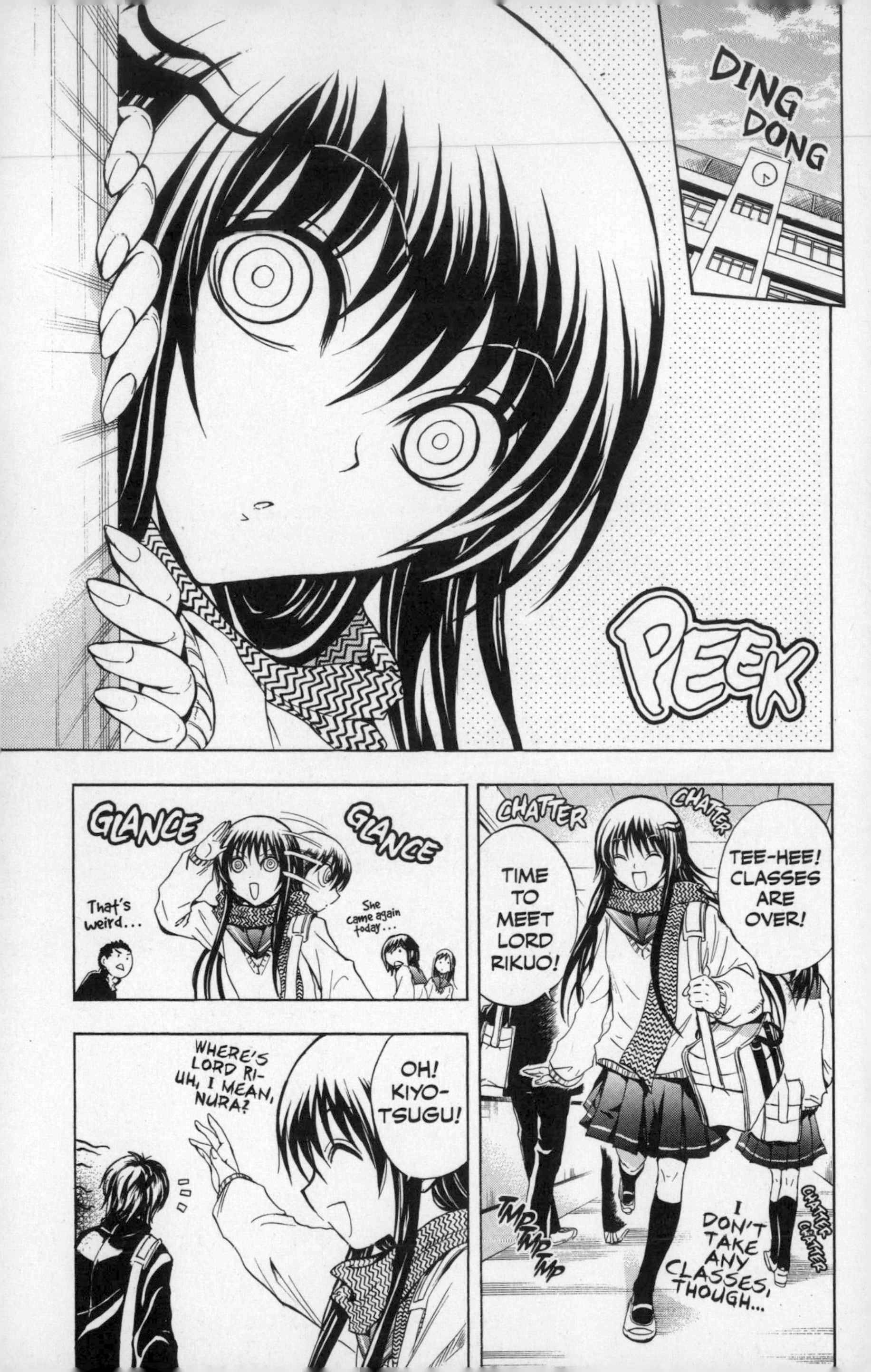
DING DONG
PEEK
CHATTER
TEE-HEE! CLASSES ARE OVER!
CHATTER
TIME TO MEET LORD RIKUO!
CHATTER CHATTER
I DON'T TAKE ANY CLASSES, THOUGH...
TMP TMP TMP
GLANCE
GLANCE
She came again today...
That's weird...
OH! KIYO-TSUGU!
WHERE'S LORD RI- UH, I MEAN, NURA?

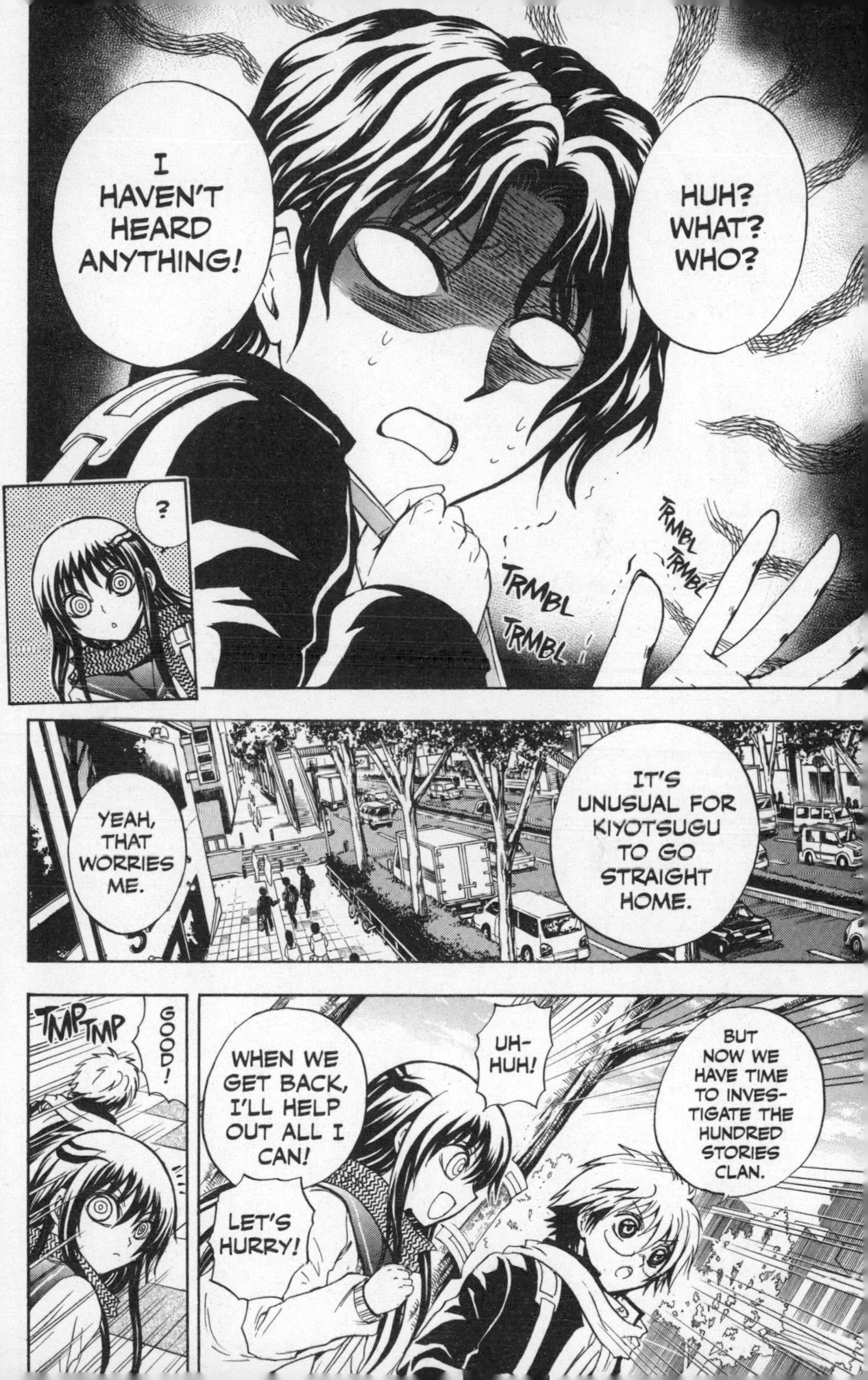
HUH? WHAT? WHO?
I HAVEN'T HEARD ANYTHING!
TRMBL TRMBL
TRMBL TRMBL
?
IT'S UNUSUAL FOR KIYOTSUGU TO GO STRAIGHT HOME.
YEAH, THAT WORRIES ME.
BUT NOW WE HAVE TIME TO INVESTIGATE THE HUNDRED STORIES CLAN.
UH-HUH!
WHEN WE GET BACK, I'LL HELP OUT ALL I CAN!
LET'S HURRY!
GOOD!
TMP TMP

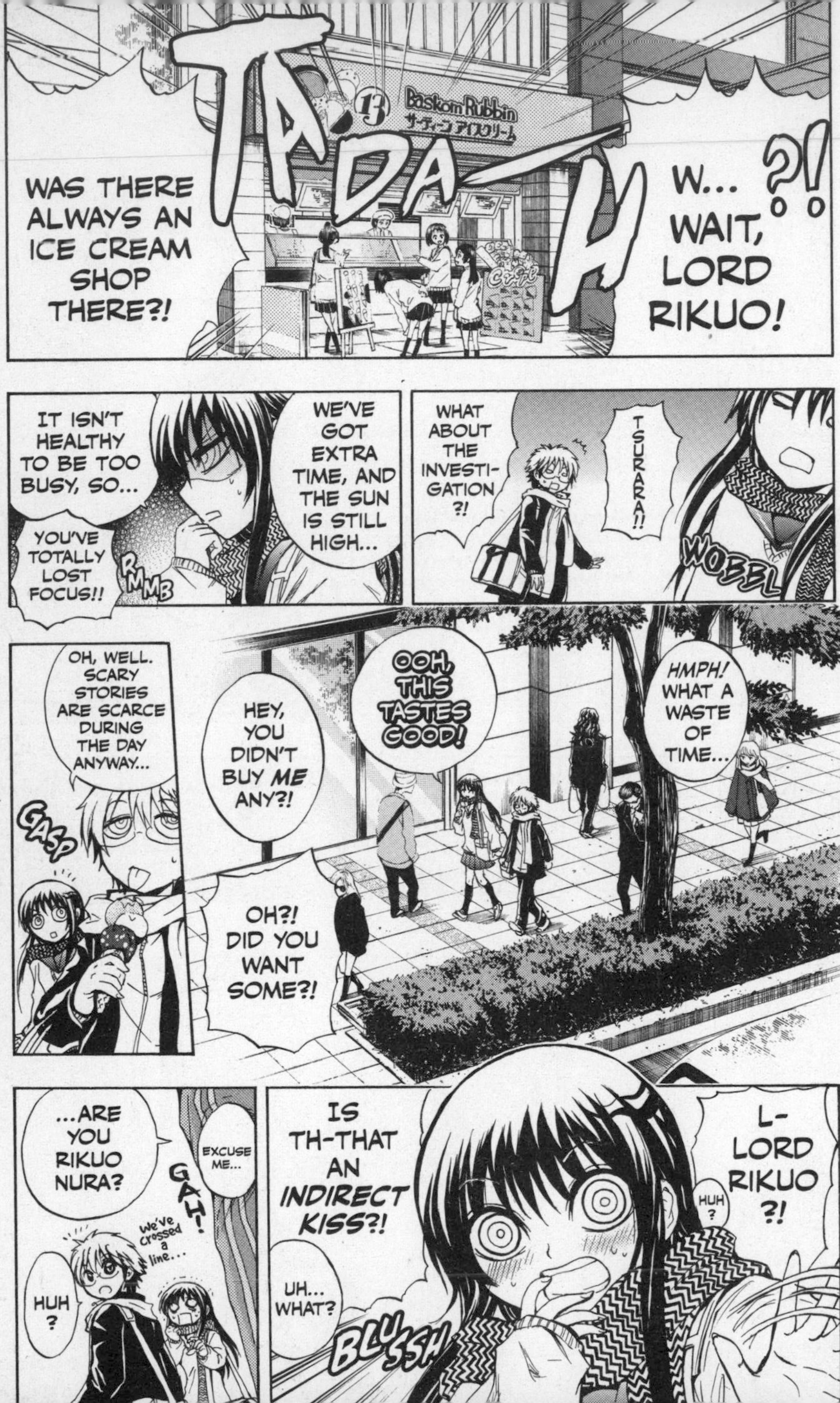
W... WAIT, LORD RIKUO!
?!
TA-DAH
Baskom Rubbin
13
サーティーン アイスクリーム
WAS THERE ALWAYS AN ICE CREAM SHOP THERE?!
TSURARA!!
WOBBL
WHAT ABOUT THE INVESTIGATION?!
WE'VE GOT EXTRA TIME, AND THE SUN IS STILL HIGH...
IT ISN'T HEALTHY TO BE TOO BUSY, SO...
YOU'VE TOTALLY LOST FOCUS!!
RMMB
HMPH! WHAT A WASTE OF TIME...
OOH, THIS TASTES GOOD!
HEY, YOU DIDN'T BUY *ME* ANY?!
OH?! DID YOU WANT SOME?!
OH, WELL. SCARY STORIES ARE SCARCE DURING THE DAY ANYWAY...
GASP
L-LORD RIKUO?!
HUH?
IS TH-THAT AN *INDIRECT KISS*?!
UH... WHAT?
BLUSSH
EXCUSE ME...
...ARE YOU RIKUO NURA?
GAH!
We've crossed a line...
HUH?

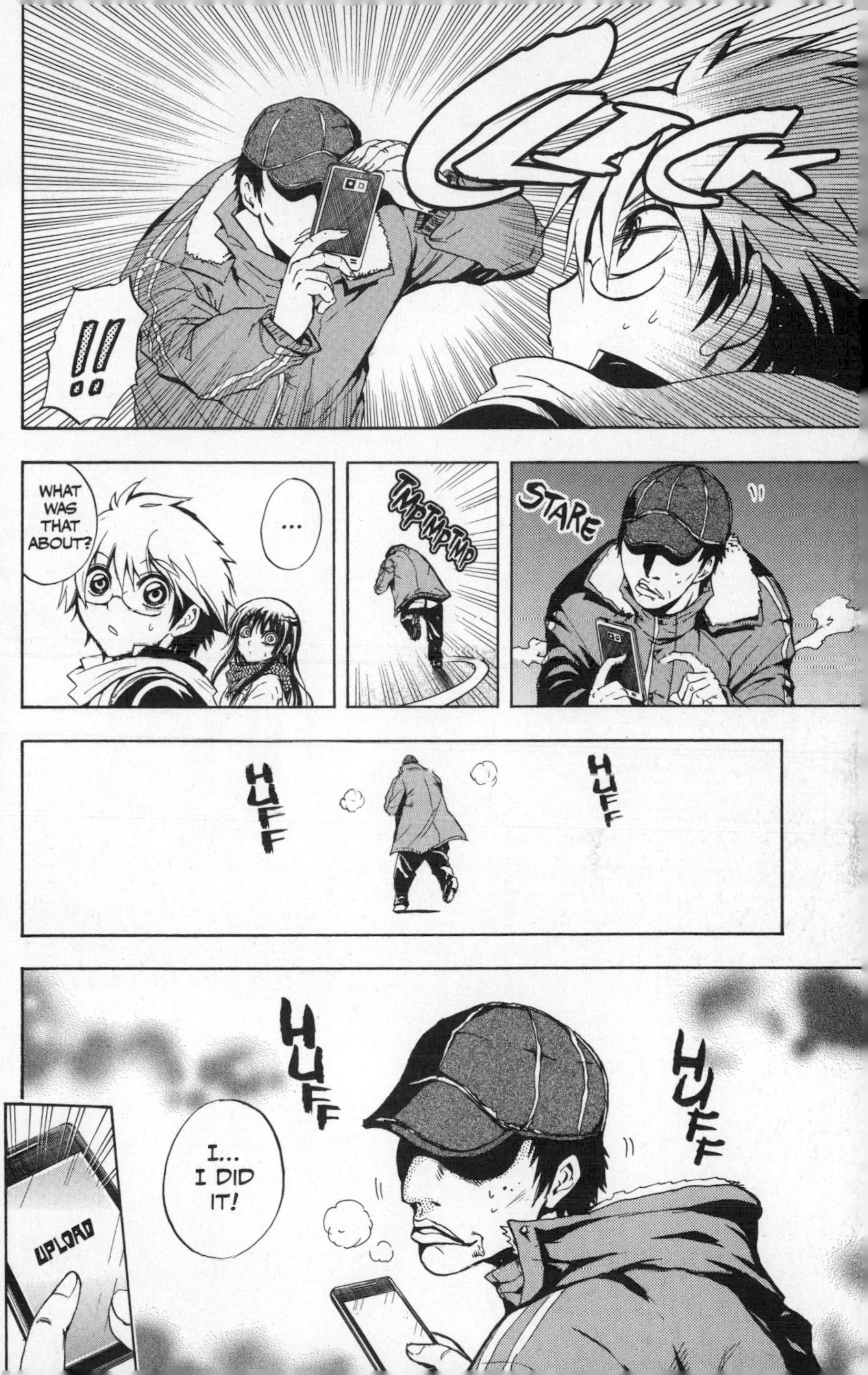
CLICK
!!
STARE
TMPTMPTMP
...
WHAT WAS THAT ABOUT?
HUFF
HUFF
HUFF
HUFF
I... I DID IT!
UPLOAD

...OF RIKUO NURA.

I SNAPPED A PIC...

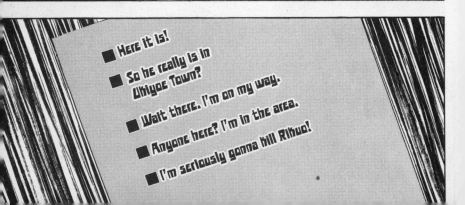

■ Here it is!

■ So he really is in Ukiyoe Town?

■ Wait there. I'm on my way.

■ Anyone here? I'm in the area.

■ I'm seriously gonna kill Rikuo!

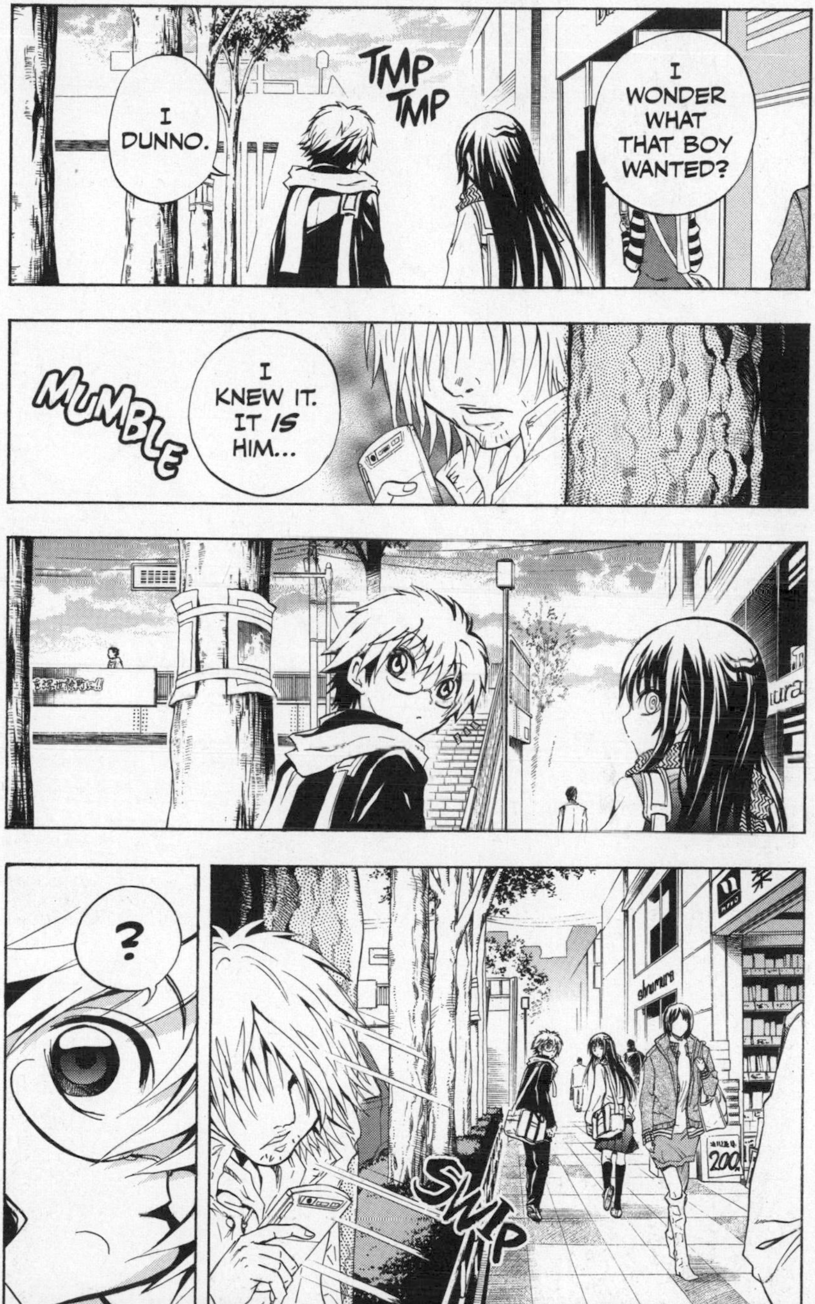
I WONDER WHAT THAT BOY WANTED?
TMP TMP
I DUNNO.
I KNEW IT. IT *IS* HIM...
MUMBLE
SWP
?

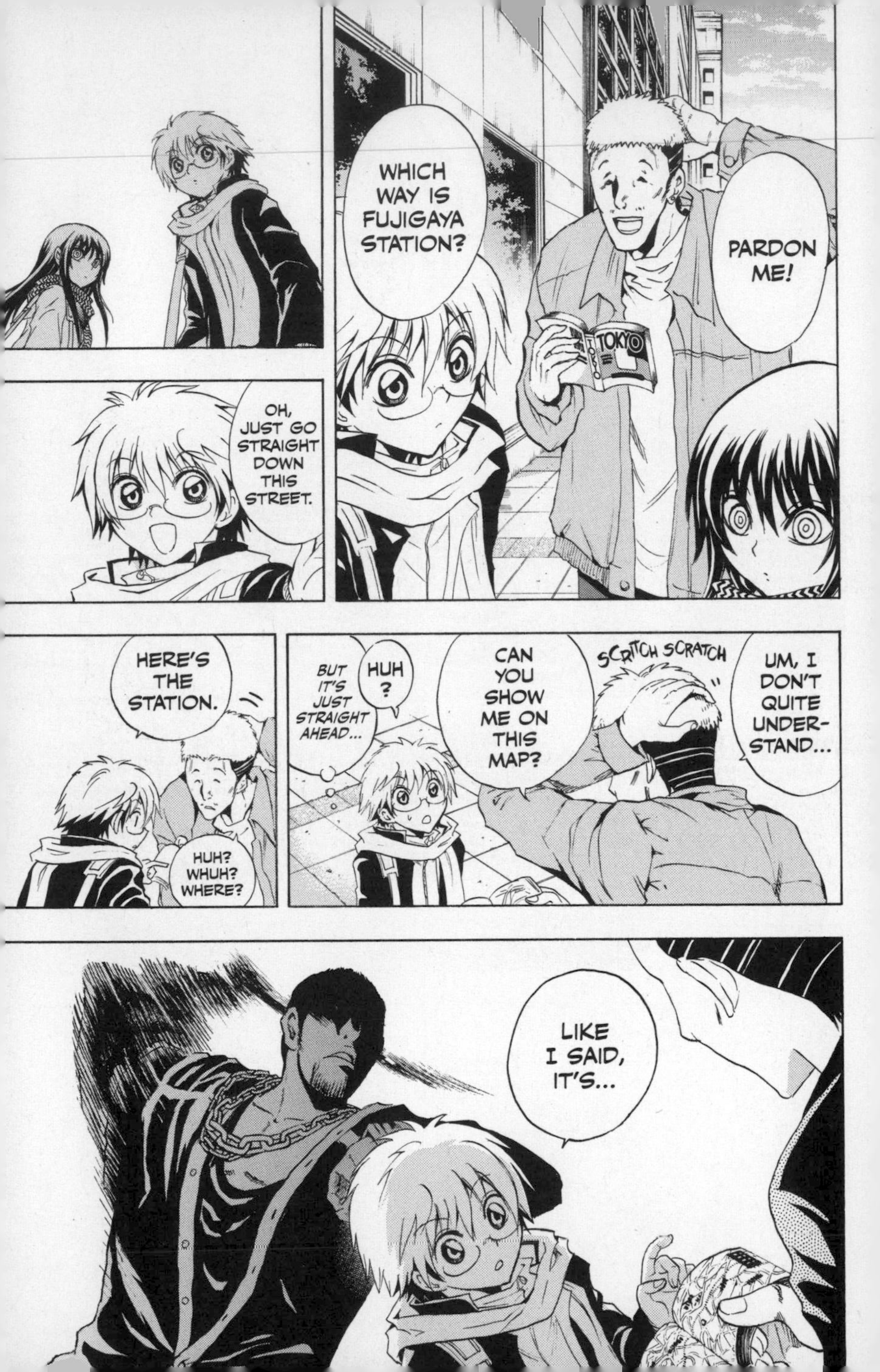
PARDON ME!
WHICH WAY IS FUJIGAYA STATION?
TOKYO
OH, JUST GO STRAIGHT DOWN THIS STREET.
UM, I DON'T QUITE UNDER-STAND...
SCRITCH SCRATCH
CAN YOU SHOW ME ON THIS MAP?
HUH?
BUT IT'S JUST STRAIGHT AHEAD...
HERE'S THE STATION.
HUH? WHUH? WHERE?
LIKE I SAID, IT'S...

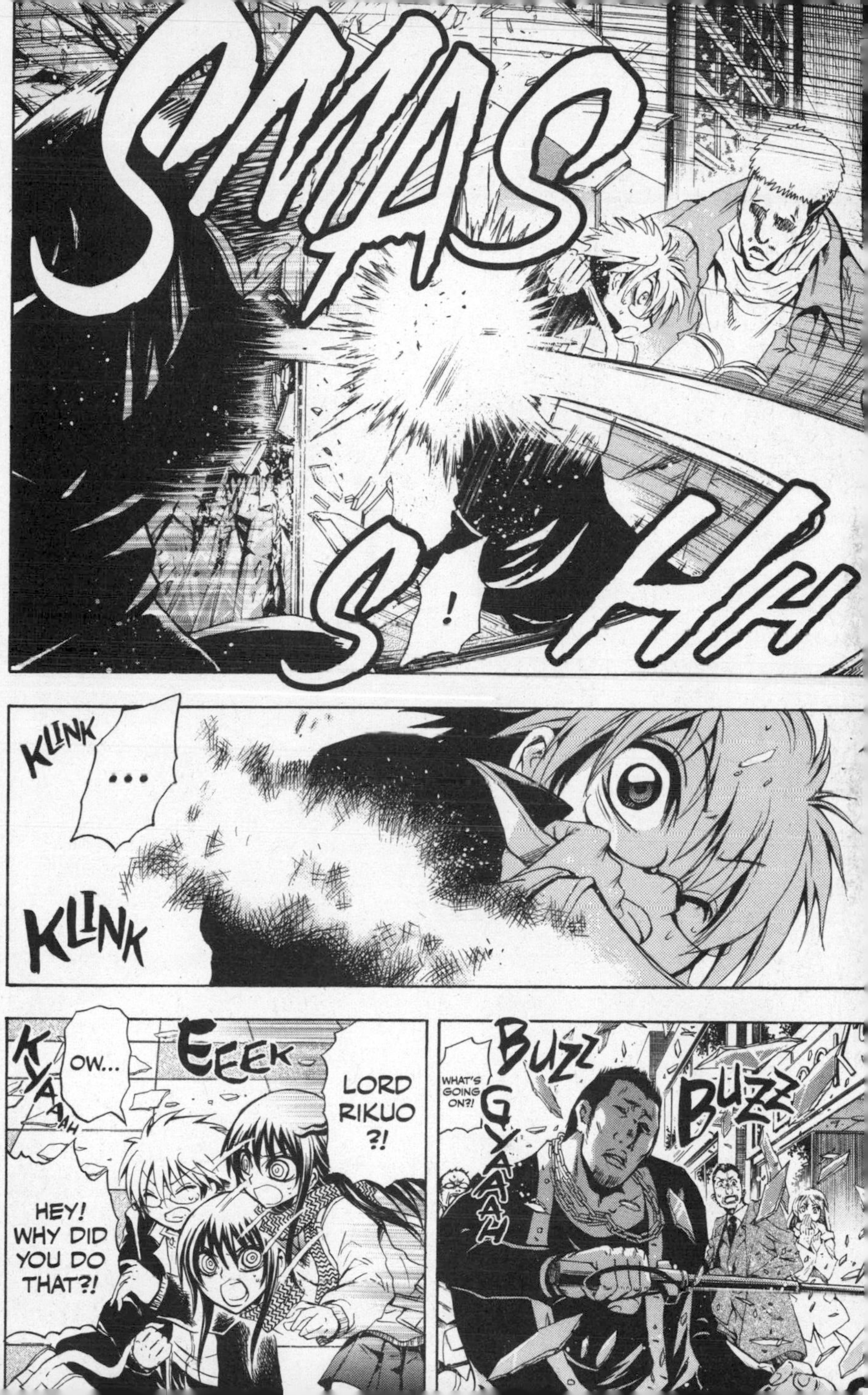
SMAS
SHH
!
...
KLINK
KLINK
BUZZ
WHAT'S GOING ON?!
GYAAAH
BUZZ
LORD RIKUO?!
EEEK
OW...
KYAAAAH
HEY! WHY DID YOU DO THAT?!

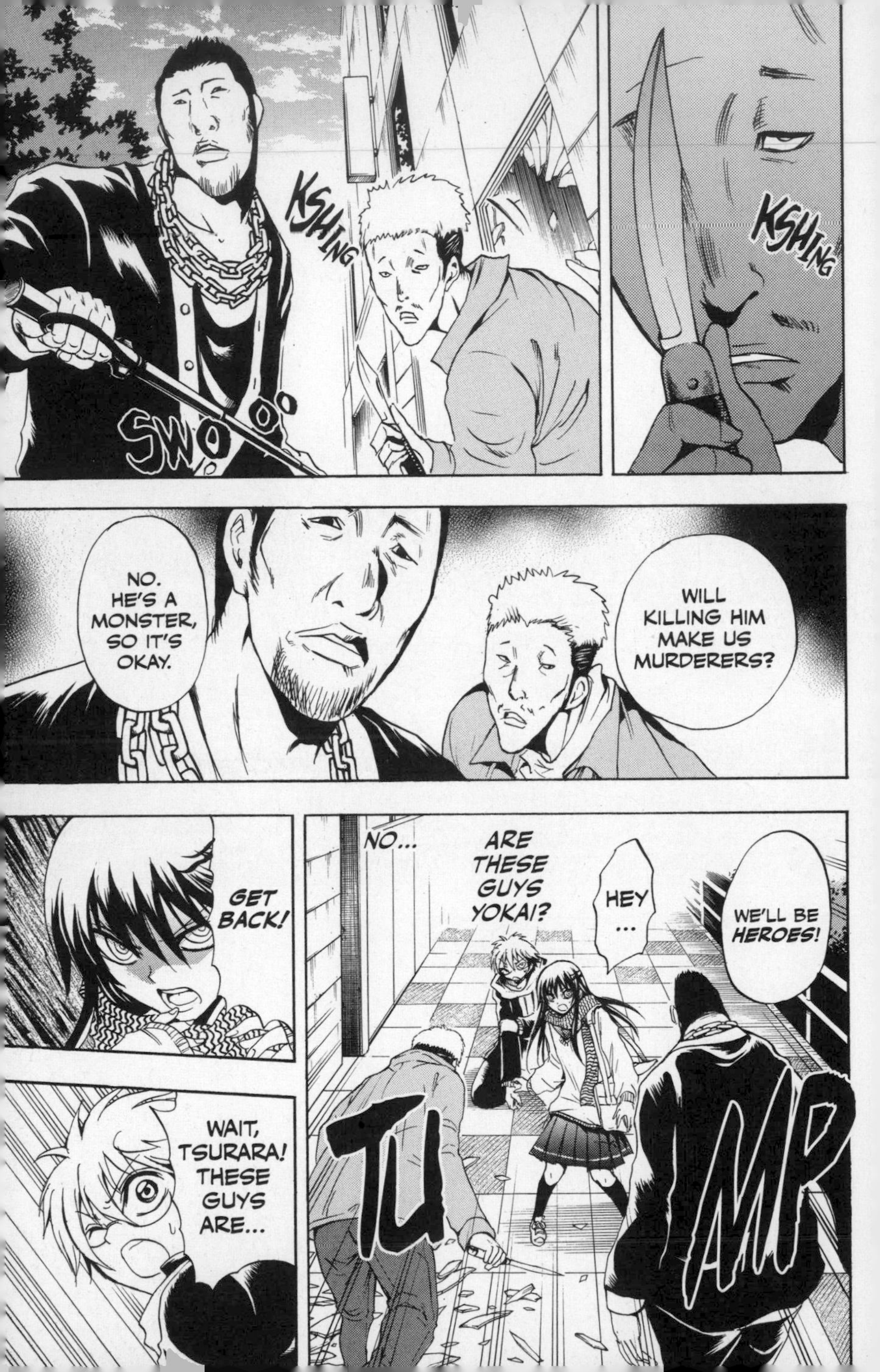
KSHING
KSHING
SWOOO
WILL KILLING HIM MAKE US MURDERERS?
NO. HE'S A MONSTER, SO IT'S OKAY.
WE'LL BE HEROES!
HEY ...
ARE THESE GUYS YOKAI?
NO...
MP
TU
GET BACK!
WAIT, TSURARA! THESE GUYS ARE...

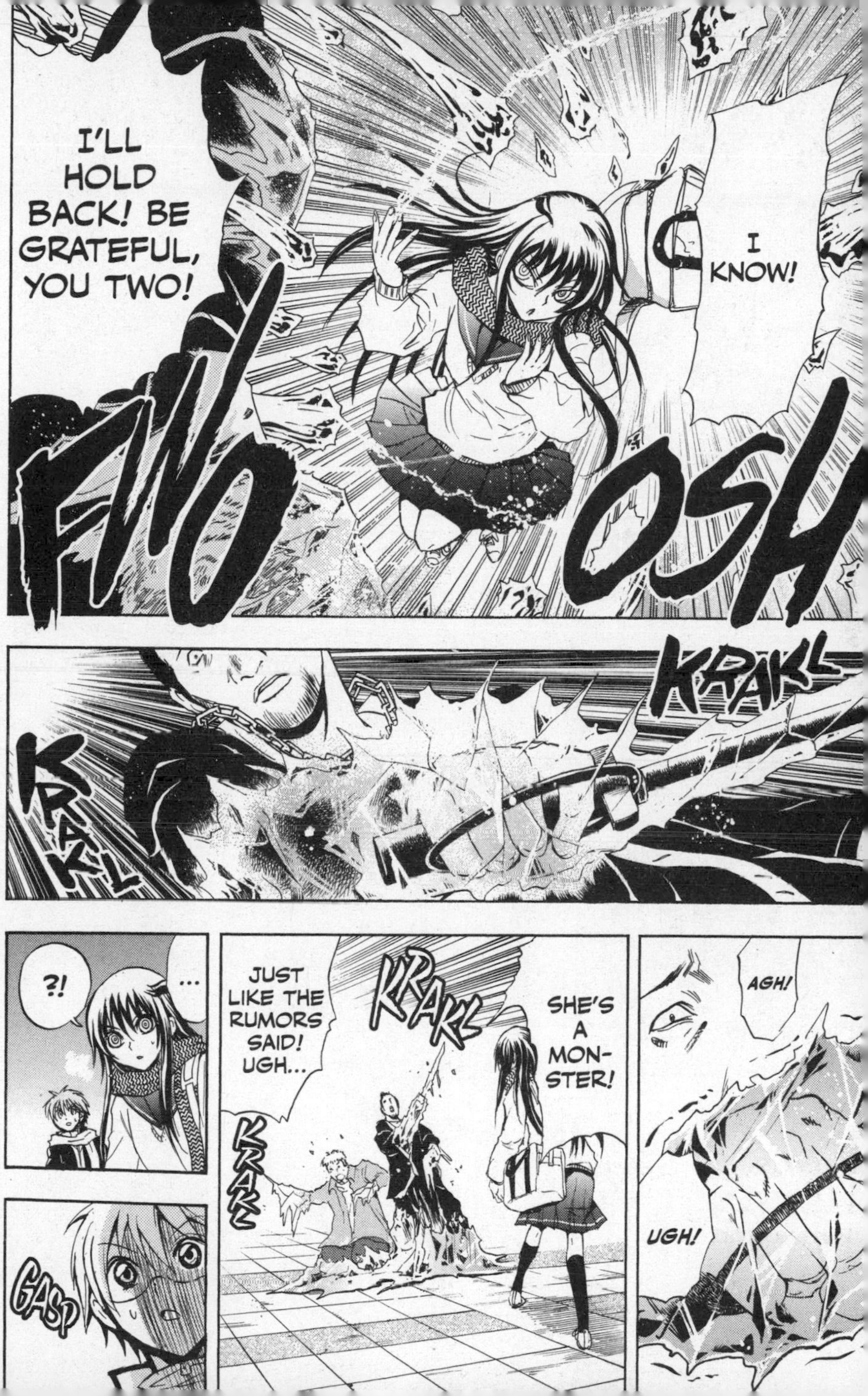
I KNOW!
I'LL HOLD BACK! BE GRATEFUL, YOU TWO!
FWOOSH
KRAKL
KRAKL
AGH!
UGH!
SHE'S A MON-STER!
KRAKL
JUST LIKE THE RUMORS SAID! UGH...
KRAKL
...
?!
GASP

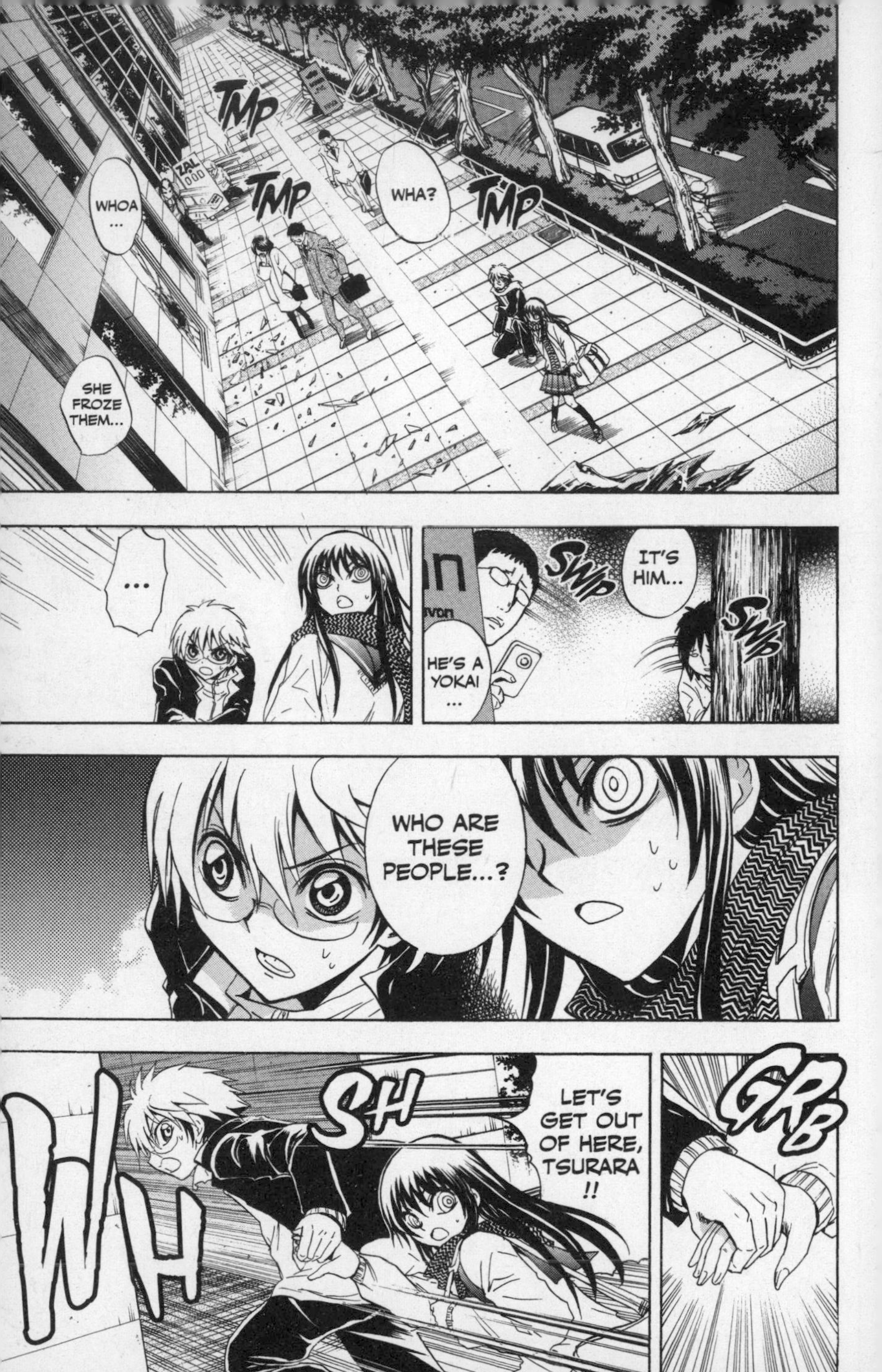
TMP
WHA?
TMP
TMP
WHOA ...
SHE FROZE THEM...
IT'S HIM...
SWIP
SWIP
HE'S A YOKAI ...
...
WHO ARE THESE PEOPLE...?
GRB
LET'S GET OUT OF HERE, TSURARA !!
SH
WH

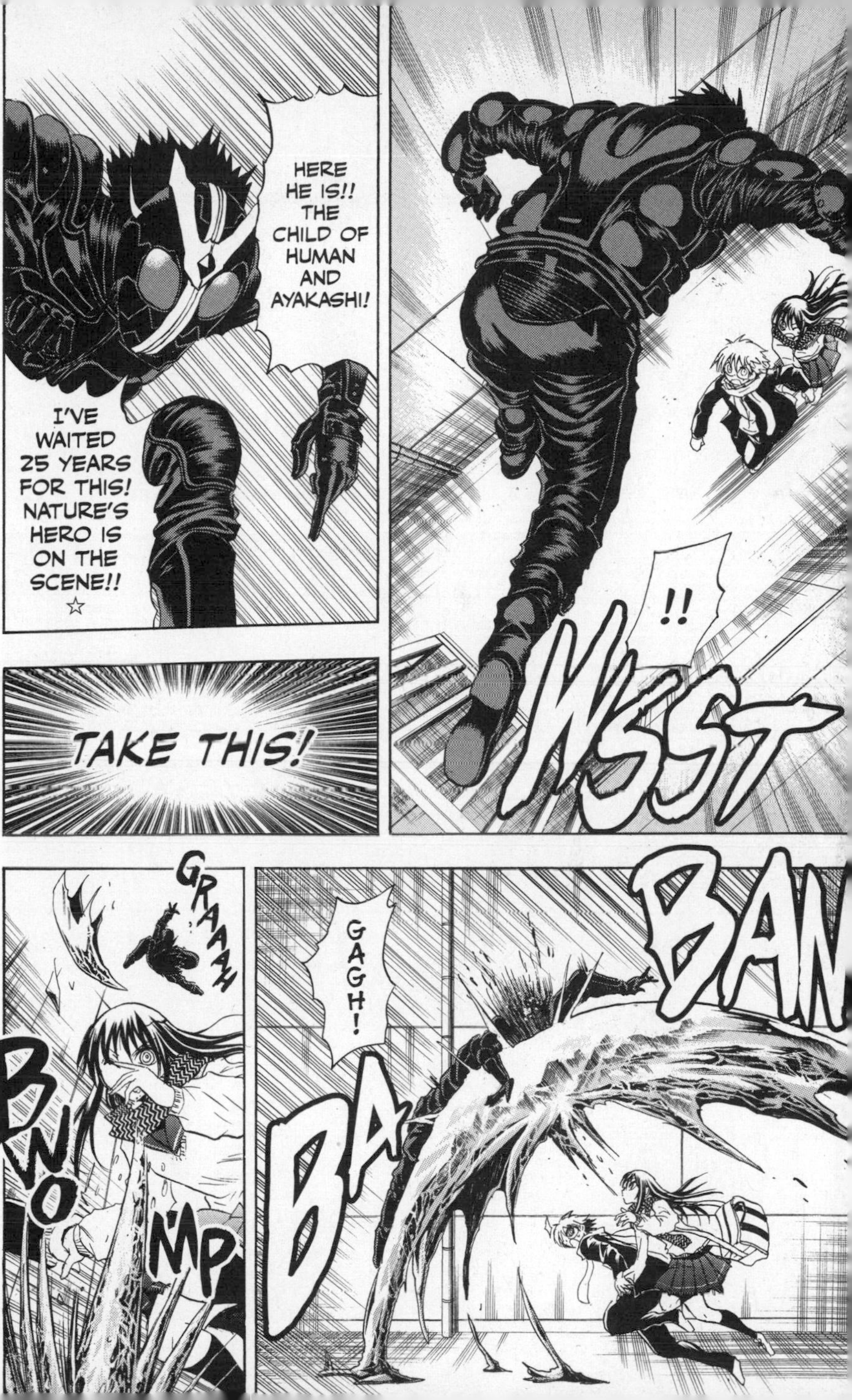
!!
WSST
HERE HE IS!! THE CHILD OF HUMAN AND AYAKASHI!
I'VE WAITED 25 YEARS FOR THIS! NATURE'S HERO IS ON THE SCENE!! ☆
TAKE THIS!
BAN
GAGH!
BA
GRAAAH
BWOMP

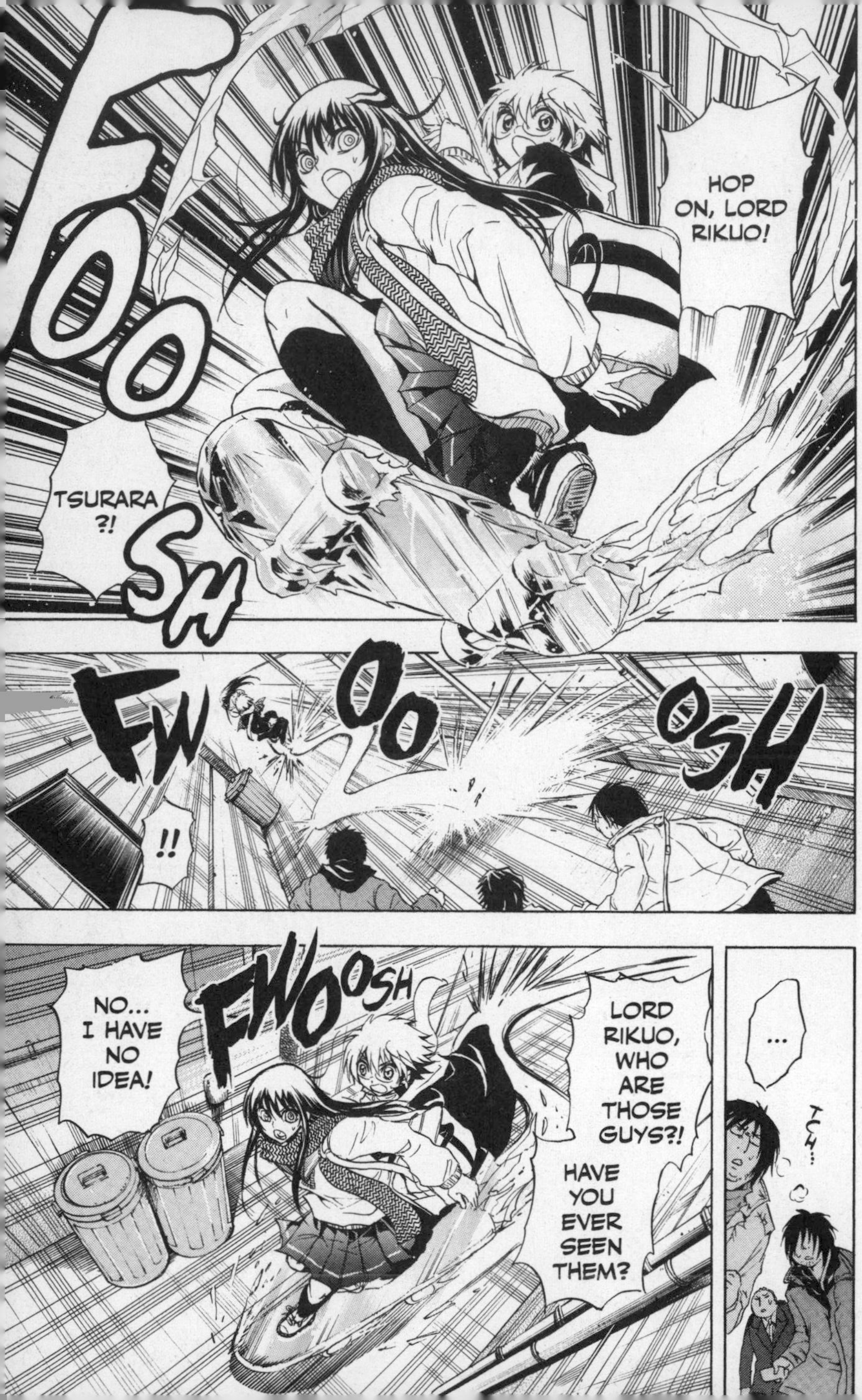
HOP ON, LORD RIKUO!
TSURARA ?!
FWOOOSH
!!
...
TCH...
LORD RIKUO, WHO ARE THOSE GUYS?!
HAVE YOU EVER SEEN THEM?
FWOOSH
NO... I HAVE NO IDEA!

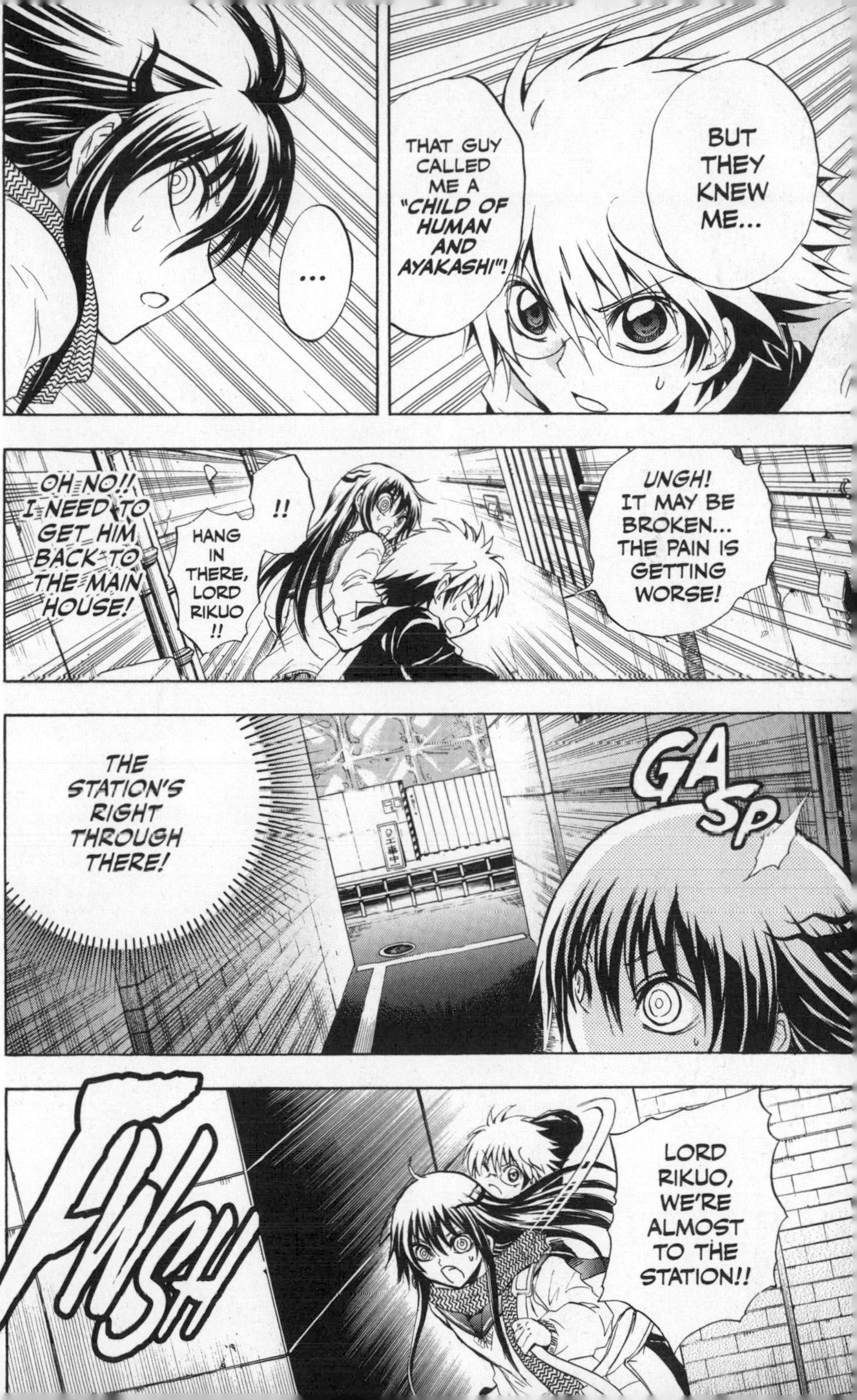
BUT THEY KNEW ME...
THAT GUY CALLED ME A "CHILD OF HUMAN AND AYAKASHI"!
...
UNGH! IT MAY BE BROKEN... THE PAIN IS GETTING WORSE!
!!
HANG IN THERE, LORD RIKUO!!
OH NO!! I NEED TO GET HIM BACK TO THE MAIN HOUSE!
GASP
THE STATION'S RIGHT THROUGH THERE!
LORD RIKUO, WE'RE ALMOST TO THE STATION!!
FWSH

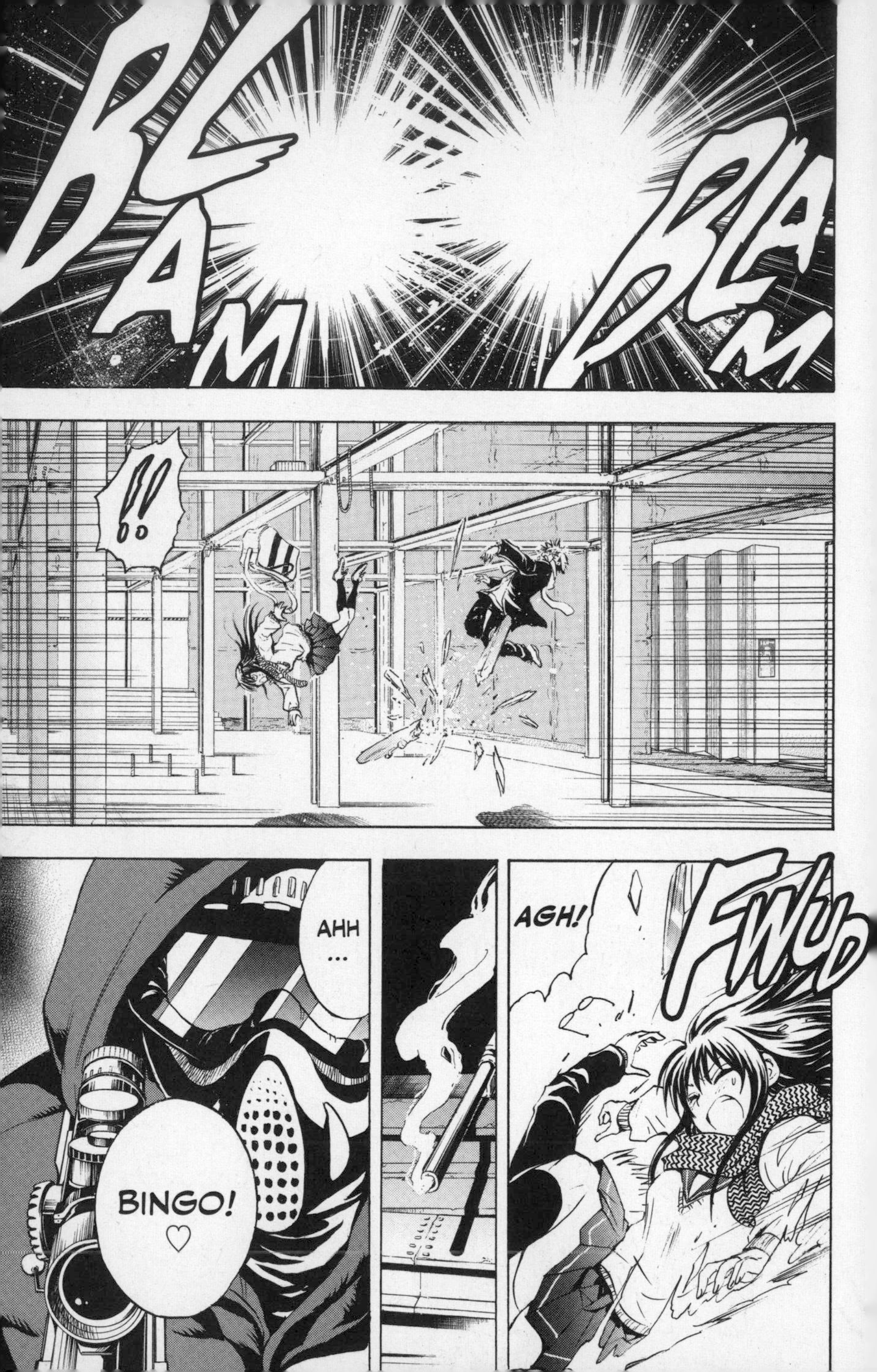
BLAM
BLAM
!!
FWUD
AGH!
AHH ...
BINGO! ♡

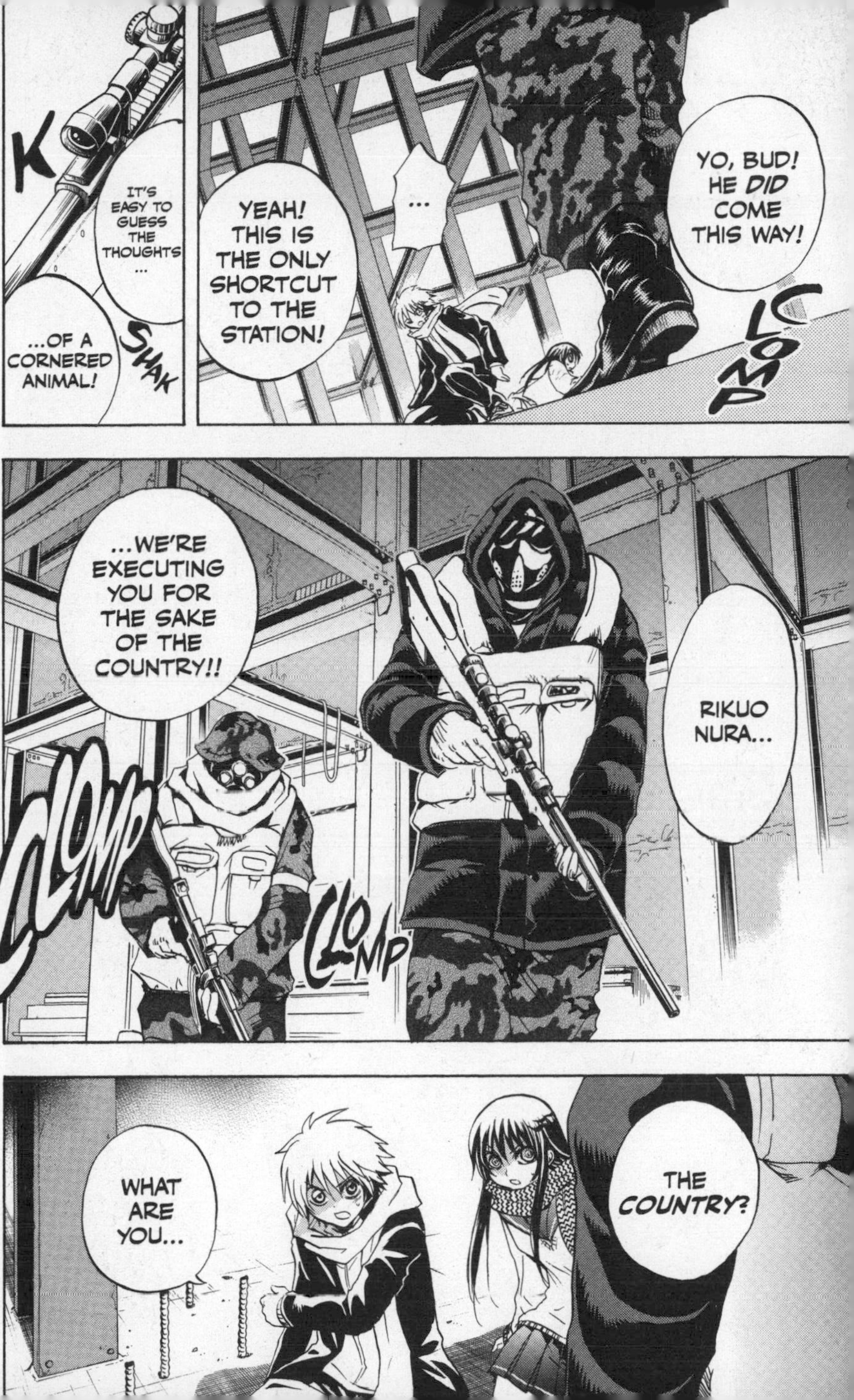
YO, BUD! HE *DID* COME THIS WAY!
CLOMP
...
YEAH! THIS IS THE ONLY SHORTCUT TO THE STATION!
K
IT'S EASY TO GUESS THE THOUGHTS...
SHAK
...OF A CORNERED ANIMAL!
RIKUO NURA...
...WE'RE EXECUTING YOU FOR THE SAKE OF THE COUNTRY!!
CLOMP
CLOMP
THE *COUNTRY?*
WHAT ARE YOU...

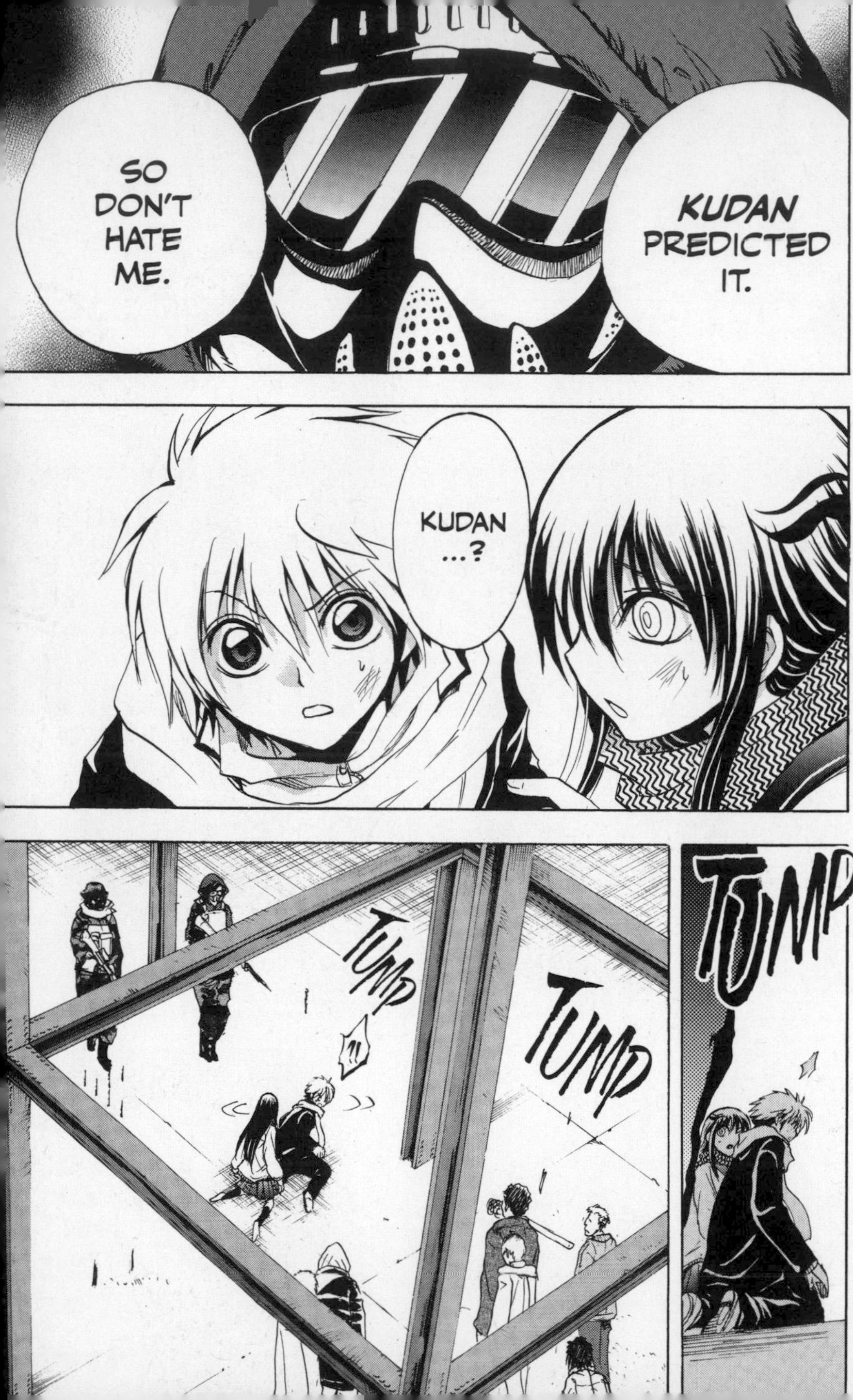
KUDAN PREDICTED IT.
SO DON'T HATE ME.
KUDAN ...?
TUMP
TUMP
TUMP
?!

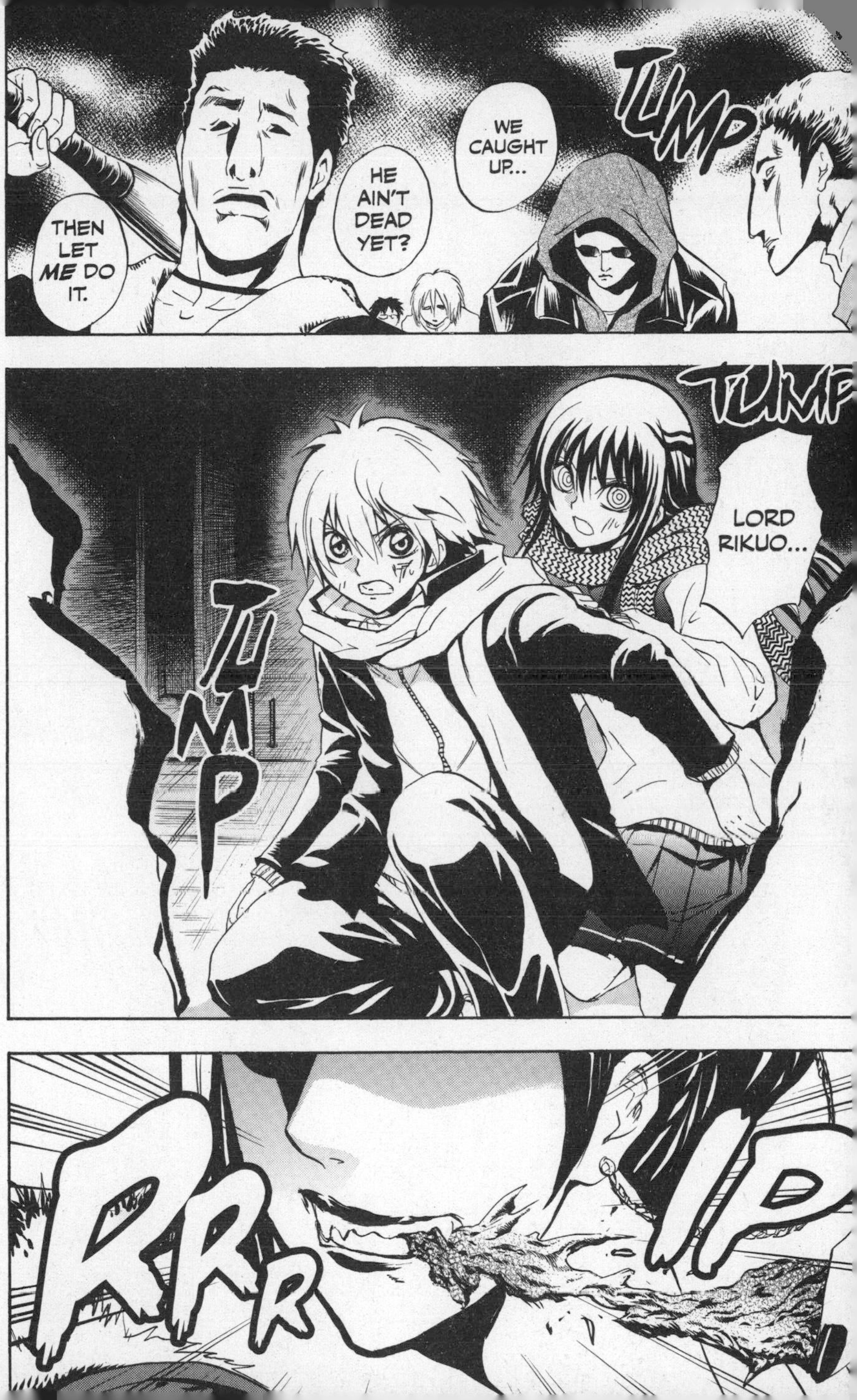
TUMP
WE CAUGHT UP...
HE AIN'T DEAD YET?
THEN LET *ME* DO IT.
TUMP
LORD RIKUO...
TUMP
RRRIP

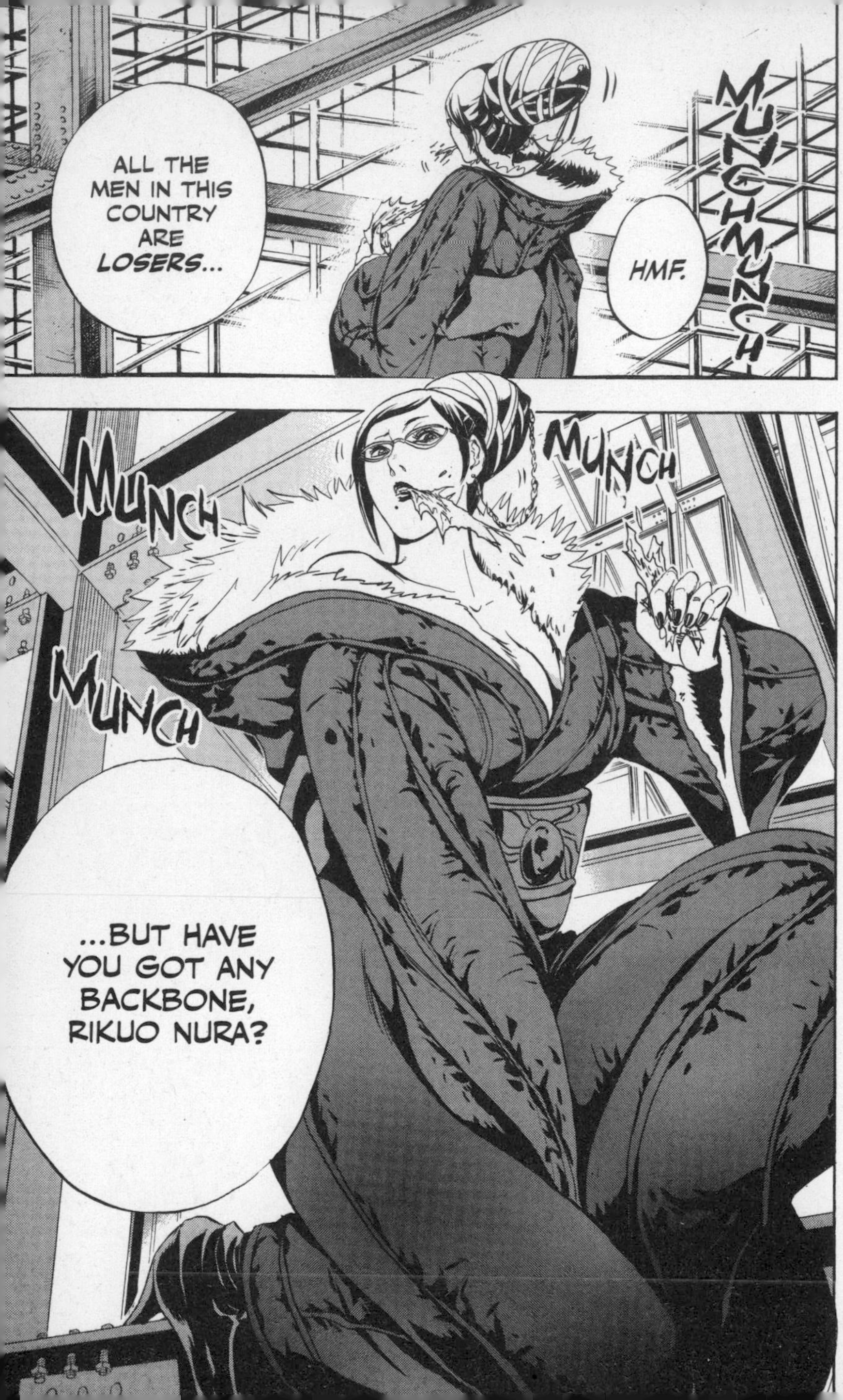
MUNCHMUNCH!
HMF.
ALL THE MEN IN THIS COUNTRY ARE *LOSERS*...
MUNCH
MUNCH
MUNCH
...BUT HAVE YOU GOT ANY BACKBONE, RIKUO NURA?

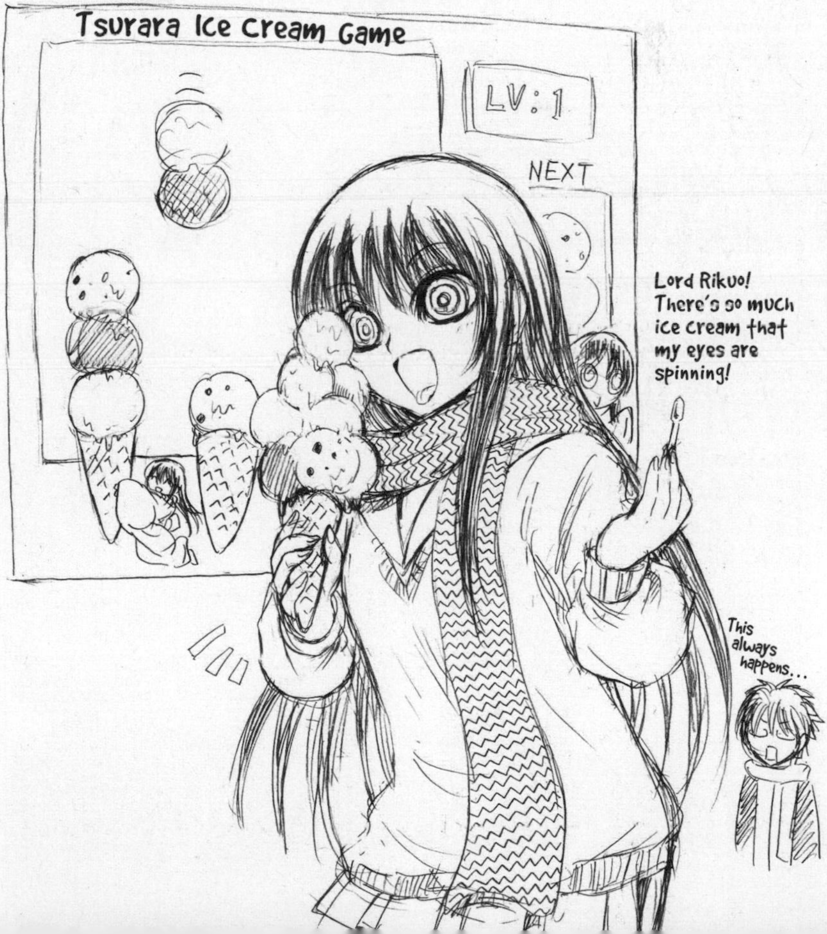
Tsurara Ice Cream Game
LV: 1
NEXT
Lord Rikuo! There's so much ice cream that my eyes are spinning!
This always happens...

Act 161: Foul Feeder

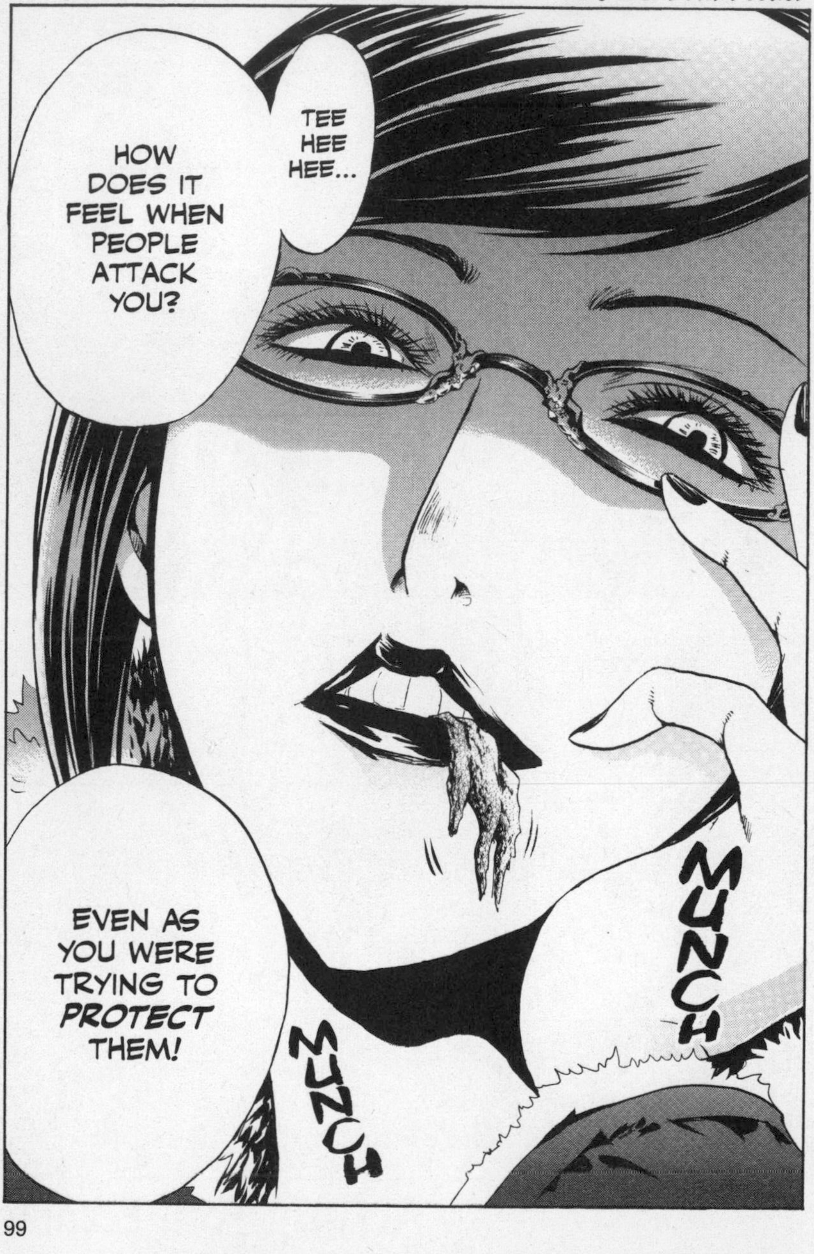
TEE HEE HEE...
HOW DOES IT FEEL WHEN PEOPLE ATTACK YOU?
MUNCH
MUNCH
EVEN AS YOU WERE TRYING TO *PROTECT* THEM!

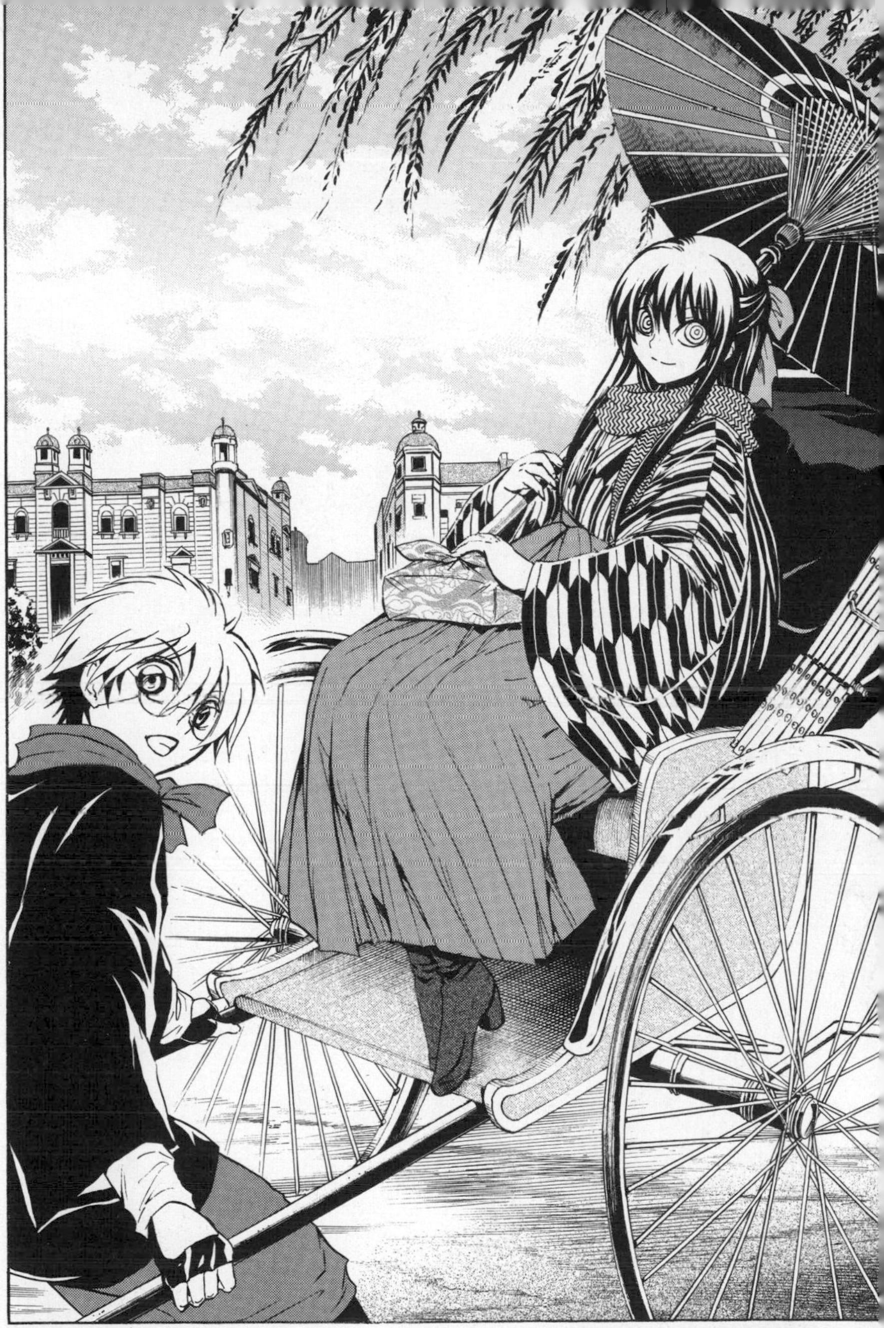

Act 161: Foul Feeder

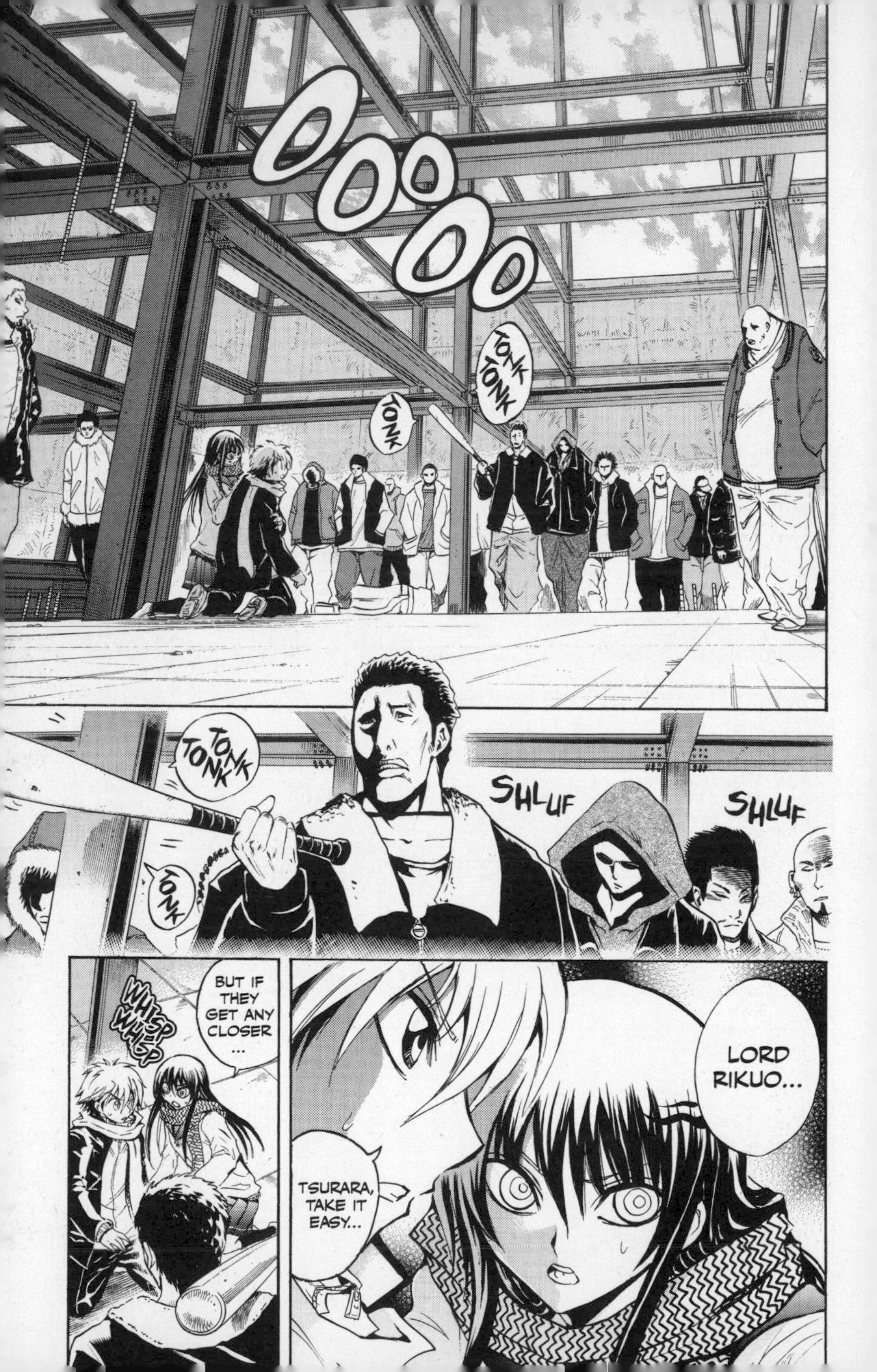
OOOOO
TONK TONK
TONK
SHLUF
SHLUF
TONK TONK
TONK
LORD RIKUO...
TSURARA, TAKE IT EASY...
BUT IF THEY GET ANY CLOSER ...
WHISP WHISP

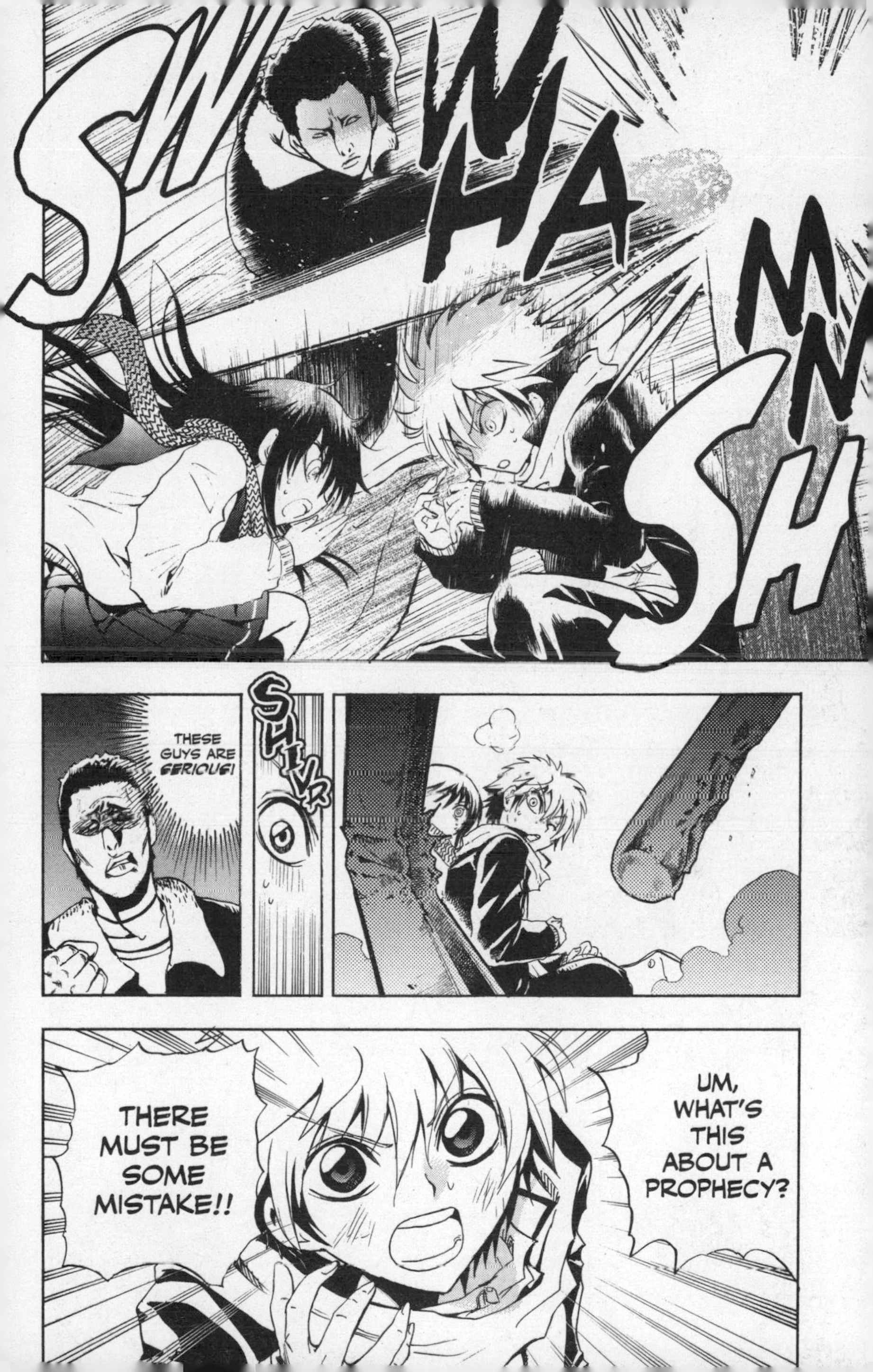
SHIVR
THESE GUYS ARE SERIOUS!
UM, WHAT'S THIS ABOUT A PROPHECY?
THERE MUST BE SOME MISTAKE!!

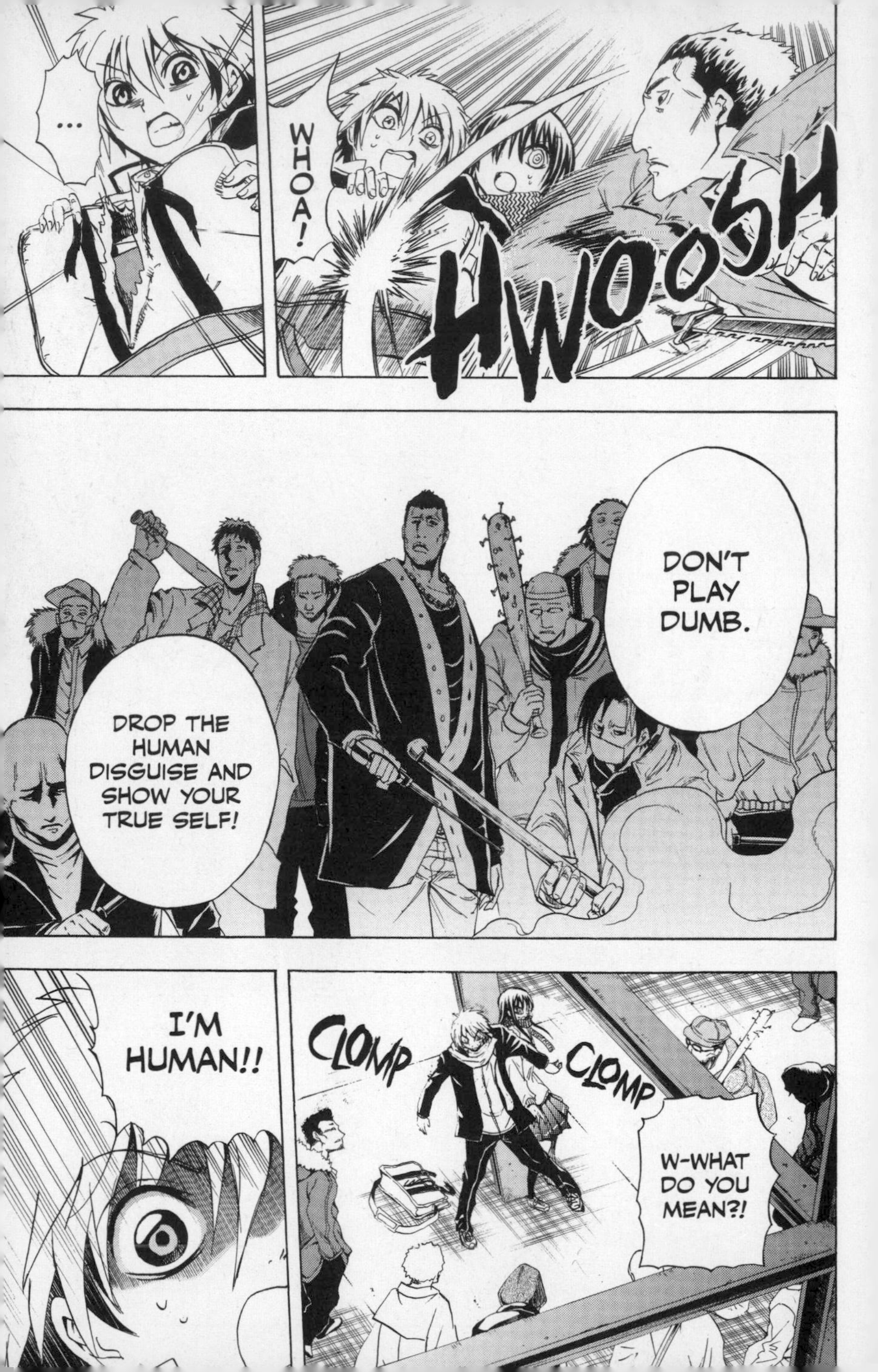
WHOA!
HWOOSH
...
DON'T PLAY DUMB.
DROP THE HUMAN DISGUISE AND SHOW YOUR TRUE SELF!
CLOMP
CLOMP
W-WHAT DO YOU MEAN?!
I'M HUMAN!!

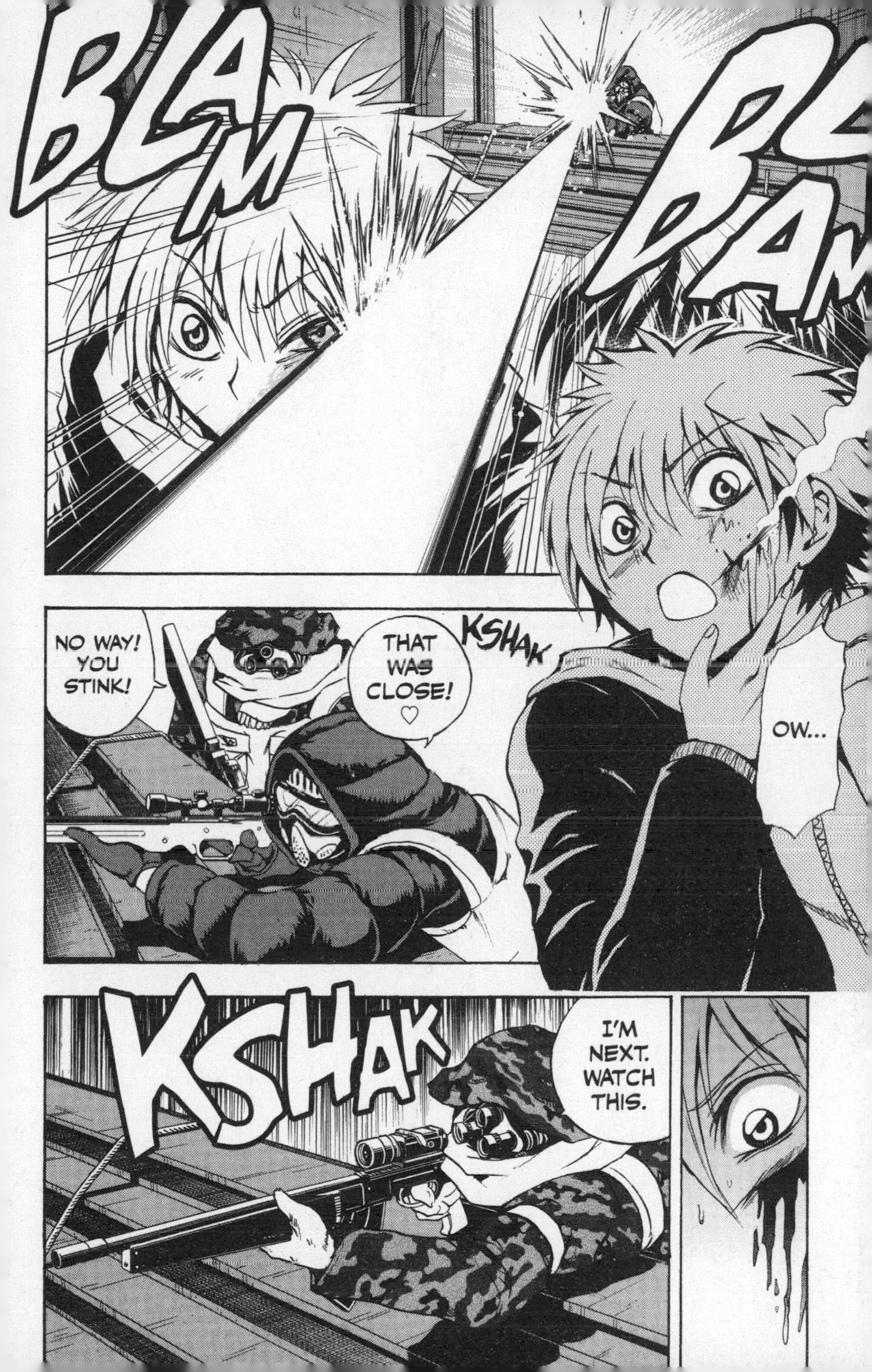
BLAM
BLAM
OW...
KSHAK
THAT WAS CLOSE! ♡
NO WAY! YOU STINK!
I'M NEXT. WATCH THIS.
KSHAK

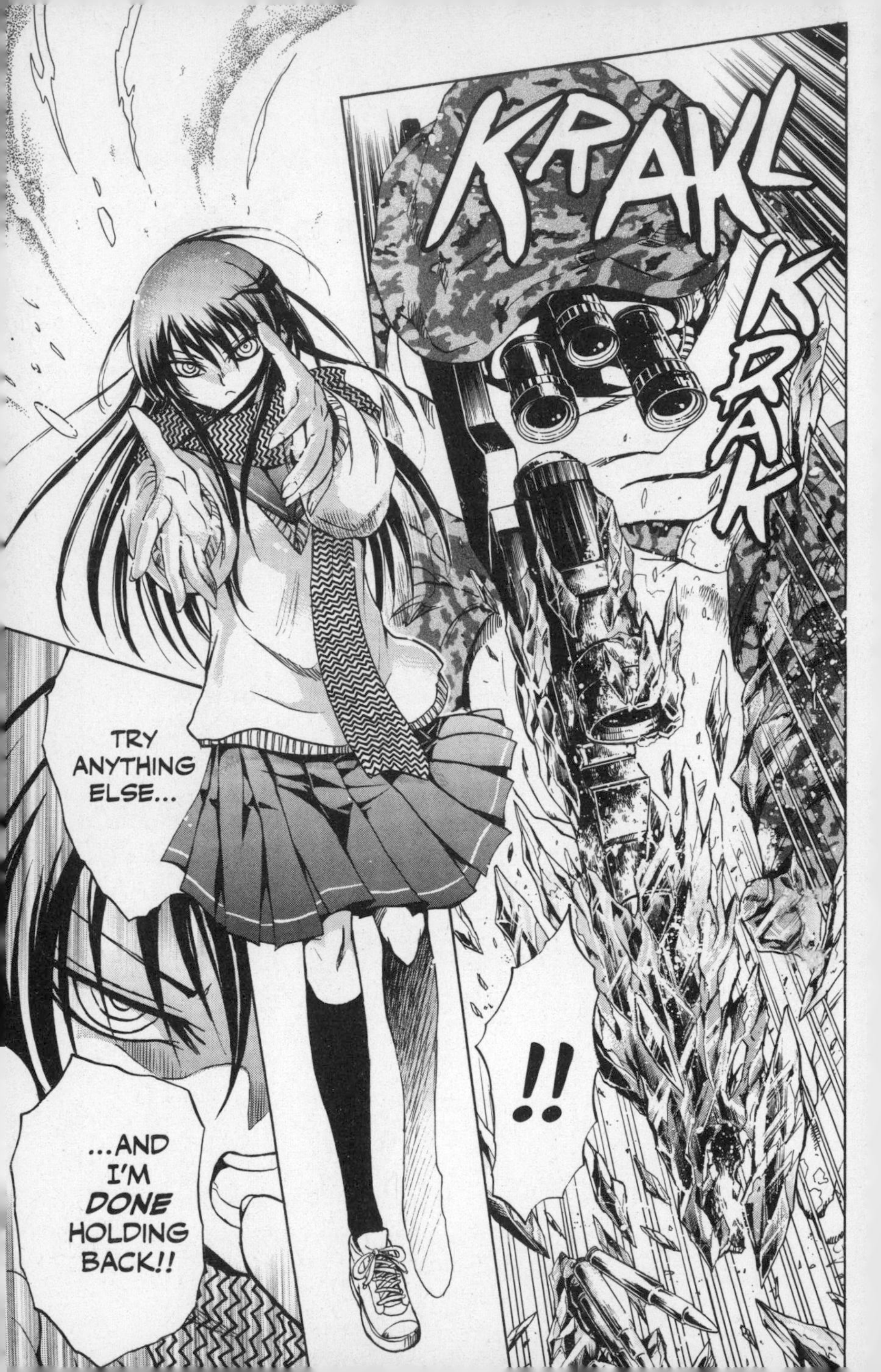
KRAKL
KRAK
!!
TRY ANYTHING ELSE...
...AND I'M *DONE* HOLDING BACK!!

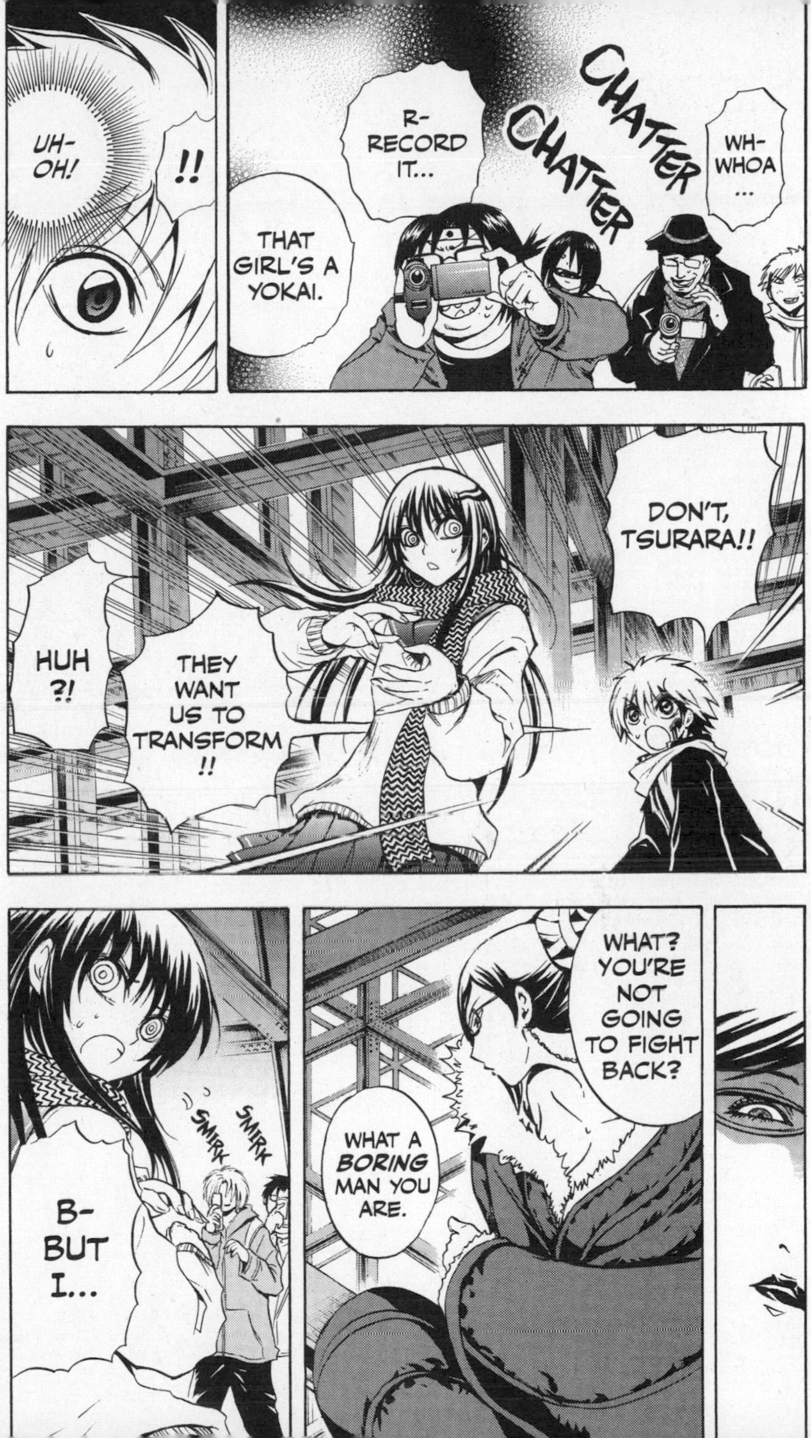
WH-WHOA ...
CHATTER
CHATTER
R-RECORD IT...
THAT GIRL'S A YOKAI.
!!
UH-OH!
DON'T, TSURARA!!
THEY WANT US TO TRANSFORM!!
HUH?!
WHAT? YOU'RE NOT GOING TO FIGHT BACK?
WHAT A *BORING* MAN YOU ARE.
SMIRK
SMIRK
B-BUT I...

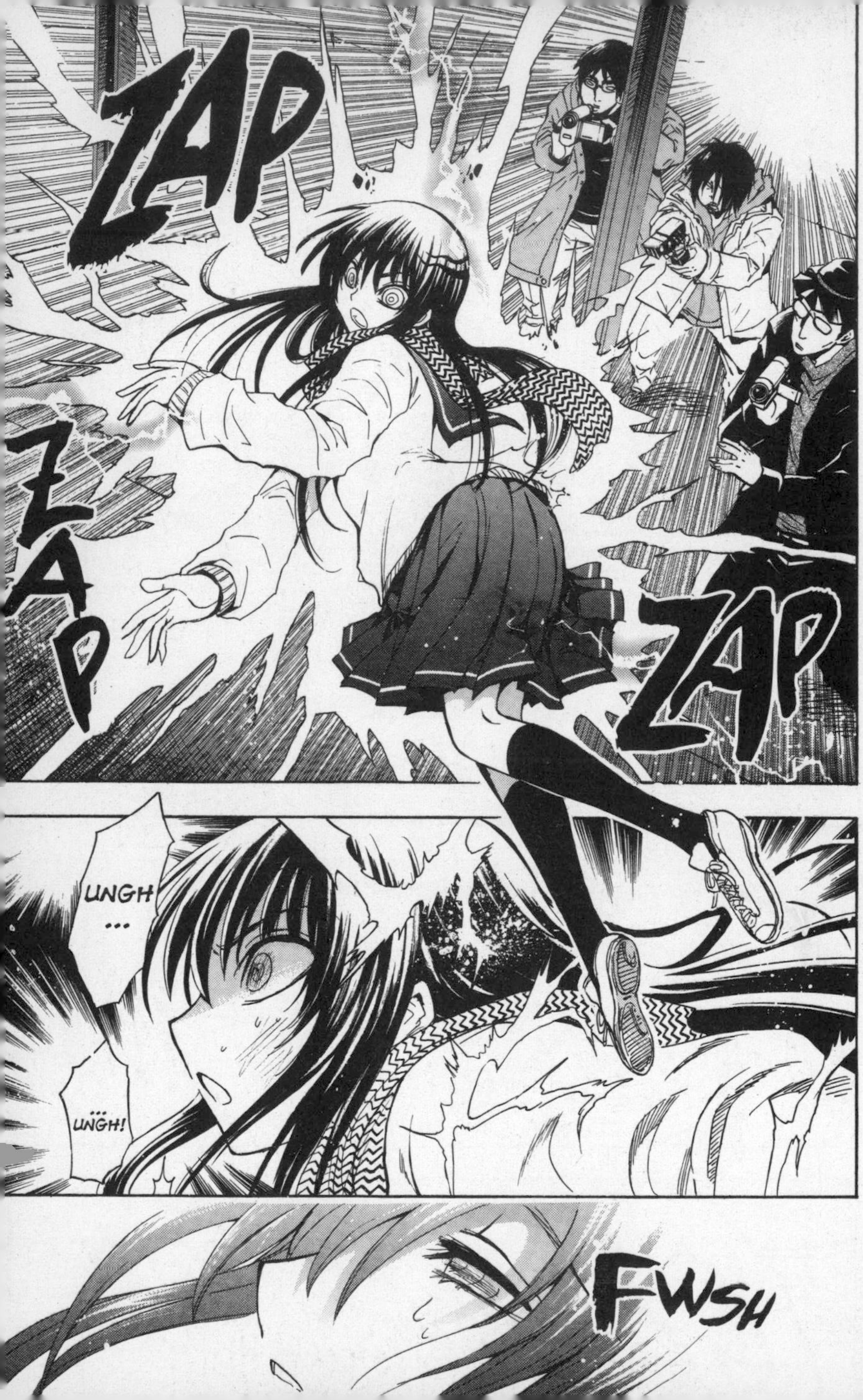
ZAP
ZAP
ZAP
UNGH ...
... UNGH!
FWSH

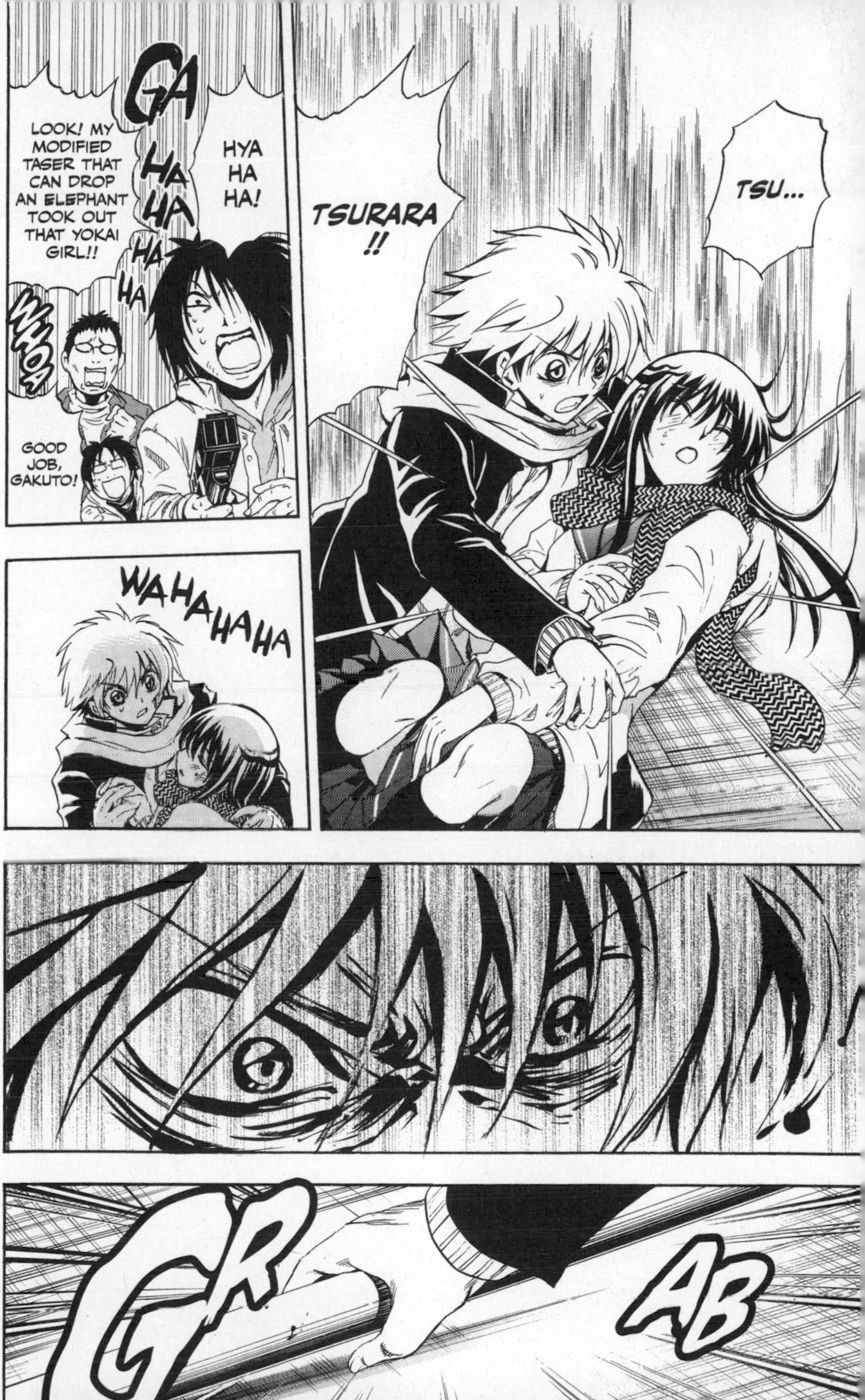
TSU...
TSURARA !!
GAHAHAHAHAHA
HYA HA HA!
LOOK! MY MODIFIED TASER THAT CAN DROP AN ELEPHANT TOOK OUT THAT YOKAI GIRL!!
WHOA
GOOD JOB, GAKUTO!
WAHAHAHAHA
GR
AB

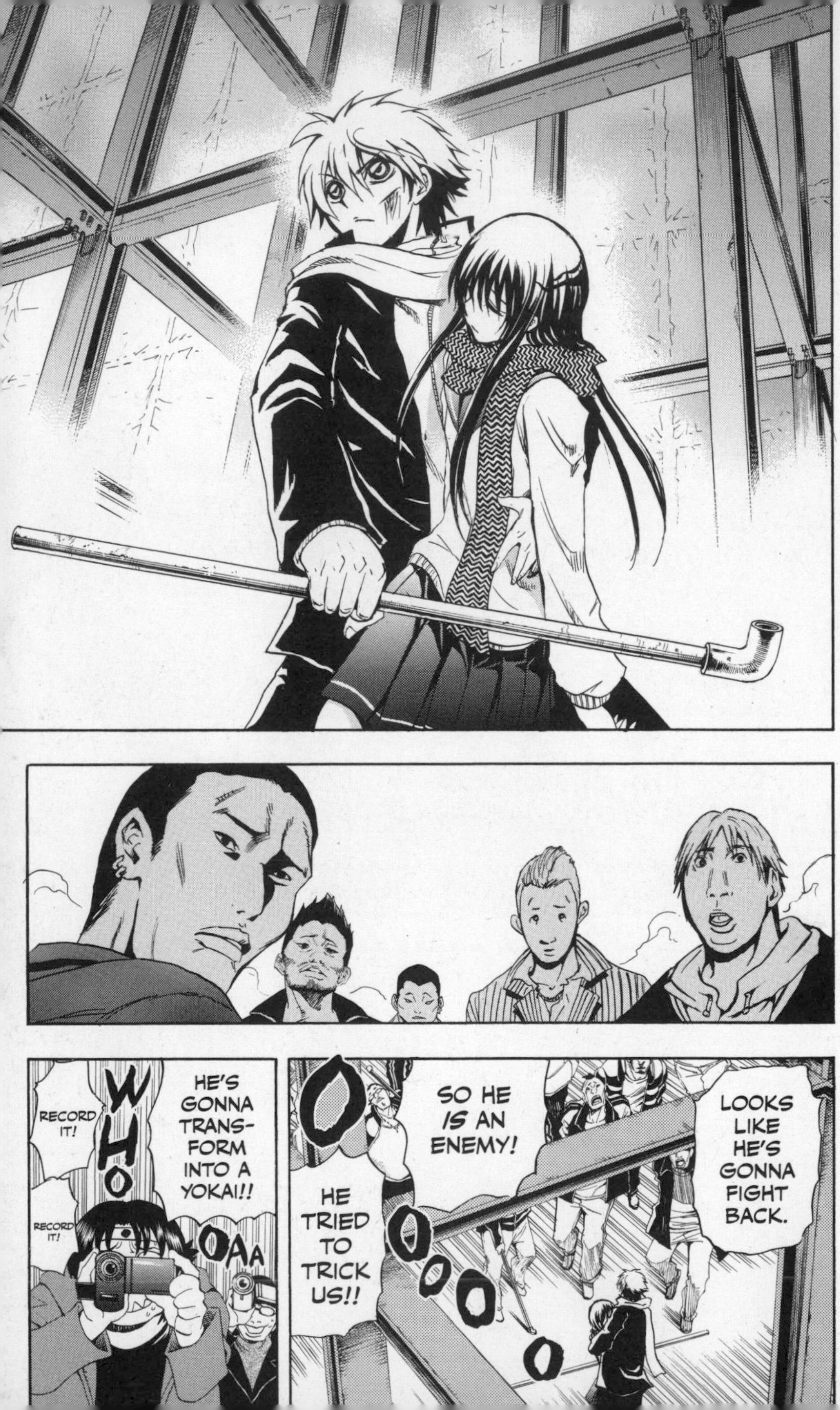
LOOKS LIKE HE'S GONNA FIGHT BACK.
SO HE *IS* AN ENEMY!
HE TRIED TO TRICK US!!
HE'S GONNA TRANS-FORM INTO A YOKAI!!
WHO
RECORD IT!
OAA
RECORD IT!

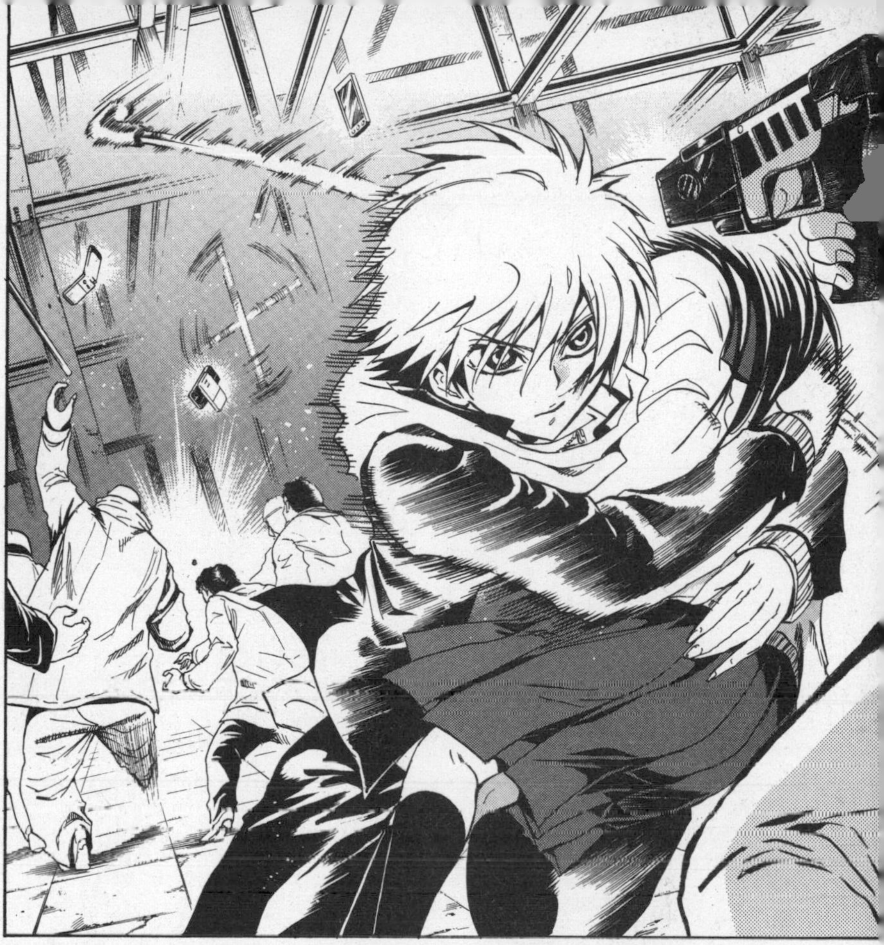
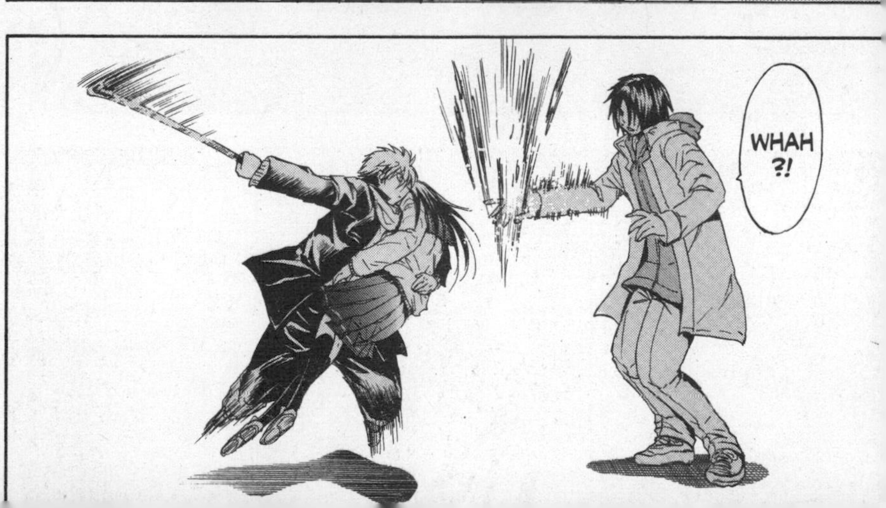
WHAH ?!

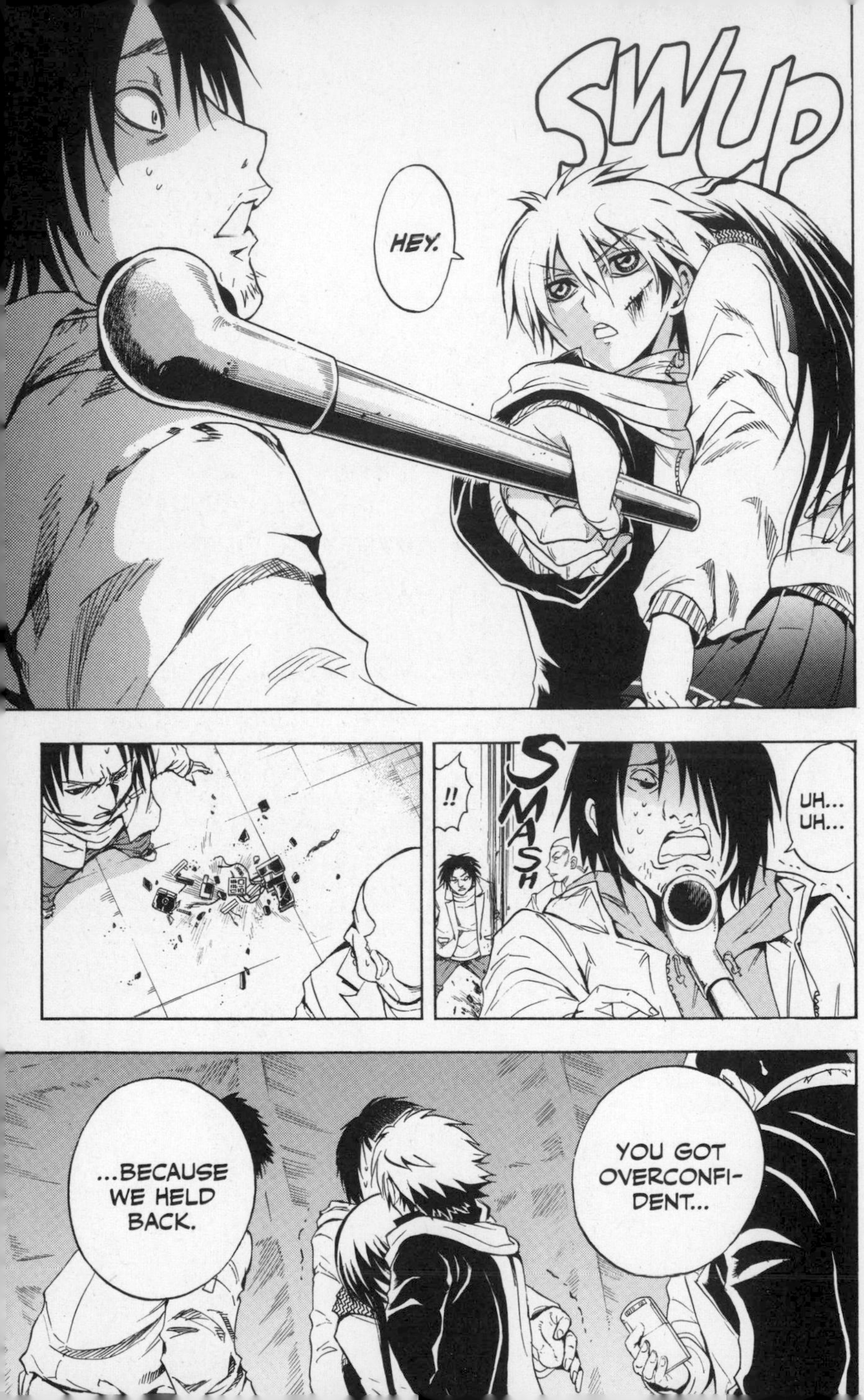
SWUP
HEY.
UH... UH...
SMASH
!!
YOU GOT OVERCONFI- DENT...
...BECAUSE WE HELD BACK.

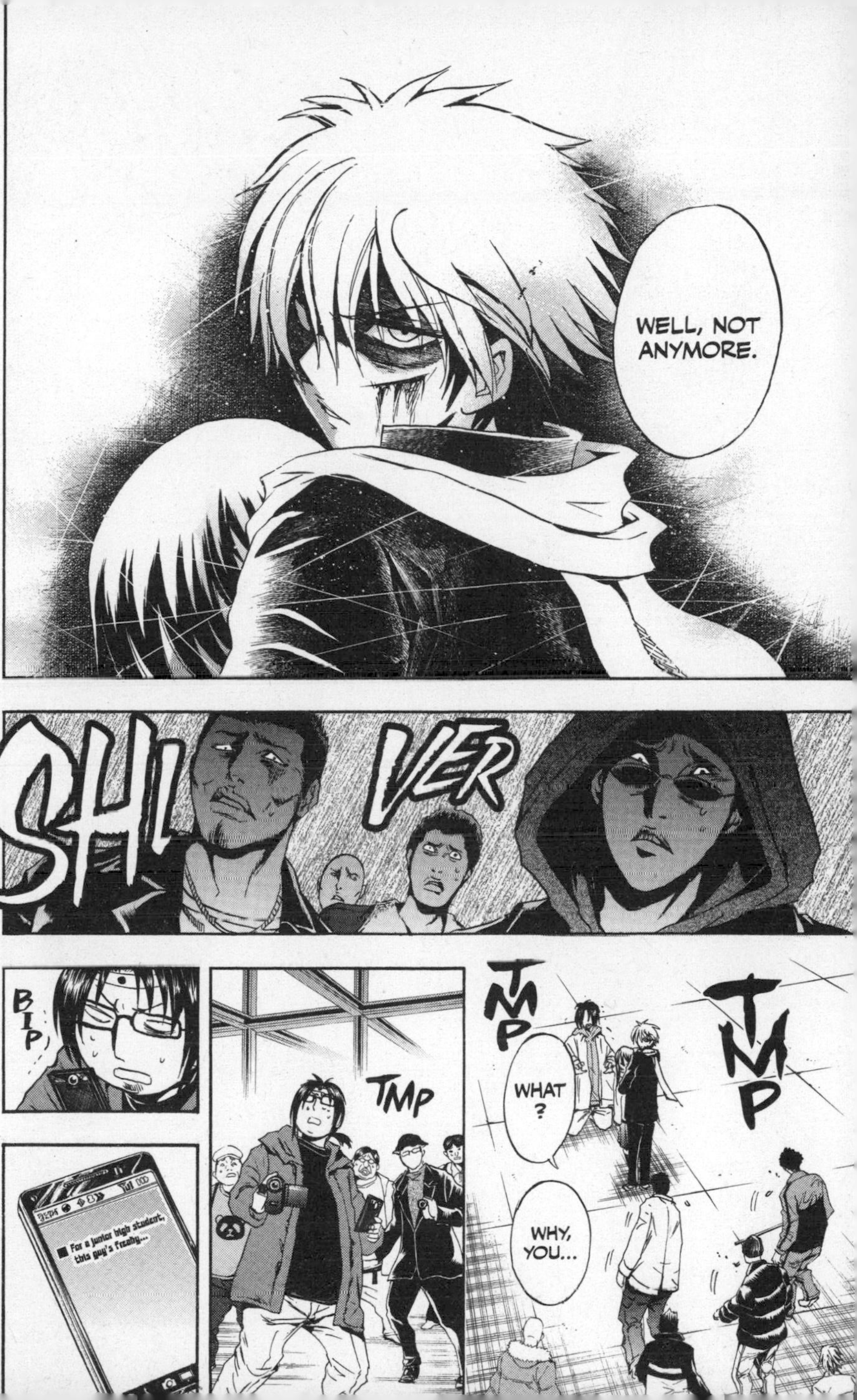
WELL, NOT ANYMORE.
SHIVER
TMP
TMP
WHAT?
WHY, YOU...
TMP
BIP
For a junior high student, this guy's freaky...

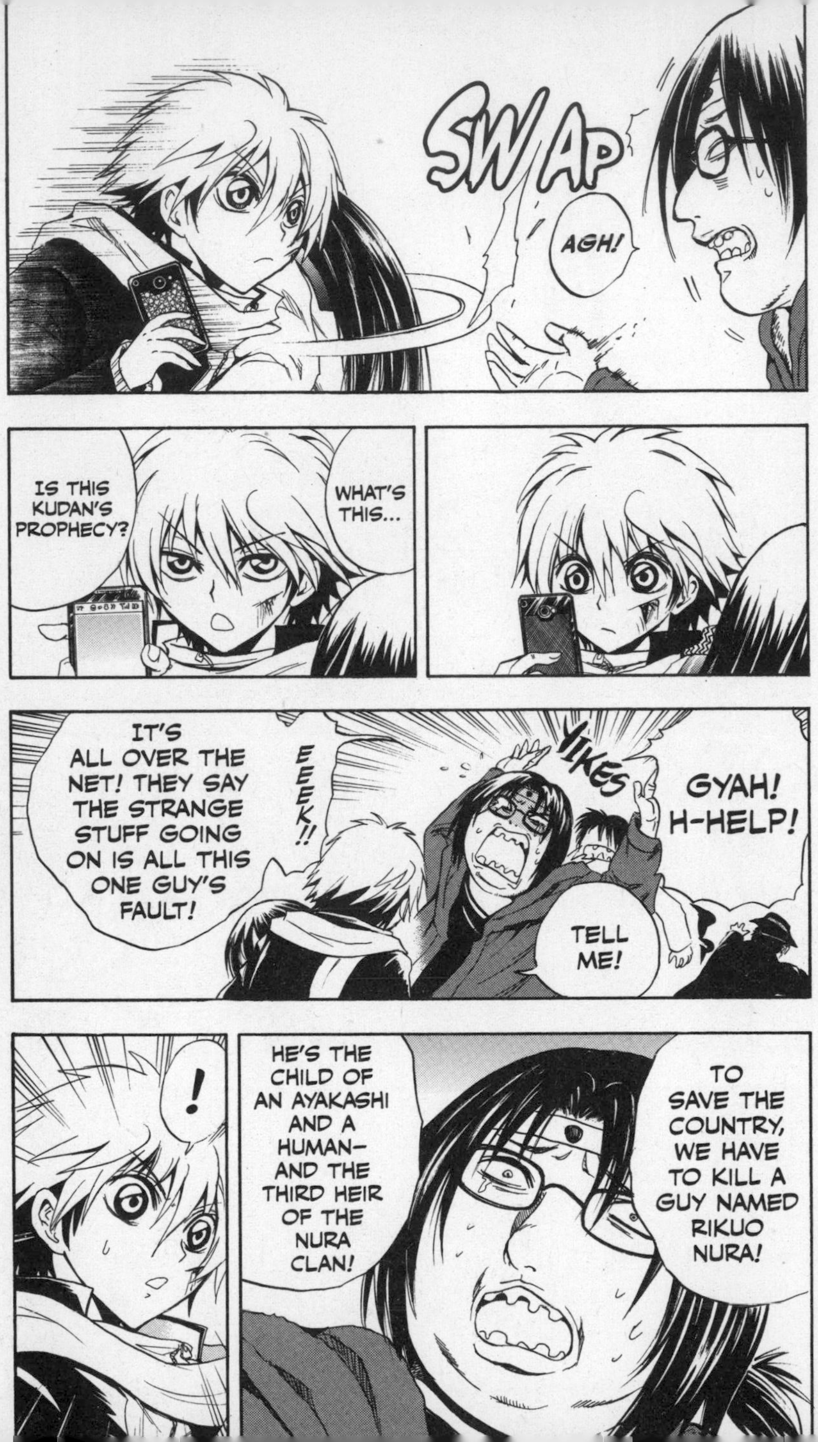
SWAP
AGH!
WHAT'S THIS...
IS THIS KUDAN'S PROPHECY?
GYAH! H-HELP!
YIKES
TELL ME!
EEEK!!
IT'S ALL OVER THE NET! THEY SAY THE STRANGE STUFF GOING ON IS ALL THIS ONE GUY'S FAULT!
TO SAVE THE COUNTRY, WE HAVE TO KILL A GUY NAMED RIKUO NURA!
HE'S THE CHILD OF AN AYAKASHI AND A HUMAN— AND THE THIRD HEIR OF THE NURA CLAN!
!

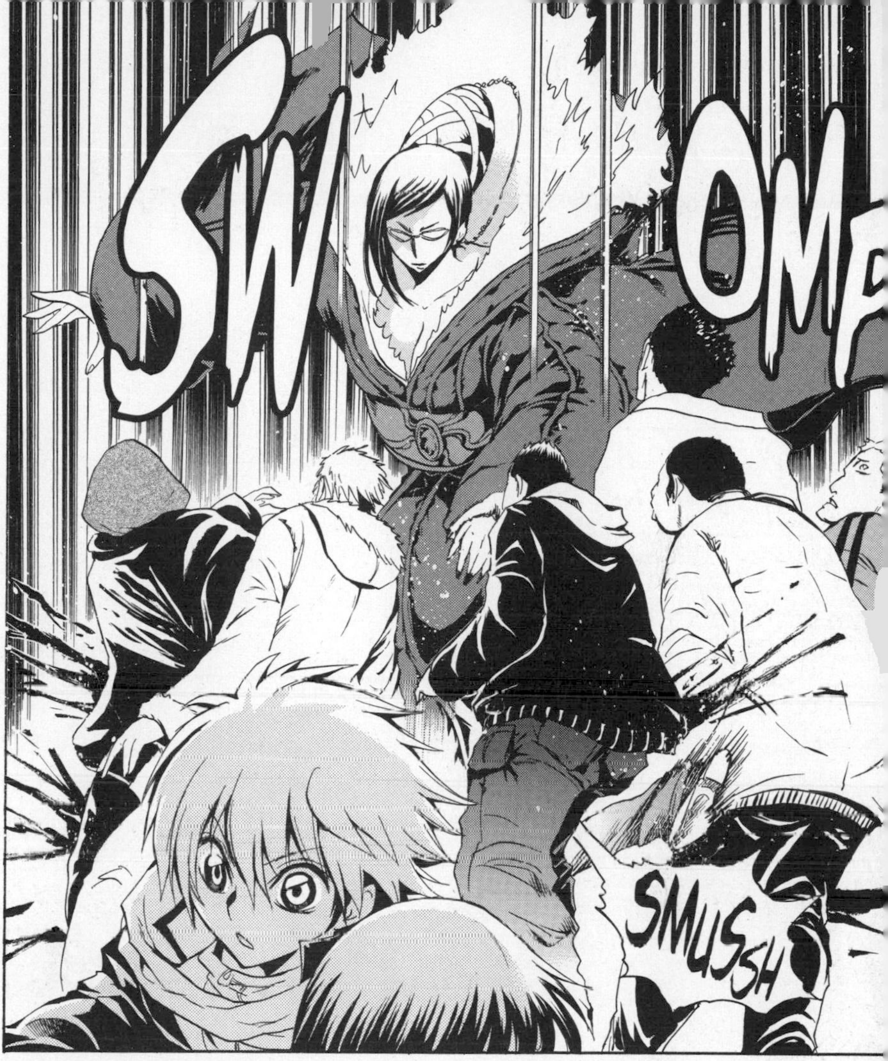
SW
OM
SMUSSH
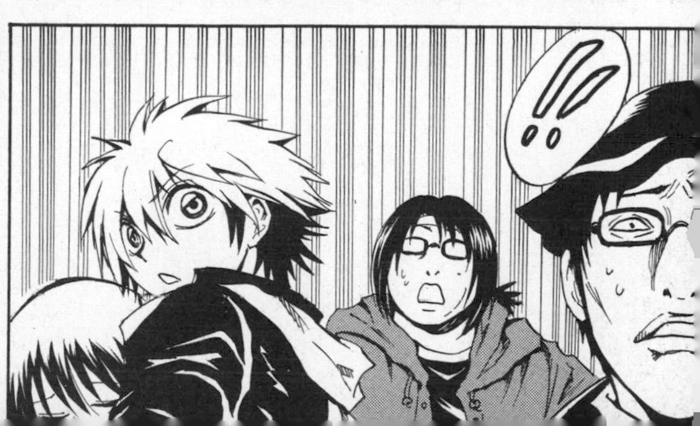
!!
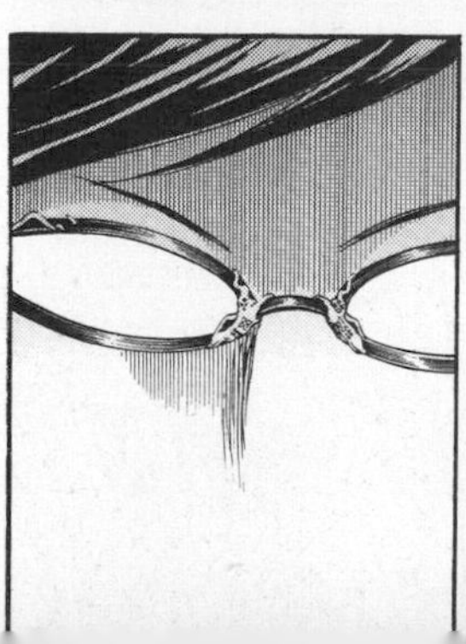

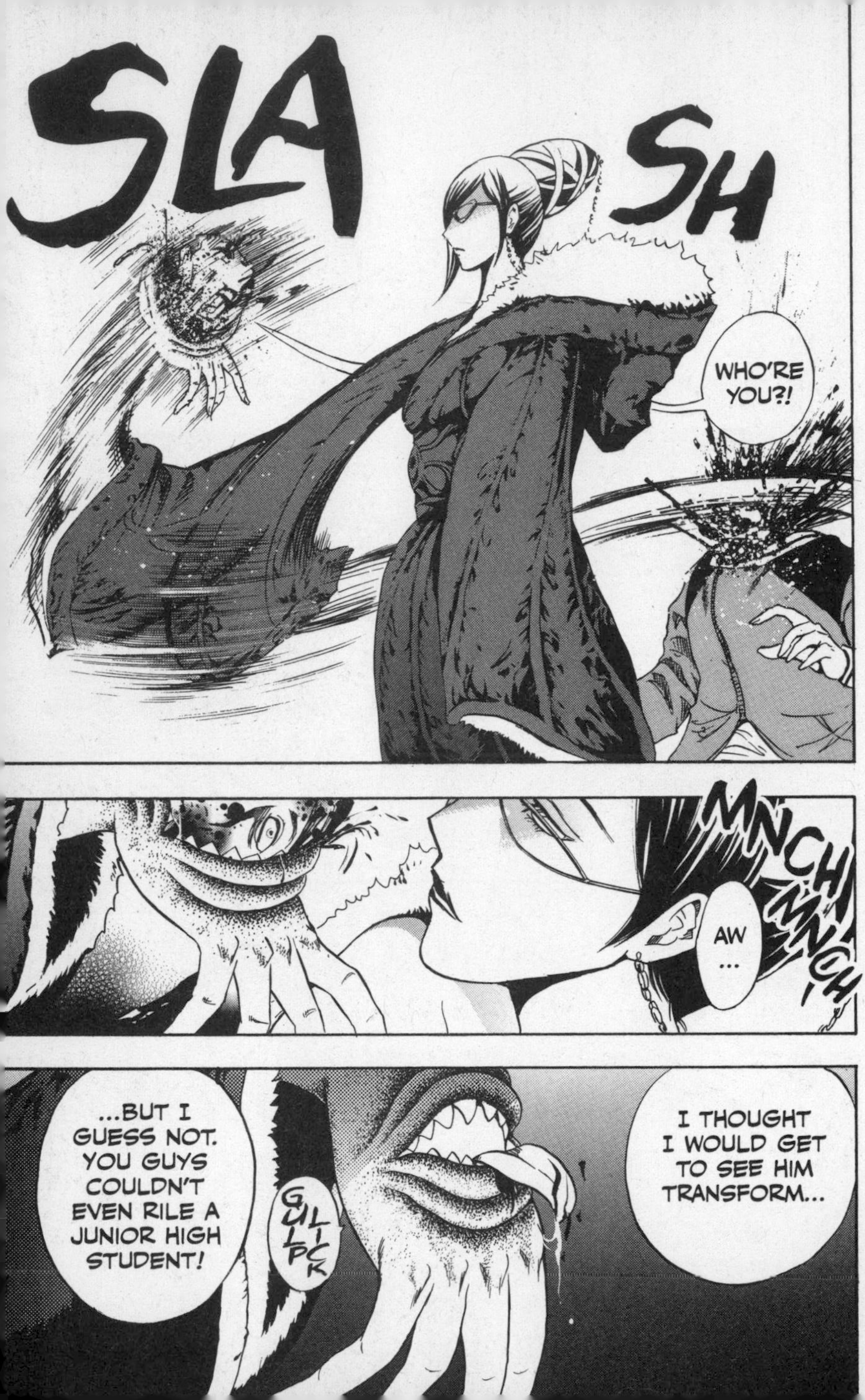
SLASH
WHO'RE YOU?!
MNCH MNCH MNCH
AW ...
I THOUGHT I WOULD GET TO SEE HIM TRANSFORM...
GULP
LICK
...BUT I GUESS NOT. YOU GUYS COULDN'T EVEN RILE A JUNIOR HIGH STUDENT!

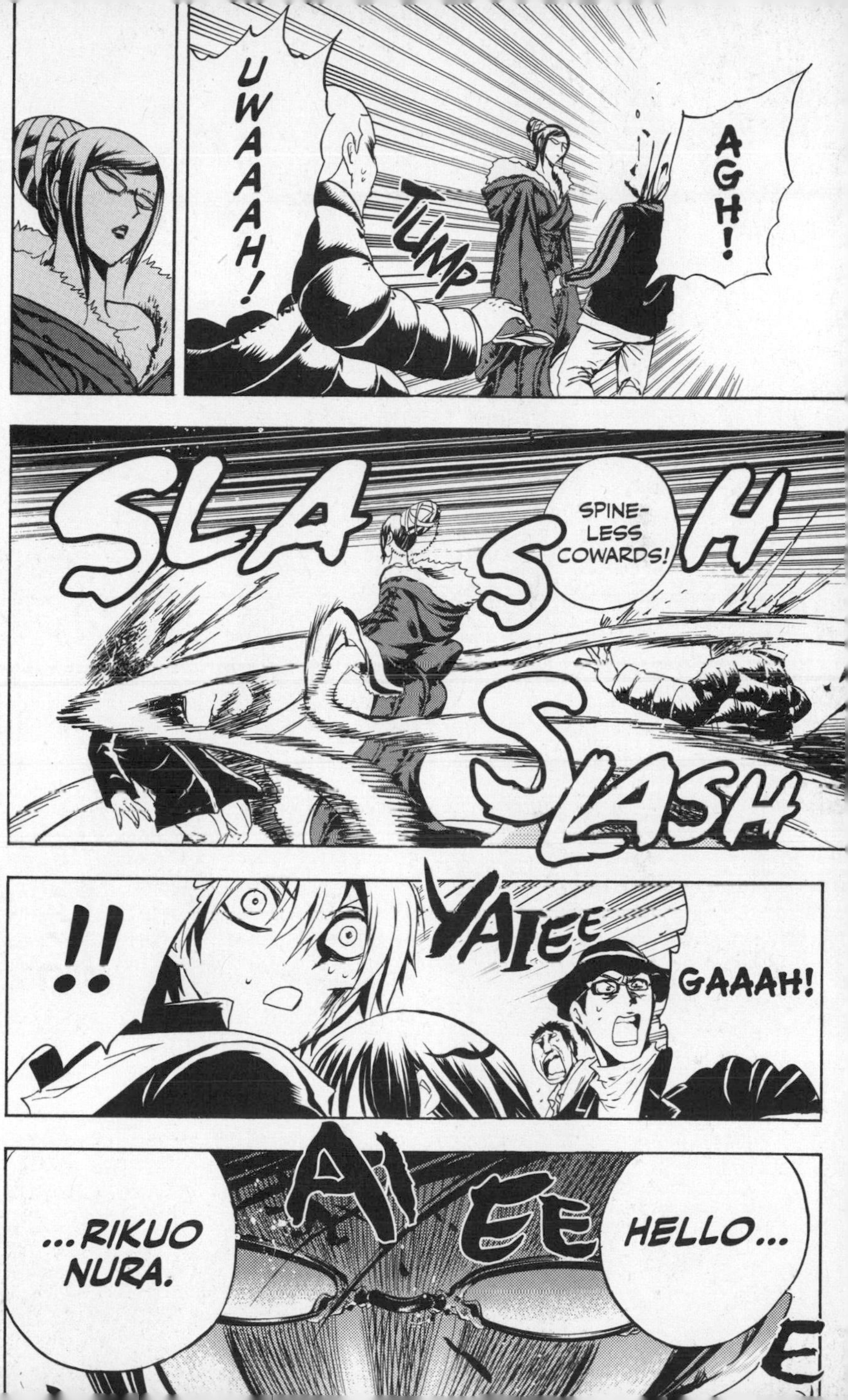
AGH!
TUMP
UWAAAAH!
SLASH
SPINE-LESS COWARDS!
SLASH
GAAAH!
YAIEE
!!
HELLO...
AIEEE
...RIKUO NURA.

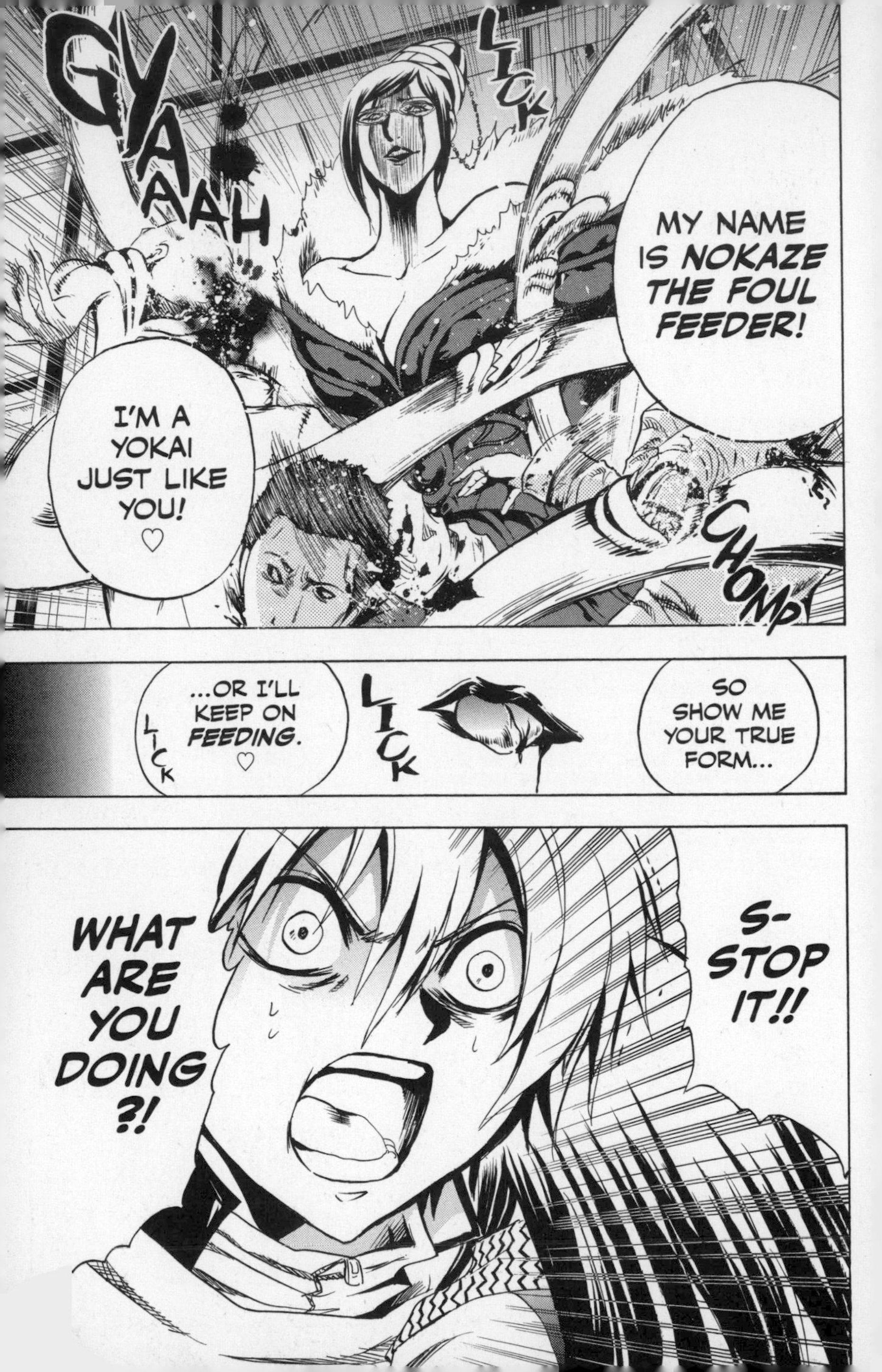
LICK
MY NAME IS NOKAZE THE FOUL FEEDER!
GYAAAH
I'M A YOKAI JUST LIKE YOU! ♡
CHOMP
SO SHOW ME YOUR TRUE FORM...
LICK
...OR I'LL KEEP ON FEEDING. ♡
LICK
S-STOP IT!!
WHAT ARE YOU DOING?!

NURA: RISE OF THE YOKAI CLAN

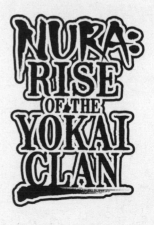

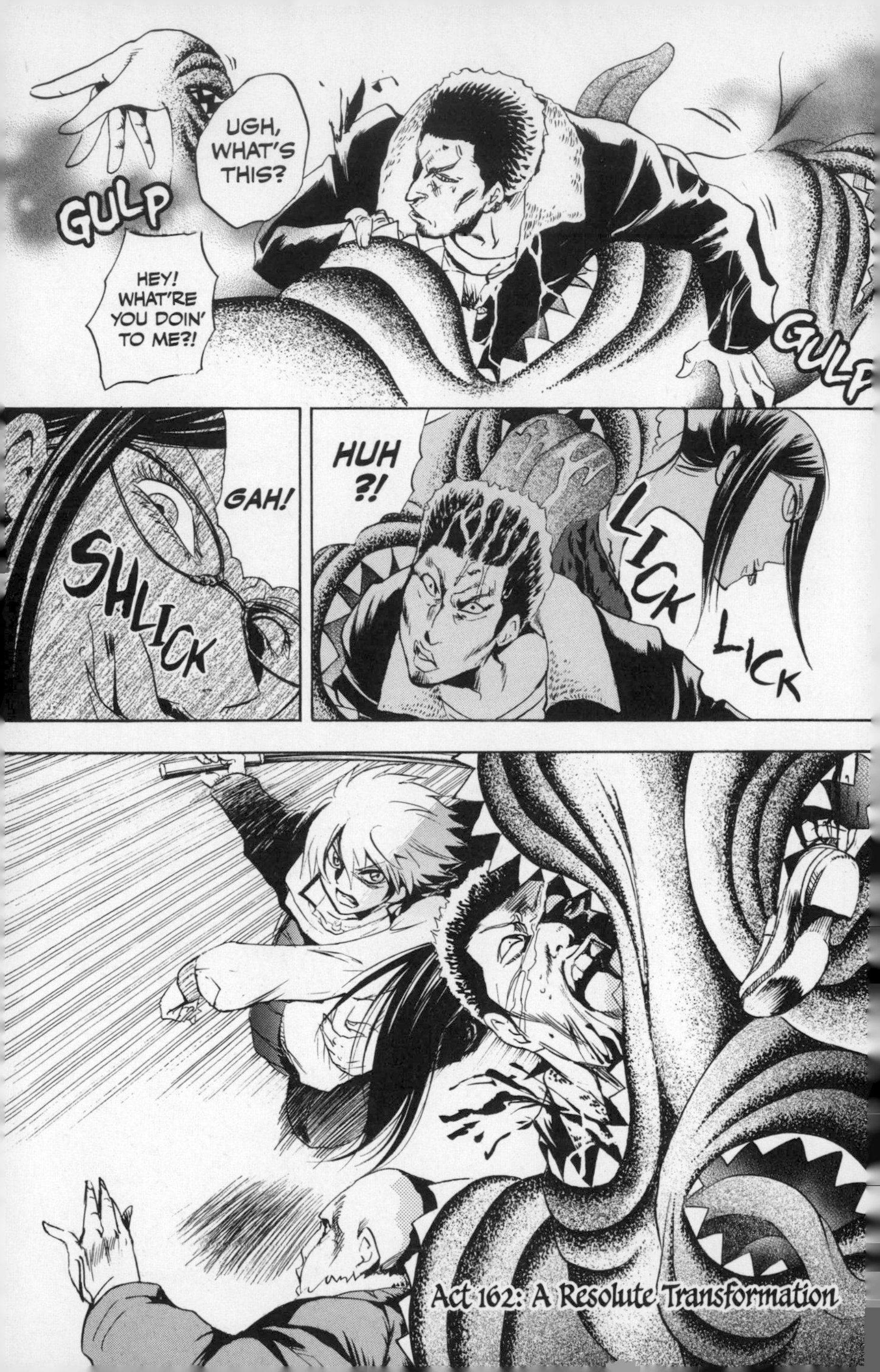
UGH, WHAT'S THIS?
GULP
HEY! WHAT'RE YOU DOIN' TO ME?!
GULP
HUH ?!
LICK
LICK
GAH!
SHLICK
Act 162: A Resolute Transformation

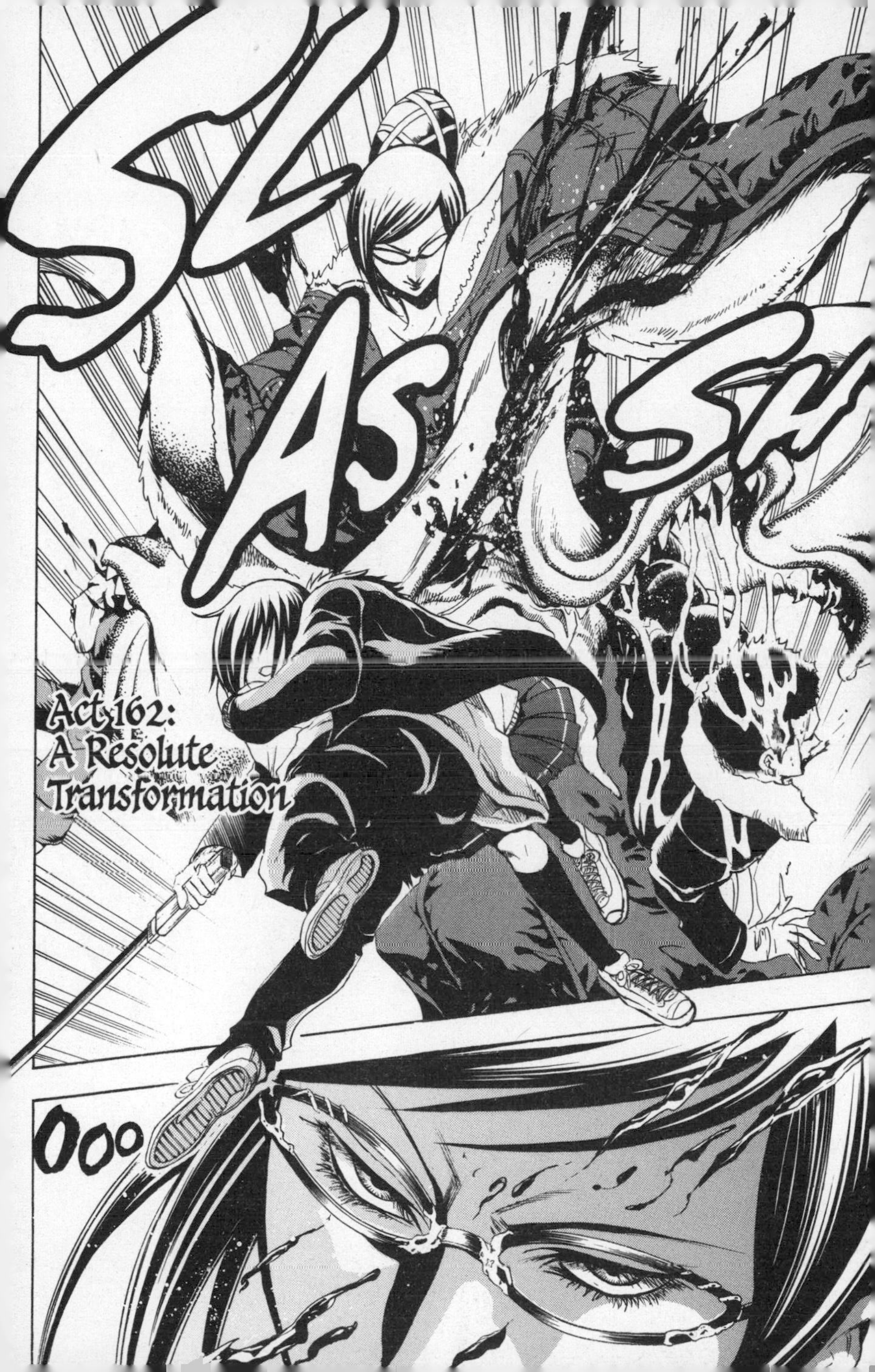
SLASH
Act 162:
A Resolute
Transformation
Ooo

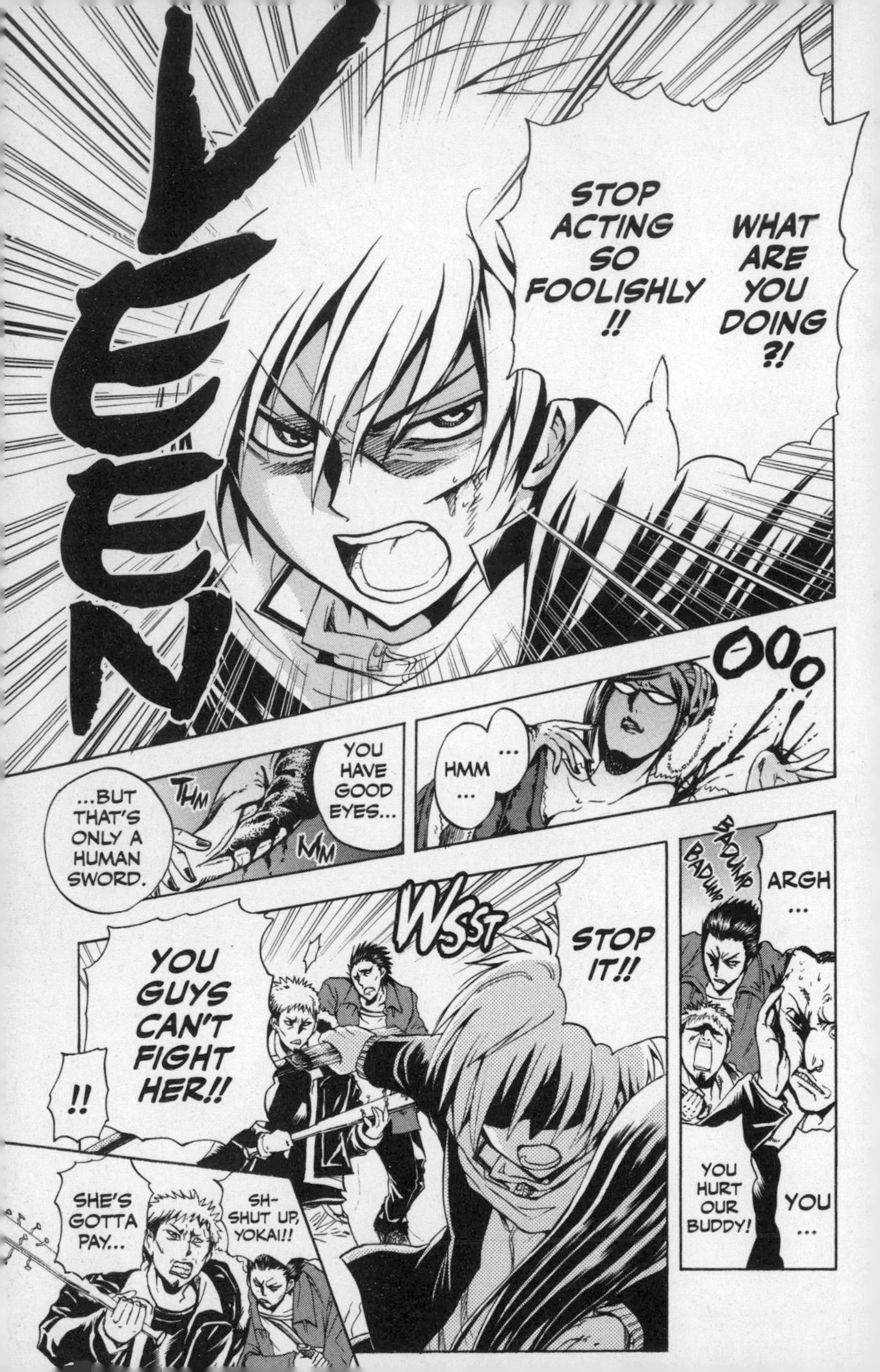
WHAT ARE YOU DOING?!
STOP ACTING SO FOOLISHLY!!
OOO
... HMM ...
YOU HAVE GOOD EYES...
THM
MM
...BUT THAT'S ONLY A HUMAN SWORD.
BADUMP BADUMP
ARGH ...
YOU ...
YOU HURT OUR BUDDY!
STOP IT!!
WSST
YOU GUYS CAN'T FIGHT HER!!
!!
SH- SHUT UP, YOKAI!!
SHE'S GOTTA PAY...

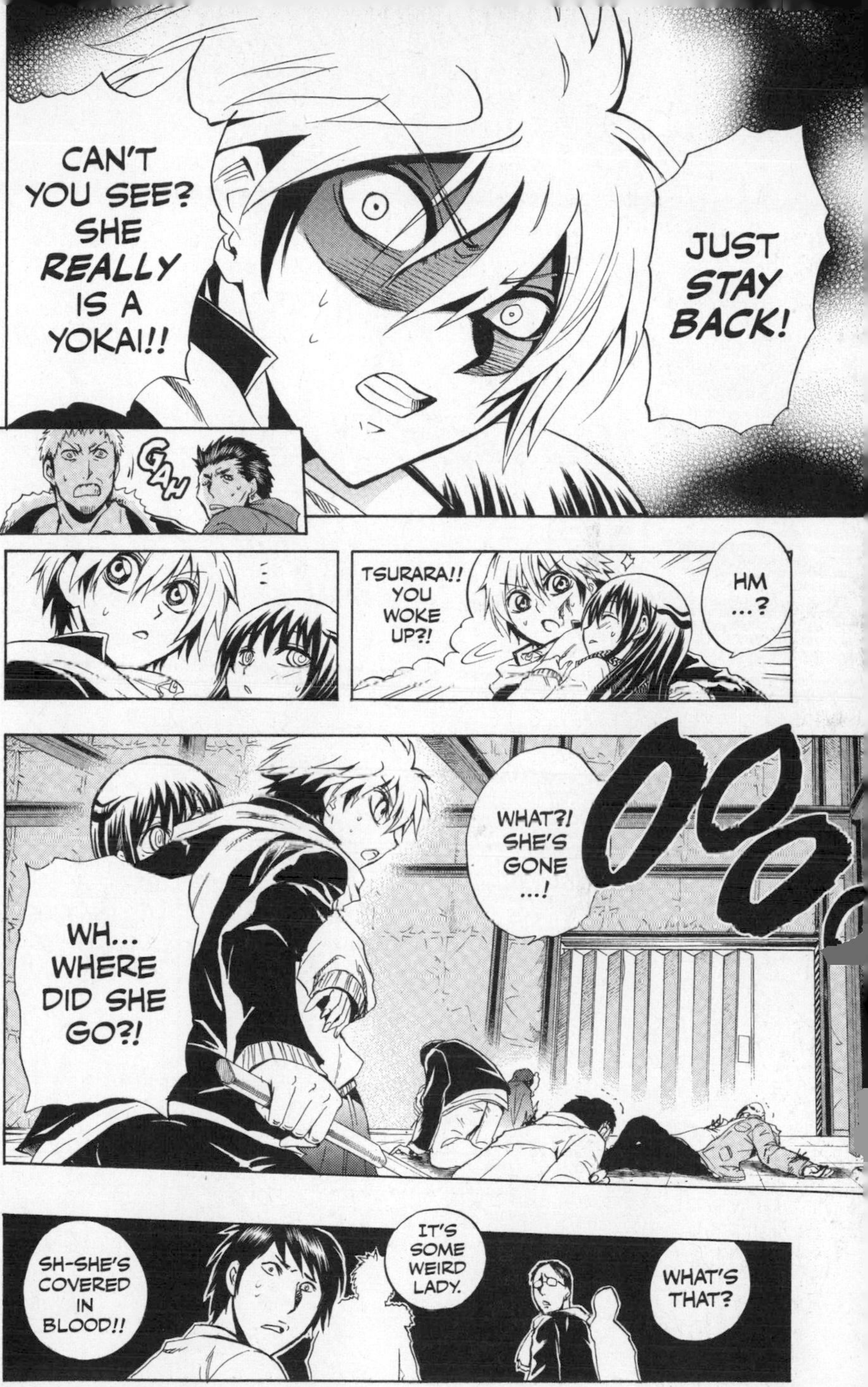
JUST STAY BACK!
CAN'T YOU SEE? SHE REALLY IS A YOKAI!!
GAH
HM ...?
TSURARA!! YOU WOKE UP?!
OOO
WHAT?! SHE'S GONE ...!
WH... WHERE DID SHE GO?!
WHAT'S THAT?
IT'S SOME WEIRD LADY.
SH-SHE'S COVERED IN BLOOD!!

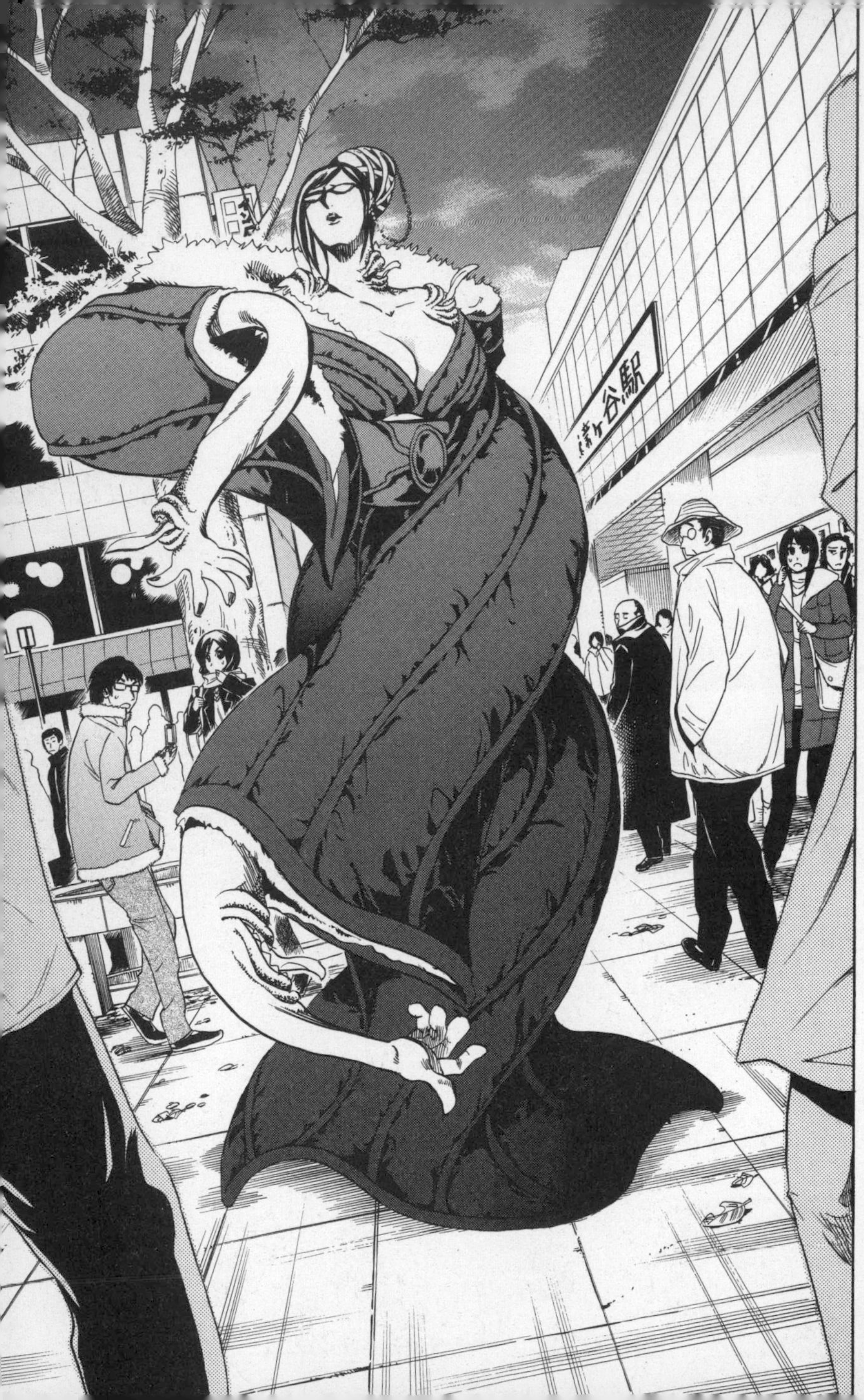
ヶ谷駅

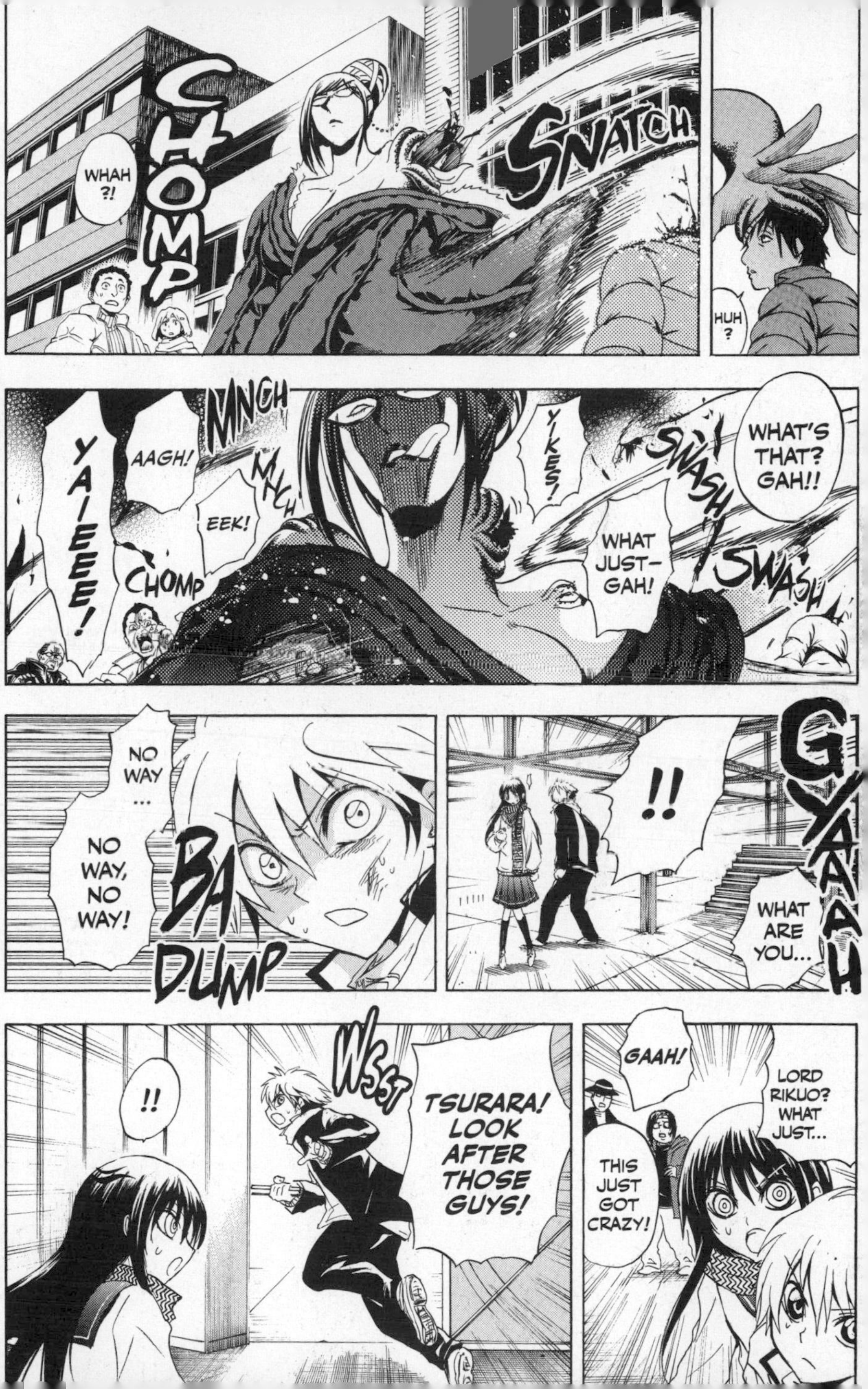
HUH ?
SNATCH
CHOMP
WHAH ?!
WHAT'S THAT? GAH!!
SWASH
SWASH
YIKES!
WHAT JUST— GAH!
MNCH
MNCH
AAGH!
EEK!
YAIEEEE!
CHOMP
GYAAAH
!!
WHAT ARE YOU...
NO WAY ...
NO WAY, NO WAY!
BA DUMP
LORD RIKUO? WHAT JUST...
GAAH!
THIS JUST GOT CRAZY!
TSURARA! LOOK AFTER THOSE GUYS!
WSSST
!!

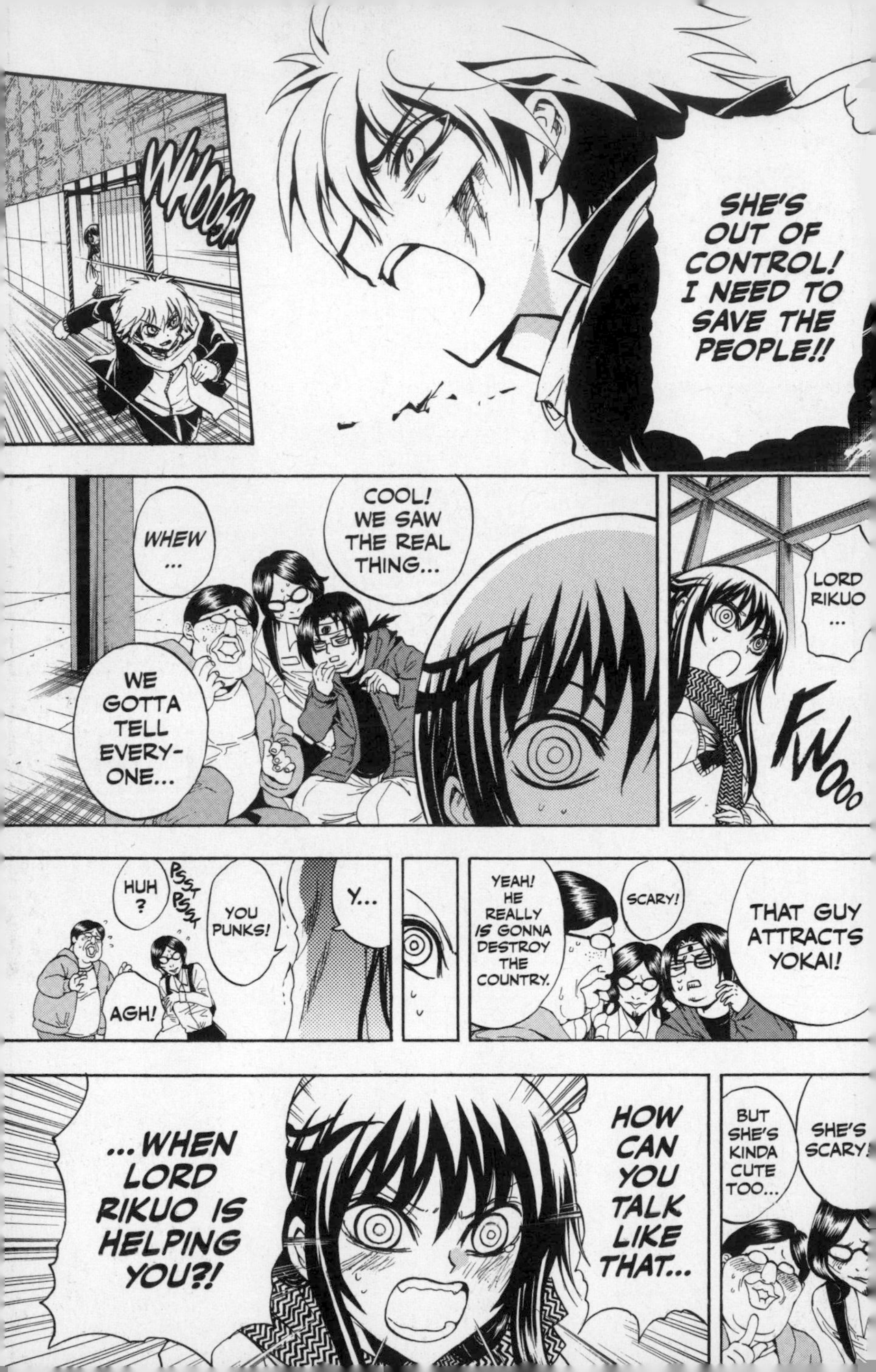
SHE'S OUT OF CONTROL! I NEED TO SAVE THE PEOPLE!!
WHOOSH
LORD RIKUO ...
FWOOO
COOL! WE SAW THE REAL THING...
WHEW ...
WE GOTTA TELL EVERY-ONE...
THAT GUY ATTRACTS YOKAI!
SCARY!
YEAH! HE REALLY IS GONNA DESTROY THE COUNTRY.
Y...
YOU PUNKS!
PSST PSST
HUH ?
AGH!
SHE'S SCARY!
BUT SHE'S KINDA CUTE TOO...
HOW CAN YOU TALK LIKE THAT...
...WHEN LORD RIKUO IS HELPING YOU?!

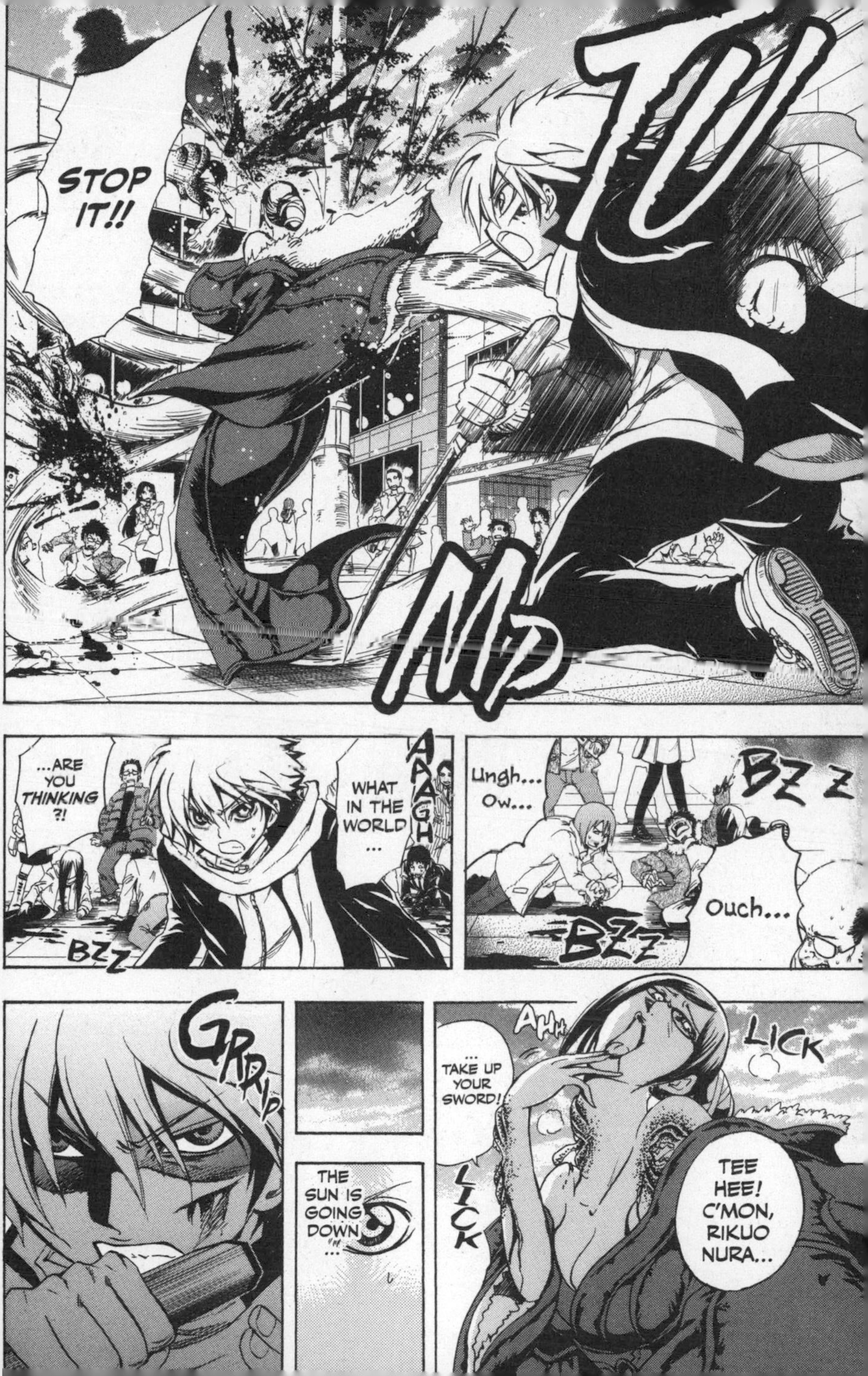
STOP IT!!
Ungh... Ow...
BZZ Z
BZZ
Ouch...
AAAGH
WHAT IN THE WORLD ...
...ARE YOU THINKING ?!
BZZ
AHH
LICK
... TAKE UP YOUR SWORD!
LICK
TEE HEE! C'MON, RIKUO NURA...
THE SUN IS GOING DOWN ...

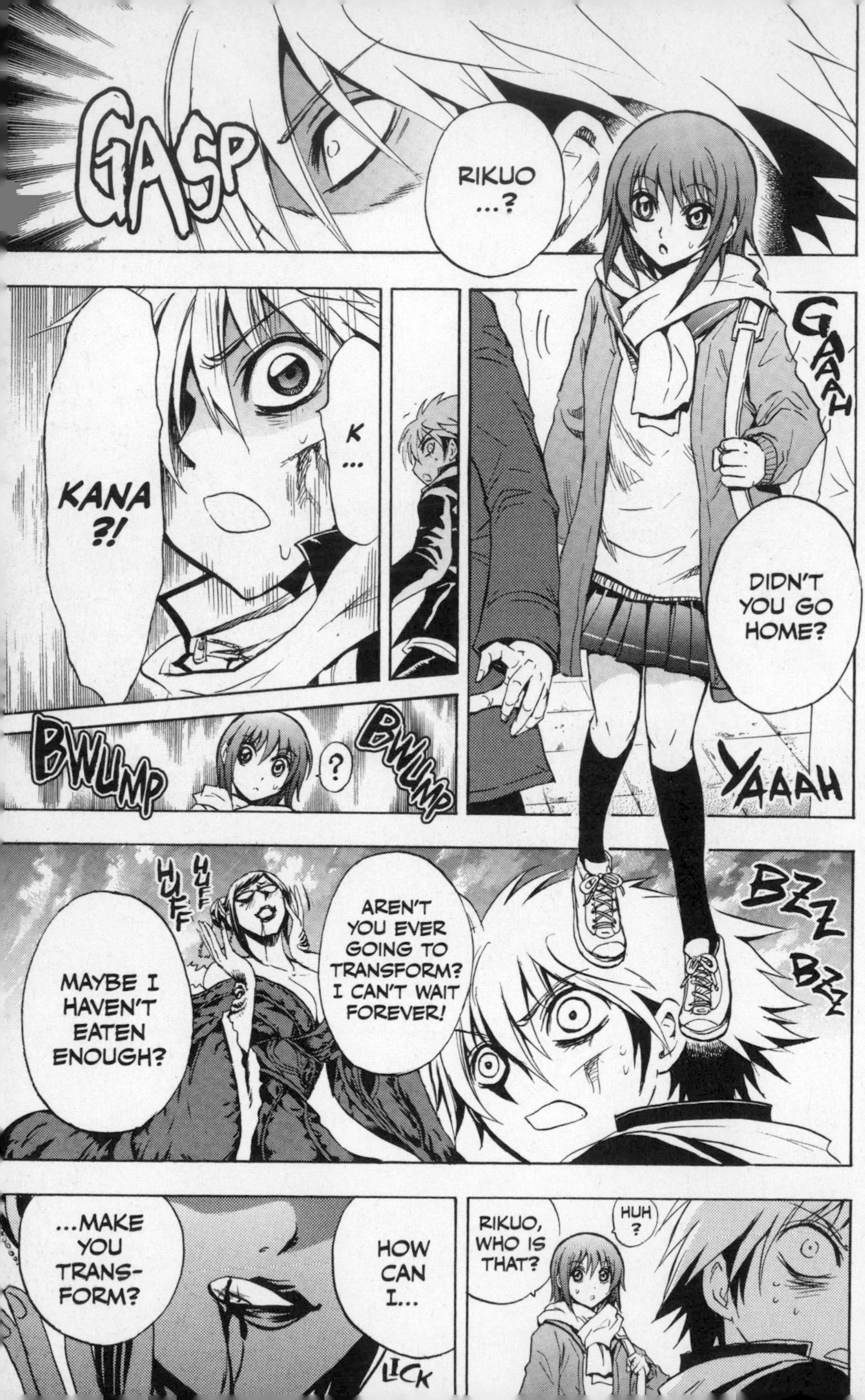
RIKUO ...?
GASP
GAAAH
DIDN'T YOU GO HOME?
YAAAH
K ...
KANA ?!
BWUMP
?
BWUMP
BZZ
BZZ
AREN'T YOU EVER GOING TO TRANSFORM? I CAN'T WAIT FOREVER!
HUFF
HUFF
MAYBE I HAVEN'T EATEN ENOUGH?
HUH ?
RIKUO, WHO IS THAT?
HOW CAN I...
...MAKE YOU TRANS-FORM?
LICK

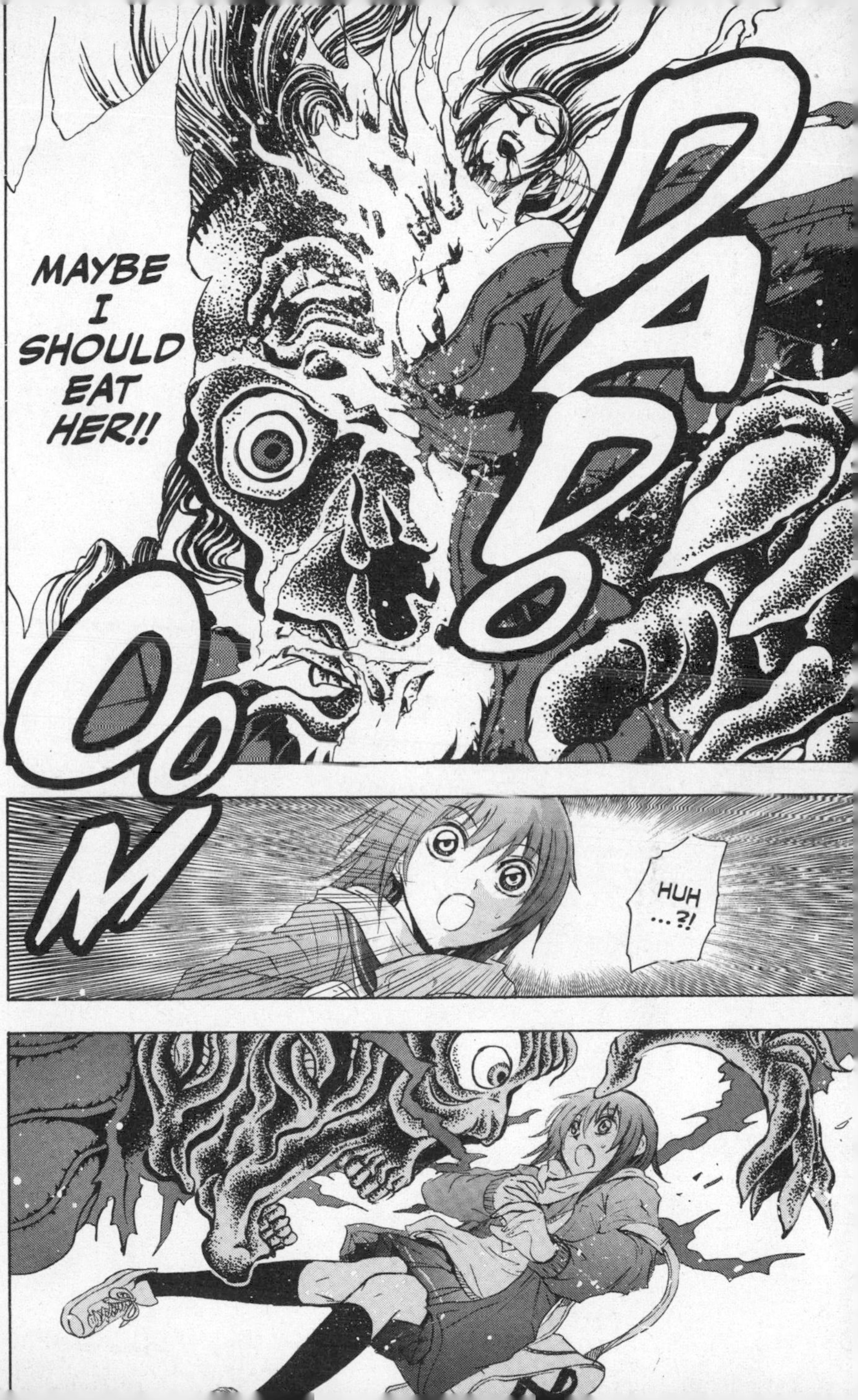
MAYBE I SHOULD EAT HER!!
DADOOOM!
HUH ...?!

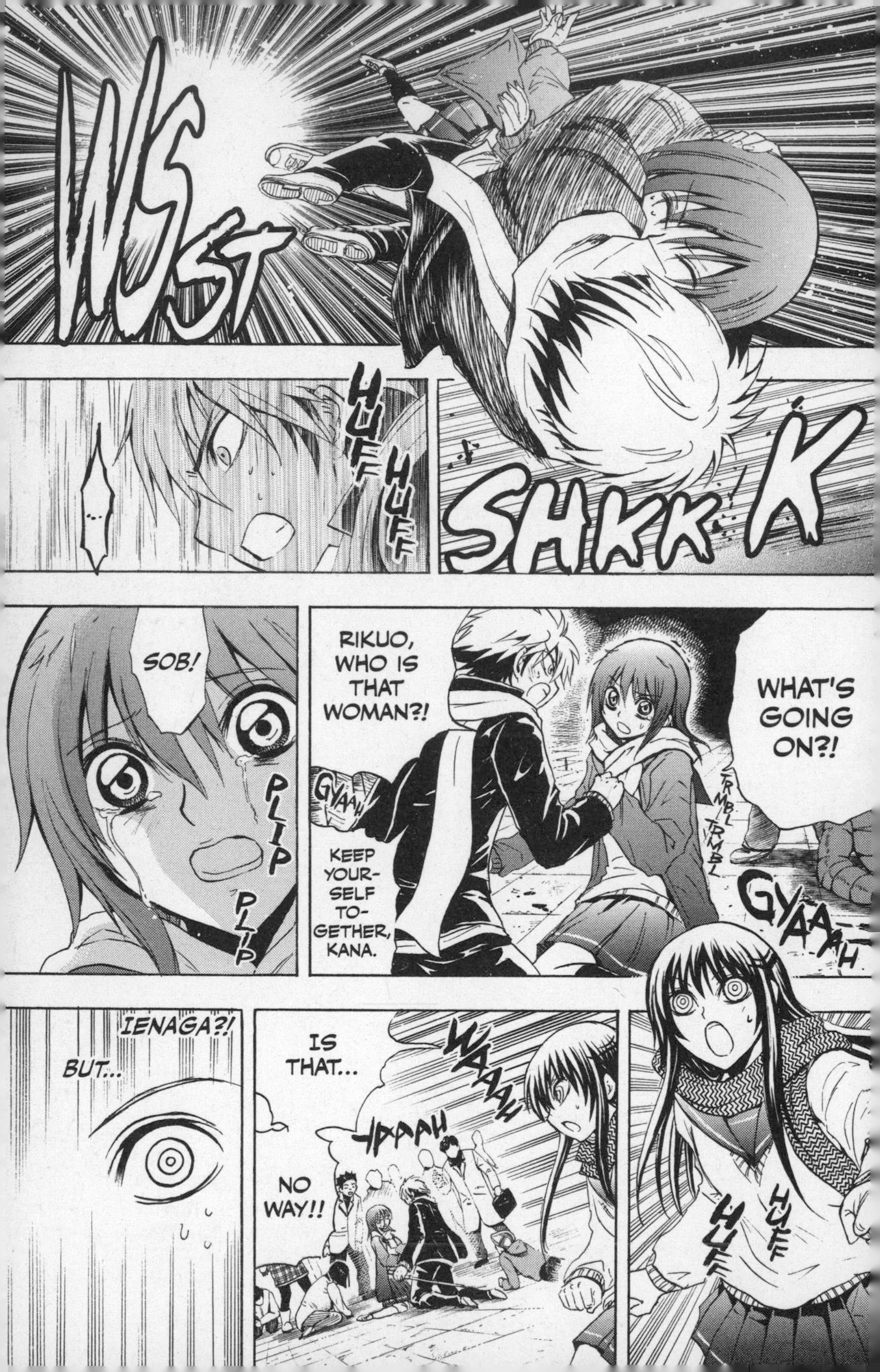
WSST
SHKK K
HUFF HUFF
...
WHAT'S GOING ON?!
TRMBL TRMBL
GYAAAH
RIKUO, WHO IS THAT WOMAN?!
GYAAH
KEEP YOURSELF TOGETHER, KANA.
SOB!
PLIP PLIP
HUFF HUFF
IS THAT...
NO WAY!!
IENAGA?!
BUT...

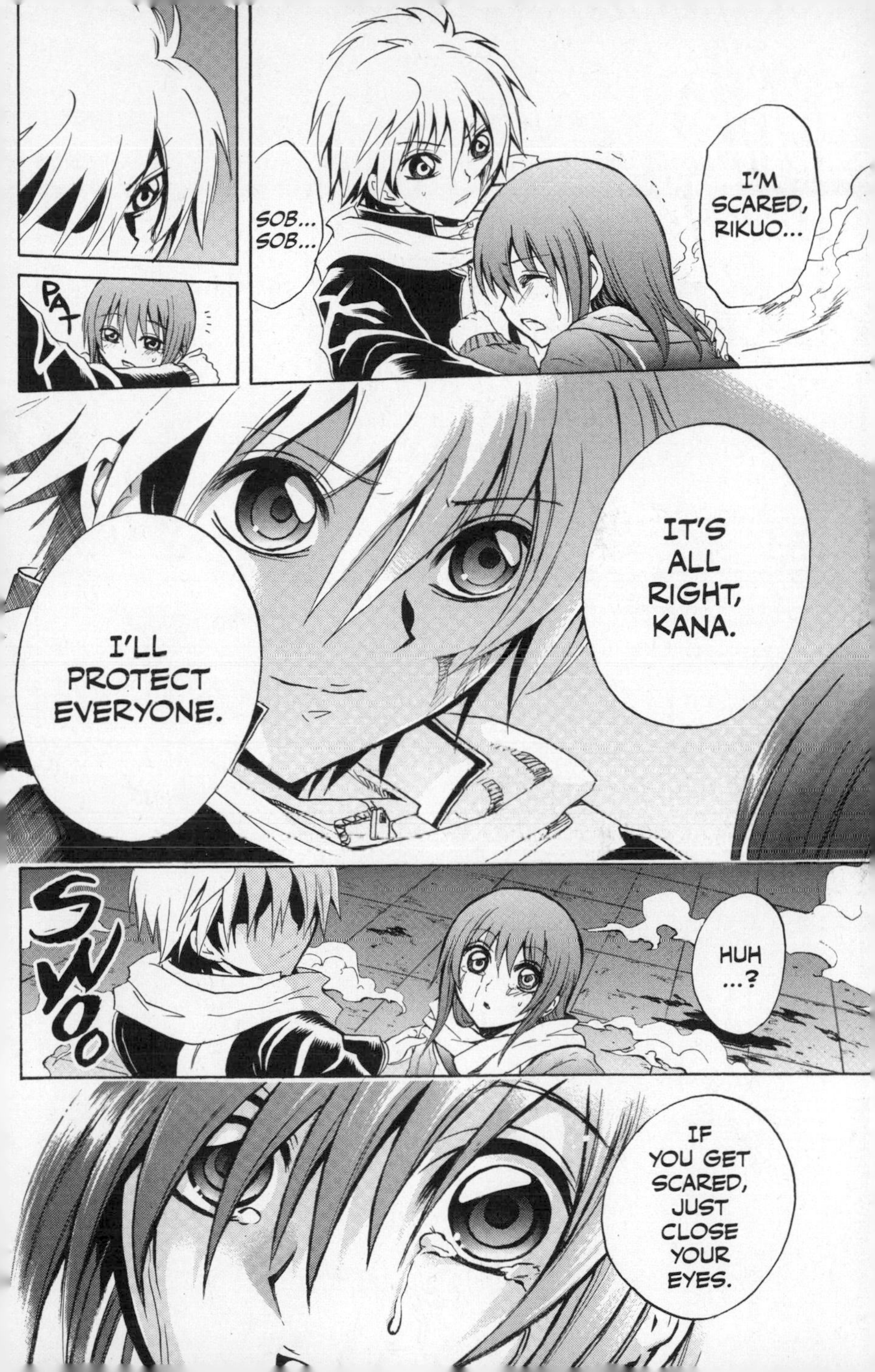
I'M SCARED, RIKUO...
SOB... SOB...
PAT
IT'S ALL RIGHT, KANA.
I'LL PROTECT EVERYONE.
HUH ...?
SWOO
IF YOU GET SCARED, JUST CLOSE YOUR EYES.

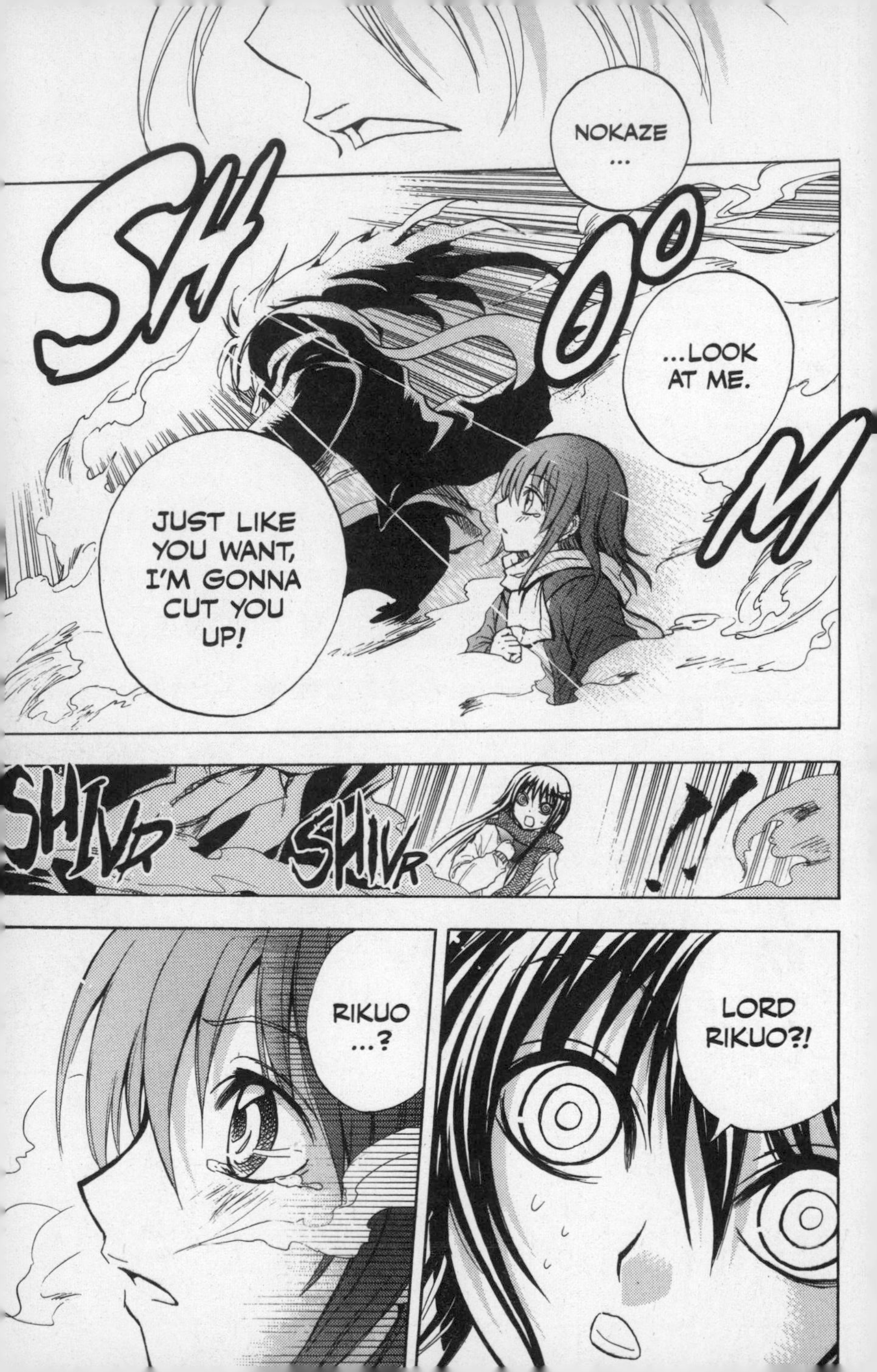
NOKAZE ...
...LOOK AT ME.
SHOOOM
JUST LIKE YOU WANT, I'M GONNA CUT YOU UP!
!!
SHIVR
SHIVR
LORD RIKUO?!
RIKUO ...?

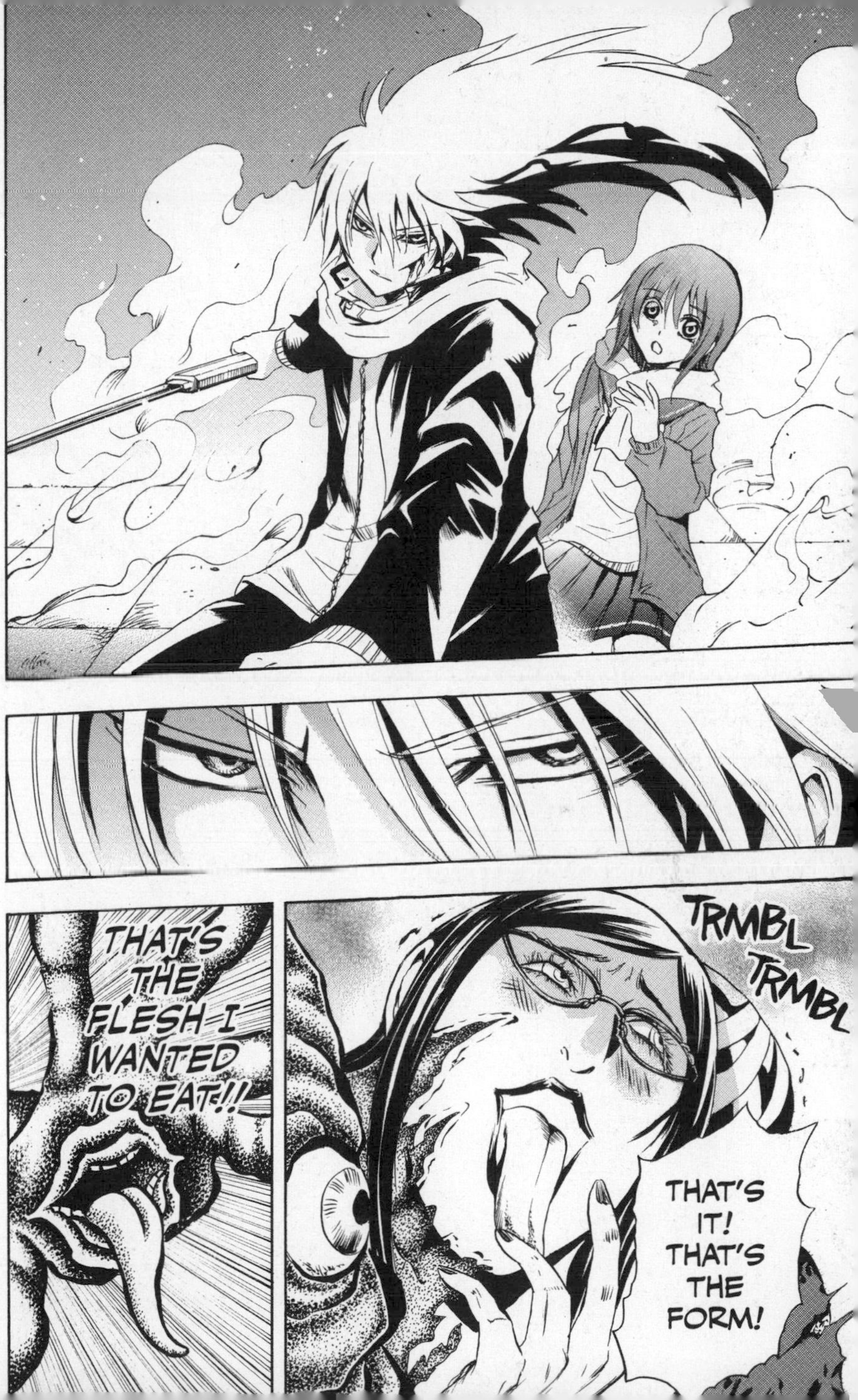
TRMBL TRMBL
THAT'S IT! THAT'S THE FORM!
THAT'S THE FLESH I WANTED TO EAT!!

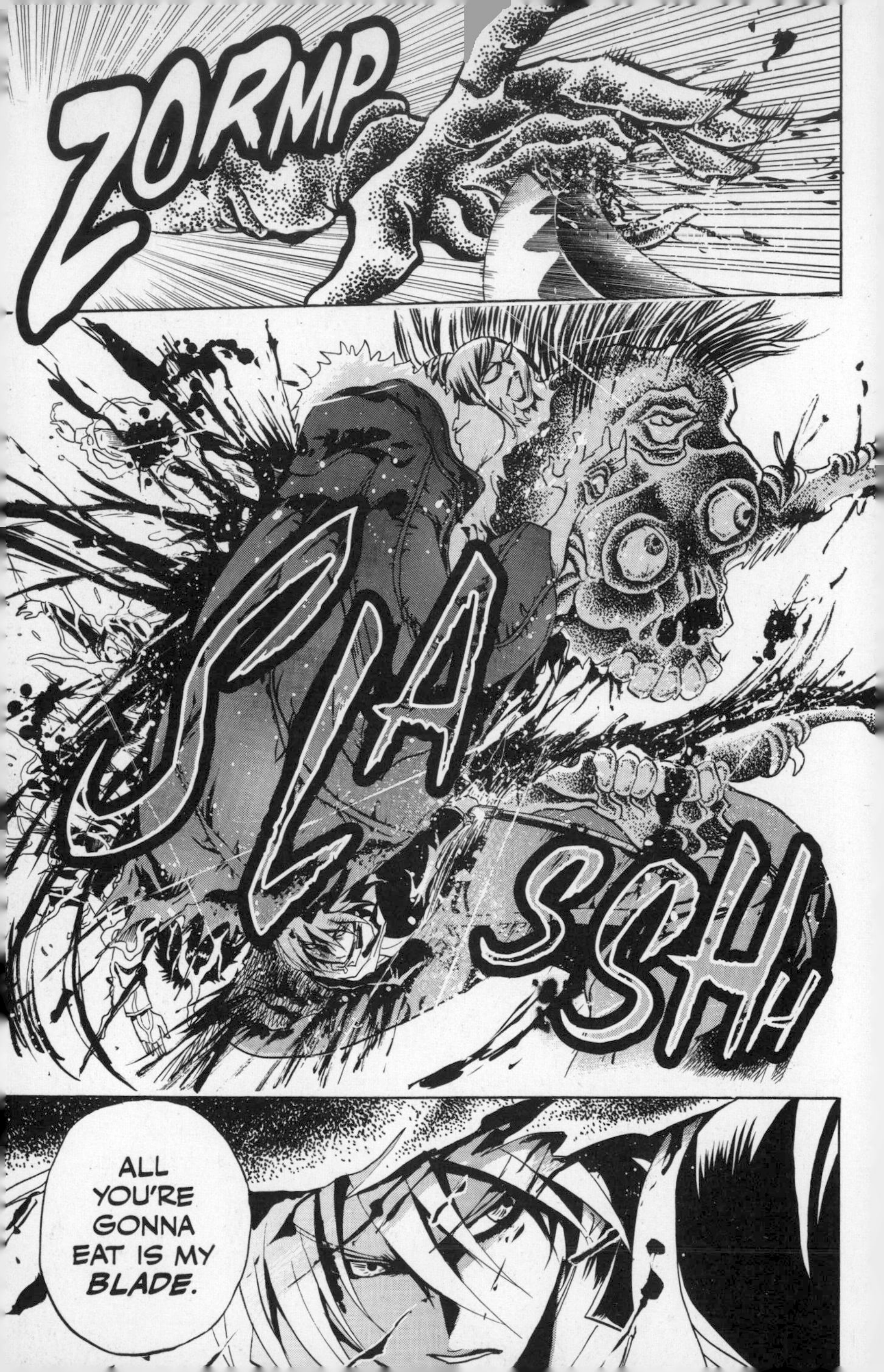
ZORMP
SLASSHH
ALL YOU'RE GONNA EAT IS MY *BLADE*.

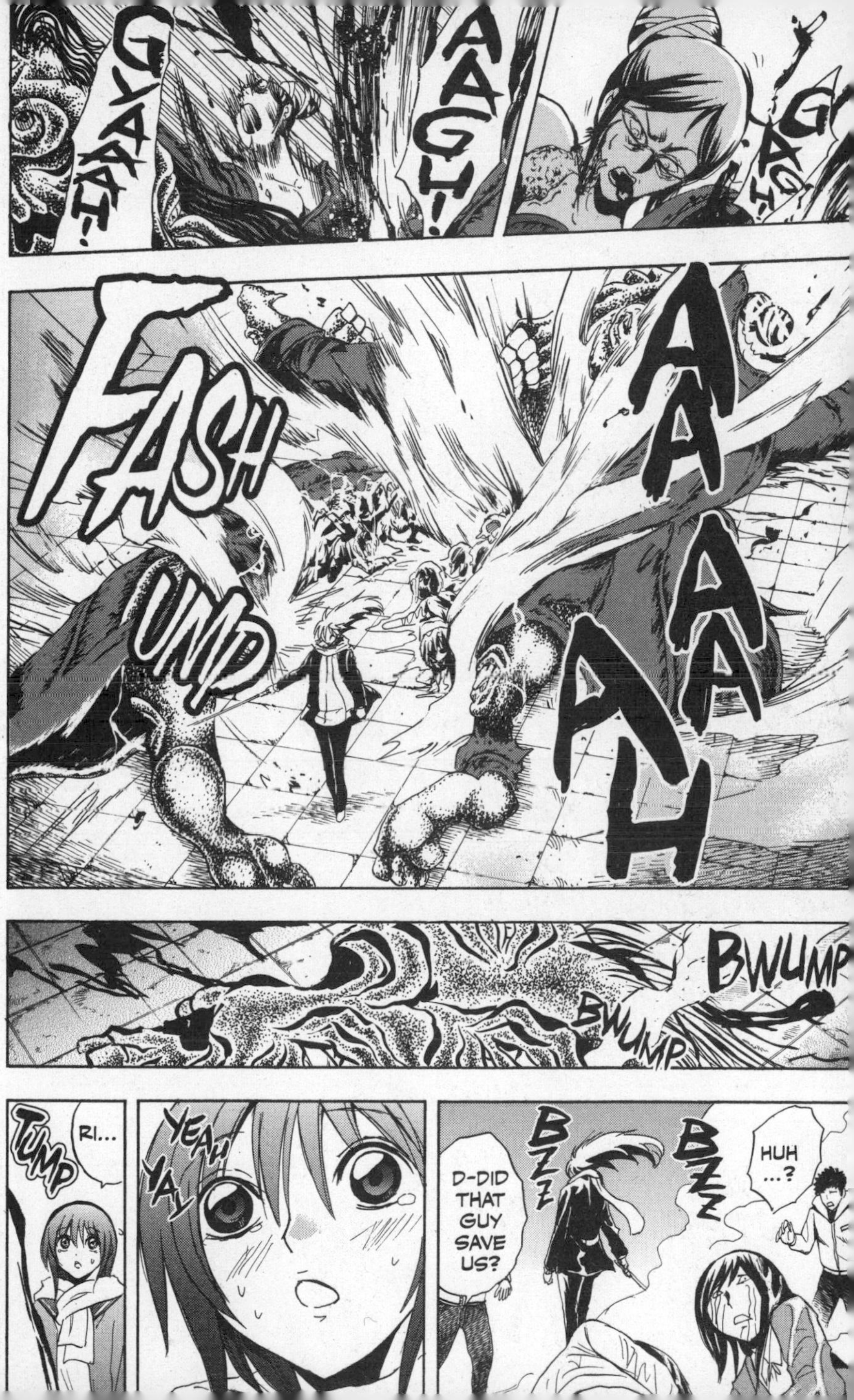
GAGH!
AAGH!
GYAAAH!
AAAAAH
FASH
UMP
BWUMP
BWUMP
HUH ...?
BZZZ
BZZZ
D-DID THAT GUY SAVE US?
YEAH YAY
RI...
TUMP

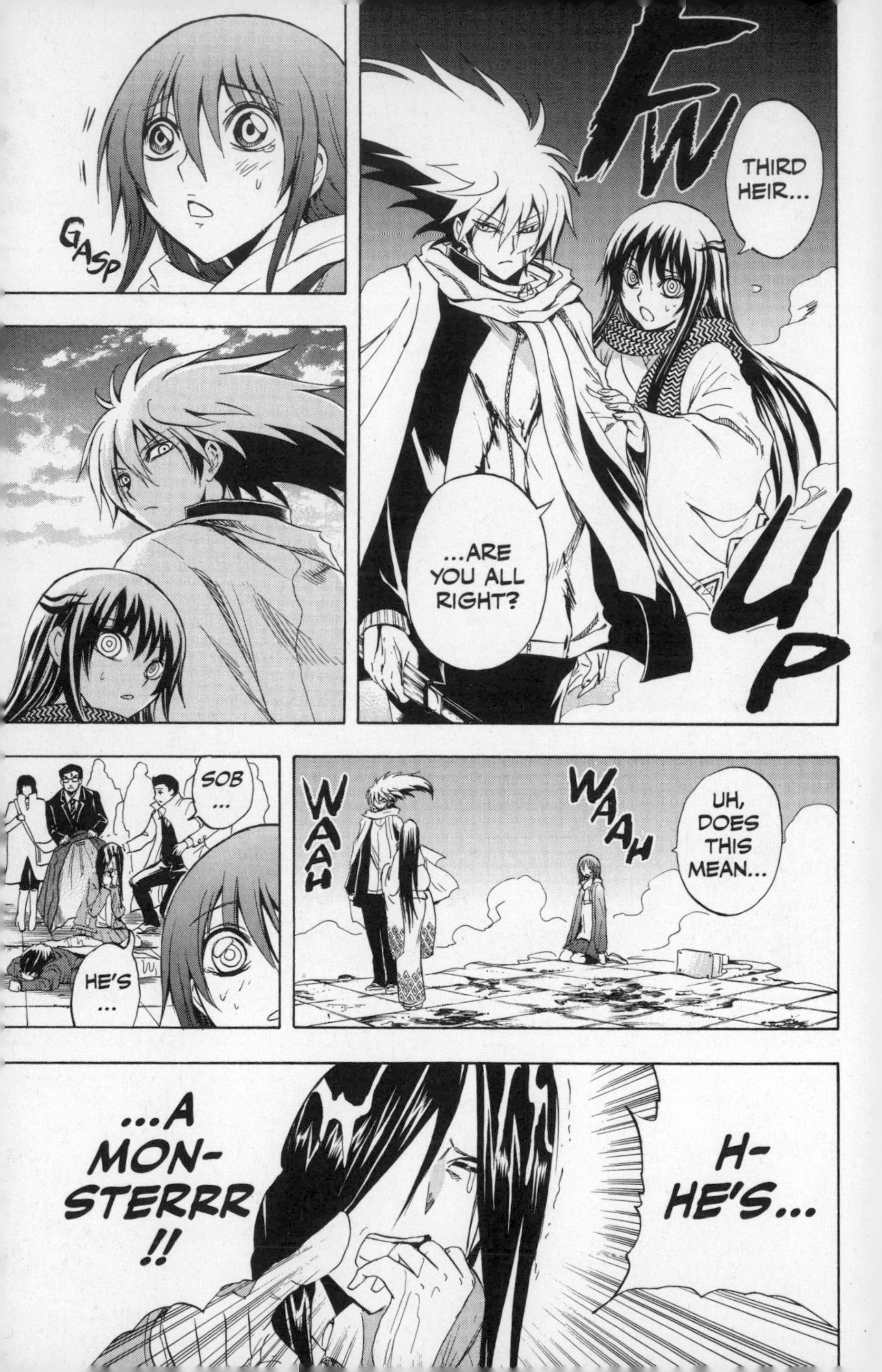
FW
THIRD HEIR...
...ARE YOU ALL RIGHT?
UP
GASP
WAAH
WAAH
UH, DOES THIS MEAN...
SOB ...
HE'S ...
H-HE'S...
...A MON-STERRR!!

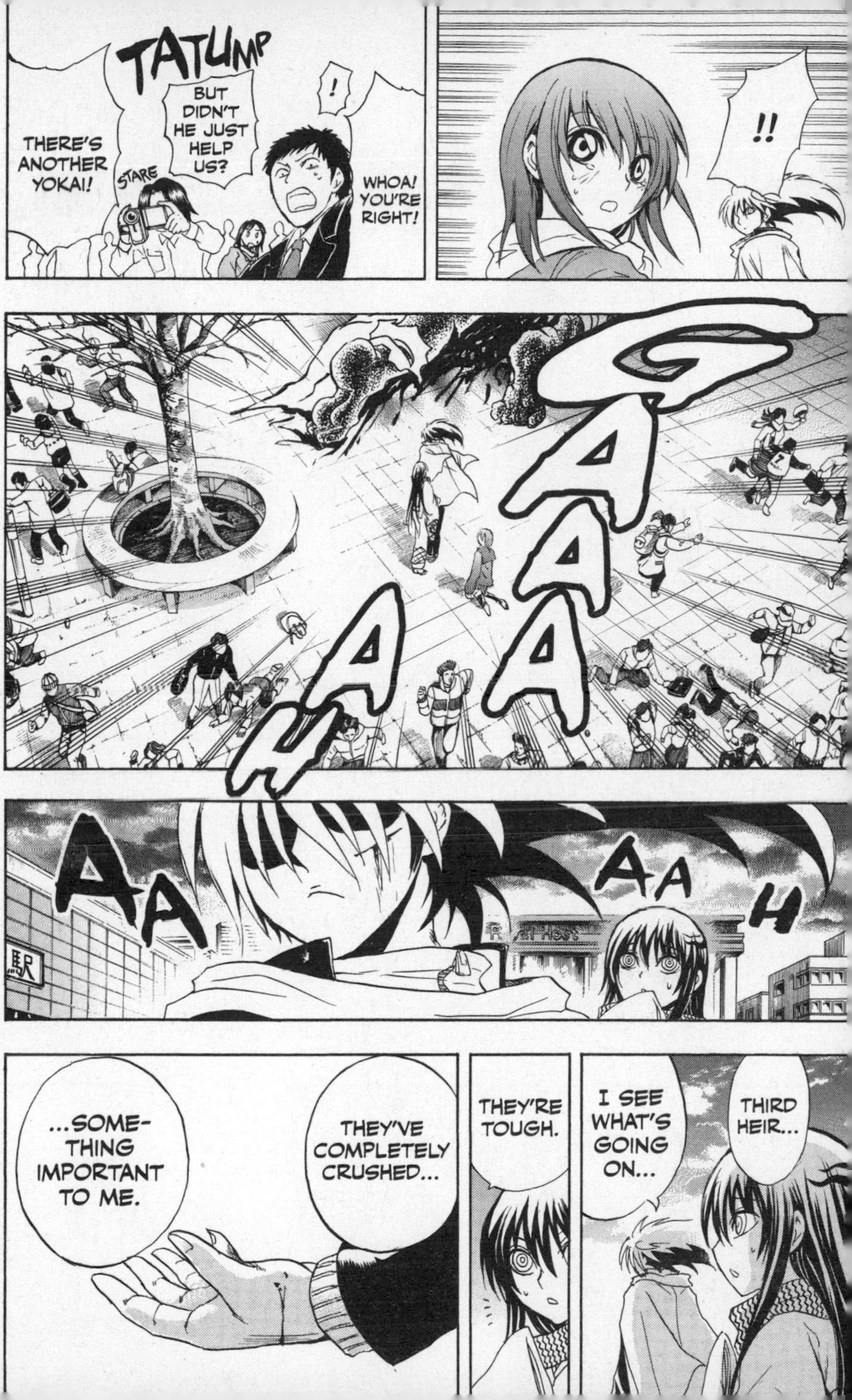
!!
!
TATUMP
BUT DIDN'T HE JUST HELP US?
WHOA! YOU'RE RIGHT!
THERE'S ANOTHER YOKAI!
STARE
GAAAAH
AAH
AA
駅
THIRD HEIR...
I SEE WHAT'S GOING ON...
THEY'RE TOUGH.
THEY'VE COMPLETELY CRUSHED...
...SOME-THING IMPORTANT TO ME.

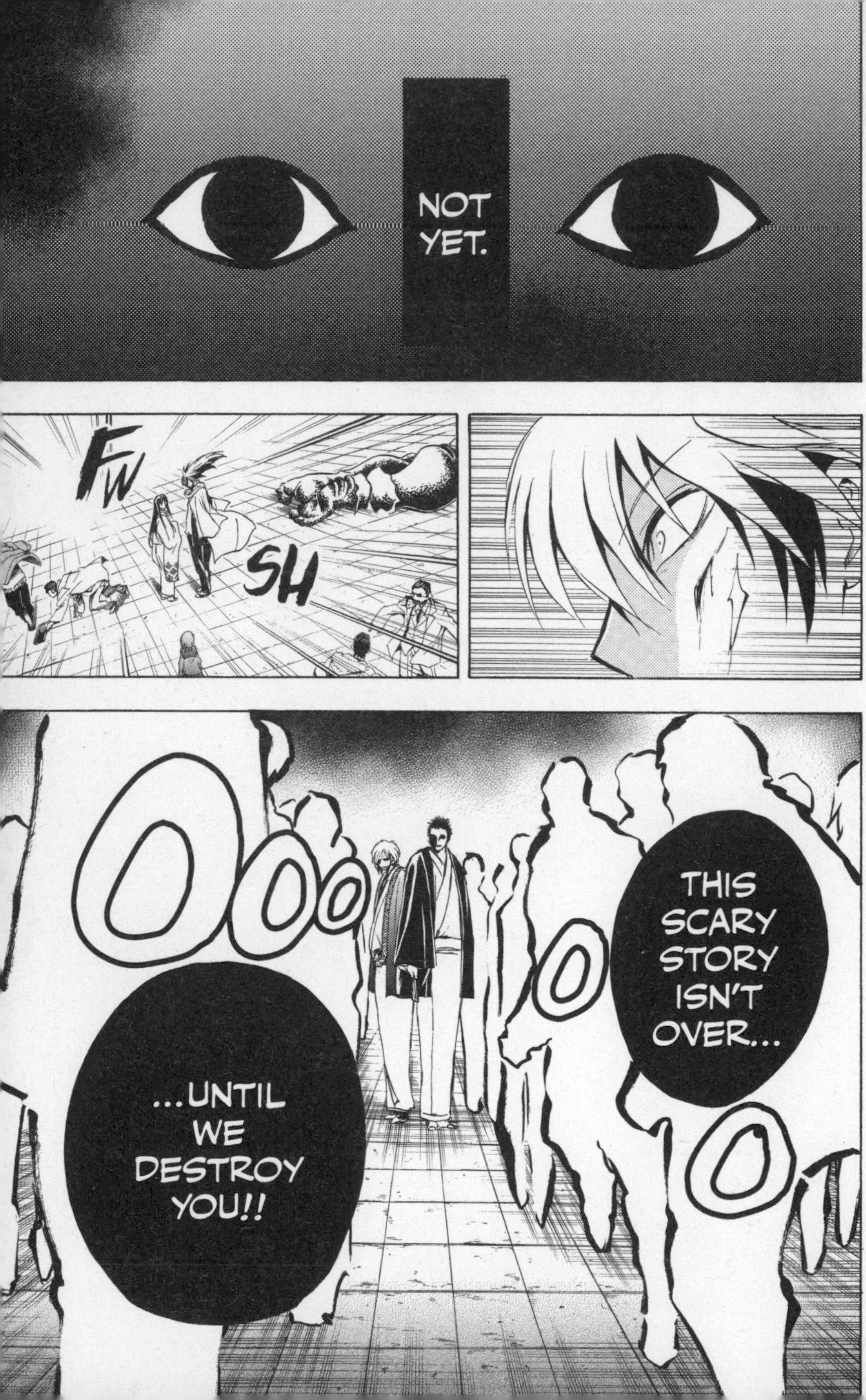
NOT YET.
FWSH
THIS SCARY STORY ISN'T OVER...
...UNTIL WE DESTROY YOU!!

Act 163: Tokyo Tag

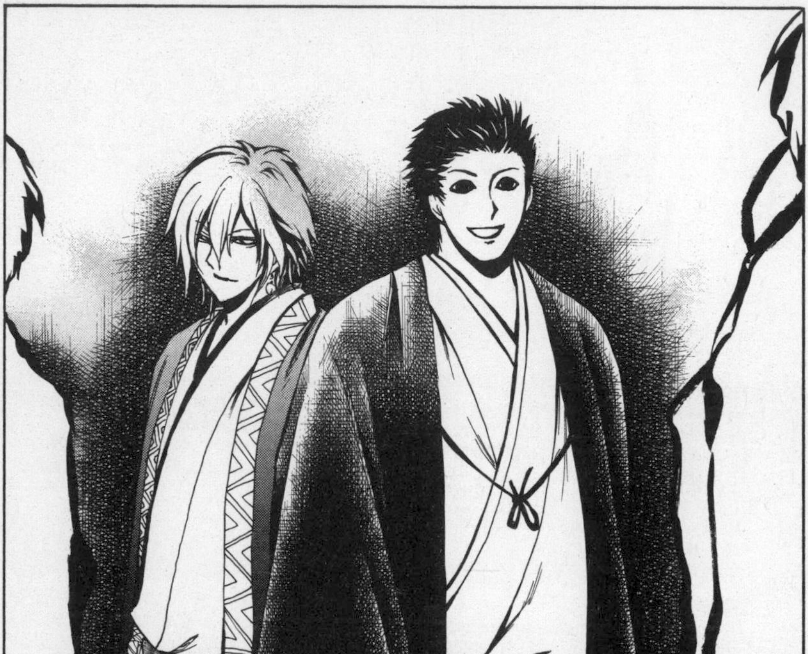

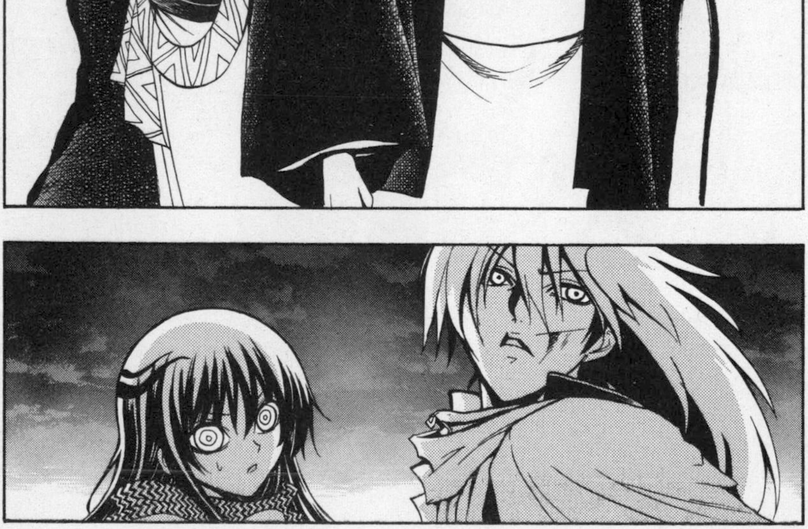

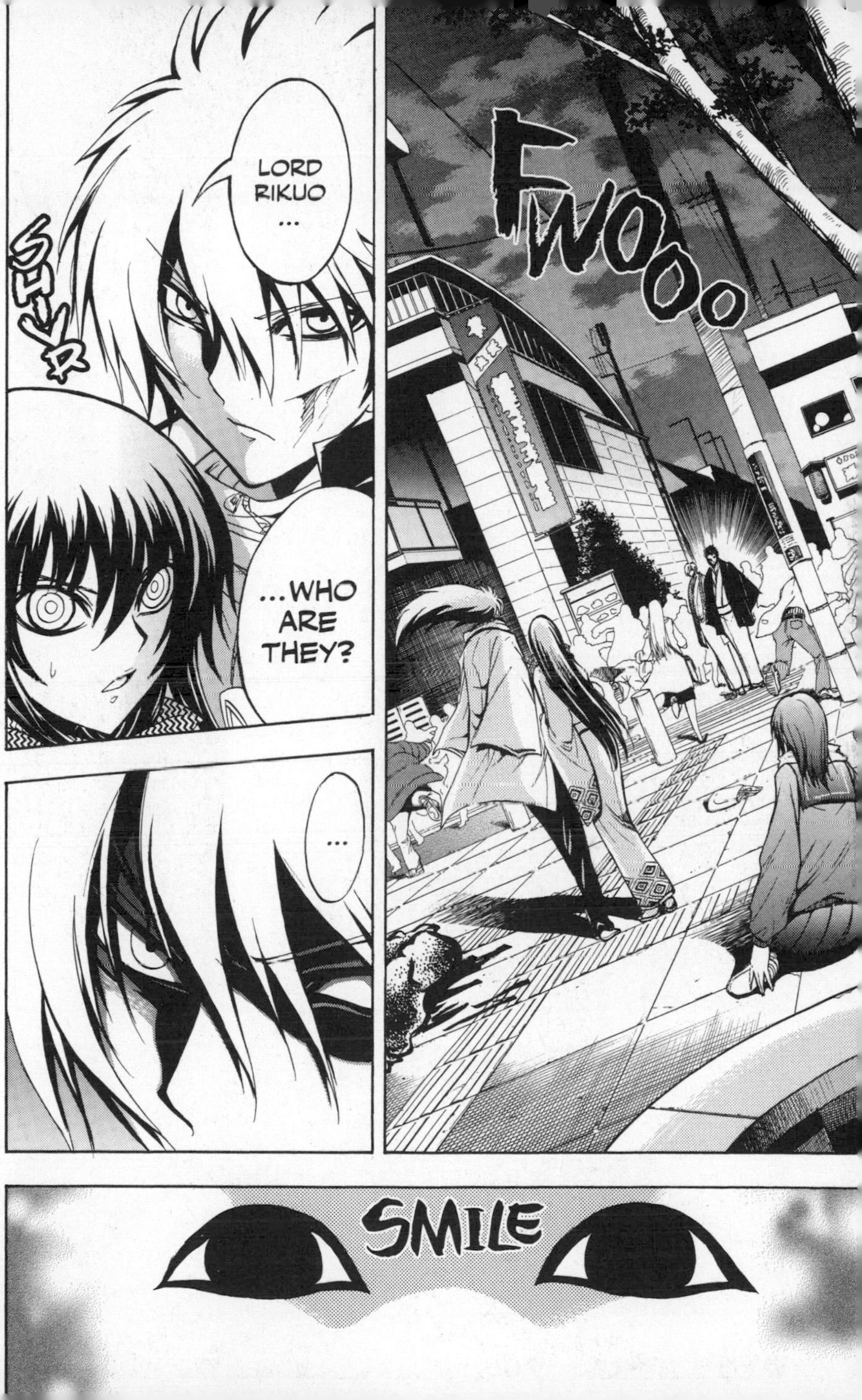
FWOOO
LORD RIKUO ...
...WHO ARE THEY?
...
SMILE

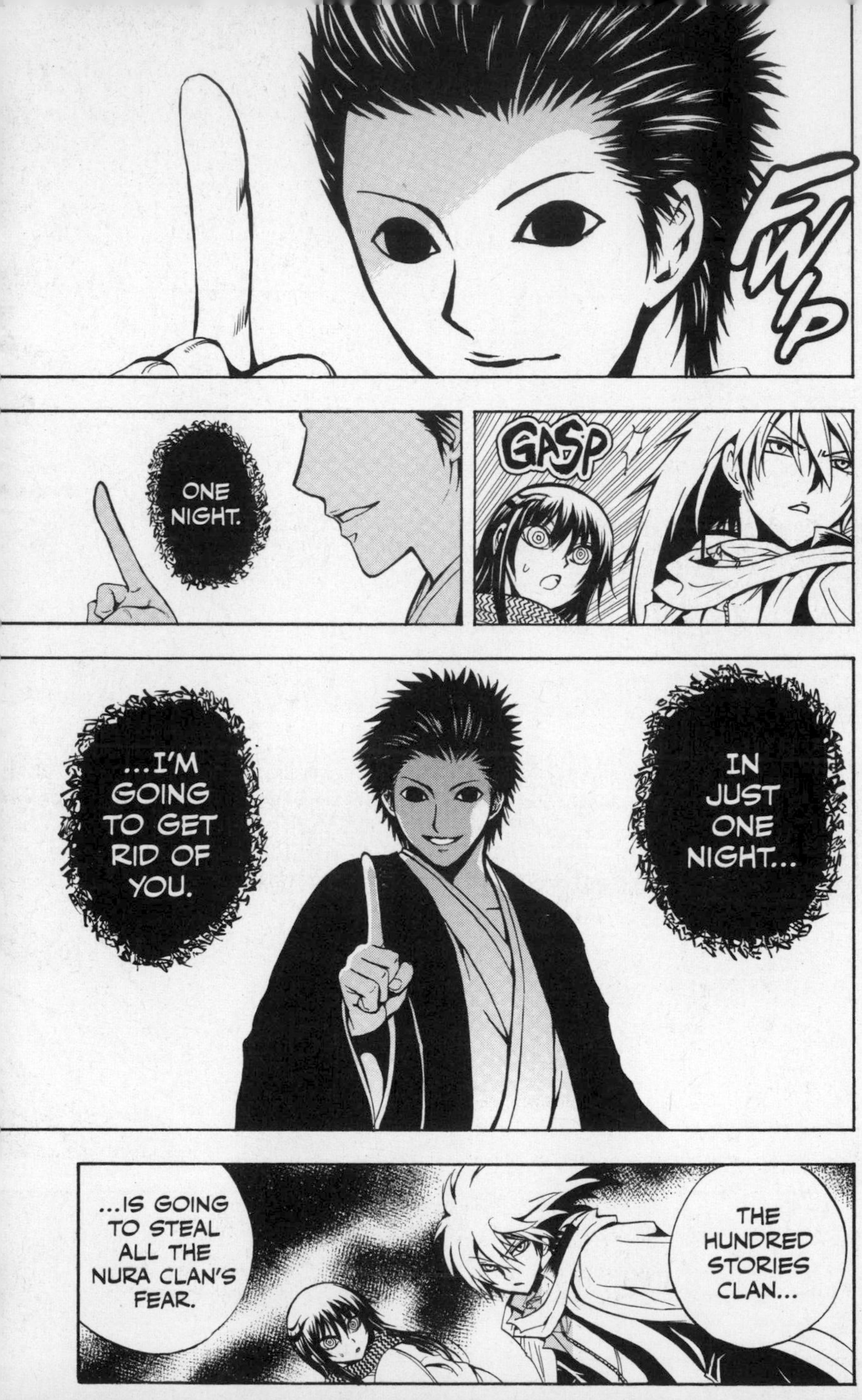
FWIP
GASP
ONE NIGHT.
IN JUST ONE NIGHT...
...I'M GOING TO GET RID OF YOU.
THE HUNDRED STORIES CLAN...
...IS GOING TO STEAL ALL THE NURA CLAN'S FEAR.

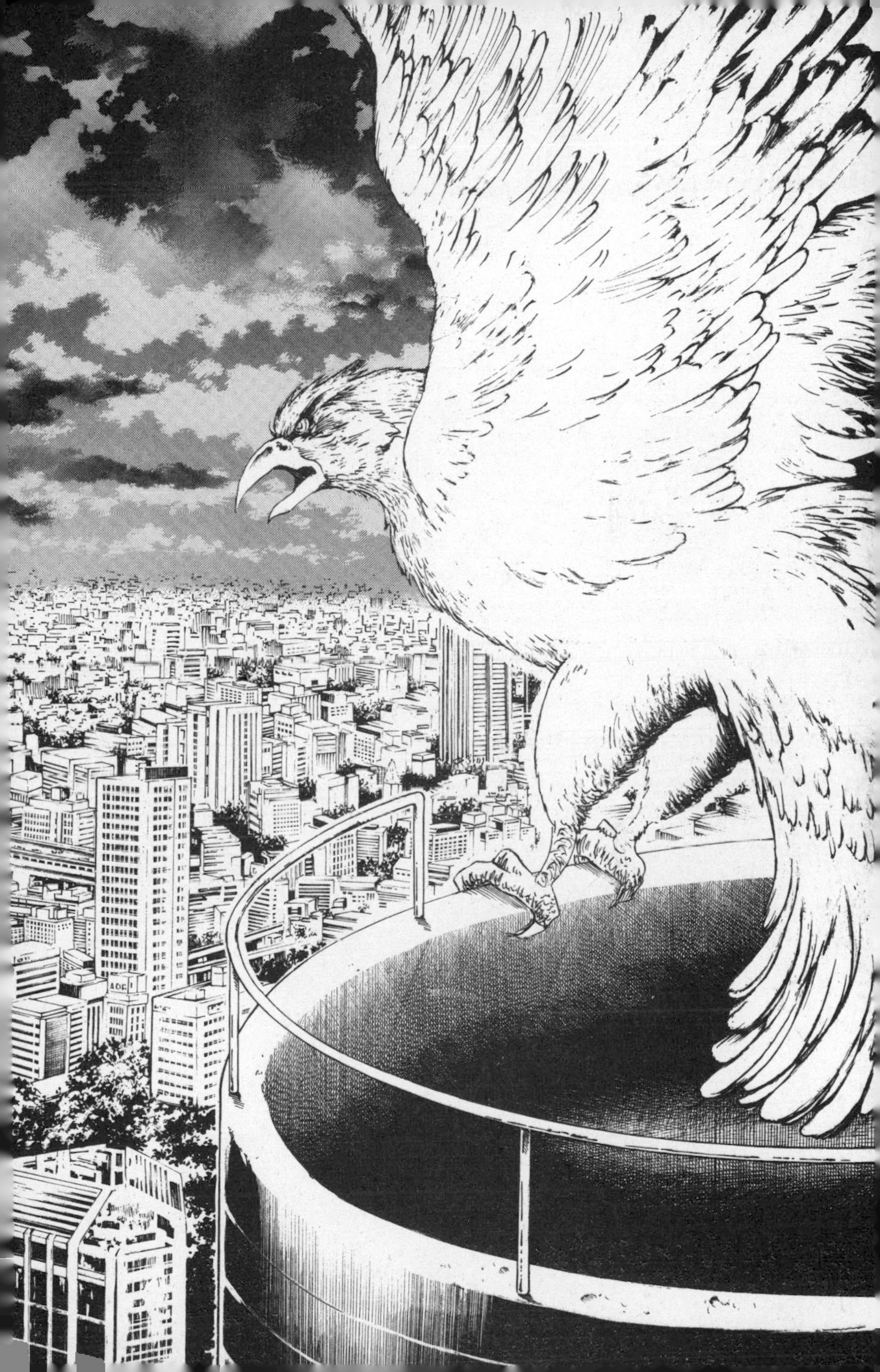

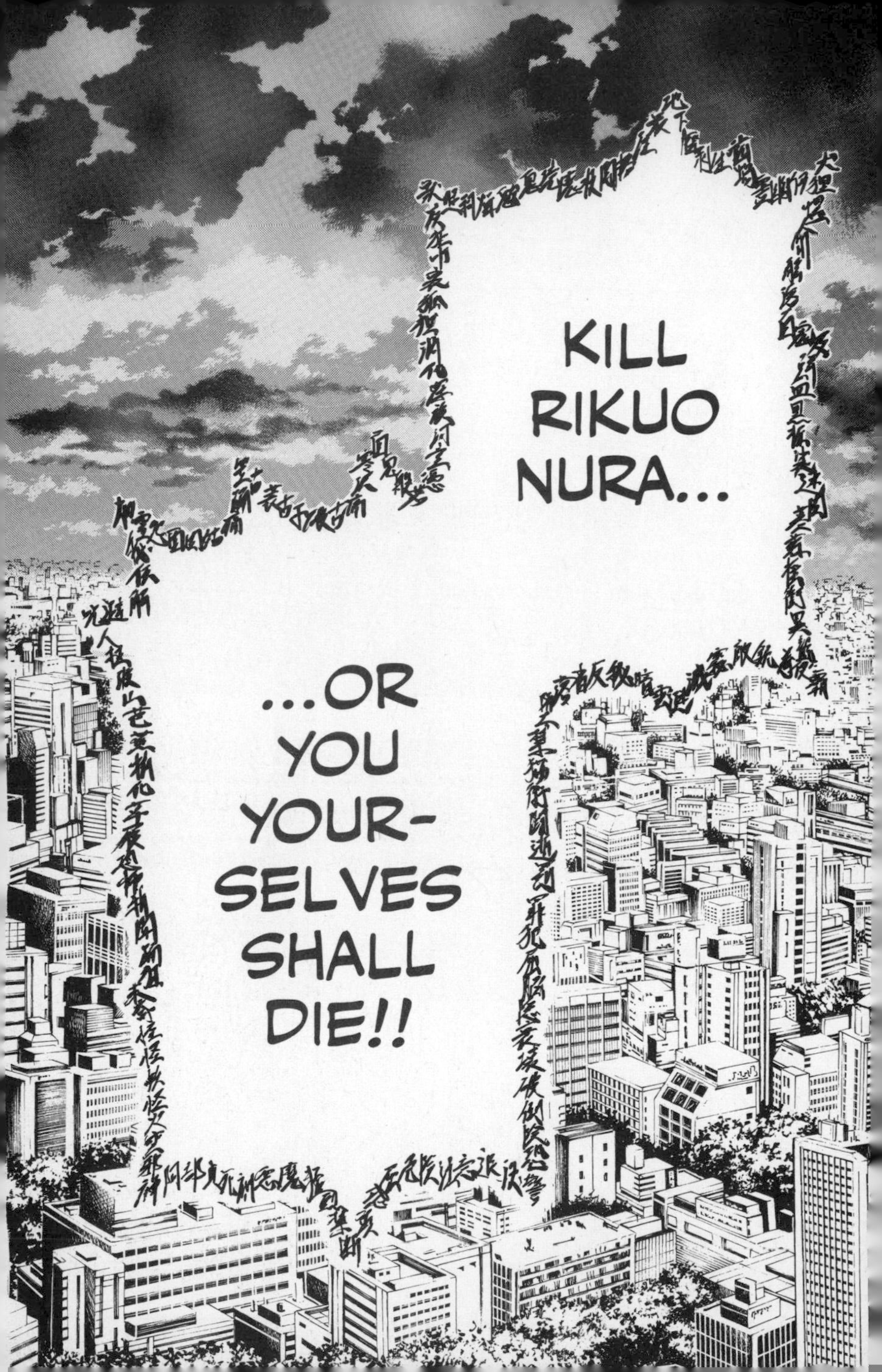
KILL RIKUO NURA...
...OR YOU YOUR-SELVES SHALL DIE!!

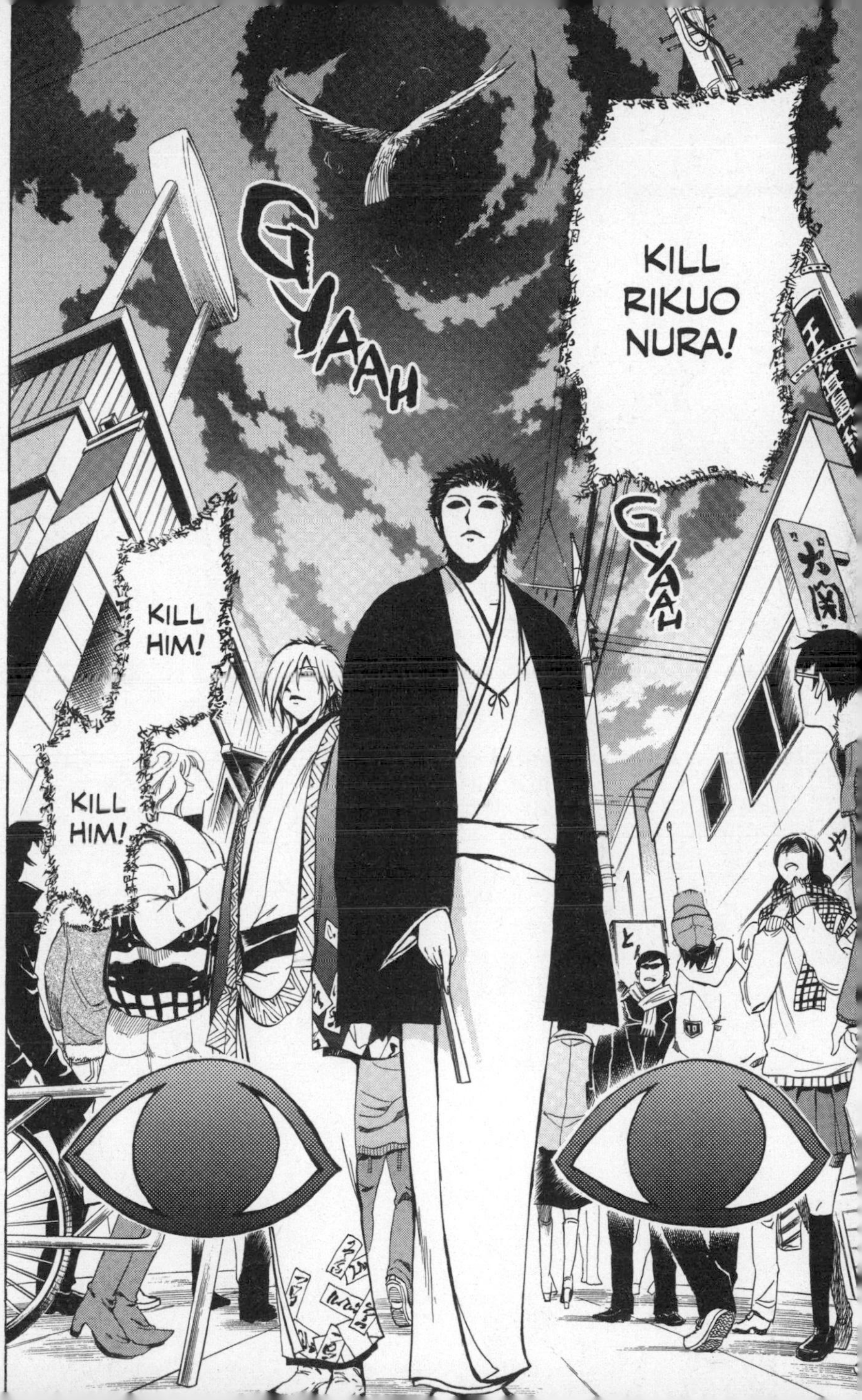
KILL RIKUO NURA!
GYAAH
GYAAH
KILL HIM!
KILL HIM!

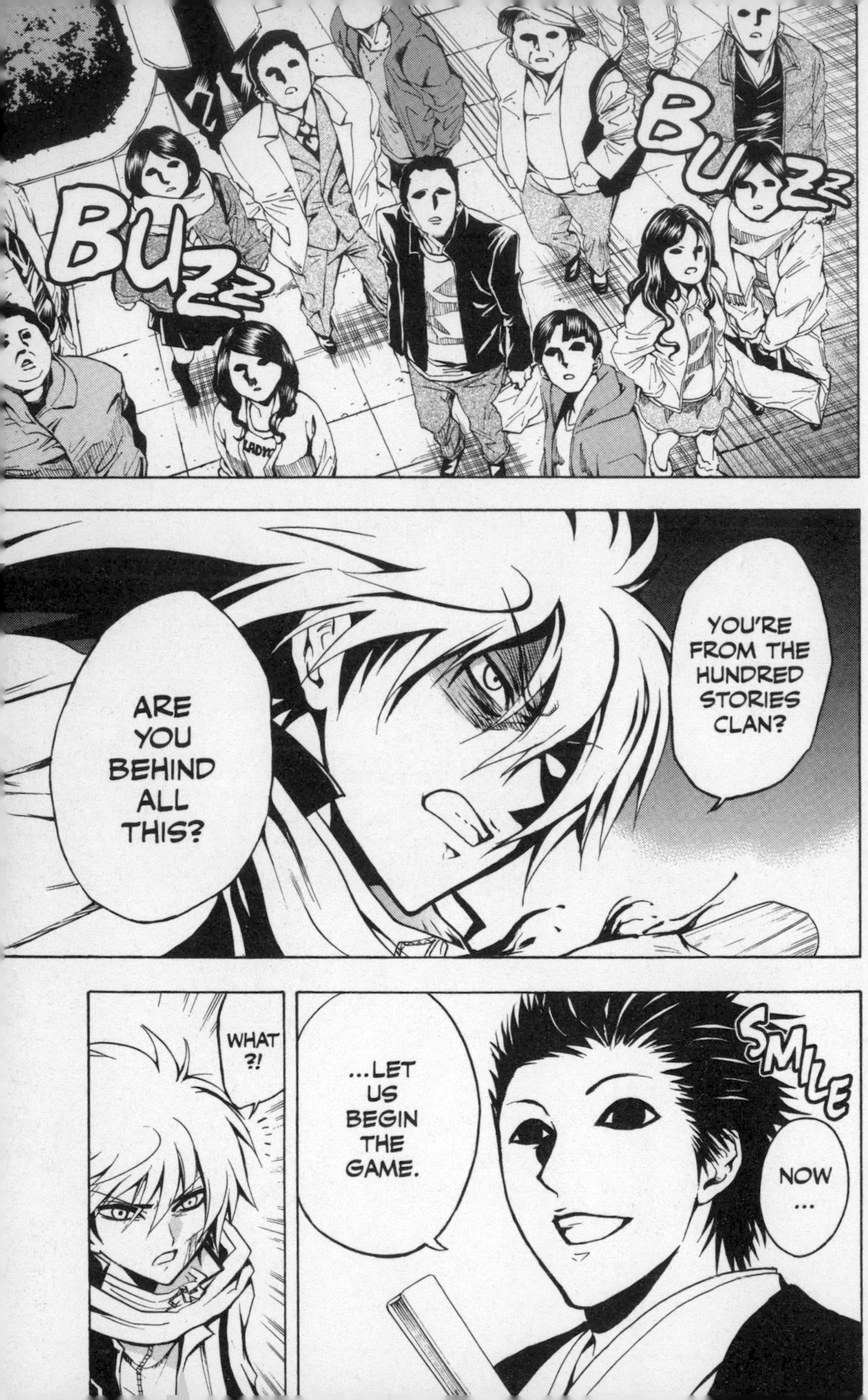
BUZZ
BUZZ
YOU'RE FROM THE HUNDRED STORIES CLAN?
ARE YOU BEHIND ALL THIS?
SMILE
NOW...
...LET US BEGIN THE GAME.
WHAT?!

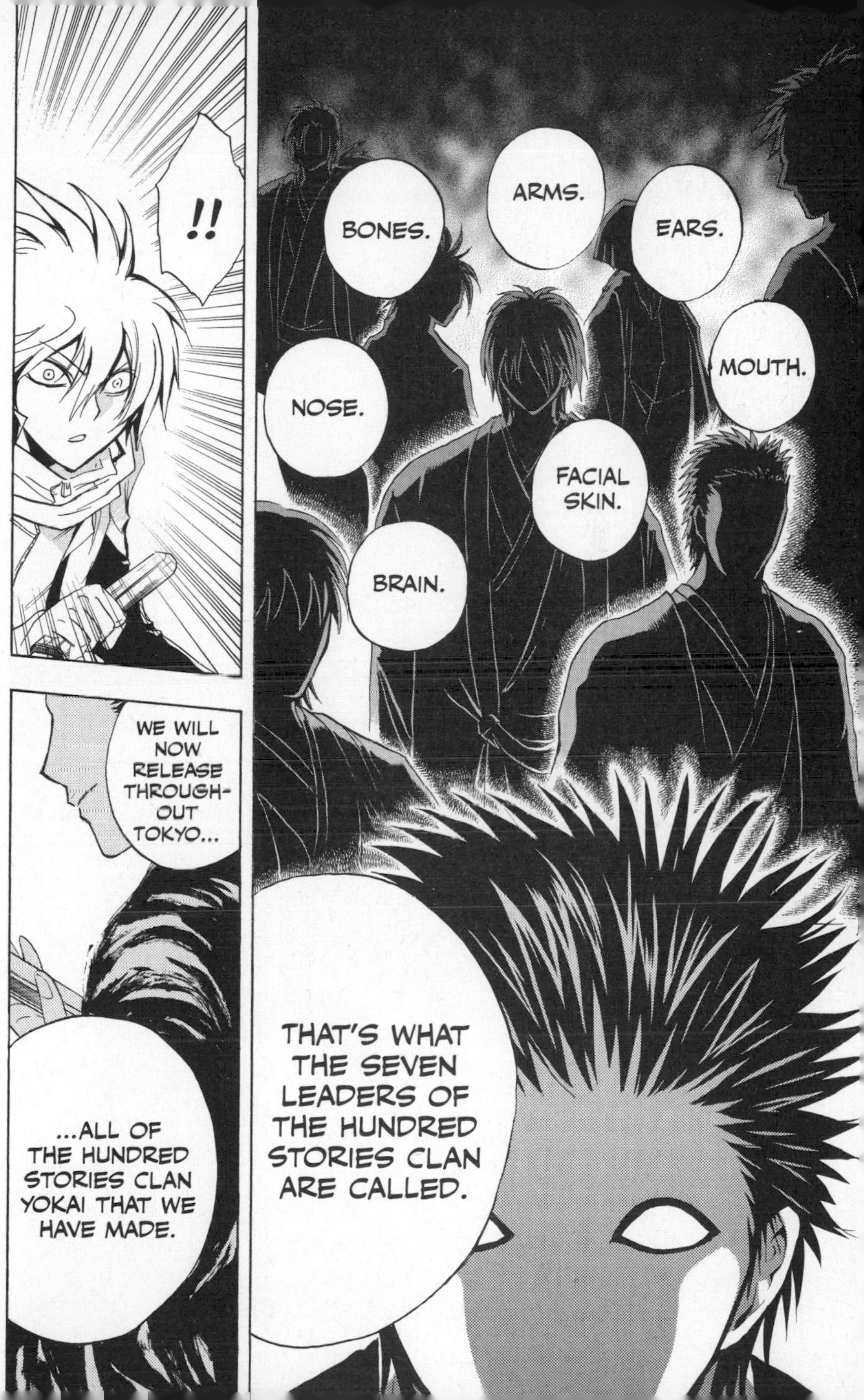
EARS.
ARMS.
BONES.
MOUTH.
NOSE.
FACIAL SKIN.
BRAIN.
THAT'S WHAT THE SEVEN LEADERS OF THE HUNDRED STORIES CLAN ARE CALLED.
!!
WE WILL NOW RELEASE THROUGH-OUT TOKYO...
...ALL OF THE HUNDRED STORIES CLAN YOKAI THAT WE HAVE MADE.

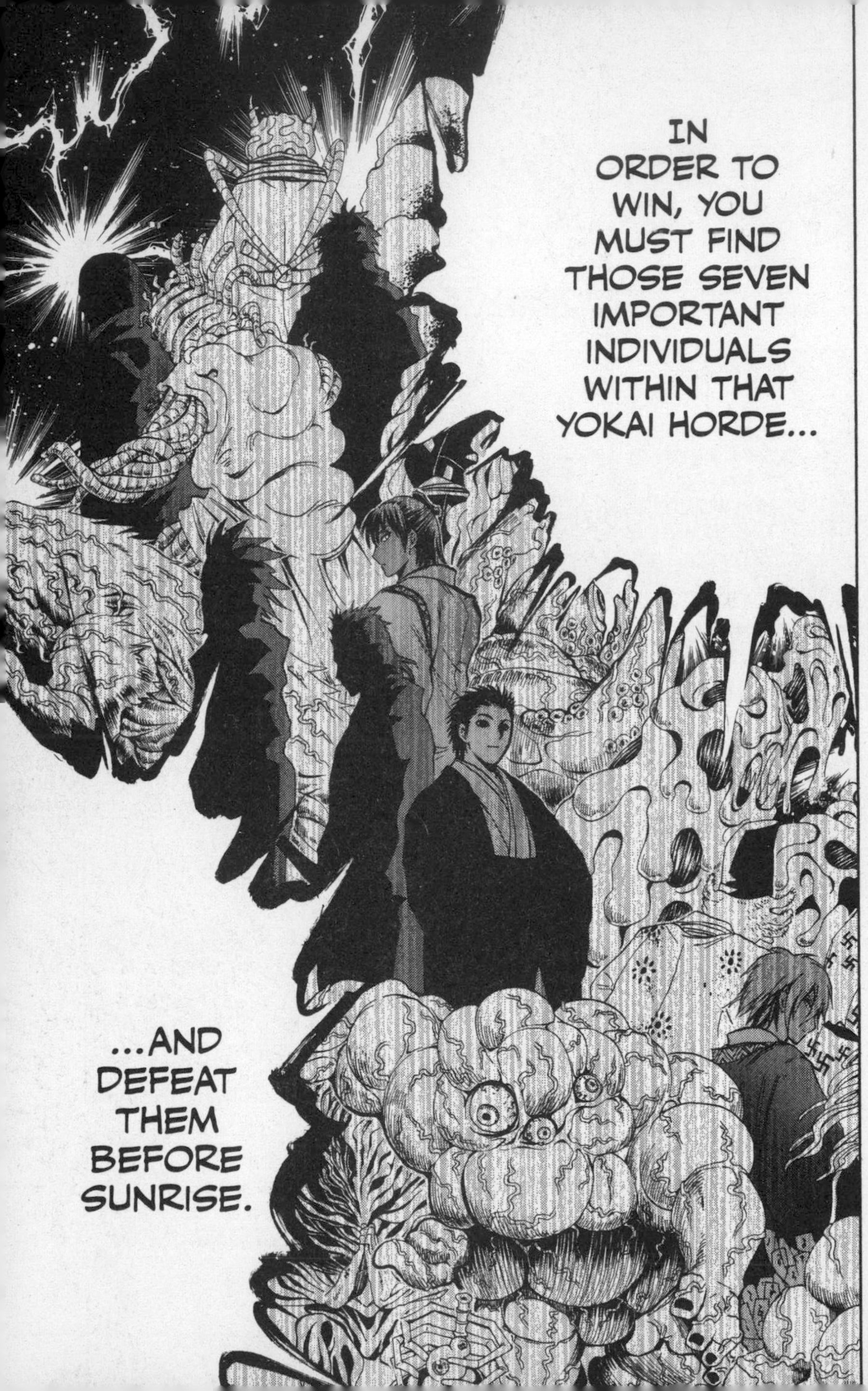
IN ORDER TO WIN, YOU MUST FIND THOSE SEVEN IMPORTANT INDIVIDUALS WITHIN THAT YOKAI HORDE...
...AND DEFEAT THEM BEFORE SUNRISE.

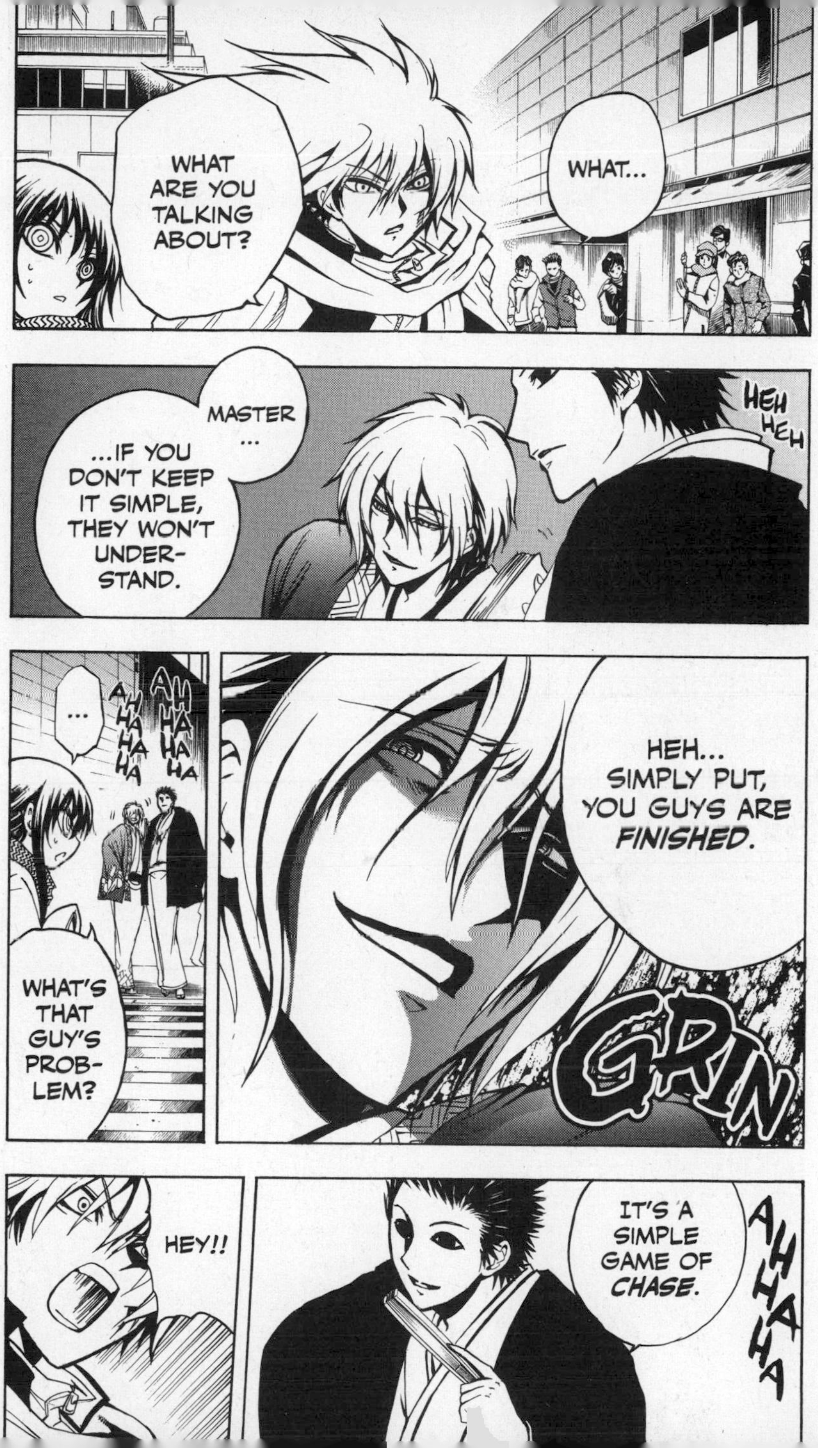
WHAT...
WHAT ARE YOU TALKING ABOUT?
HEH HEH
MASTER ...
...IF YOU DON'T KEEP IT SIMPLE, THEY WON'T UNDER-STAND.
HEH... SIMPLY PUT, YOU GUYS ARE *FINISHED*.
GRIN
AH HA HA HA
AH HA HA HA
...
WHAT'S THAT GUY'S PROB-LEM?
AHHAHAHA
IT'S A SIMPLE GAME OF *CHASE*.
HEY!!

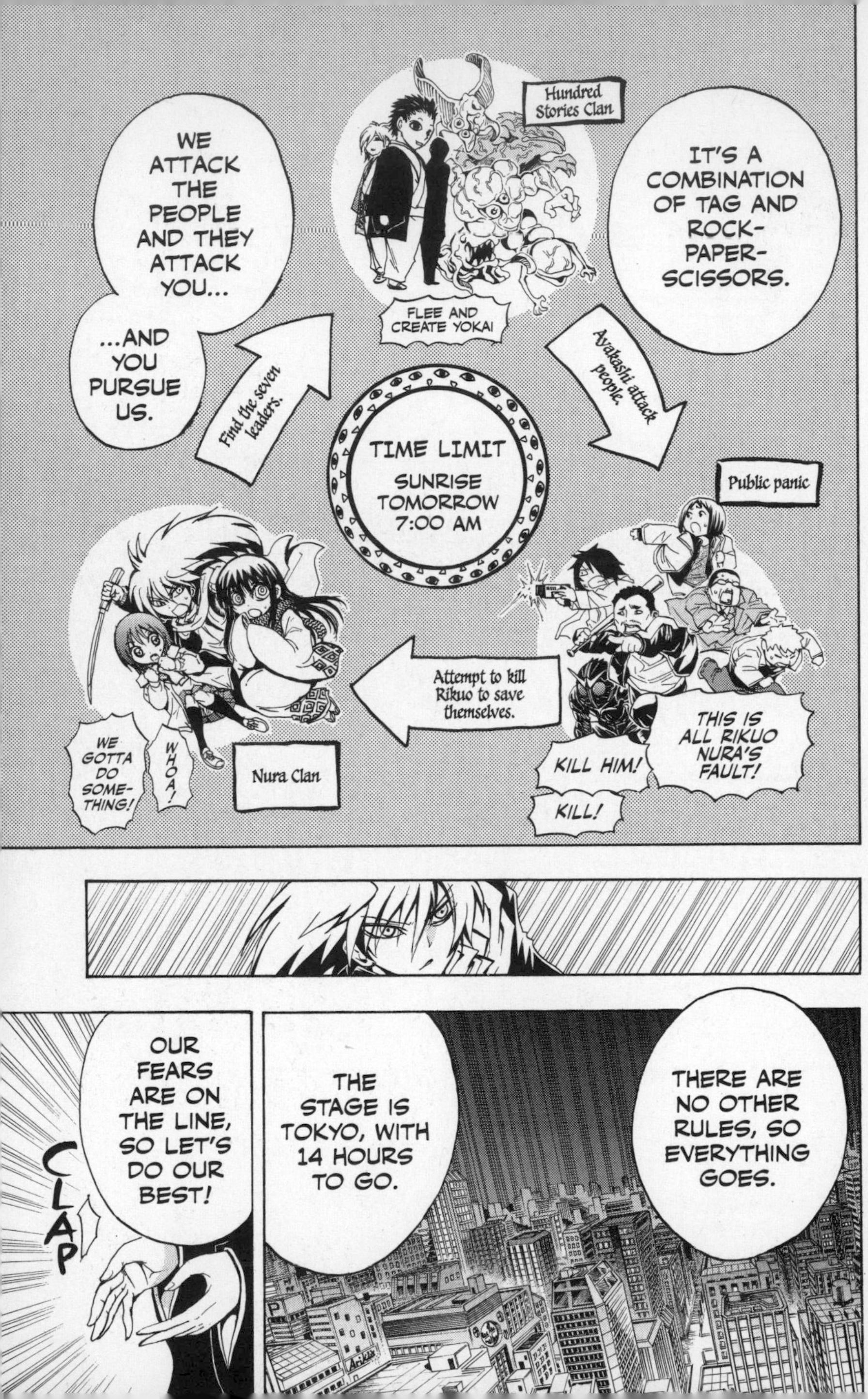
Hundred Stories Clan
IT'S A COMBINATION OF TAG AND ROCK-PAPER-SCISSORS.
WE ATTACK THE PEOPLE AND THEY ATTACK YOU...
...AND YOU PURSUE US.
FLEE AND CREATE YOKAI
Ayakashi attack people.
Find the seven leaders.
TIME LIMIT
SUNRISE TOMORROW 7:00 AM
Public panic
THIS IS ALL RIKUO NURA'S FAULT!
KILL HIM!
KILL!
Attempt to kill Rikuo to save themselves.
Nura Clan
WHOA!
WE GOTTA DO SOME-THING!
THERE ARE NO OTHER RULES, SO EVERYTHING GOES.
THE STAGE IS TOKYO, WITH 14 HOURS TO GO.
OUR FEARS ARE ON THE LINE, SO LET'S DO OUR BEST!
CLAP

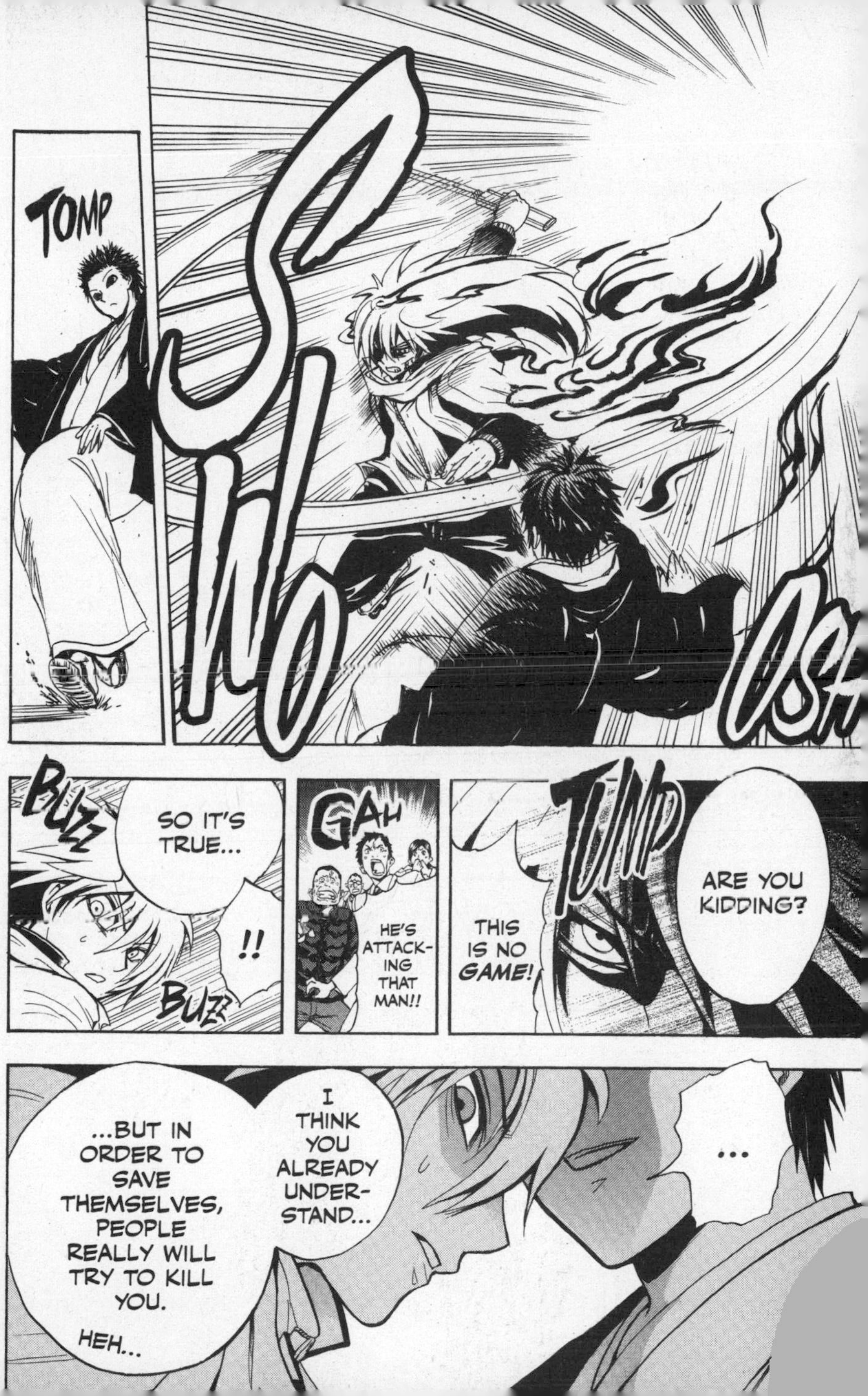
SWOOSH
TOMP
TUMP
ARE YOU KIDDING?
THIS IS NO GAME!
GAH
HE'S ATTACKING THAT MAN!!
BUZZ
SO IT'S TRUE...
!!
BUZZ
...
I THINK YOU ALREADY UNDERSTAND...
...BUT IN ORDER TO SAVE THEMSELVES, PEOPLE REALLY WILL TRY TO KILL YOU.
HEH...

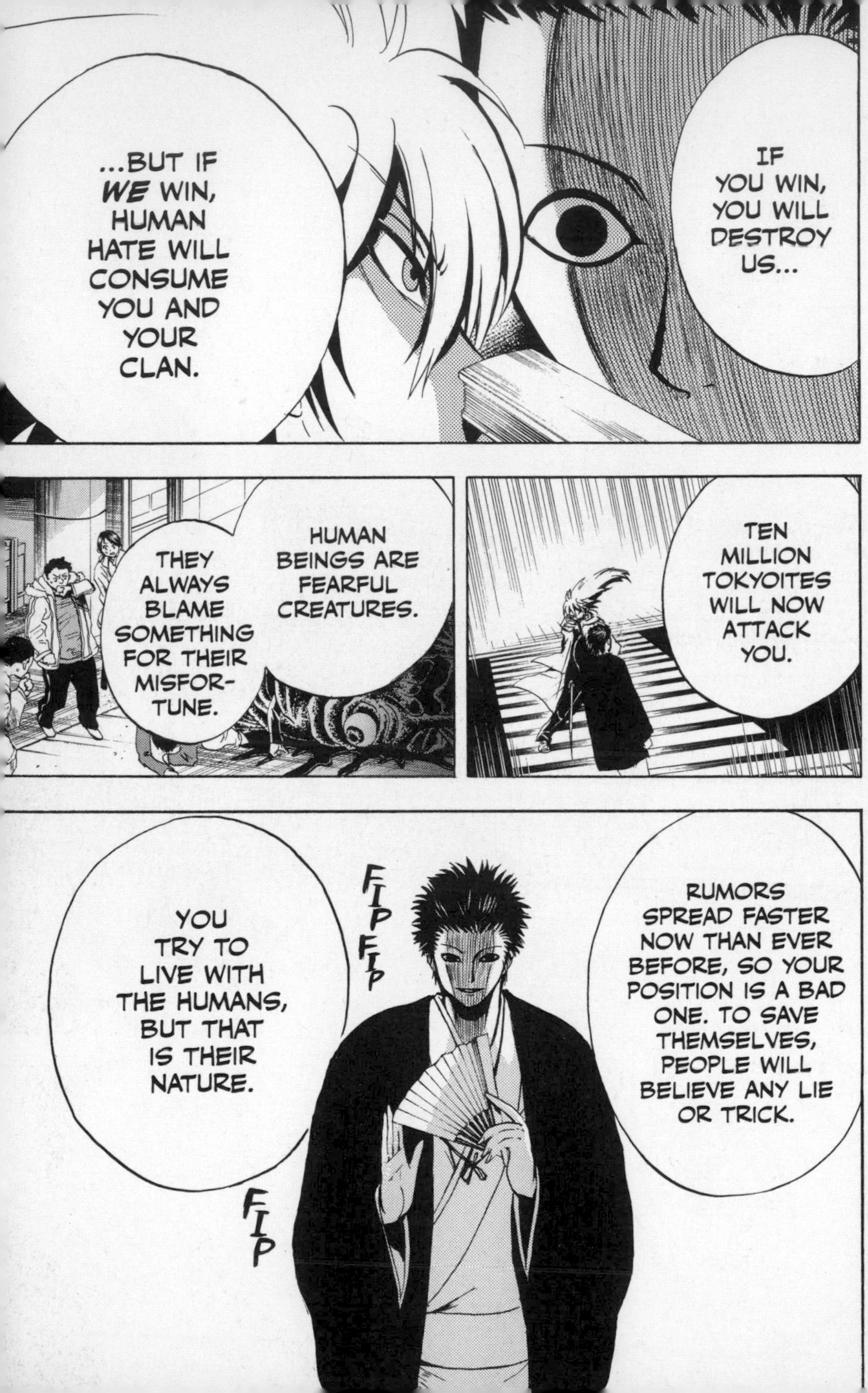
IF YOU WIN, YOU WILL DESTROY US...
...BUT IF *WE* WIN, HUMAN HATE WILL CONSUME YOU AND YOUR CLAN.
TEN MILLION TOKYOITES WILL NOW ATTACK YOU.
HUMAN BEINGS ARE FEARFUL CREATURES.
THEY ALWAYS BLAME SOMETHING FOR THEIR MISFOR-TUNE.
RUMORS SPREAD FASTER NOW THAN EVER BEFORE, SO YOUR POSITION IS A BAD ONE. TO SAVE THEMSELVES, PEOPLE WILL BELIEVE ANY LIE OR TRICK.
FIP FIP
YOU TRY TO LIVE WITH THE HUMANS, BUT THAT IS THEIR NATURE.
FIP

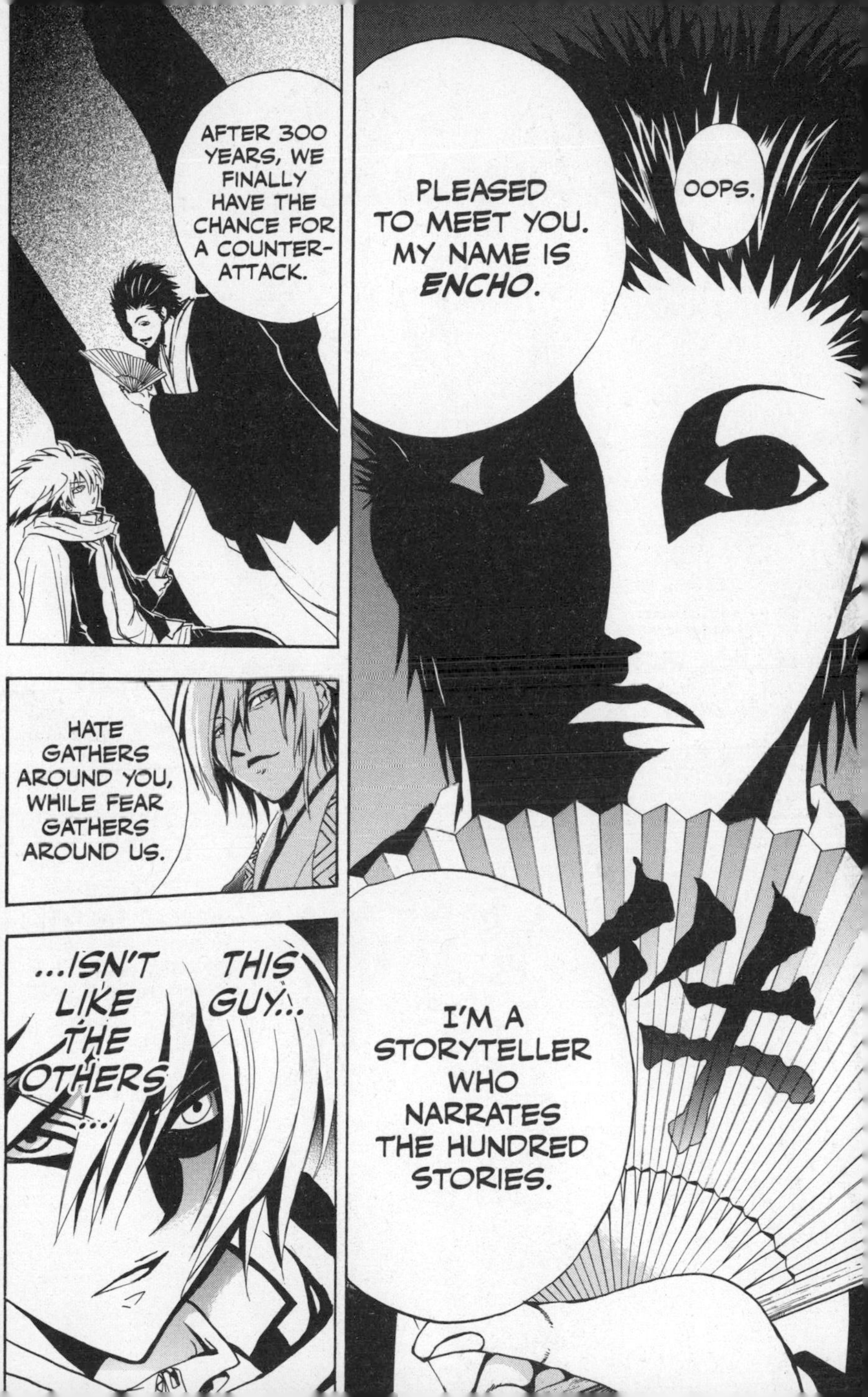
OOPS.
PLEASED TO MEET YOU. MY NAME IS *ENCHO*.
I'M A STORYTELLER WHO NARRATES THE HUNDRED STORIES.
AFTER 300 YEARS, WE FINALLY HAVE THE CHANCE FOR A COUNTER-ATTACK.
HATE GATHERS AROUND YOU, WHILE FEAR GATHERS AROUND US.
THIS GUY...
...ISN'T LIKE THE OTHERS...

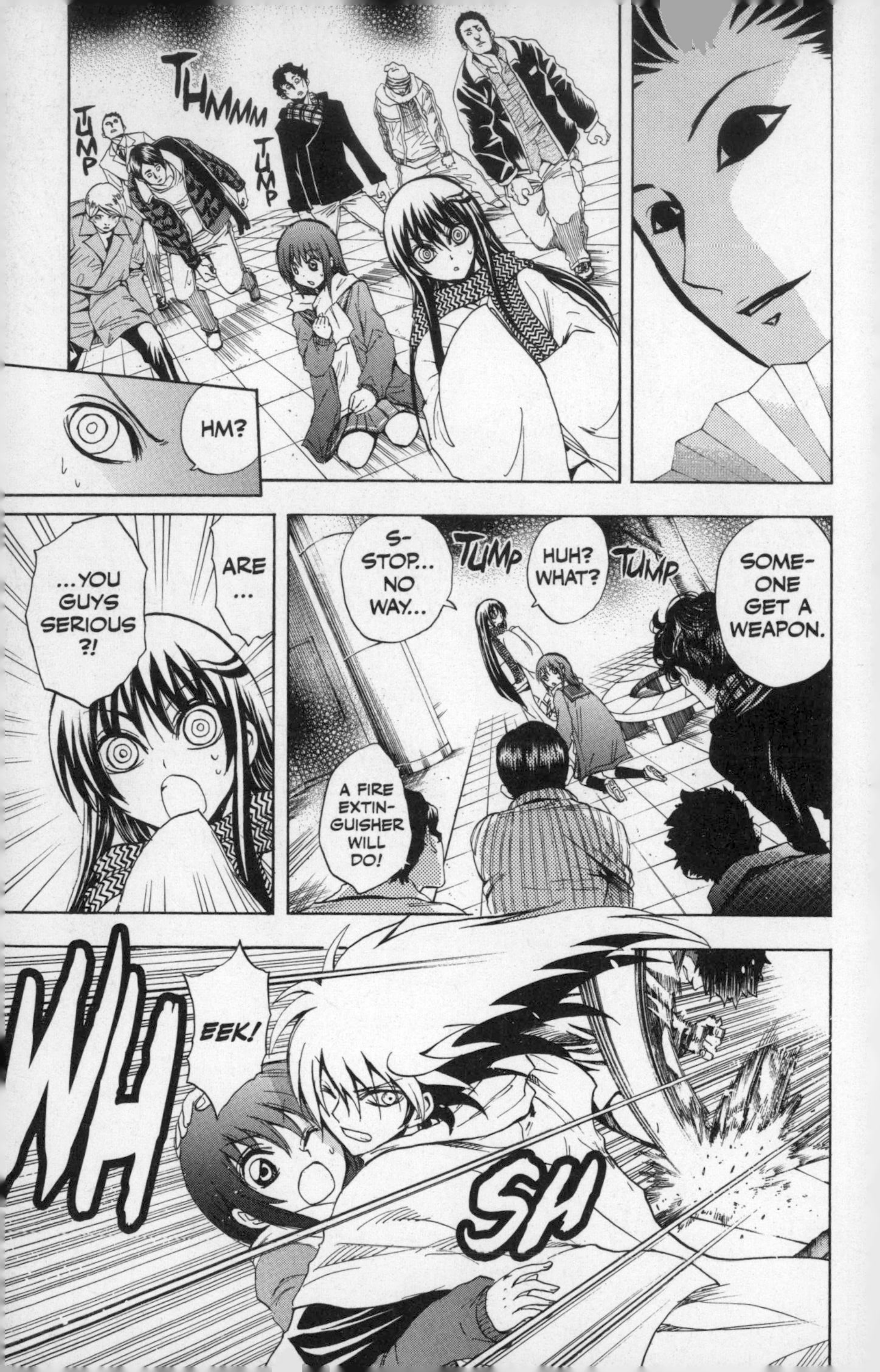
THMMM
TUMP
TUMP
HM?
SOME-ONE GET A WEAPON.
TUMP
HUH? WHAT?
TUMP
S-STOP... NO WAY...
A FIRE EXTIN-GUISHER WILL DO!
ARE ...
...YOU GUYS SERIOUS ?!
EEK!
WH
SH

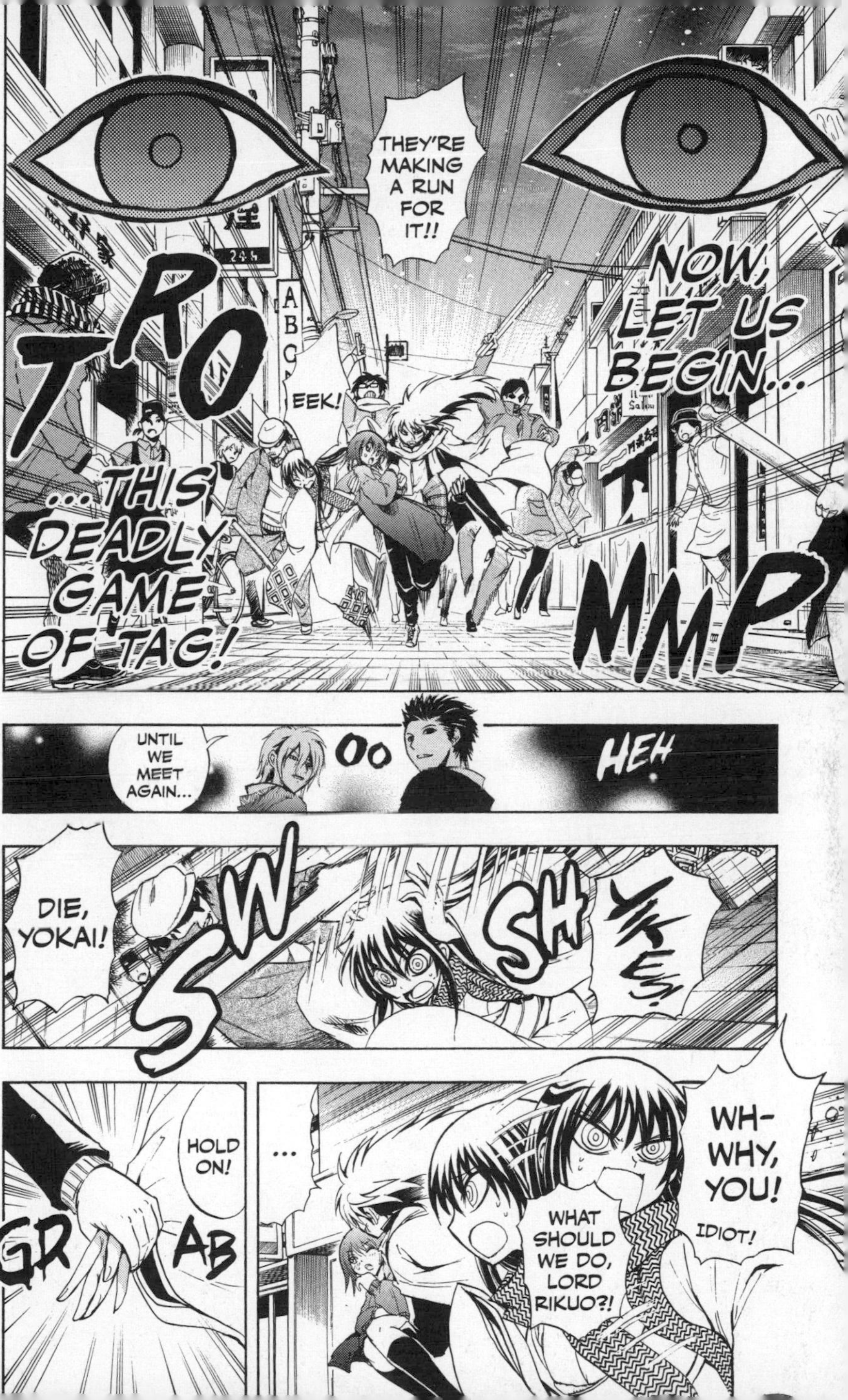
NOW, LET US BEGIN...
THEY'RE MAKING A RUN FOR IT!!
EEK!
TRO
...THIS DEADLY GAME OF TAG!
MMP
HEH
OO
UNTIL WE MEET AGAIN...
YIKES!
SH
W
S
DIE, YOKAI!
WH- WHY, YOU!
IDIOT!
WHAT SHOULD WE DO, LORD RIKUO?!
...
HOLD ON!
GR
AB

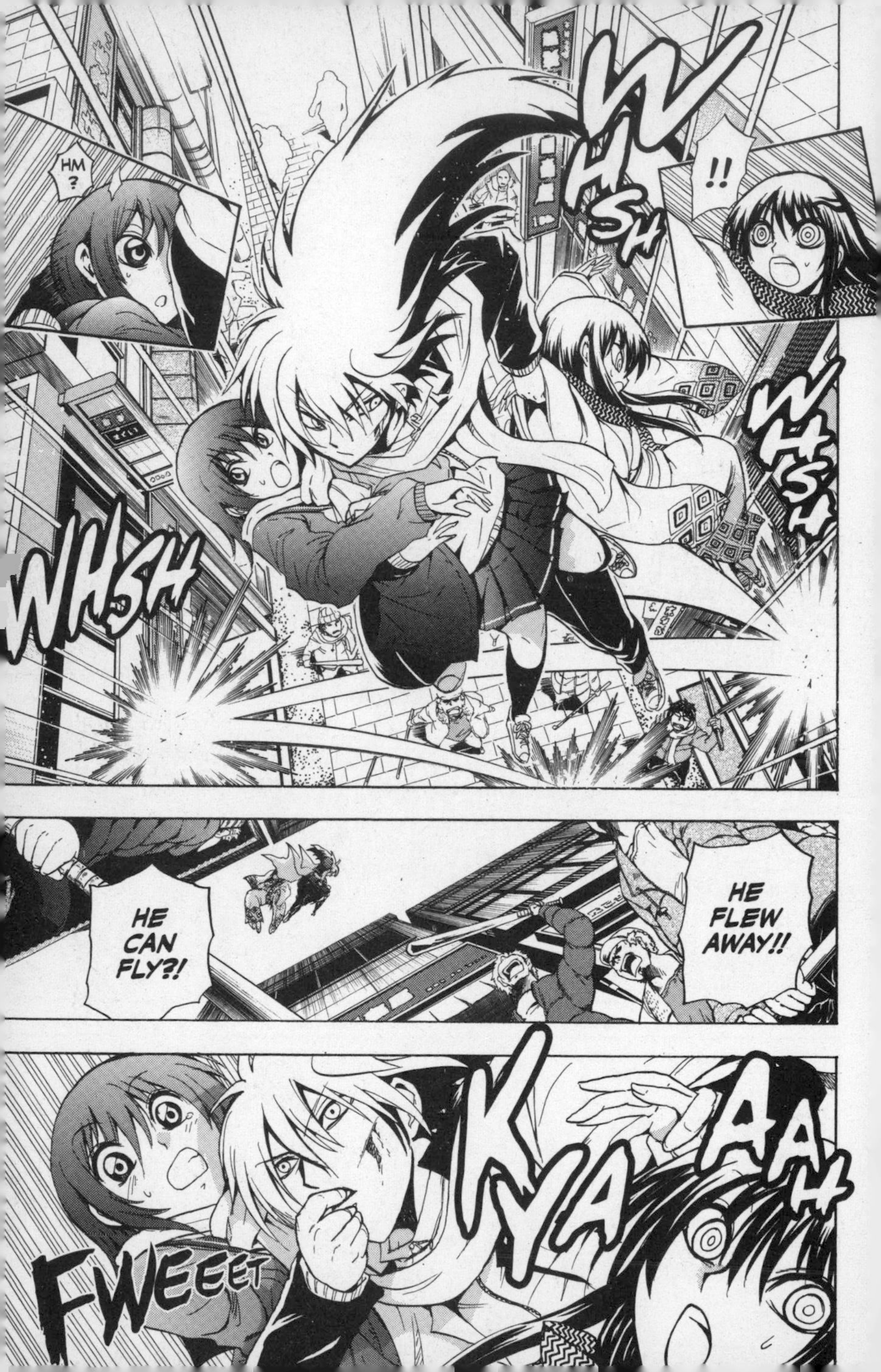
!!
WHSH
WHSH
HM ?
WHSH
HE FLEW AWAY!!
HE CAN FLY?!
KYAAAH
FWEEEET

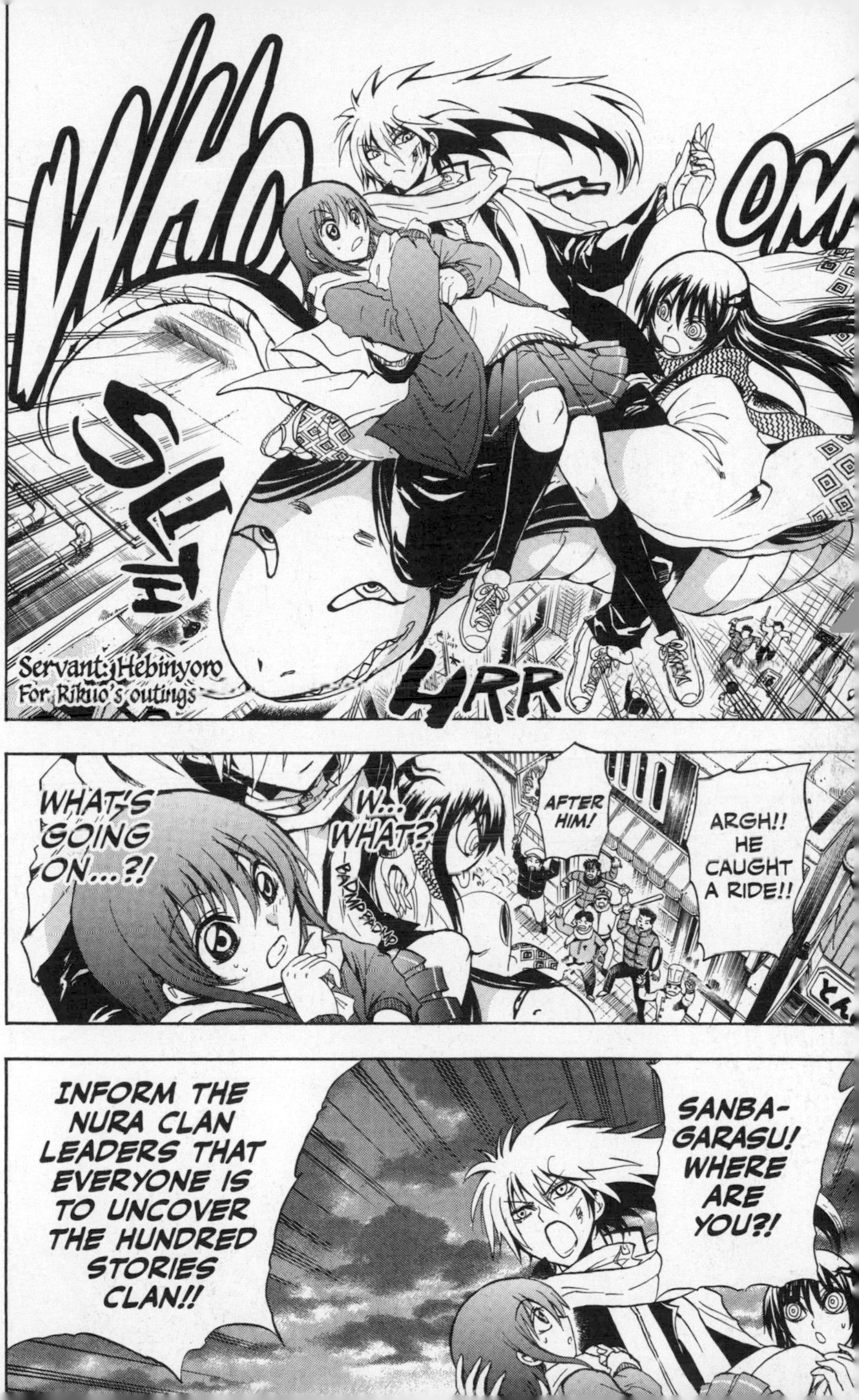
Servant: Hebinyoro
For Rikuo's outings
SLITH
ARGH!! HE CAUGHT A RIDE!!
AFTER HIM!
W... WHAT?
WHAT'S GOING ON...?!
SANBA-GARASU! WHERE ARE YOU?!
INFORM THE NURA CLAN LEADERS THAT EVERYONE IS TO UNCOVER THE HUNDRED STORIES CLAN!!

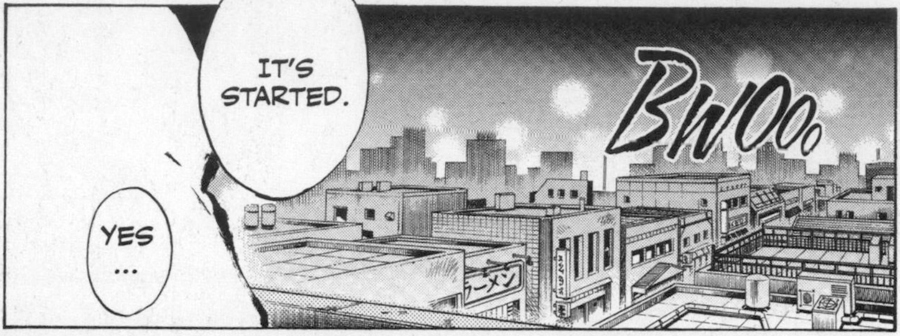
BWOoo
IT'S STARTED.
YES ...

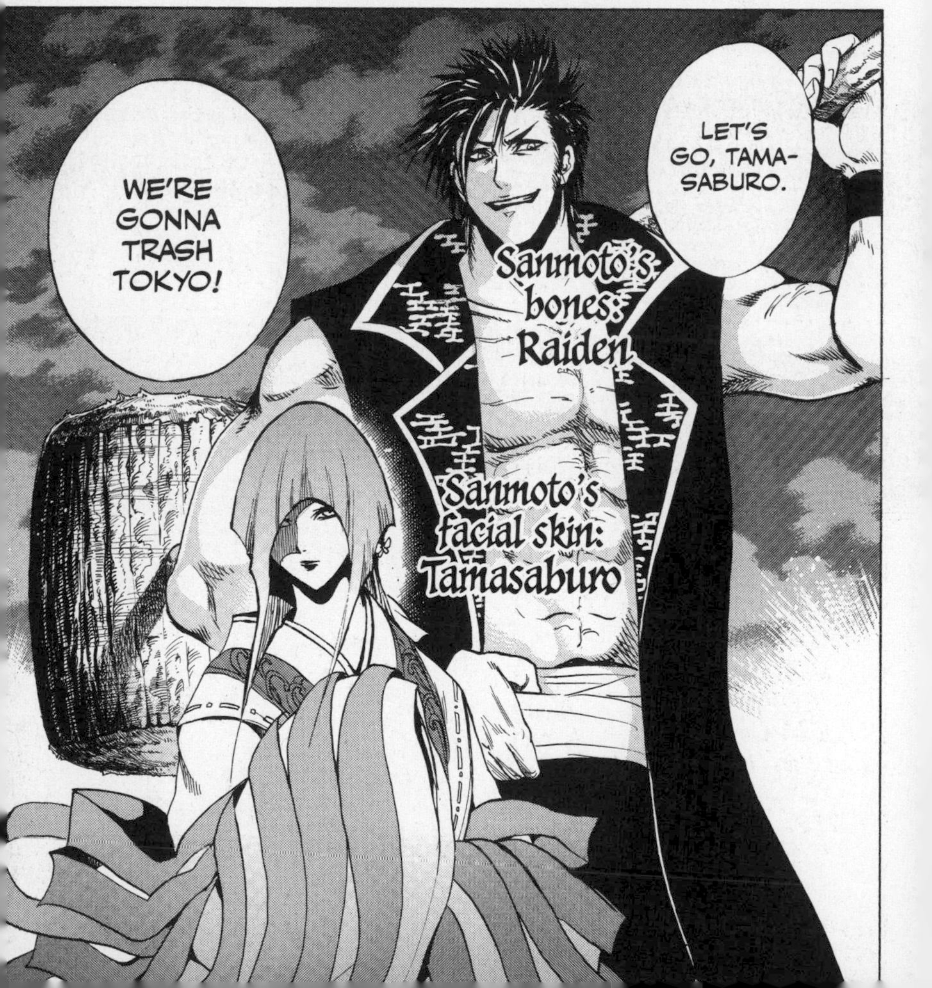
LET'S GO, TAMA-SABURO.
WE'RE GONNA TRASH TOKYO!
Sanmoto's bones: Raiden
Sanmoto's facial skin: Tamasaburo

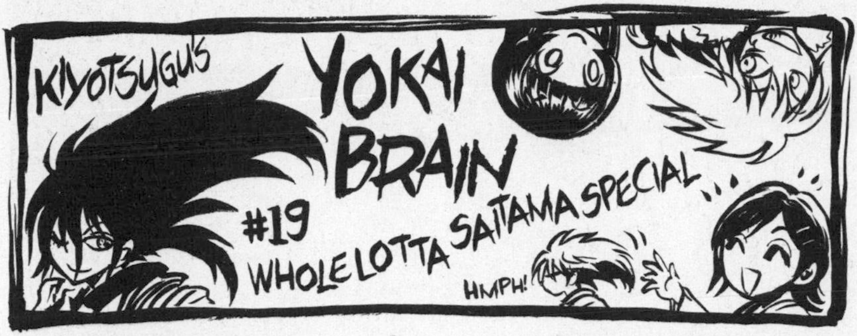
KIYOTSUGU'S
YOKAI BRAIN
#19
WHOLE LOTTA SAITAMA SPECIAL
HMPH!

Q: HOW OLD WAS PRINCESS YO WHEN SHE MET NURARIHYON? *–S.R., SAITAMA PREFECTURE*

YO: I WAS 15!

Q: HAS AWASHIMA EVER FELT LIKE BEING MACHO? *–NAGARESAKURA, IBARAKI PREFECTURE*

AWASHIMA: HAVEN'T YOU? I SURE HAVE! BUT ONLY WHEN I'M A MAN!

Q: THIS QUESTION IS FOR GYUKI AND GOZUMARU!! WHAT WOULD YOU DO IF MEZUMARU DRAGGED YOU INTO SOMETHING UNIMAGINABLE? ANSWER HONESTLY!! *–MAYU YAMADA, SAITAMA PREFECTURE*

OZUMARU: SOMETHING UNIMAGINABLE? LIKE WHAT?

GYUKI: DON'T THINK ABOUT IT. THIS IS ABOUT HEART! SHE WANTS YOU TO ANSWER HONESTLY—FROM THE HEART!

OZUMARU: THAT'S MEAN!

Q: HOW OLD WAS HIDEMOTO KEIKAIN WHEN HE DIED? *–AKIRA NURA, NAGASAKI PREFECTURE*

RTEENTH: I LIVED PRETTY LONG! ♡ BECAUSE I MYSELF WASN'T CURSED! ♡

Q: THIS QUESTION'S FOR PATO! CAN PATO TELL FORTUNES WITH HIS CRYSTAL BALL? *–MILK CALCIUM, NIIGATA PREFECTURE*

PATO: YES, I CAN!! NATTO-KOZO'S FUTURE IS... YEP, IT'S SMELLY!!

Q: I KNOW THAT RYUJI IS IN HIGH SCHOOL, BUT IS MAMIRU IN HIGH SCHOOL, TOO? I REALLY GOTTA KNOW! OH...AND RYUJI'S COOL! ♡ *–KUROKITSUNE, HIROSHIMA PREFECTURE*

RYUJI: YEAH, HE'S IN HIGH SCHOOL.

Q: RYUJI! ARE YOU DRINKING ENOUGH MILK? THERE'S STILL TIME, YOU KNOW! *–HII, CHIBA PREFECTURE*

RYUJI: MIND YOUR OWN BUSINESS!

Q: KUBINASHI OFTEN CARRIES AROUND A SHAMISEN. CAN HE PLAY IT? *–TSUCCHI, AICHI PREFECTURE*

KUBINASHI: A LITTLE. KEJORO AND SETSURA CAN PLAY BETTER, THOUGH.

Q: WHO IS THE OLDEST PERSON IN THE NURA CLAN?

GYUKI: AS FAR AS I KNOW, I AM. BUT A LOT OF GUYS DON'T KNOW HOW LONG THEY'VE BEEN AROUND.

Q: I HAVE A QUESTION FOR SAGAMI. HONESTLY, DO YOU LIKE YOUR NAME? *–NNM, SAITAMA PREFECTURE*

SAGAMI: I...DON'T LIKE IT! *(ANGRY)*

Q: EQUIP CAUSES TATTOO-LIKE MARKS TO APPEAR ON ITS USER'S BACK, BUT NURARIHYON'S MARKS ARE JUST TATTOOS, RIGHT? I MEAN, EQUIP IS A HALF-YOKAI MOVE, SO... *–FUKUOKA GEORGE, FUKUOKA PREFECTURE*

NURARIHYON: THEY'RE DIFFERENT FROM THE EQUIP MARKS.

Q: DOES WAKANA TALK TO THE NIGHTTIME RIKUO? WHAT'S THAT LIKE? *–MAO, SAITAMA PREFECTURE*

WAKANA: I WOULD LIKE TO, BUT THAT BOY GETS SO TACITURN!

Q: THIS QUESTION'S FOR RIHAN! WHY DO YOU ALWAYS CLOSE ONE EYE? *–MIO OHASHI, GIFU PREFECTURE (AND OTHERS)*

RIHAN: HA HA HA! MAYBE IT'S JUST A HABIT!

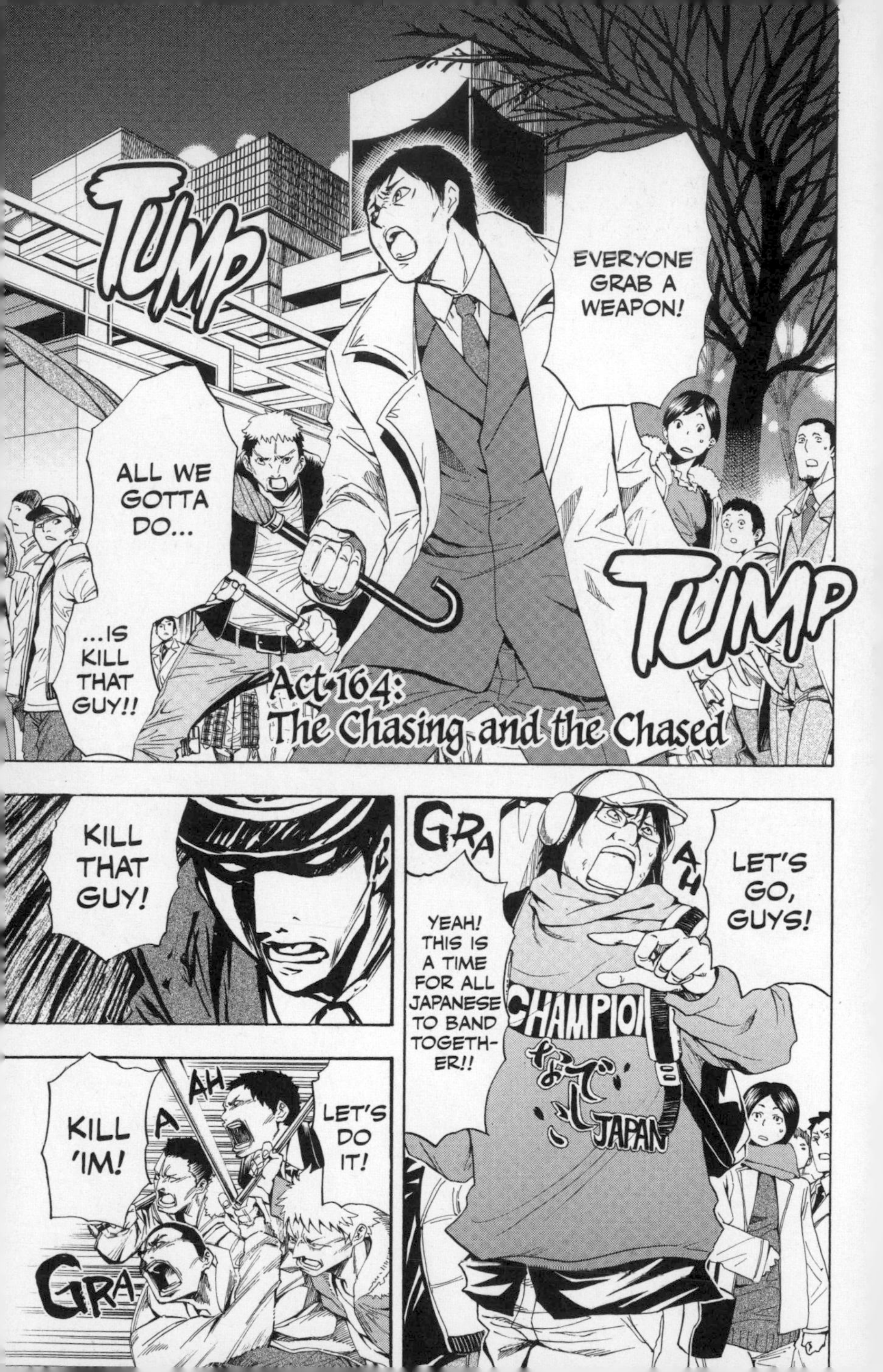
TUMP
EVERYONE GRAB A WEAPON!
TUMP
ALL WE GOTTA DO...
...IS KILL THAT GUY!!
Act 164: The Chasing and the Chased
GRA
AH
LET'S GO, GUYS!
YEAH! THIS IS A TIME FOR ALL JAPANESE TO BAND TOGETH-ER!!
CHAMPION
JAPAN
KILL THAT GUY!
LET'S DO IT!
AH
A
KILL 'IM!
GRA

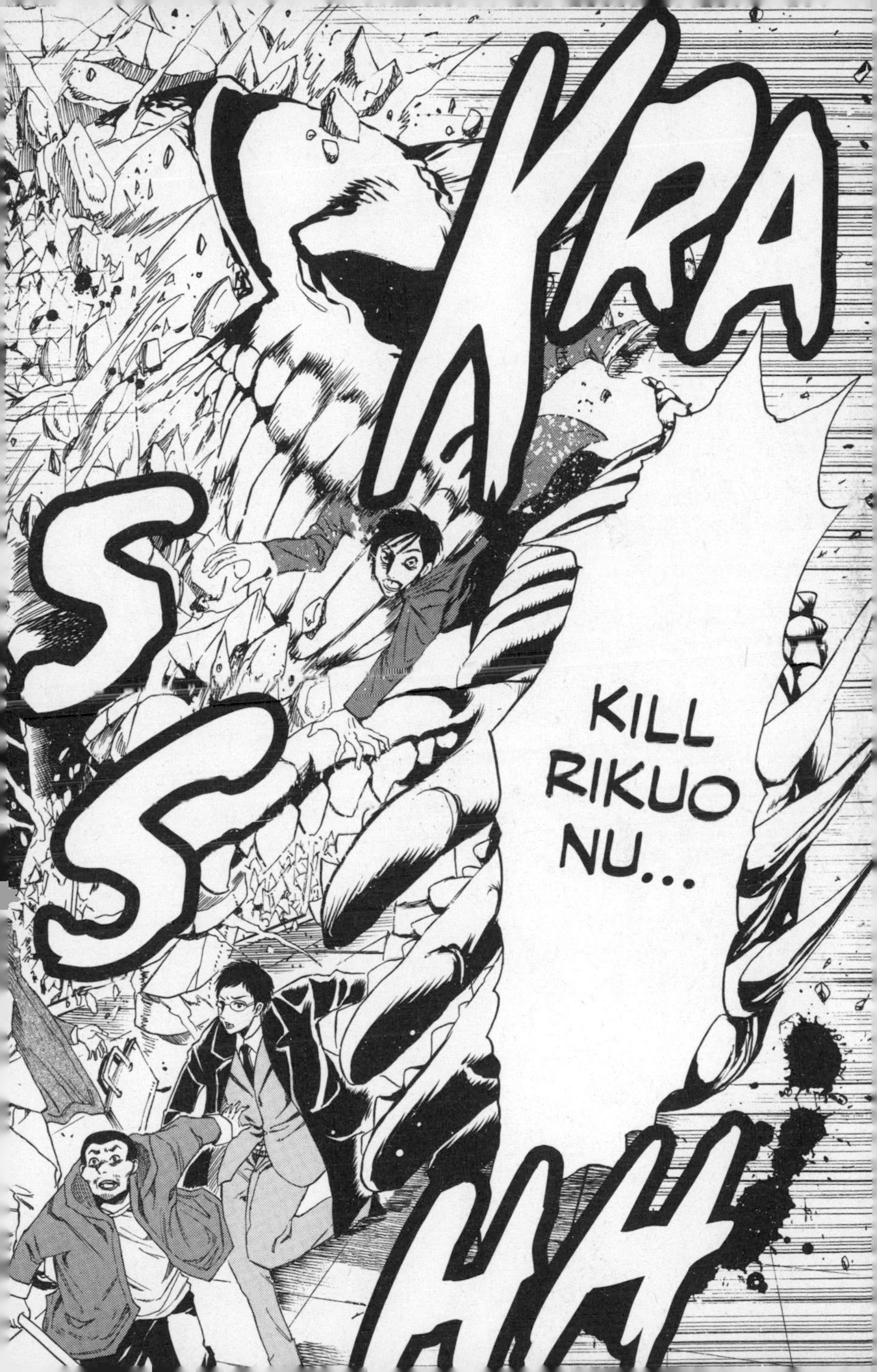
KILL RIKUO NU...

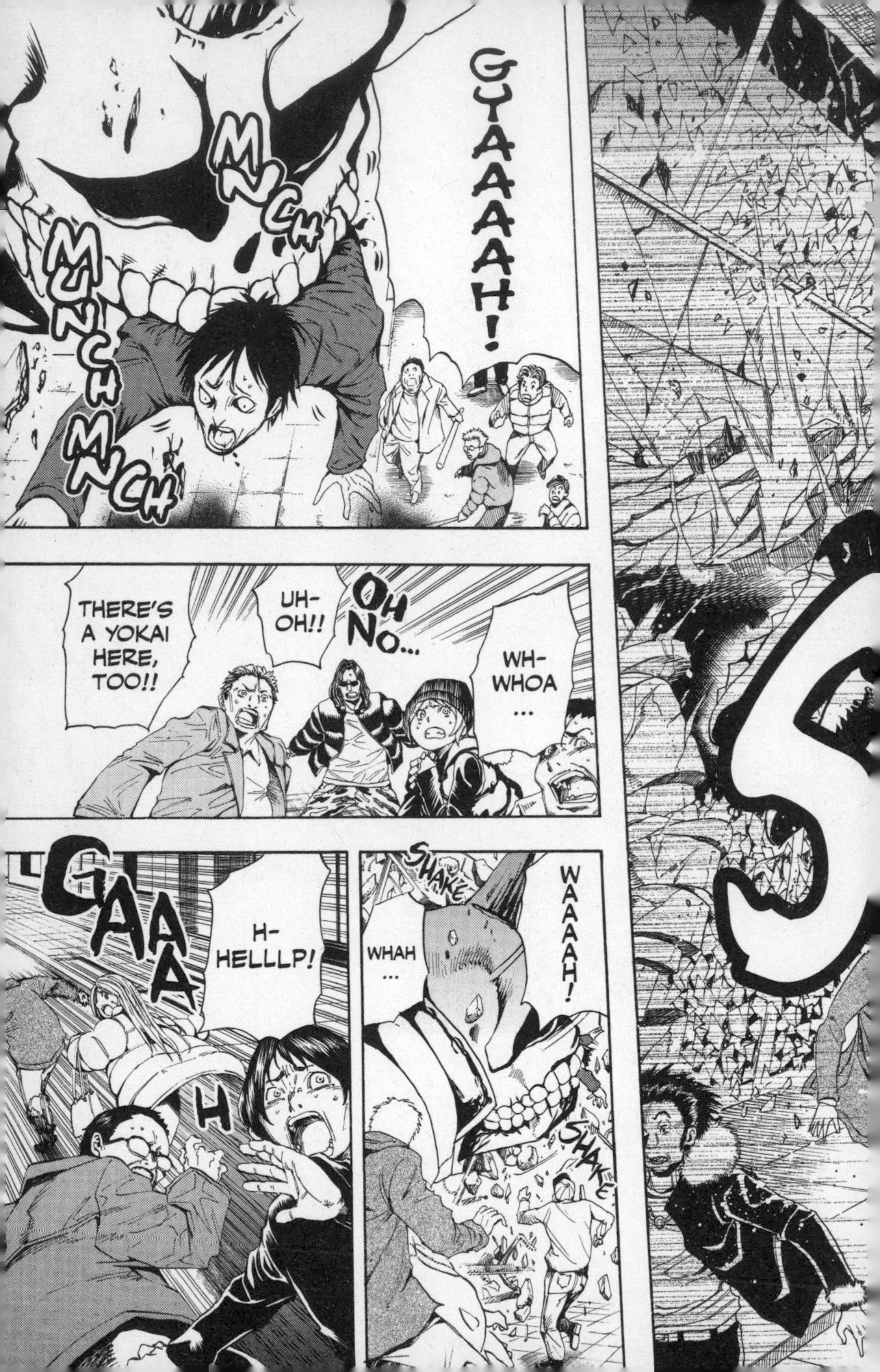
GYAAAAAH!
MUNCH
MUNCH MUNCH
MUNCH
WH-WHOA ...
OH NO...
UH-OH!!
THERE'S A YOKAI HERE, TOO!!
WAAAAAH!
SHAKE
WHAH ...
SHAKE
H-HELLLP!
GAAAH

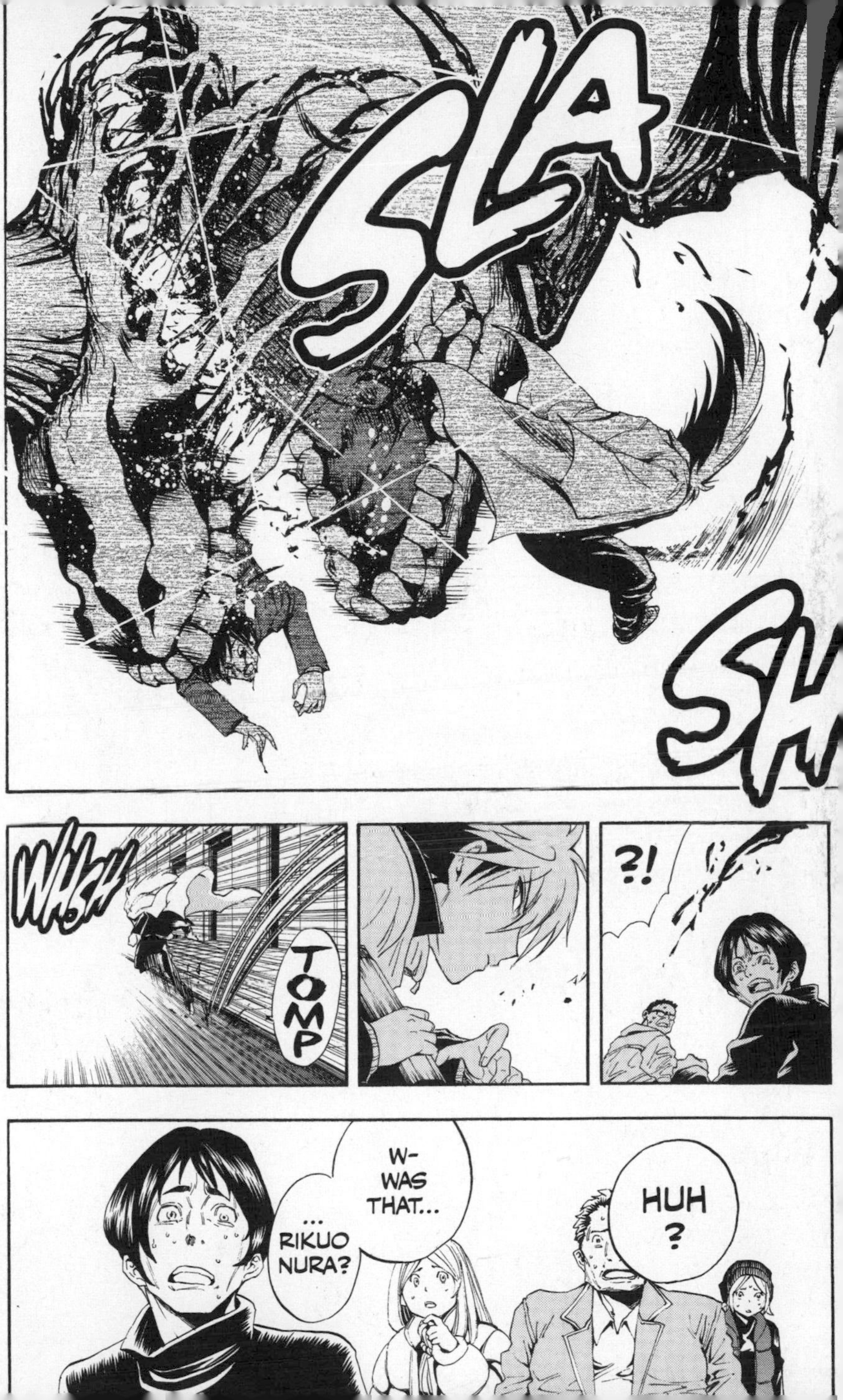
SLA
SH
?!
TOMP
WHOSH
HUH ?
W- WAS THAT...
... RIKUO NURA?

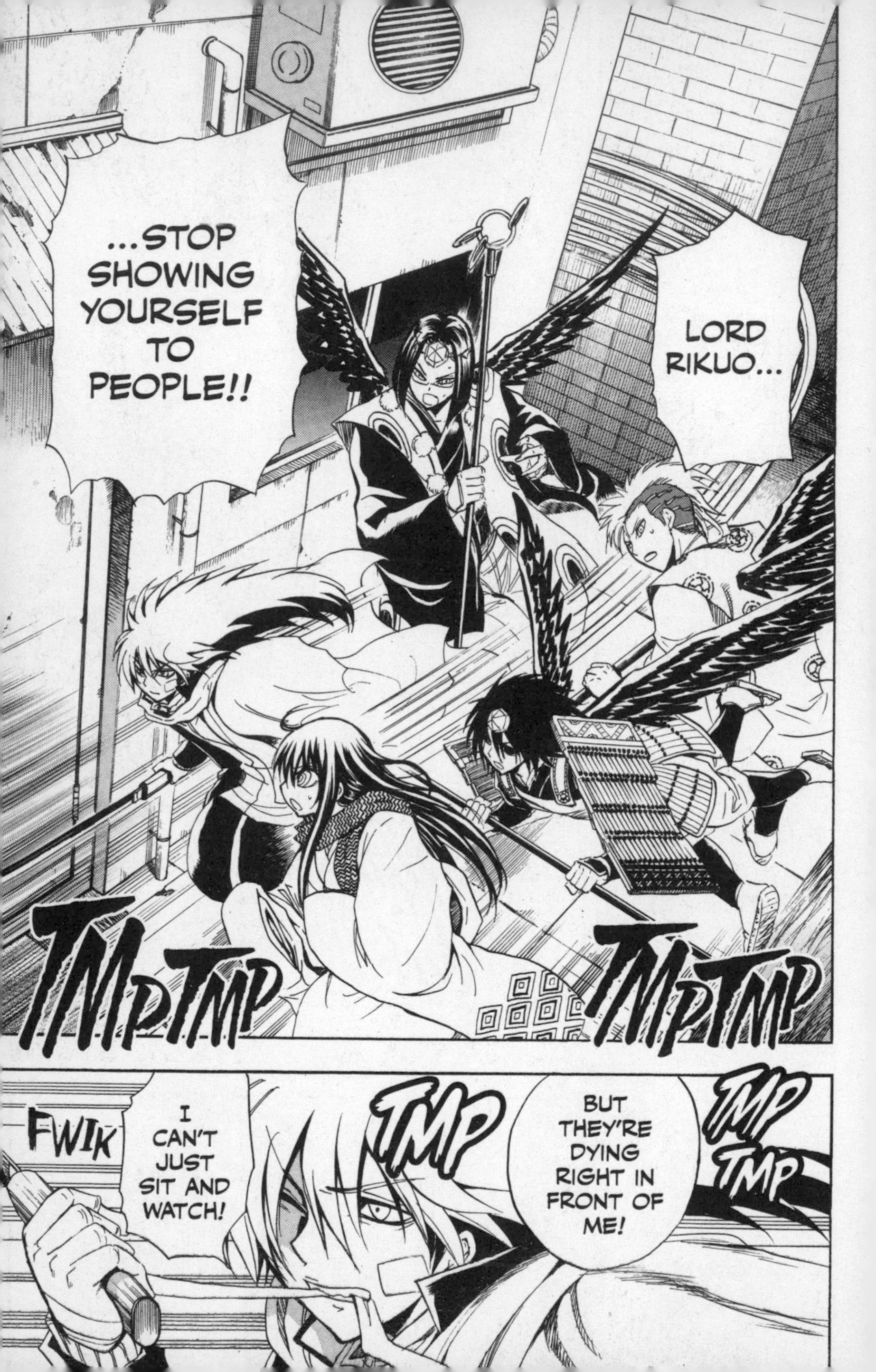
LORD RIKUO...
...STOP SHOWING YOURSELF TO PEOPLE!!
TMP TMP
TMP TMP
TMP TMP
BUT THEY'RE DYING RIGHT IN FRONT OF ME!
TMP
I CAN'T JUST SIT AND WATCH!
FWIK

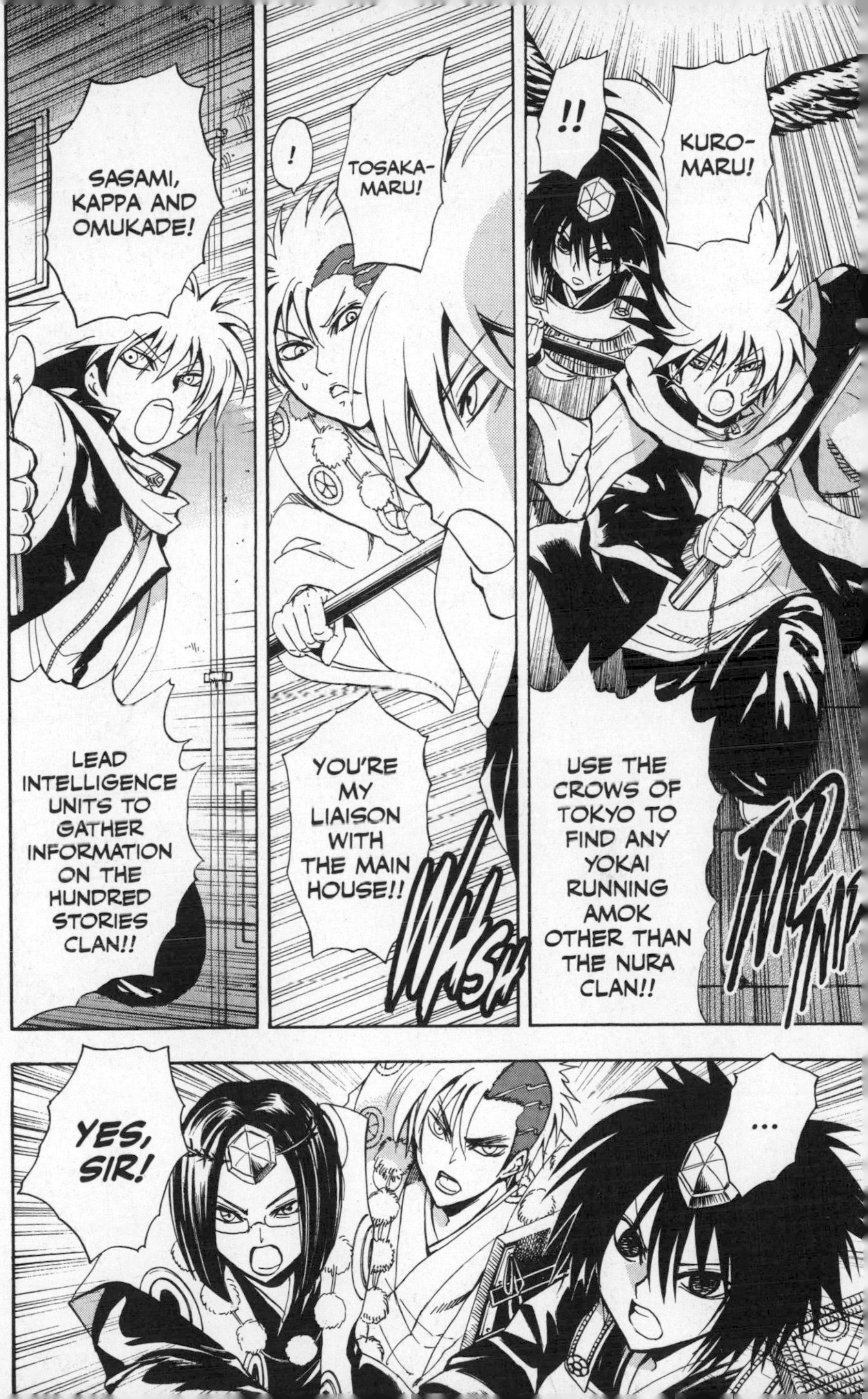
KURO-MARU!
!!
USE THE CROWS OF TOKYO TO FIND ANY YOKAI RUNNING AMOK OTHER THAN THE NURA CLAN!!
TOSAKA-MARU!
!
YOU'RE MY LIAISON WITH THE MAIN HOUSE!!
SASAMI, KAPPA AND OMUKADE!
LEAD INTELLIGENCE UNITS TO GATHER INFORMATION ON THE HUNDRED STORIES CLAN!!
...
YES, SIR!

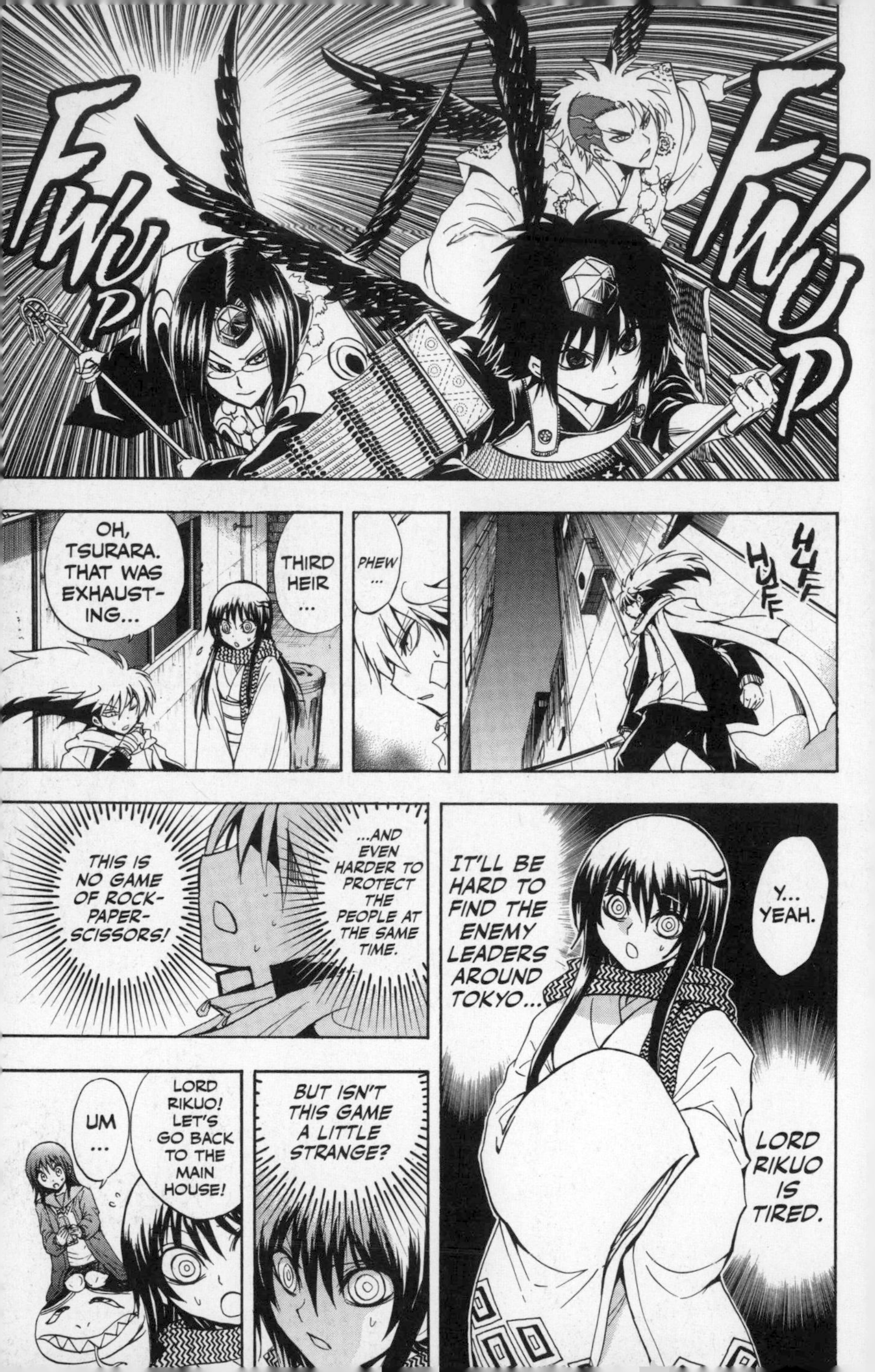
FWUP
FWUP
HUFF HUFF
PHEW ...
THIRD HEIR ...
OH, TSURARA. THAT WAS EXHAUSTING...
Y... YEAH.
IT'LL BE HARD TO FIND THE ENEMY LEADERS AROUND TOKYO...
LORD RIKUO IS TIRED.
...AND EVEN HARDER TO PROTECT THE PEOPLE AT THE SAME TIME.
THIS IS NO GAME OF ROCK-PAPER-SCISSORS!
BUT ISN'T THIS GAME A LITTLE STRANGE?
LORD RIKUO! LET'S GO BACK TO THE MAIN HOUSE!
UM ...

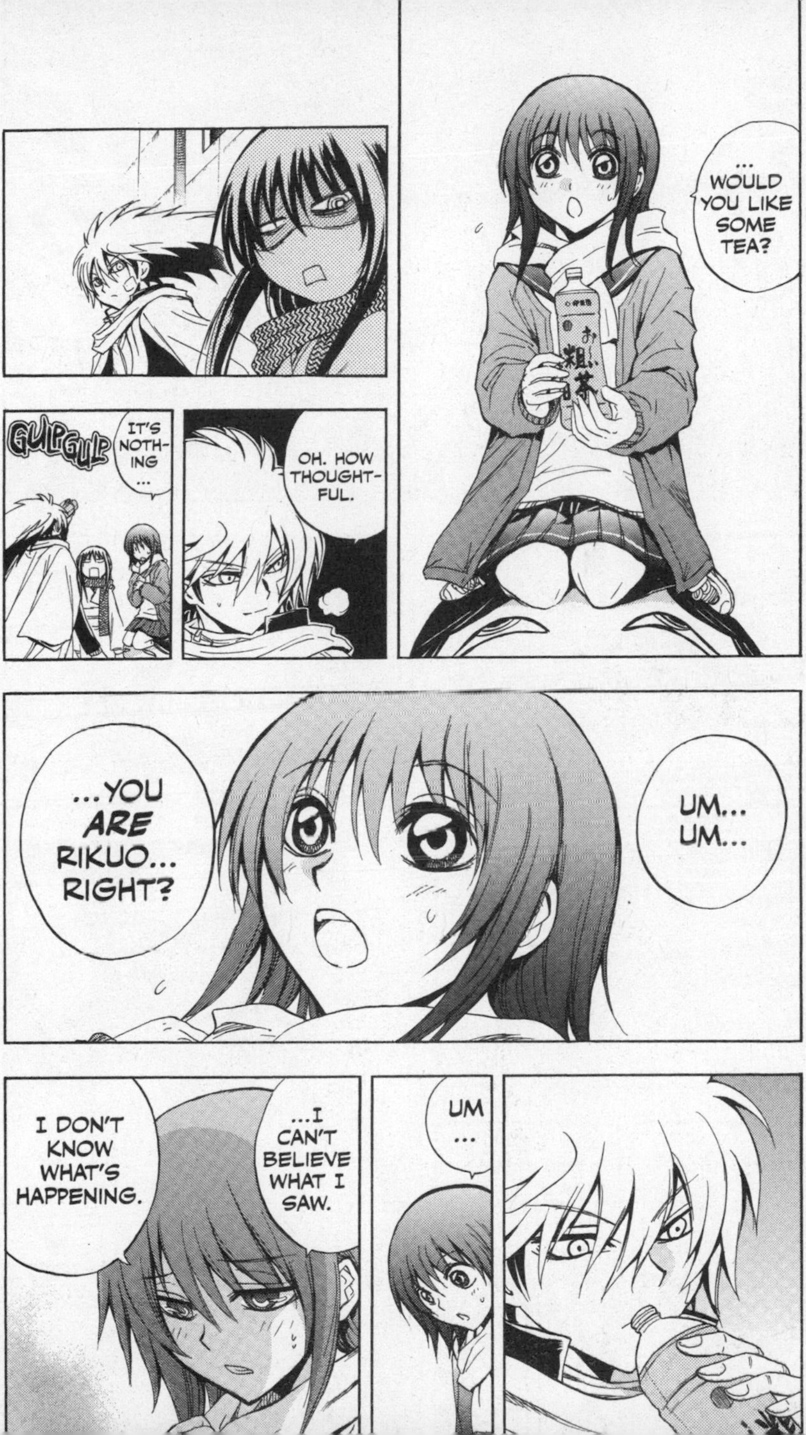

...WOULD YOU LIKE SOME TEA?
OH. HOW THOUGHTFUL.
IT'S NOTHING ...
GULPGULP
UM... UM...
...YOU ARE RIKUO... RIGHT?
UM ...
...I CAN'T BELIEVE WHAT I SAW.
I DON'T KNOW WHAT'S HAPPENING.

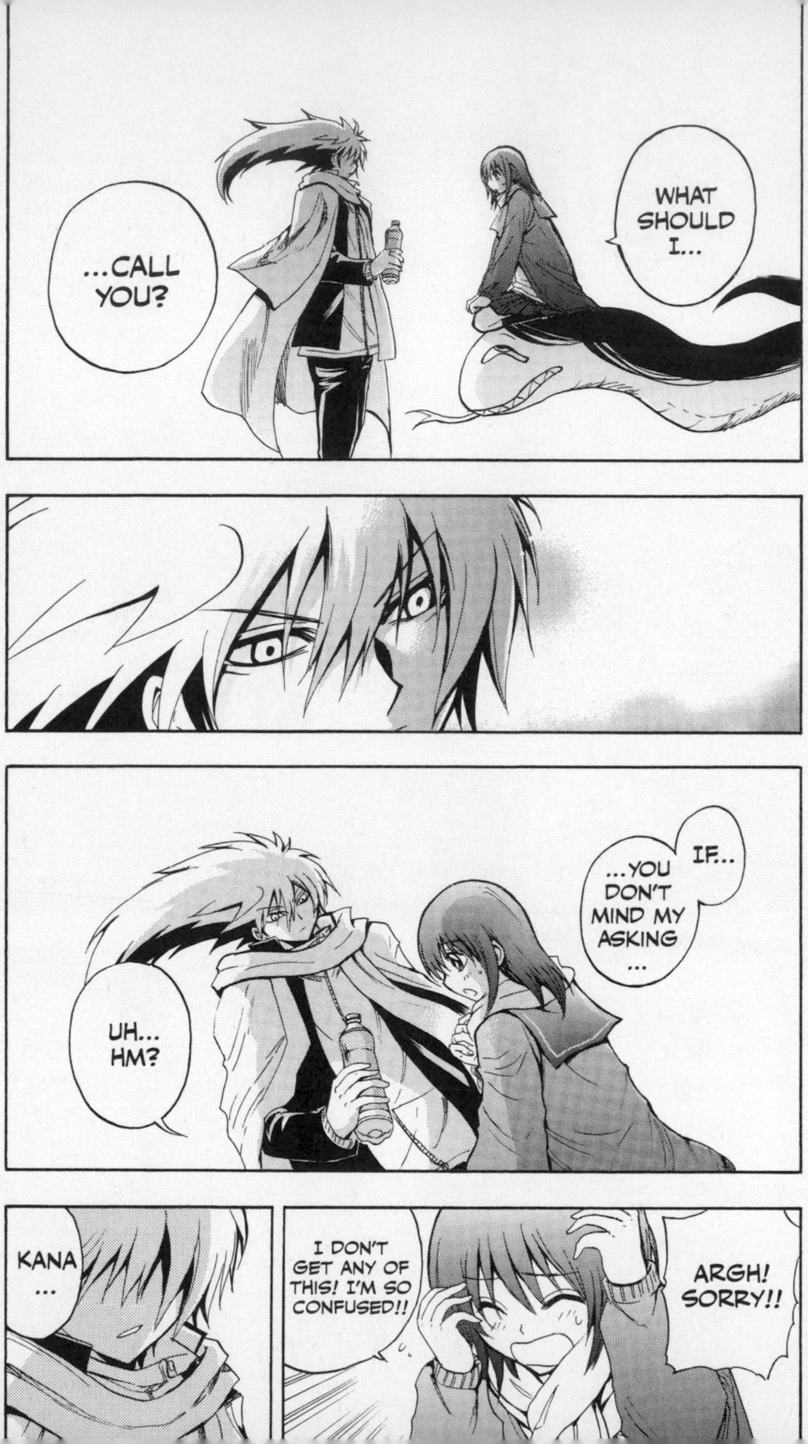
WHAT SHOULD I...
...CALL YOU?
IF...
...YOU DON'T MIND MY ASKING ...
UH... HM?
ARGH! SORRY!!
I DON'T GET ANY OF THIS! I'M SO CONFUSED!!
KANA ...

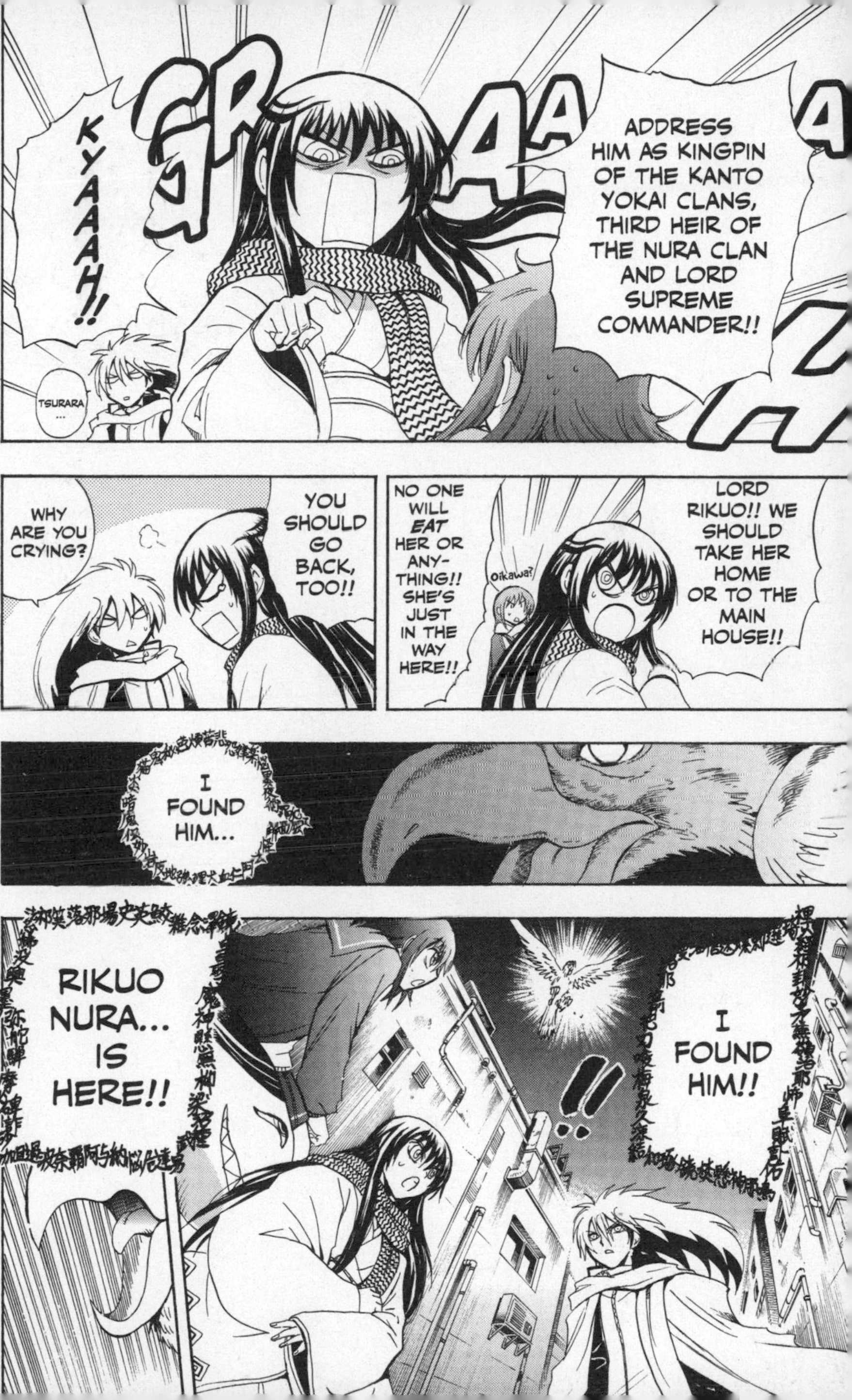
ADDRESS HIM AS KINGPIN OF THE KANTO YOKAI CLANS, THIRD HEIR OF THE NURA CLAN AND LORD SUPREME COMMANDER!!
GRAAAH
KYAAAAH!!
TSURARA...
LORD RIKUO!! WE SHOULD TAKE HER HOME OR TO THE MAIN HOUSE!!
Oikawa?
NO ONE WILL *EAT* HER OR ANYTHING!! SHE'S JUST IN THE WAY HERE!!
YOU SHOULD GO BACK, TOO!!
WHY ARE YOU CRYING?
I FOUND HIM...
I FOUND HIM!!
!!
RIKUO NURA... IS HERE!!

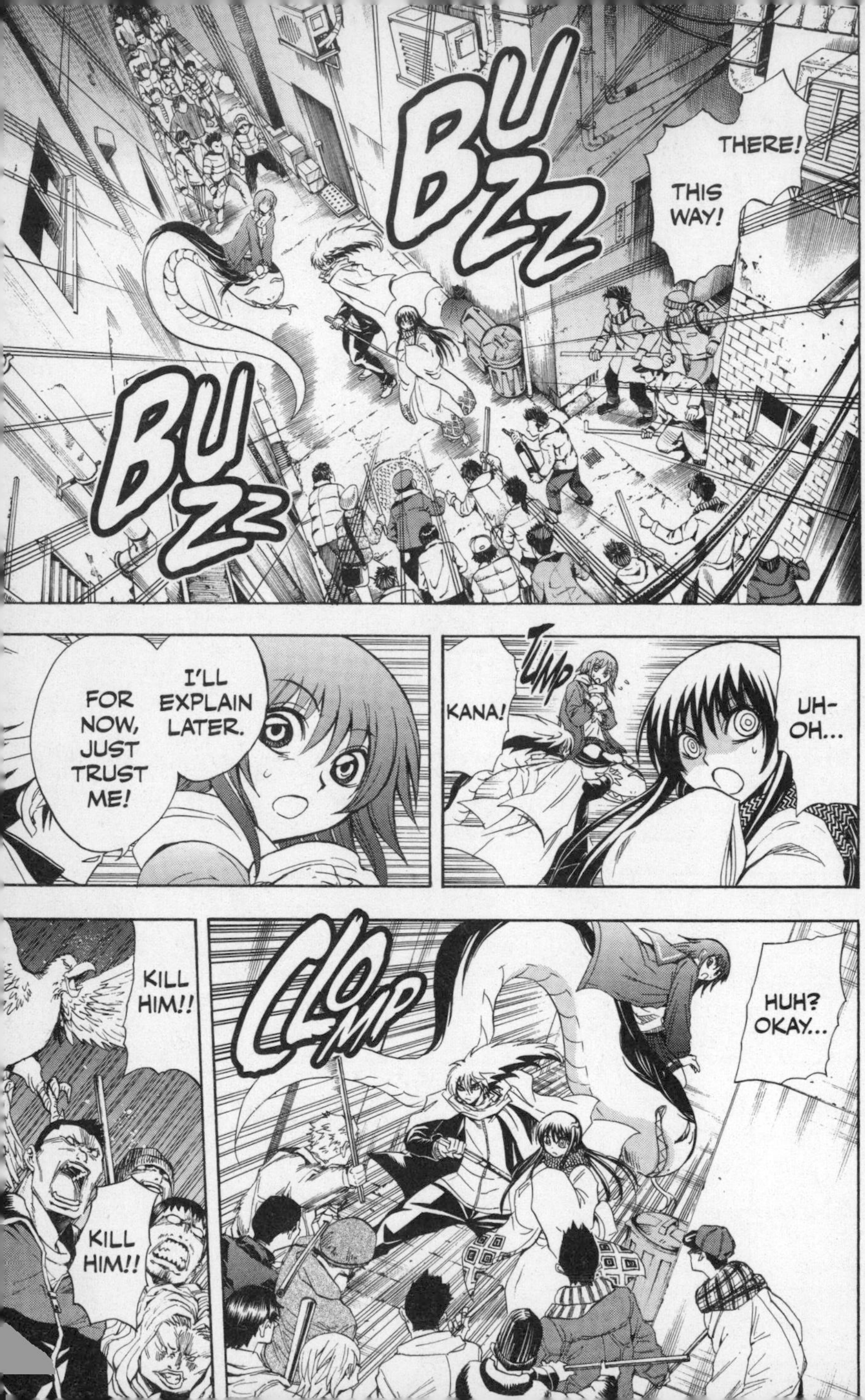
BUZZ
THERE!
THIS WAY!
BUZZ
UH-OH...
TUMP
KANA!
I'LL EXPLAIN LATER.
FOR NOW, JUST TRUST ME!
HUH? OKAY...
CLOMP
KILL HIM!!
KILL HIM!!

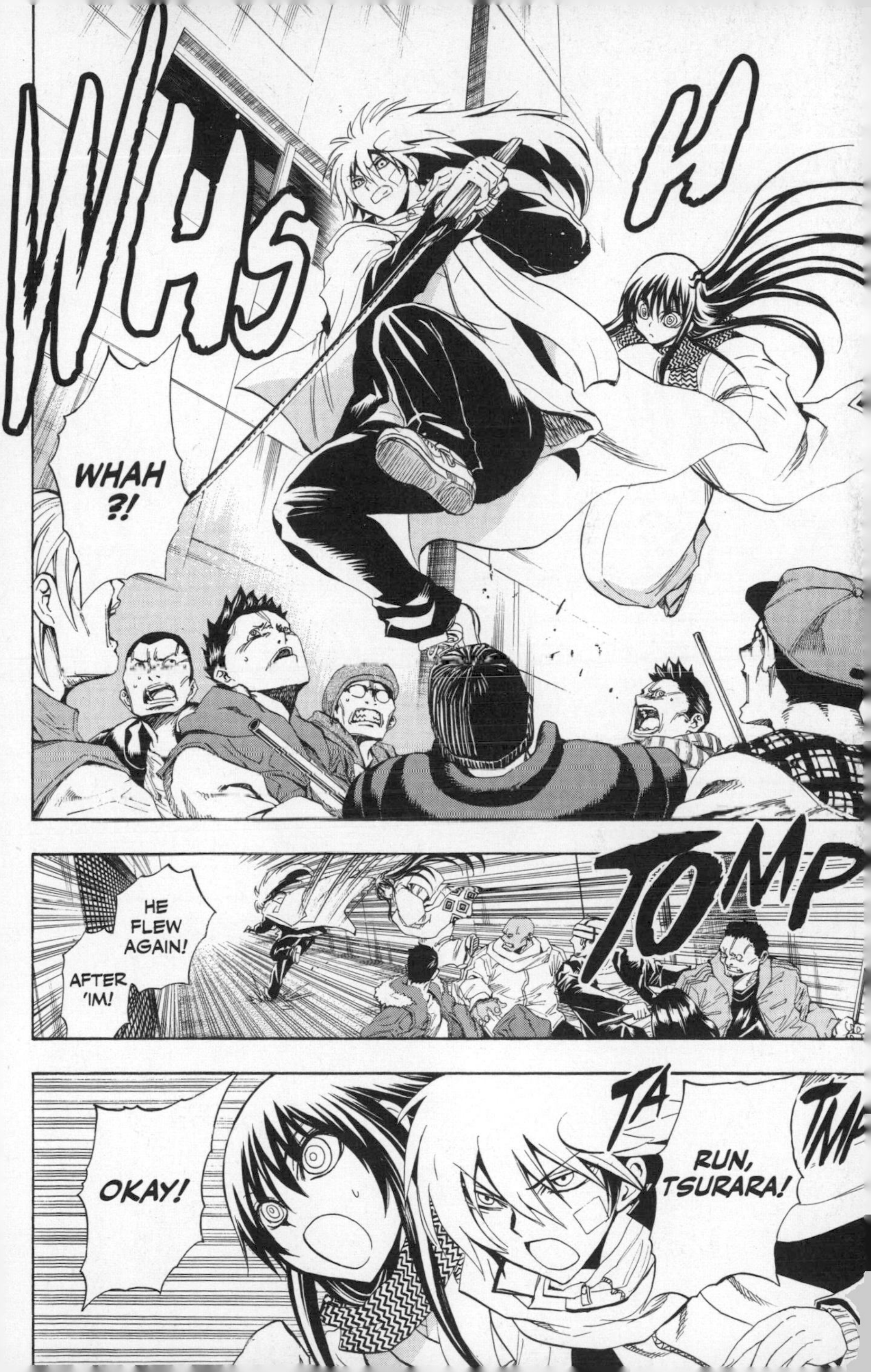
WHASH
WHAH ?!
TOMP
HE FLEW AGAIN!
AFTER 'IM!
TA
TMP
RUN, TSURARA!
OKAY!

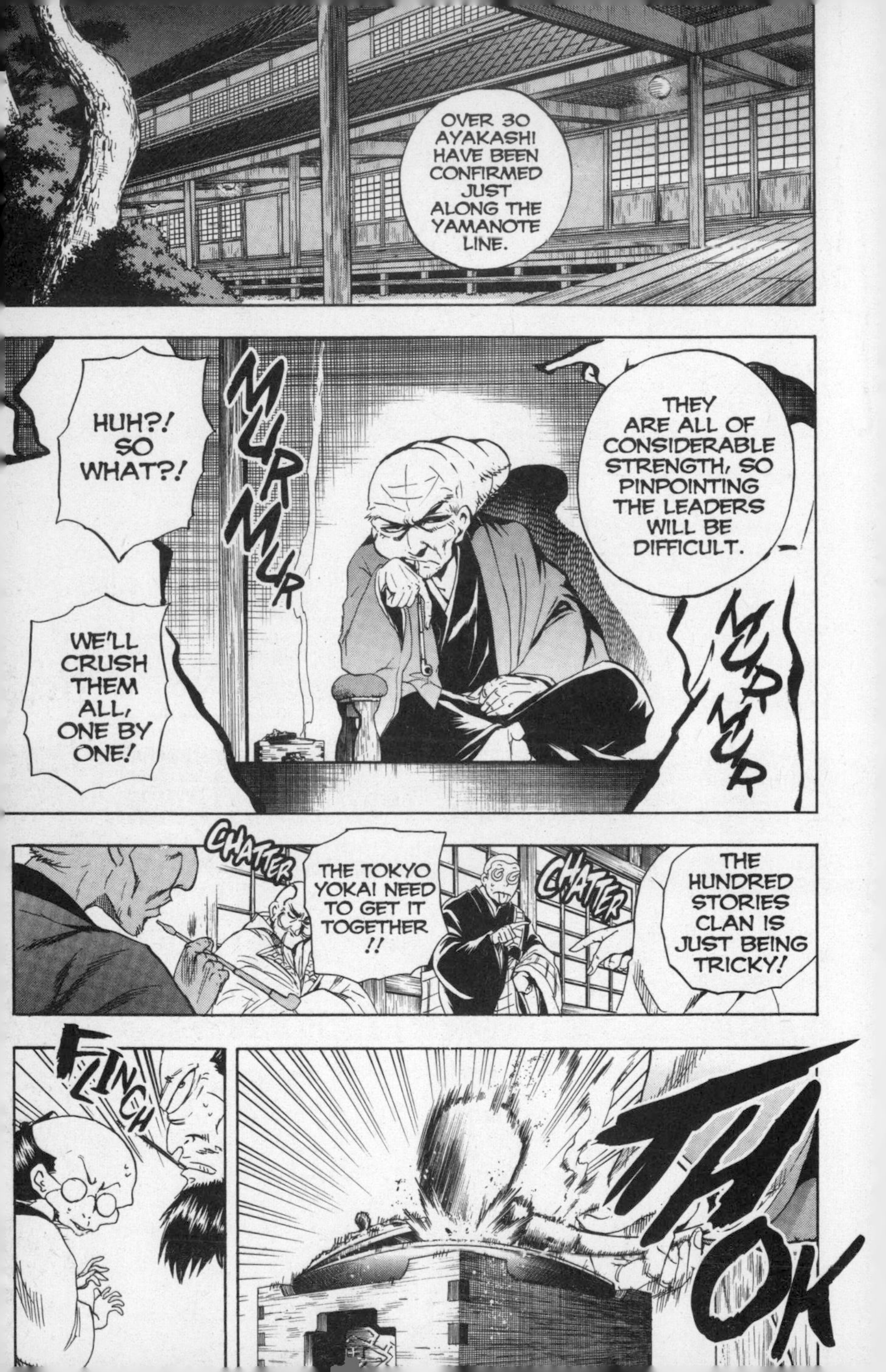
OVER 30 AYAKASHI HAVE BEEN CONFIRMED JUST ALONG THE YAMANOTE LINE.
THEY ARE ALL OF CONSIDERABLE STRENGTH, SO PINPOINTING THE LEADERS WILL BE DIFFICULT.
MURMUR
HUH?! SO WHAT?!
MURMUR
WE'LL CRUSH THEM ALL, ONE BY ONE!
THE HUNDRED STORIES CLAN IS JUST BEING TRICKY!
CHATTER
THE TOKYO YOKAI NEED TO GET IT TOGETHER!!
CHATTER
THOK
FLINCH

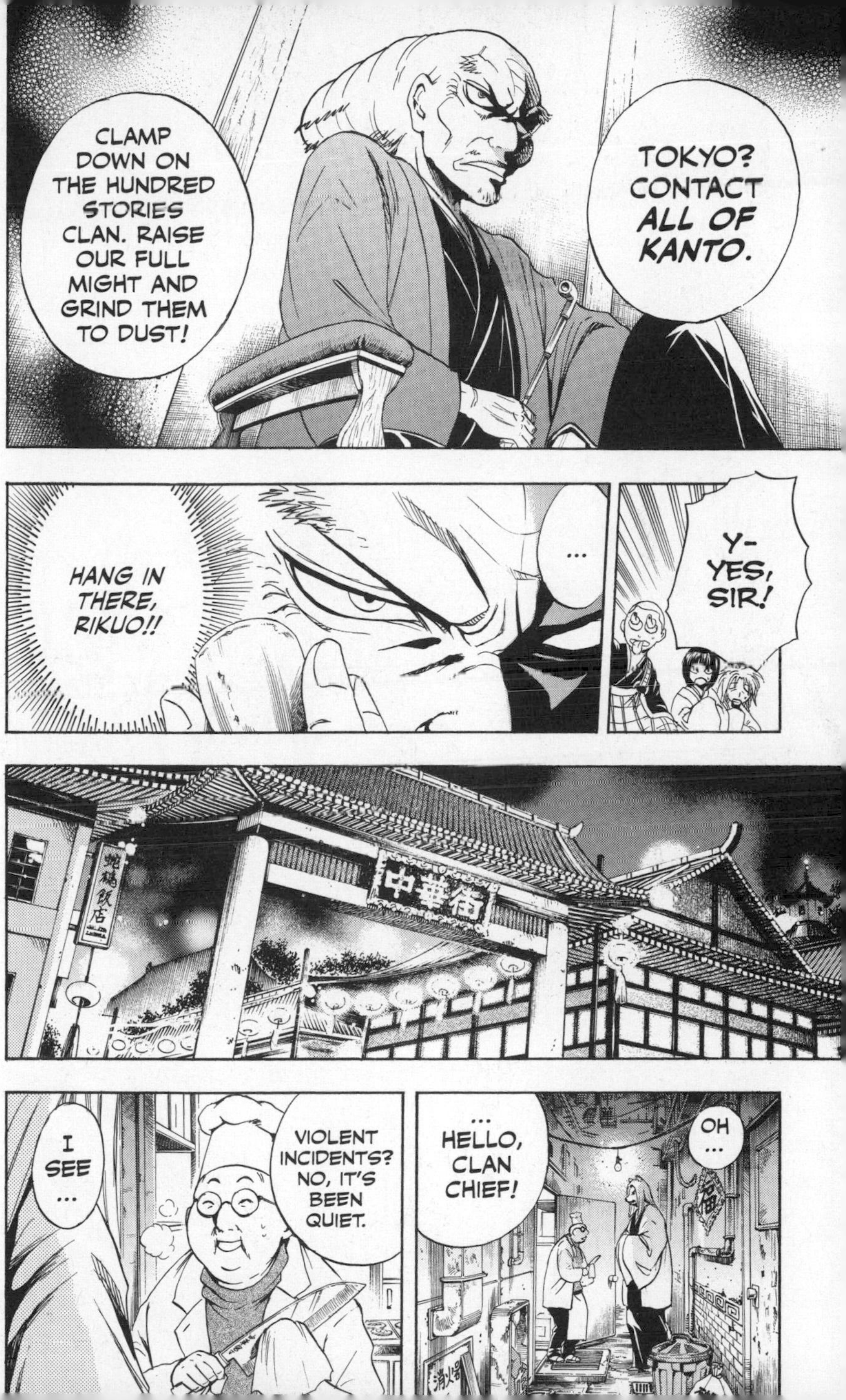
TOKYO? CONTACT ALL OF KANTO.
CLAMP DOWN ON THE HUNDRED STORIES CLAN. RAISE OUR FULL MIGHT AND GRIND THEM TO DUST!
Y-YES, SIR!
...
HANG IN THERE, RIKUO!!
中華街
OH ...
... HELLO, CLAN CHIEF!
VIOLENT INCIDENTS? NO, IT'S BEEN QUIET.
I SEE ...

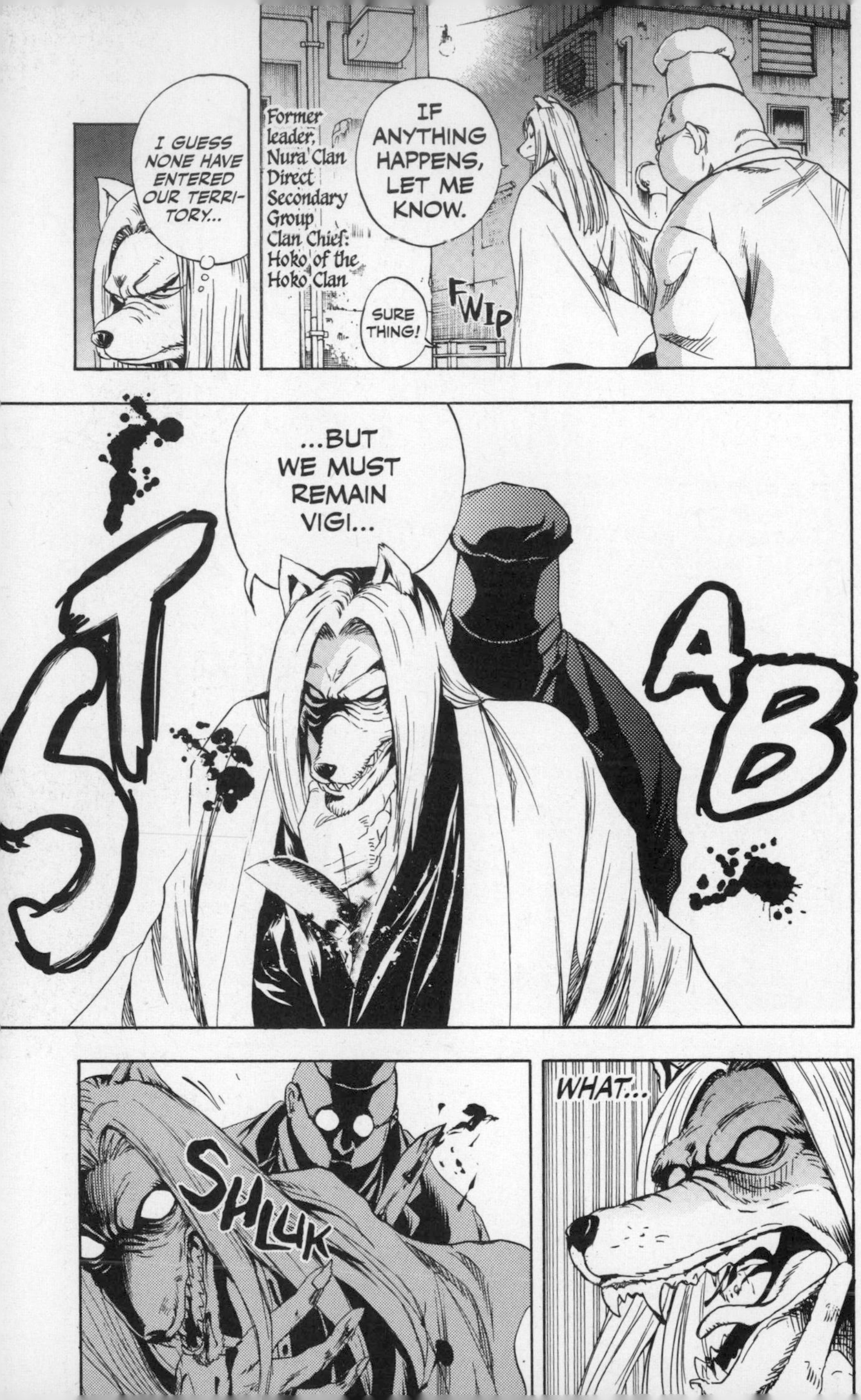
IF ANYTHING HAPPENS, LET ME KNOW.
Former leader, Nura Clan Direct Secondary Group Clan Chief: Hoko of the Hoko Clan
FWIP
SURE THING!
I GUESS NONE HAVE ENTERED OUR TERRITORY...
...BUT WE MUST REMAIN VIGI...
STAB
WHAT...
SHLUK

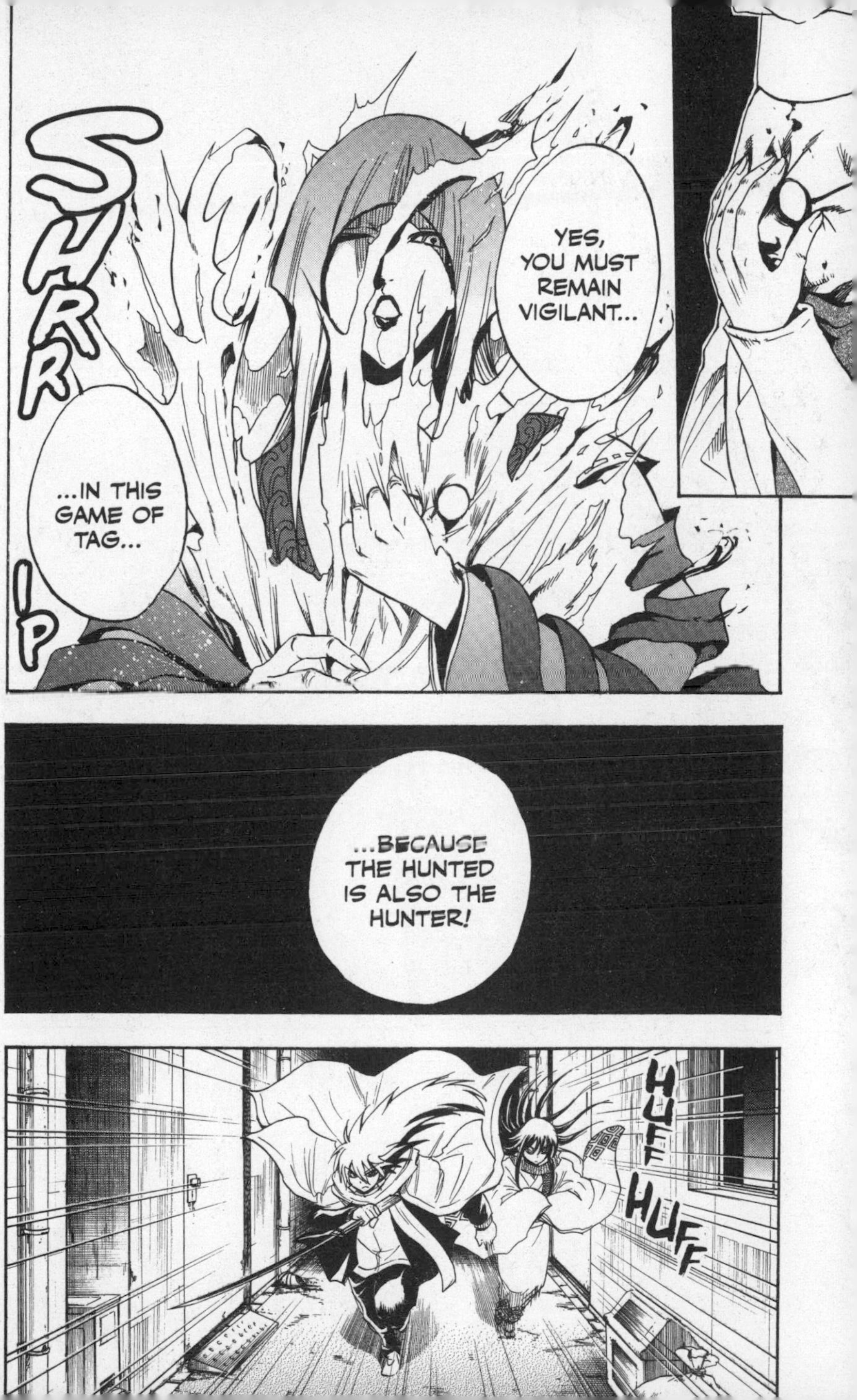
YES, YOU MUST REMAIN VIGILANT...
...IN THIS GAME OF TAG...
SHRRIP
...BECAUSE THE HUNTED IS ALSO THE HUNTER!
HUFF HUFF

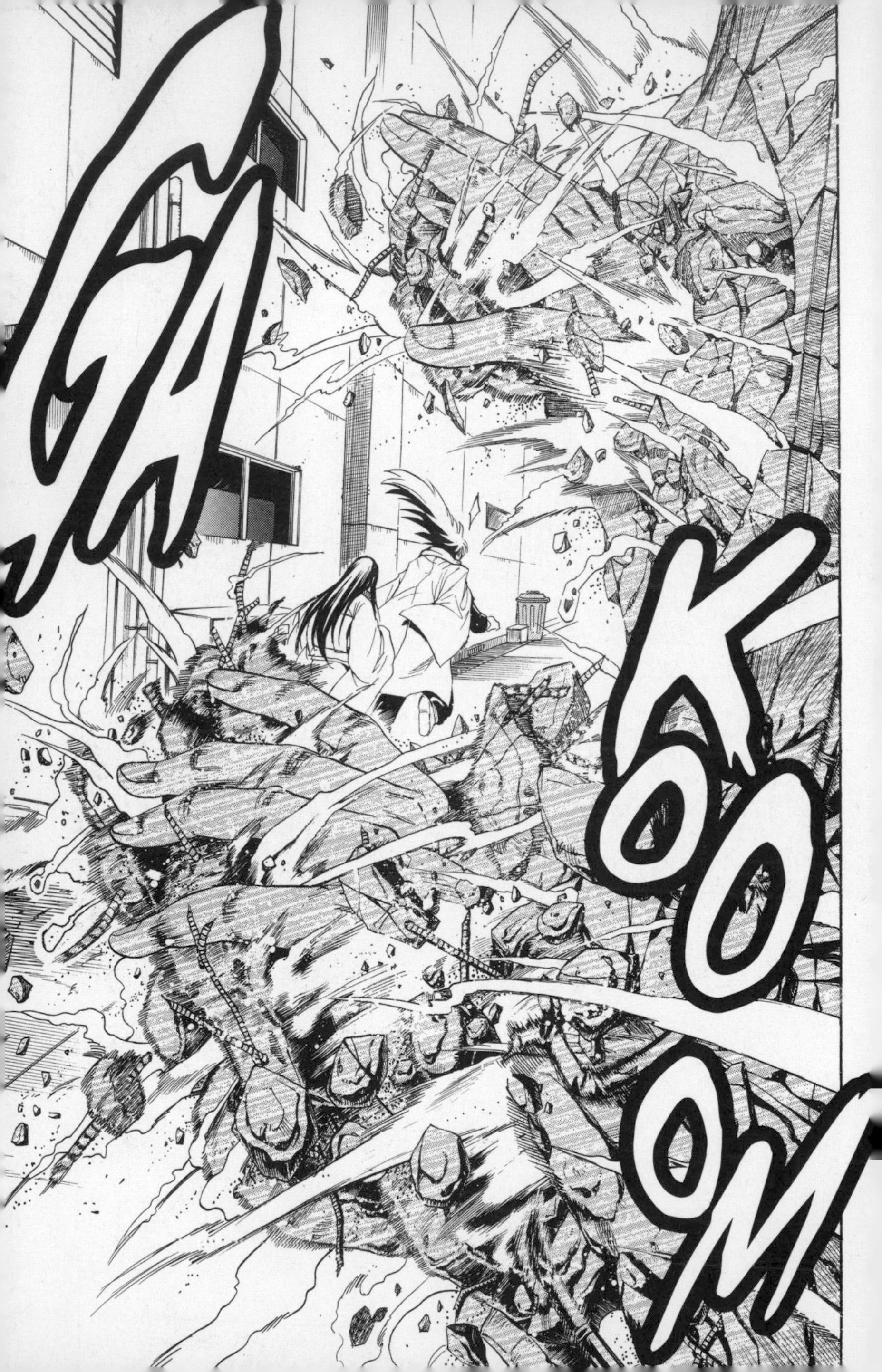
GA
KOOOM

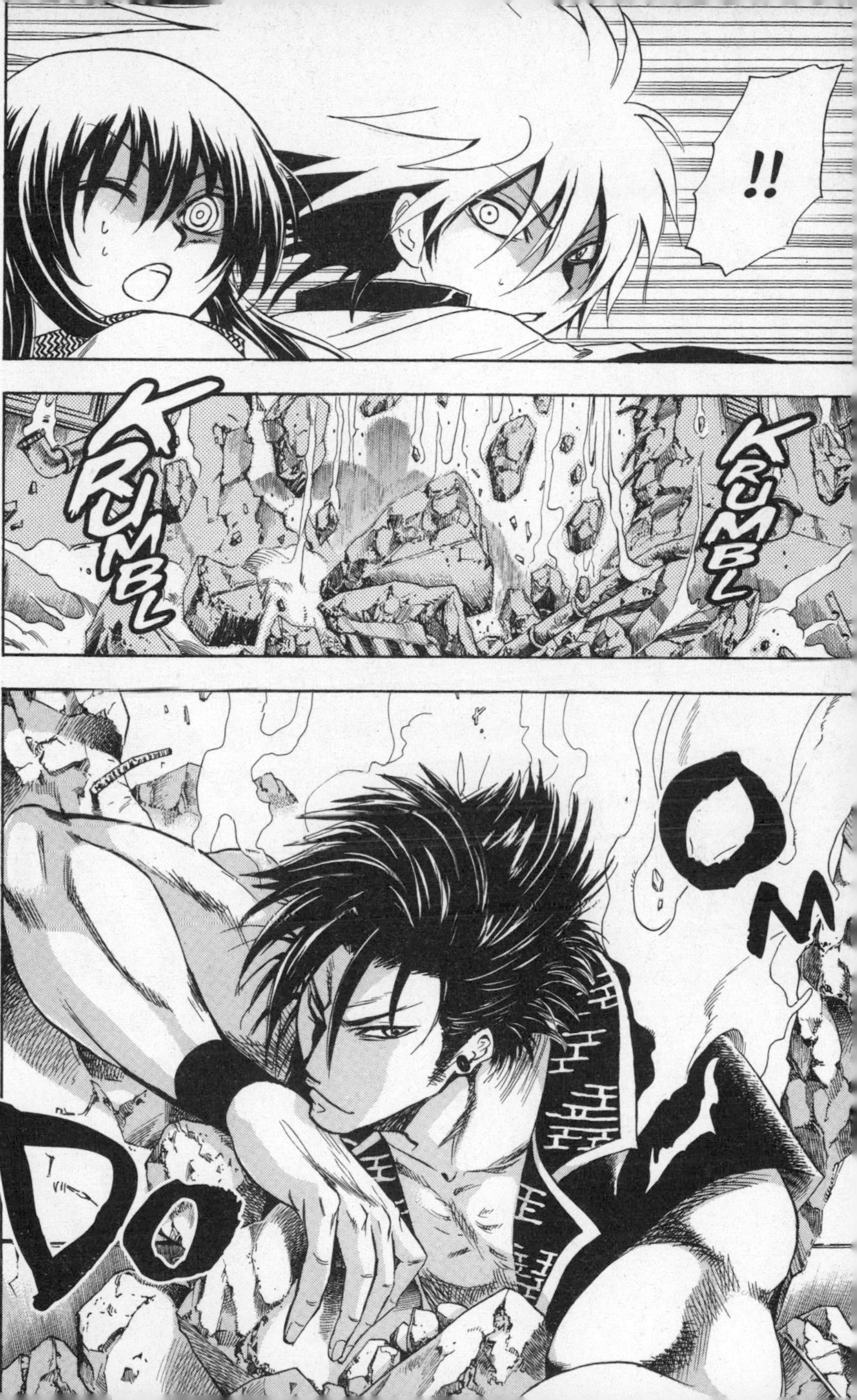
!!
KRUMBL
KRUMBL
DOOM

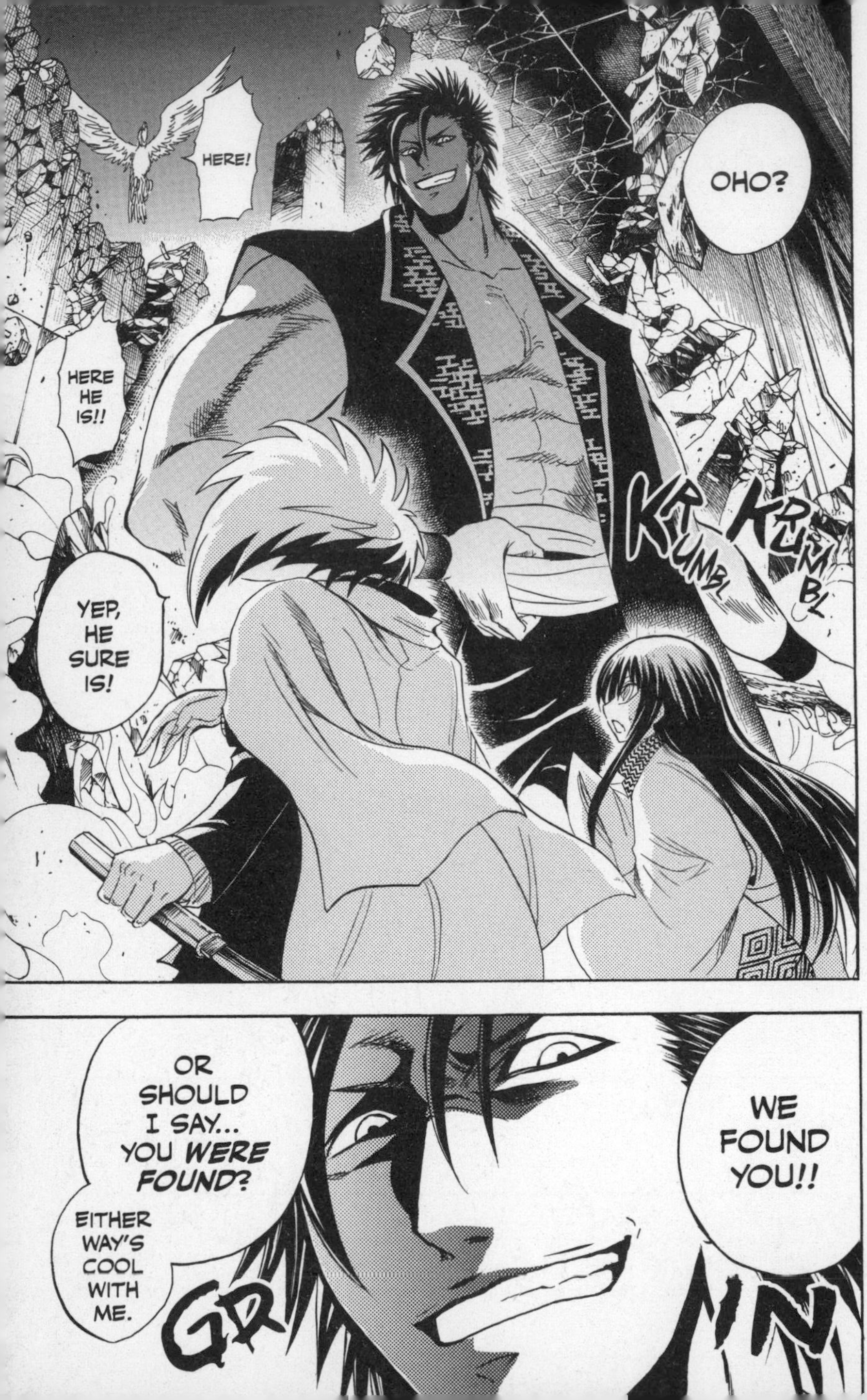
OHO?
HERE!
HERE HE IS!!
KRUMBL KRUMBL
YEP, HE SURE IS!
WE FOUND YOU!!
OR SHOULD I SAY... YOU WERE FOUND?
EITHER WAY'S COOL WITH ME.
GRIN

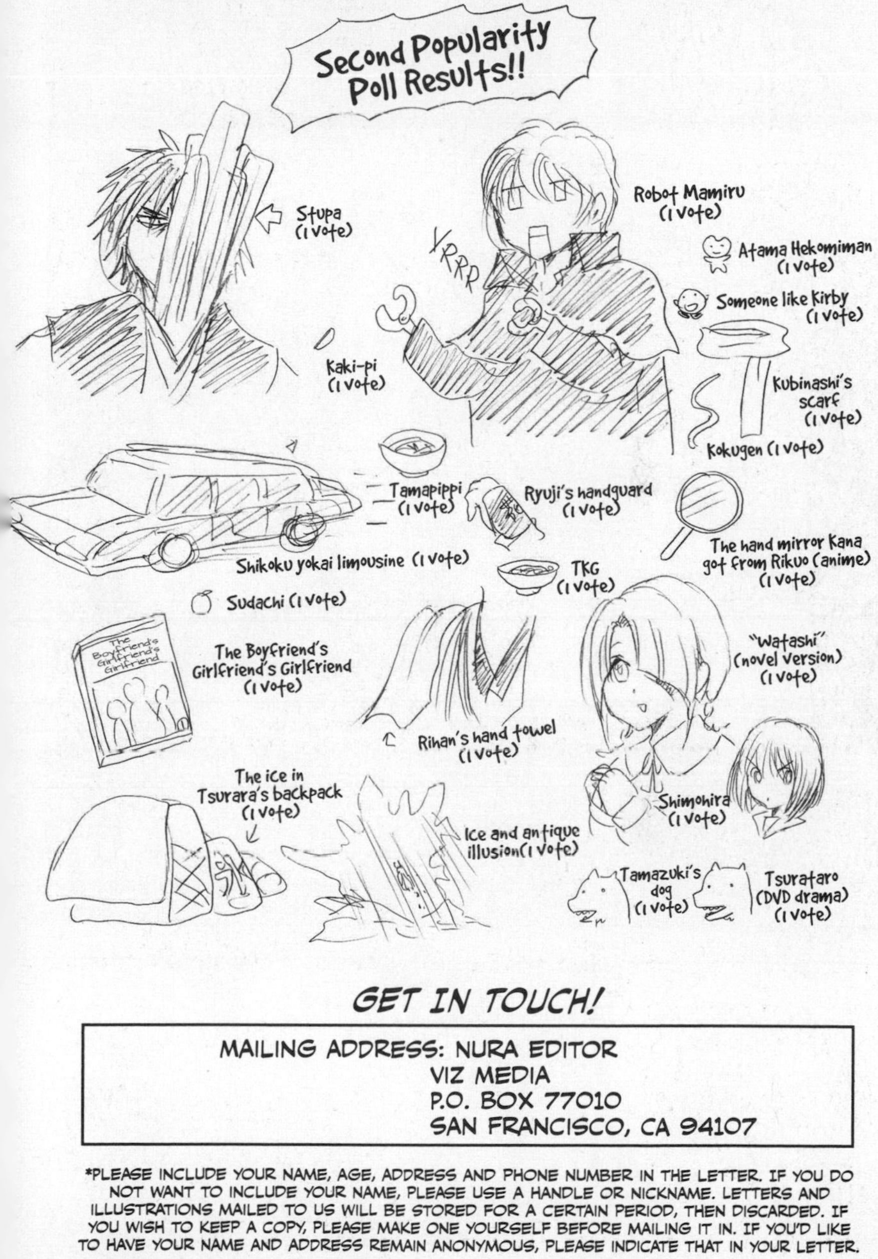

Second Popularity Poll Results!!
Stupa (1 vote)
Robot Mamiru (1 vote)
VRRR
Atama Hekomiman (1 vote)
Someone like Kirby (1 vote)
Kaki-pi (1 vote)
Kubinashi's scarf (1 vote)
Kokugen (1 vote)
Tamapippi (1 vote)
Ryuji's handguard (1 vote)
Shikoku yokai limousine (1 vote)
The hand mirror Kana got from Rikuo (anime) (1 vote)
TKG (1 vote)
Sudachi (1 vote)
The Boyfriend's Girlfriend's Girlfriend
The Boyfriend's Girlfriend's Girlfriend (1 vote)
"Watashi" (novel version) (1 vote)
Rihan's hand towel (1 vote)
The ice in Tsurara's backpack (1 vote)
Shimohira (1 vote)
Ice and antique illusion (1 vote)
Tamazuki's dog (1 vote)
Tsurataro (DVD drama) (1 vote)

GET IN TOUCH!

MAILING ADDRESS: NURA EDITOR
VIZ MEDIA
P.O. BOX 77010
SAN FRANCISCO, CA 94107

*PLEASE INCLUDE YOUR NAME, AGE, ADDRESS AND PHONE NUMBER IN THE LETTER. IF YOU DO NOT WANT TO INCLUDE YOUR NAME, PLEASE USE A HANDLE OR NICKNAME. LETTERS AND ILLUSTRATIONS MAILED TO US WILL BE STORED FOR A CERTAIN PERIOD, THEN DISCARDED. IF YOU WISH TO KEEP A COPY, PLEASE MAKE ONE YOURSELF BEFORE MAILING IT IN. IF YOU'D LIKE TO HAVE YOUR NAME AND ADDRESS REMAIN ANONYMOUS, PLEASE INDICATE THAT IN YOUR LETTER.

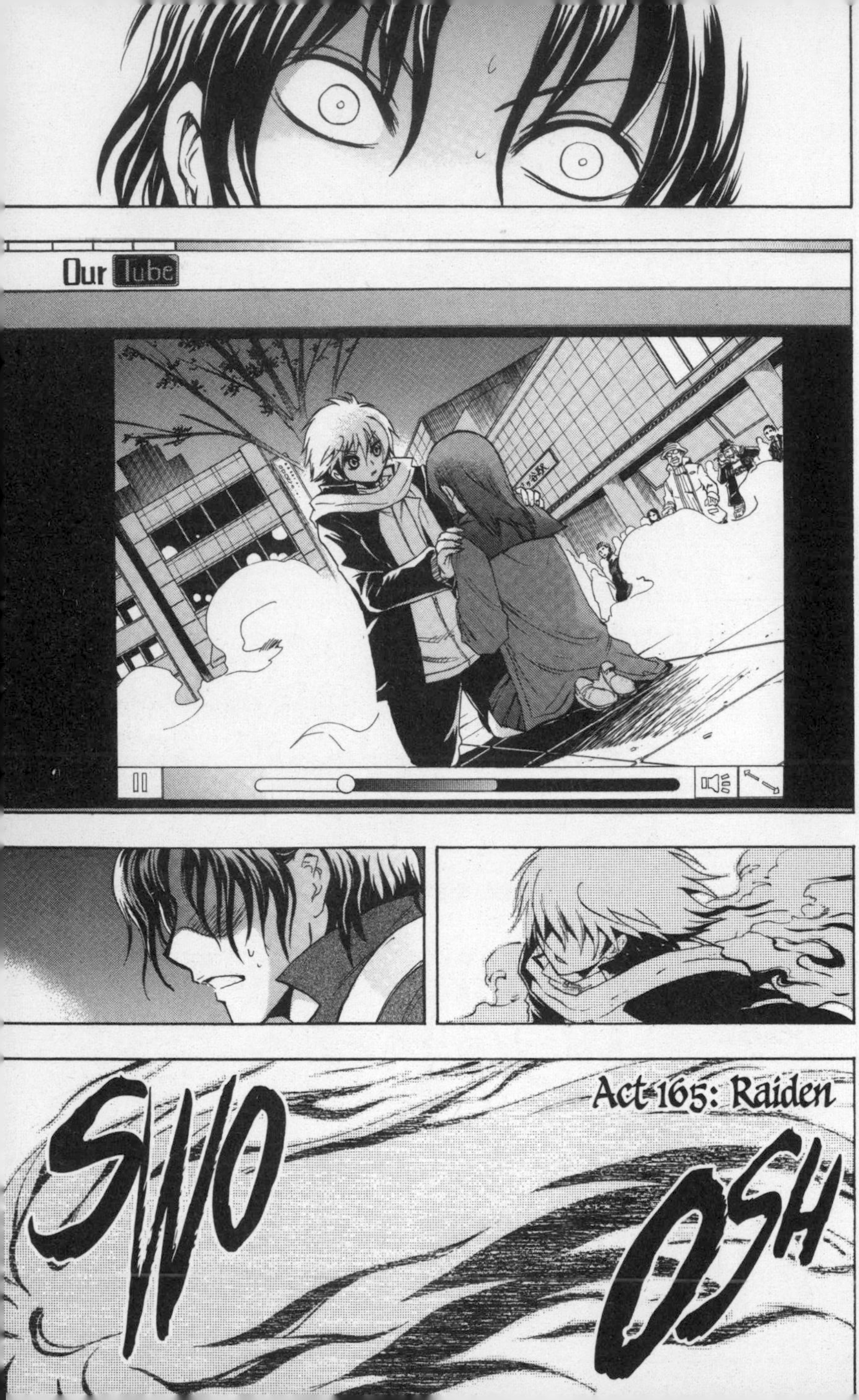
Our Tube
Act 165: Raiden
SWOOSH

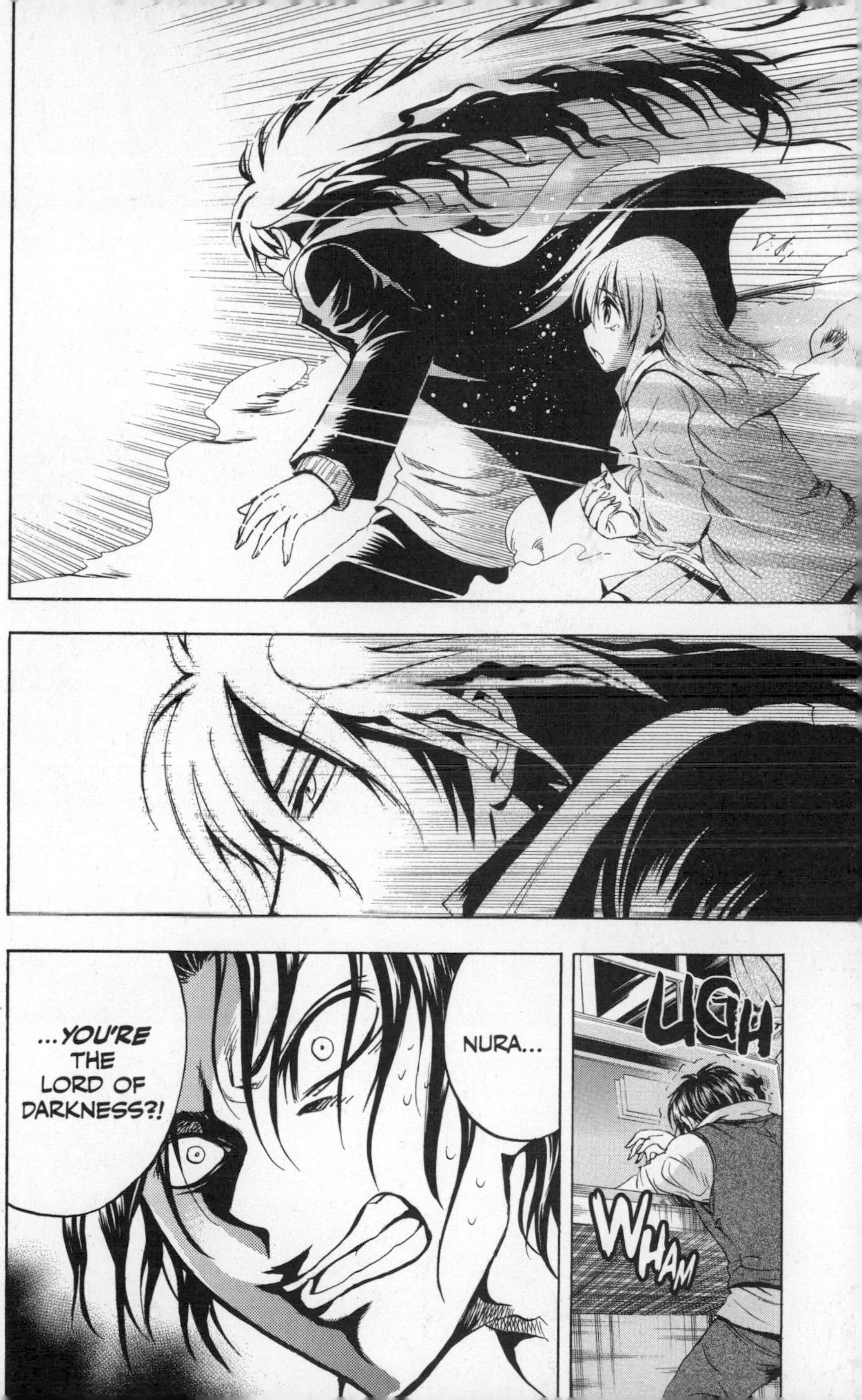
UGH
WHAM
NURA...
...YOU'RE THE LORD OF DARKNESS?!

Act 165: Raiden

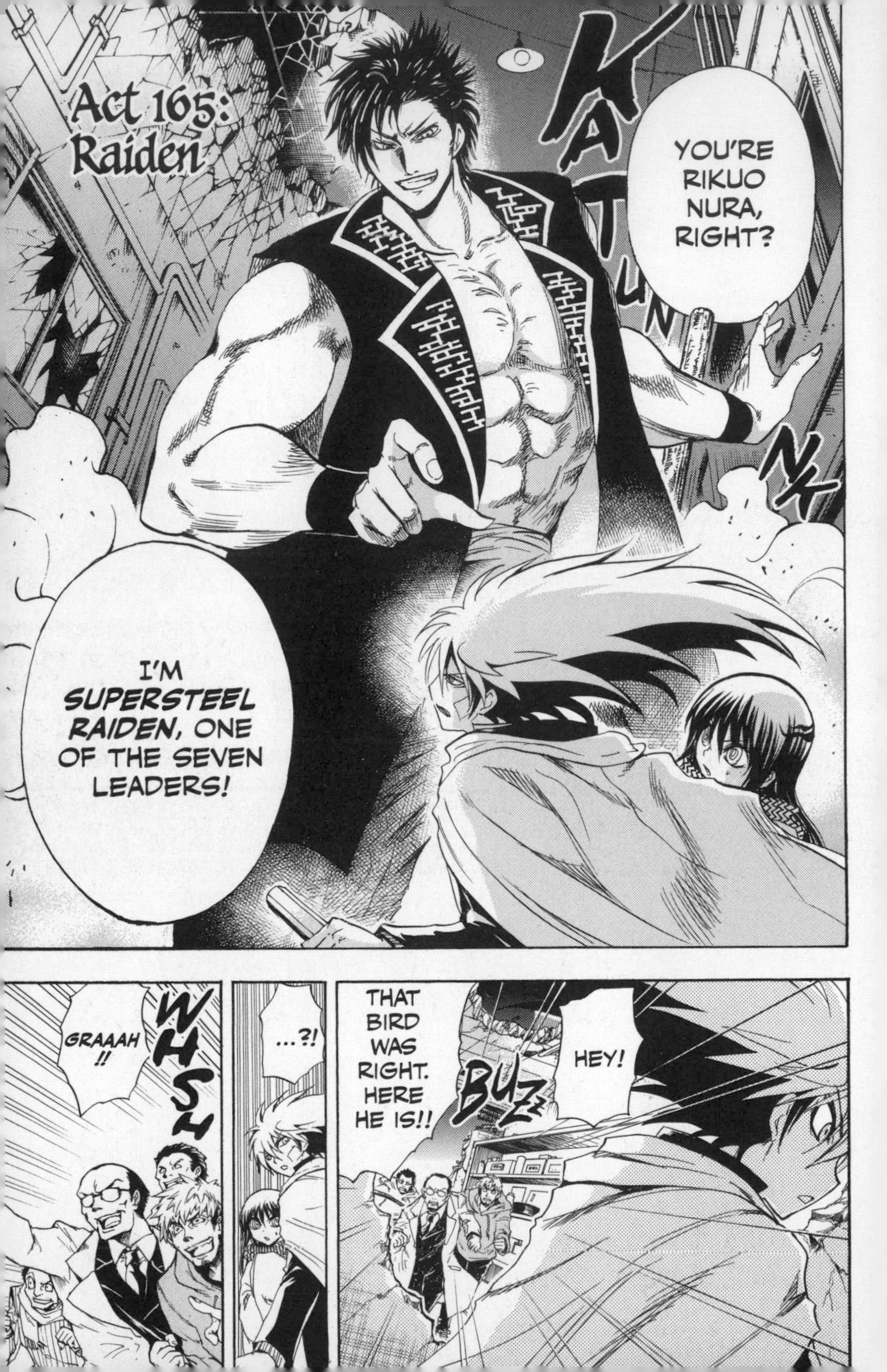
KATUNNK
YOU'RE RIKUO NURA, RIGHT?
I'M SUPERSTEEL RAIDEN, ONE OF THE SEVEN LEADERS!
HEY!
BUZZ
THAT BIRD WAS RIGHT. HERE HE IS!!
...?!
WHSH
GRAAAH!!

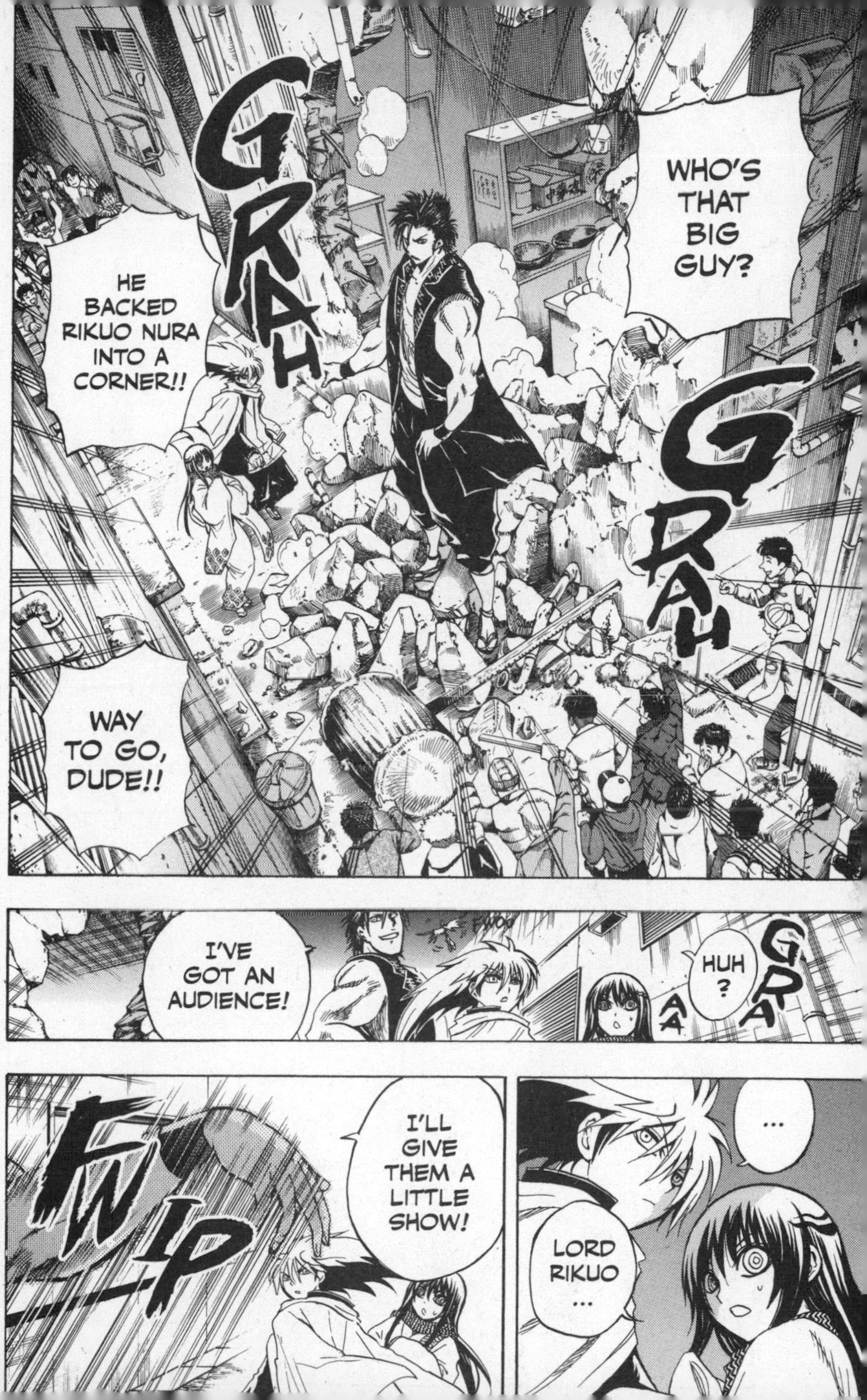
WHO'S THAT BIG GUY?
GRAH
HE BACKED RIKUO NURA INTO A CORNER!!
GRAH
WAY TO GO, DUDE!!
GRA
AA
HUH?
FWOO
I'VE GOT AN AUDIENCE!
...
LORD RIKUO ...
I'LL GIVE THEM A LITTLE SHOW!
FWIP

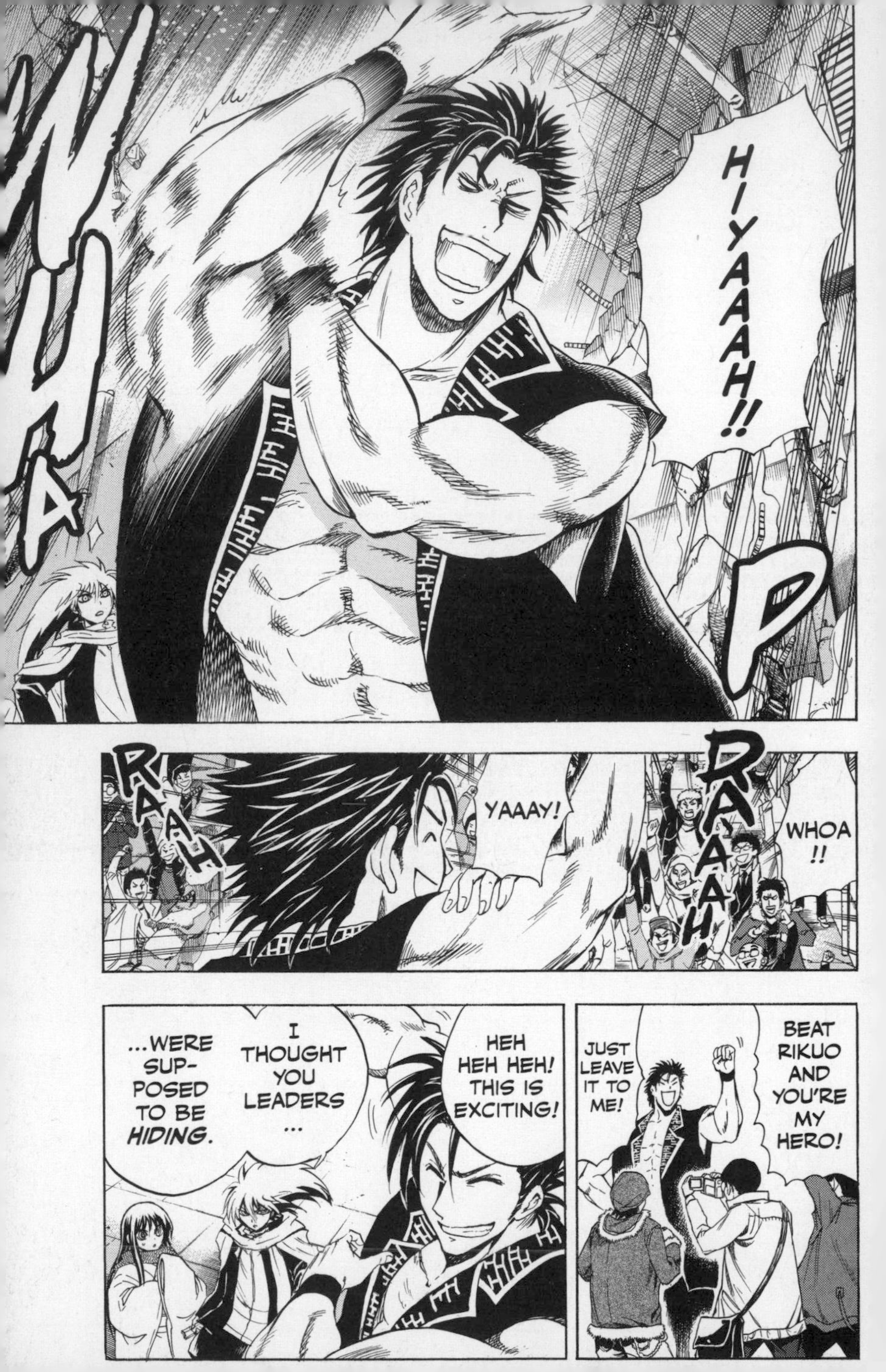
HIYAAAAH!!
WHOA !!
YAAAY!
BEAT RIKUO AND YOU'RE MY HERO!
JUST LEAVE IT TO ME!
HEH HEH HEH! THIS IS EXCITING!
I THOUGHT YOU LEADERS ...
...WERE SUP-POSED TO BE *HIDING*.

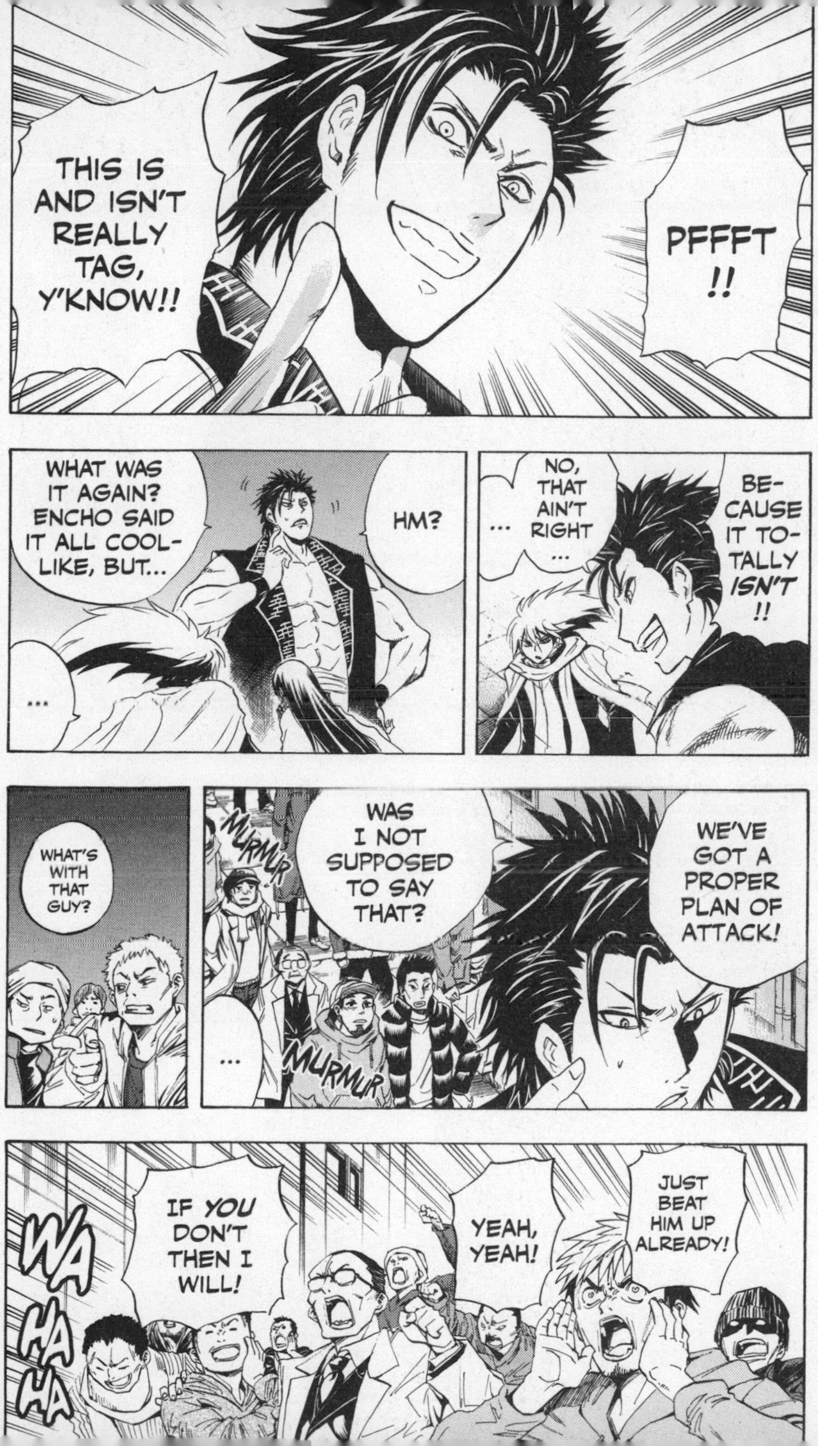
PFFFT !!
THIS IS AND ISN'T REALLY TAG, Y'KNOW!!
BE-CAUSE IT TO-TALLY *ISN'T* !!
NO, THAT AIN'T RIGHT ...
...
HM?
WHAT WAS IT AGAIN? ENCHO SAID IT ALL COOL-LIKE, BUT...
...
WE'VE GOT A PROPER PLAN OF ATTACK!
WAS I NOT SUPPOSED TO SAY THAT?
MURMUR
MURMUR
...
WHAT'S WITH THAT GUY?
JUST BEAT HIM UP ALREADY!
YEAH, YEAH!
IF *YOU* DON'T THEN I WILL!
WA HA HA HA

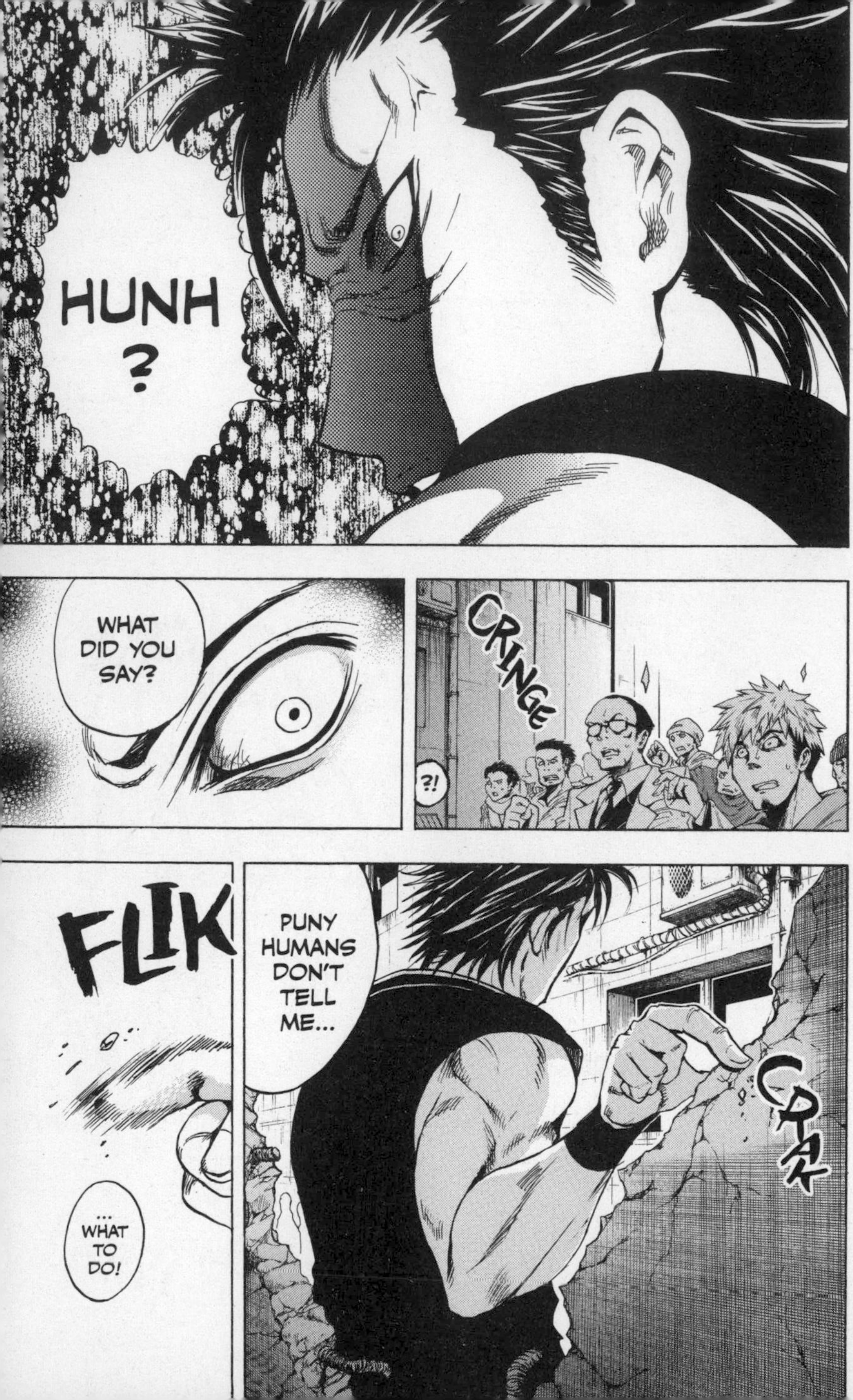
HUNH ?
CRINGE
?!
WHAT DID YOU SAY?
PUNY HUMANS DON'T TELL ME...
CRAK
FLIK
...WHAT TO DO!

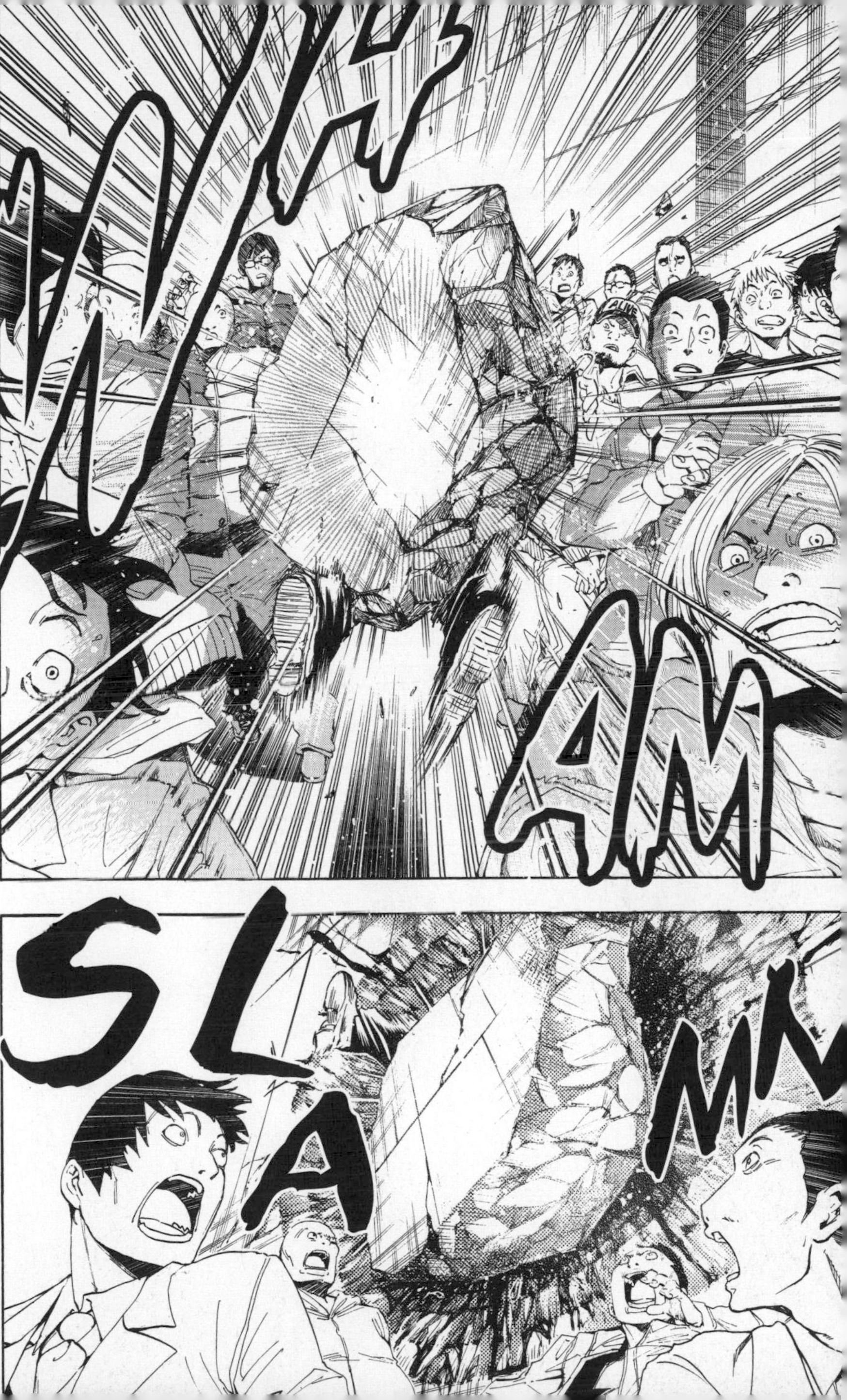
WHAM
SLAMM

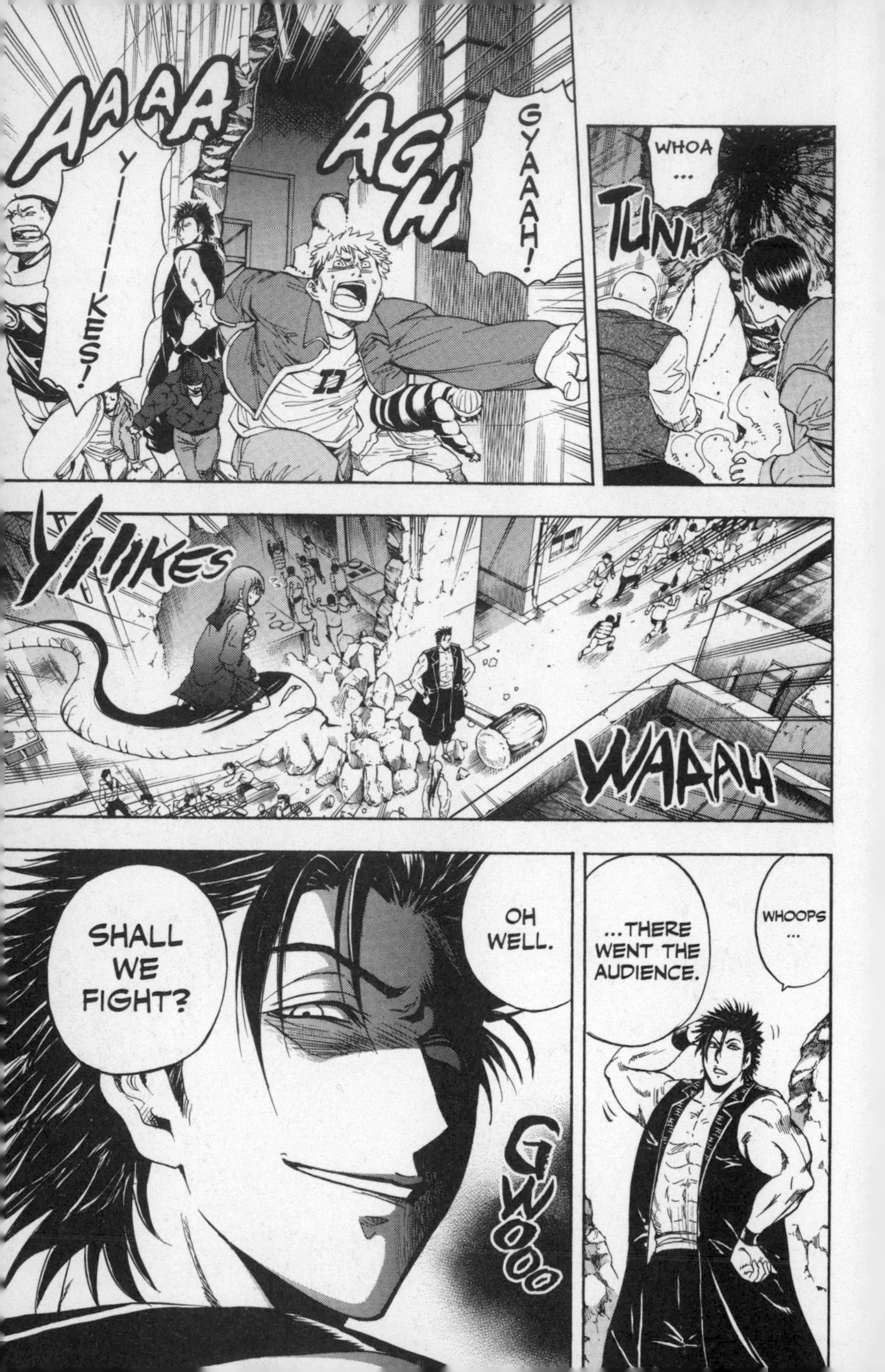
WHOA ...
TUNK
GYAAAH!
AGH
AAAA
Y-I-I-IKES!
YIIIKES
WAAAH
WHOOPS ...
...THERE WENT THE AUDIENCE.
OH WELL.
SHALL WE FIGHT?
GWOOO

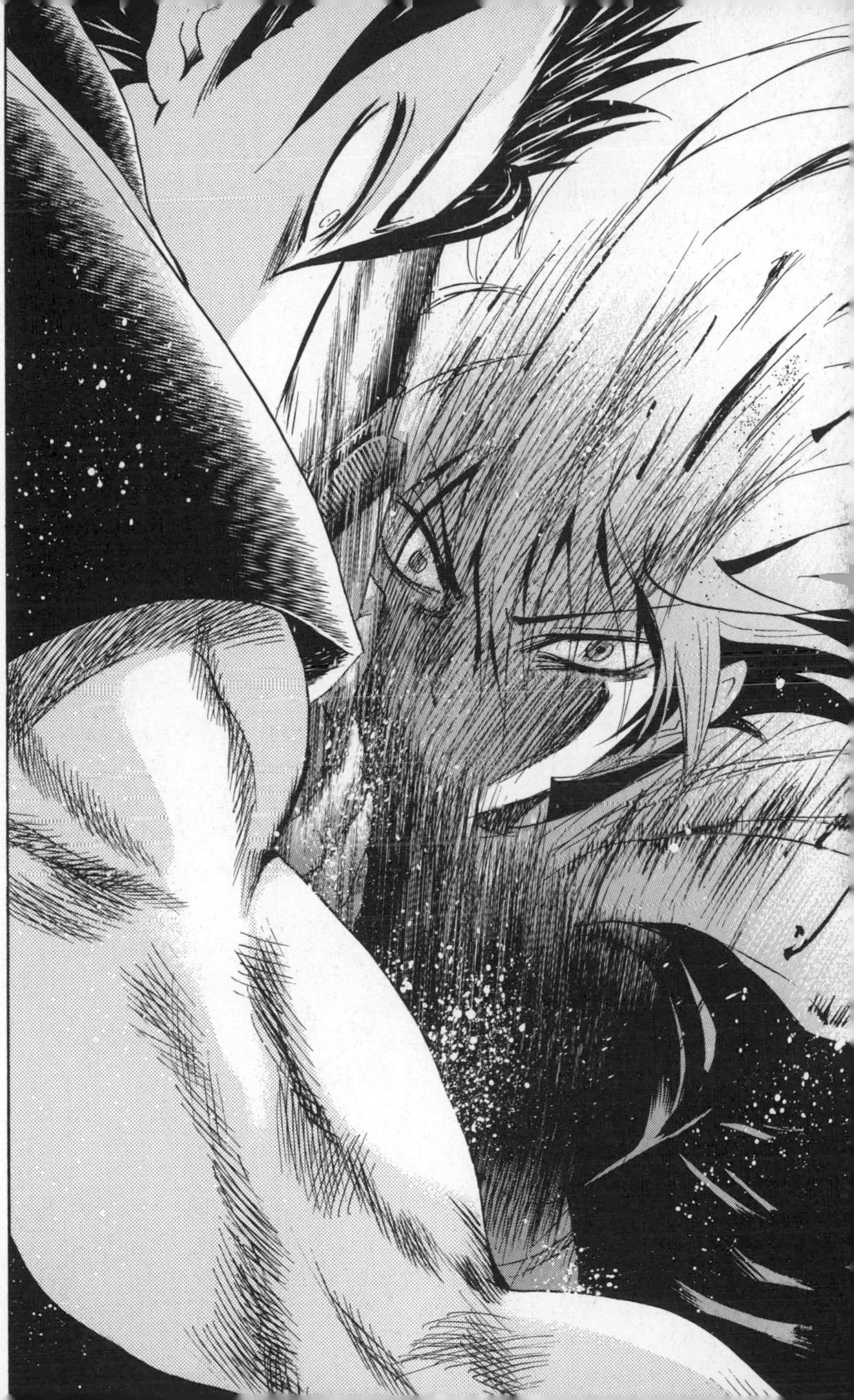

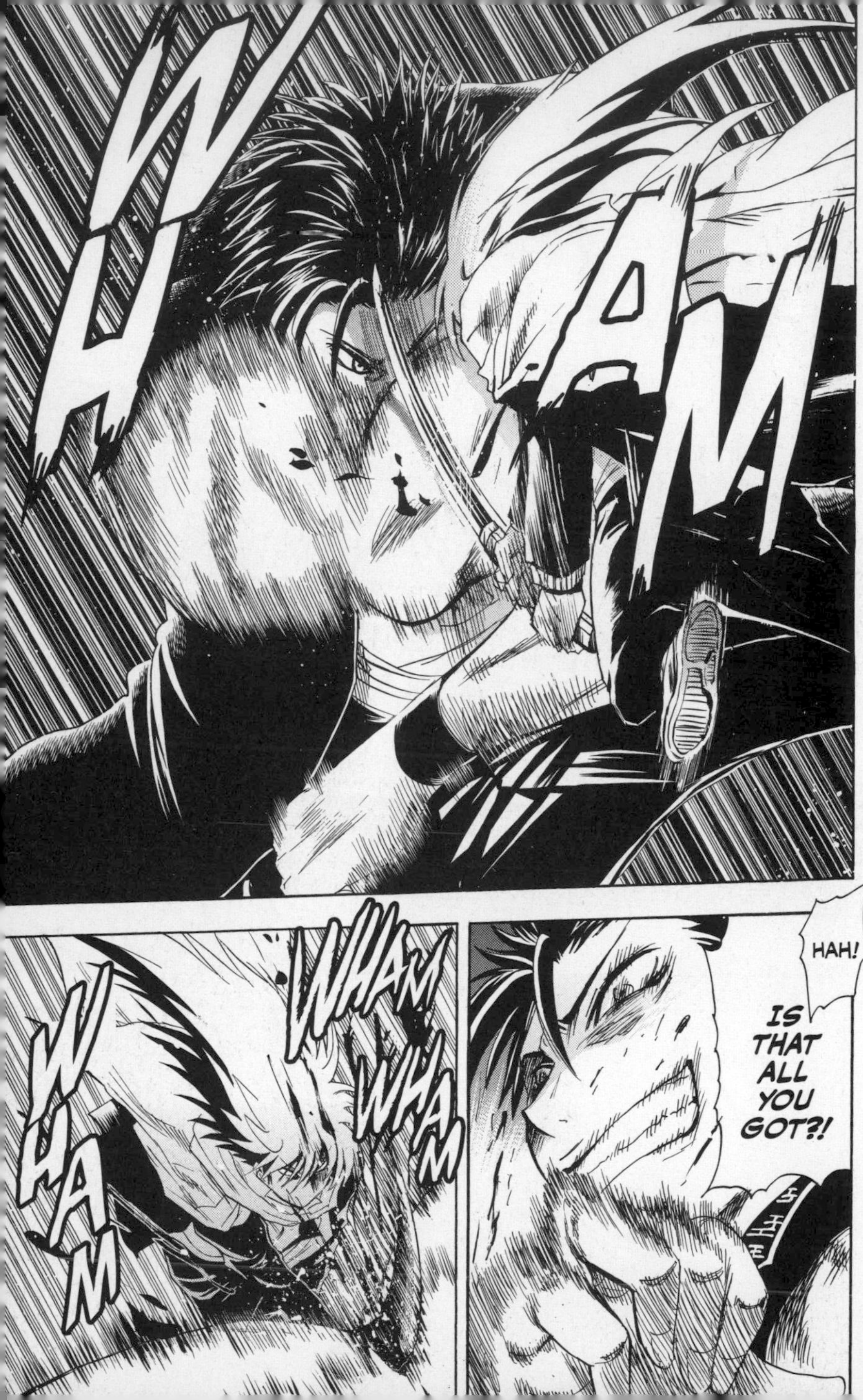
WHAM
HAH!
IS THAT ALL YOU GOT?!
WHAM
WHAM
WHAM

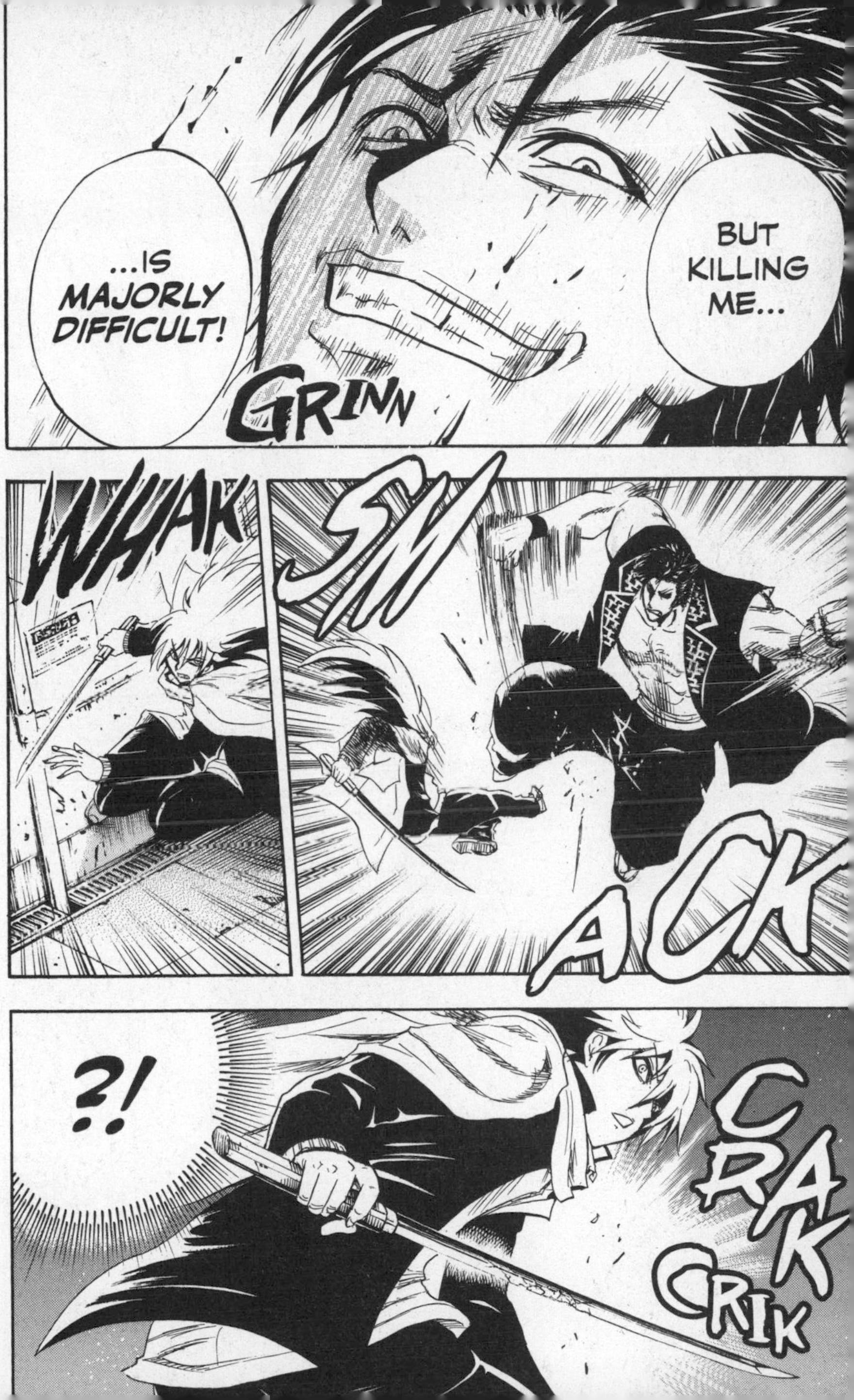
BUT KILLING ME...
...IS MAJORLY DIFFICULT!
GRINN
SM
ACK
WHAK
CRAK
CRIK
?!

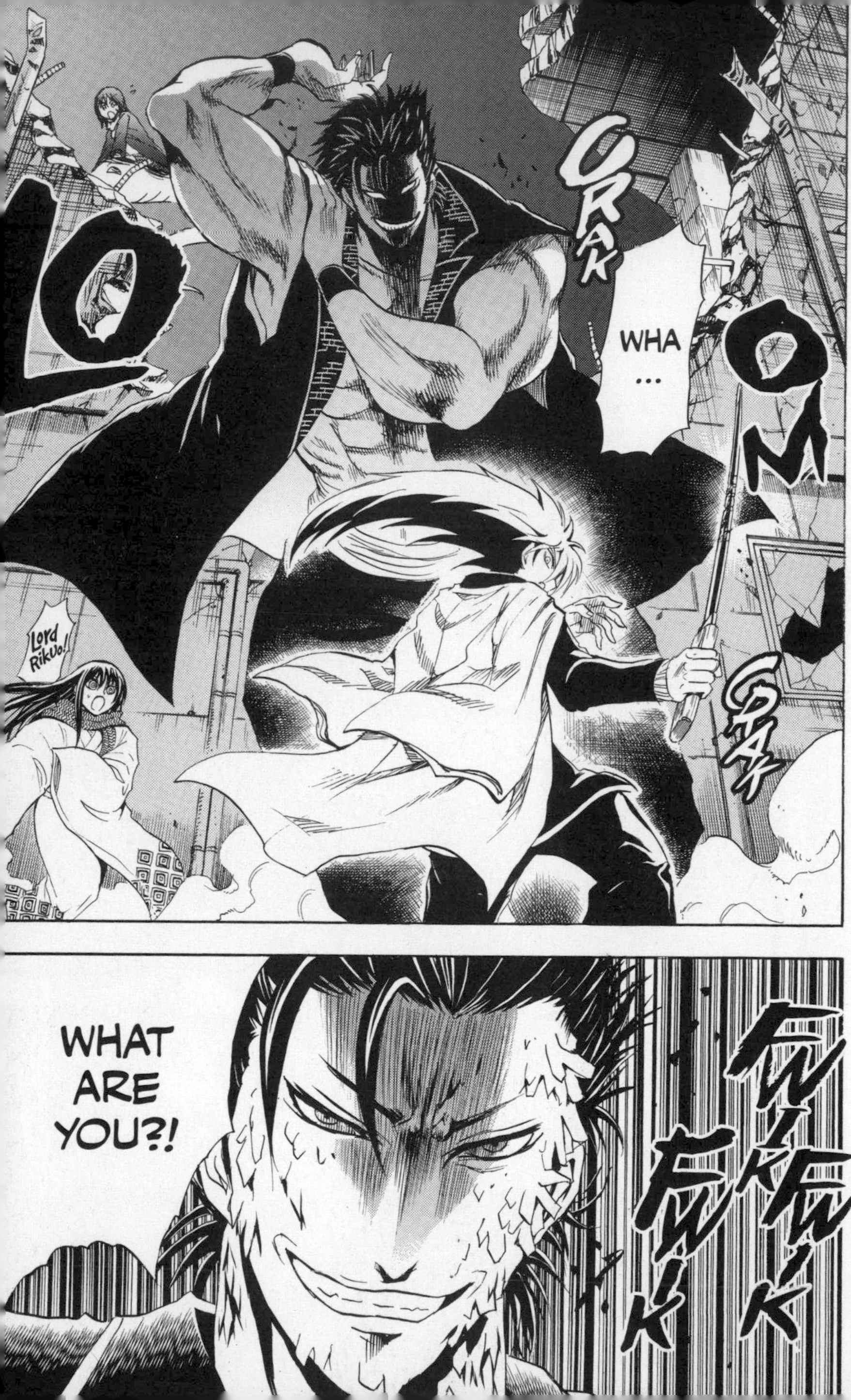
CRAK
WHA ...
CRAK
Lord Rikuo!
WHAT ARE YOU?!
FWIK FWIK

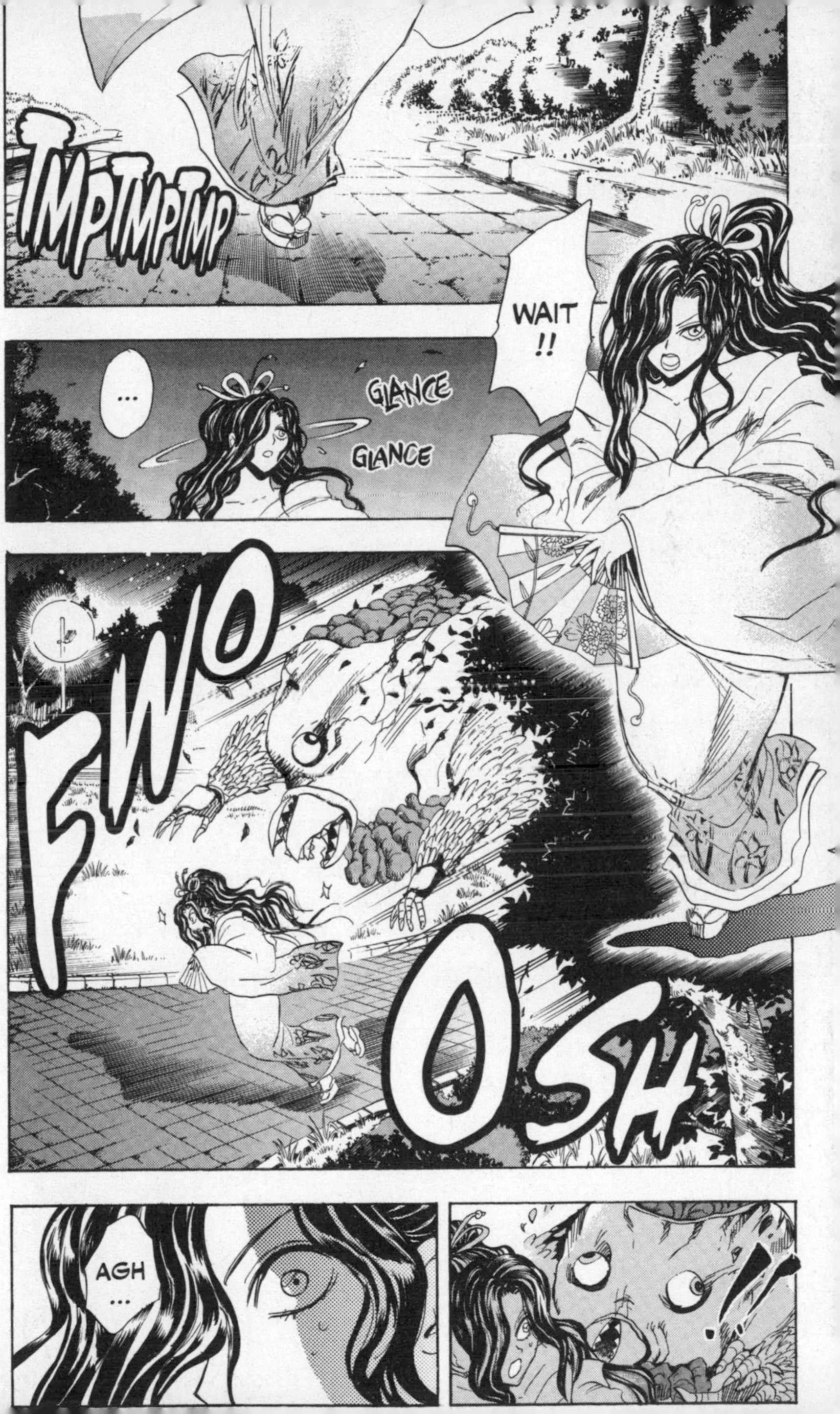
TMPTMPTMP
WAIT !!
GLANCE
GLANCE
...
FWOOSH
!
AGH ...

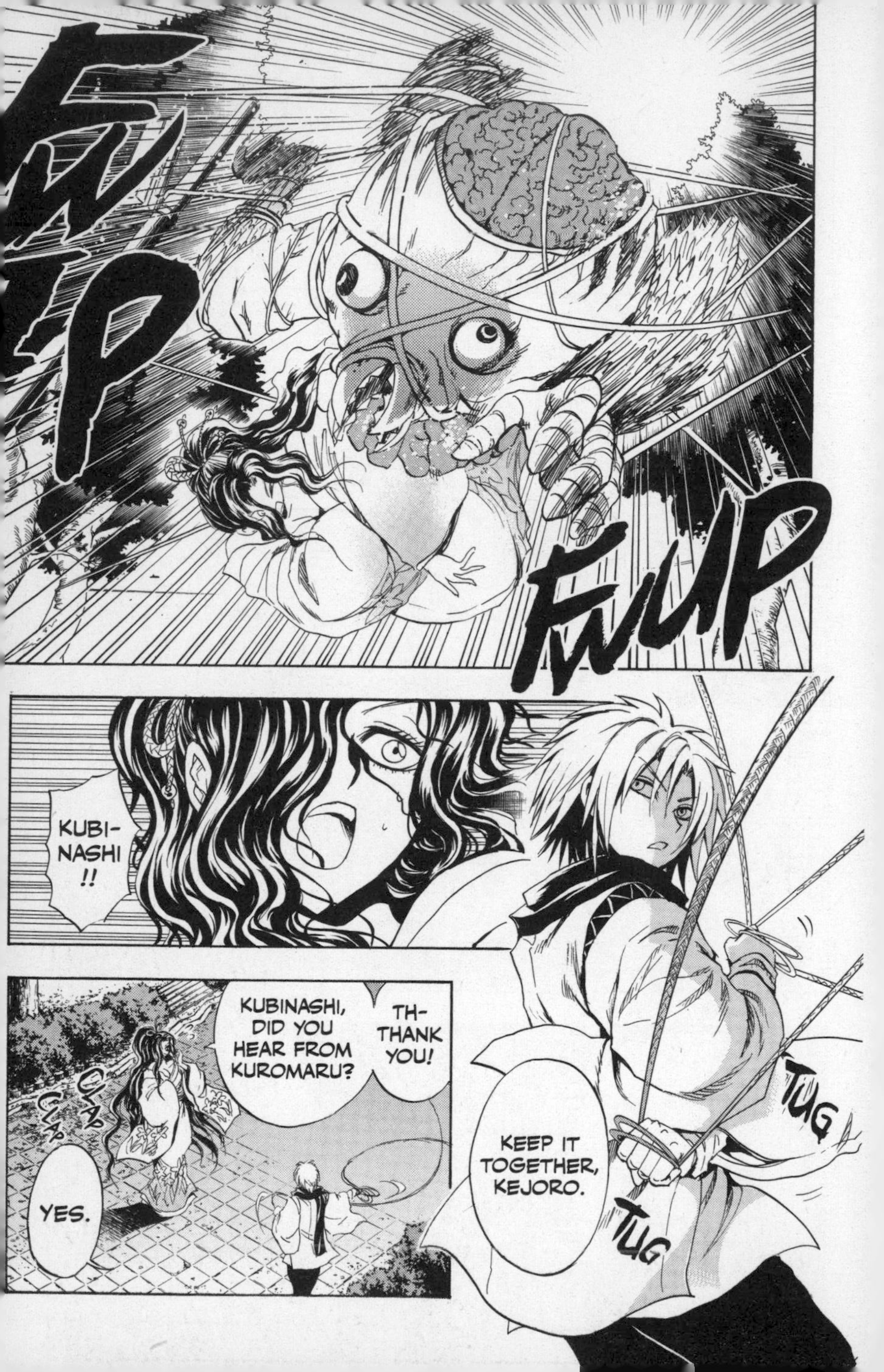
FWUP
TUG
TUG
KEEP IT TOGETHER, KEJORO.
KUBI-NASHI !!
TH-THANK YOU!
KUBINASHI, DID YOU HEAR FROM KUROMARU?
CLAP CLAP
YES.

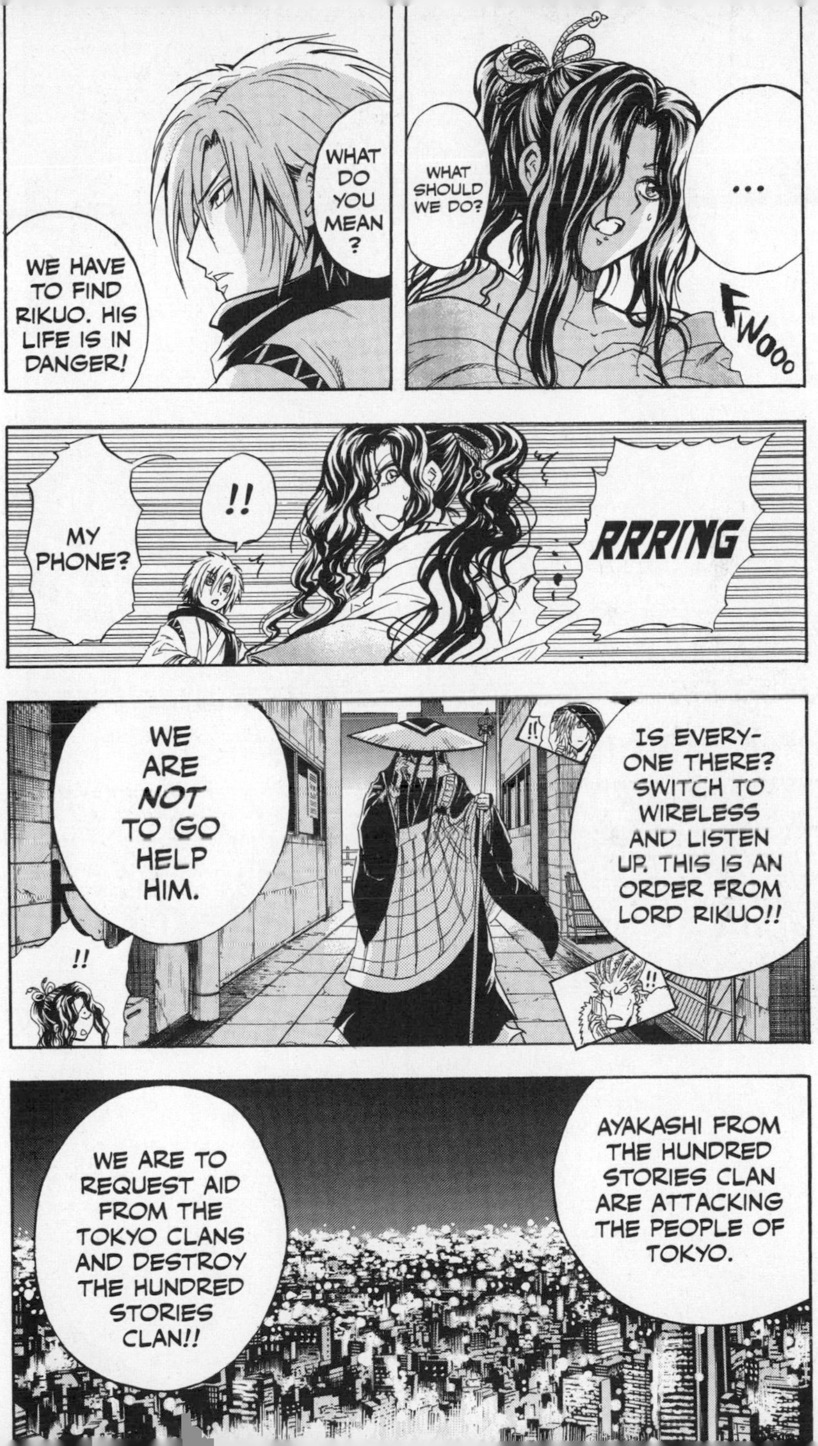
...
WHAT SHOULD WE DO?
FWOOO
WHAT DO YOU MEAN?
WE HAVE TO FIND RIKUO. HIS LIFE IS IN DANGER!
RRRING
!!
MY PHONE?
IS EVERY-ONE THERE? SWITCH TO WIRELESS AND LISTEN UP. THIS IS AN ORDER FROM LORD RIKUO!!
!!
!!
WE ARE NOT TO GO HELP HIM.
!!
AYAKASHI FROM THE HUNDRED STORIES CLAN ARE ATTACKING THE PEOPLE OF TOKYO.
WE ARE TO REQUEST AID FROM THE TOKYO CLANS AND DESTROY THE HUNDRED STORIES CLAN!!

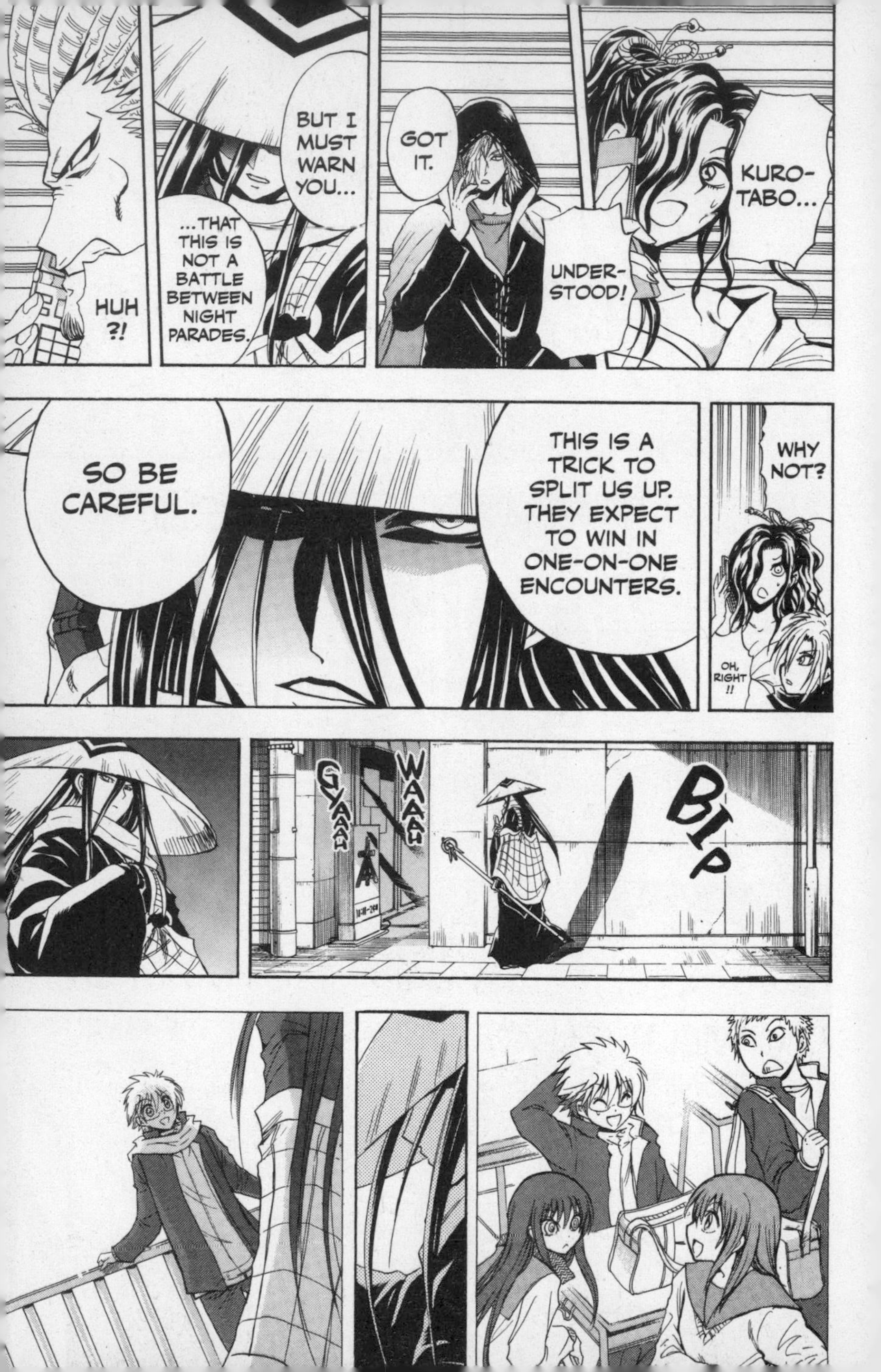
KURO-TABO...
UNDER-STOOD!
GOT IT.
BUT I MUST WARN YOU...
...THAT THIS IS NOT A BATTLE BETWEEN NIGHT PARADES.
HUH ?!
WHY NOT?
OH, RIGHT !!
THIS IS A TRICK TO SPLIT US UP. THEY EXPECT TO WIN IN ONE-ON-ONE ENCOUNTERS.
SO BE CAREFUL.
BIP
WAAAH
GYAAAH

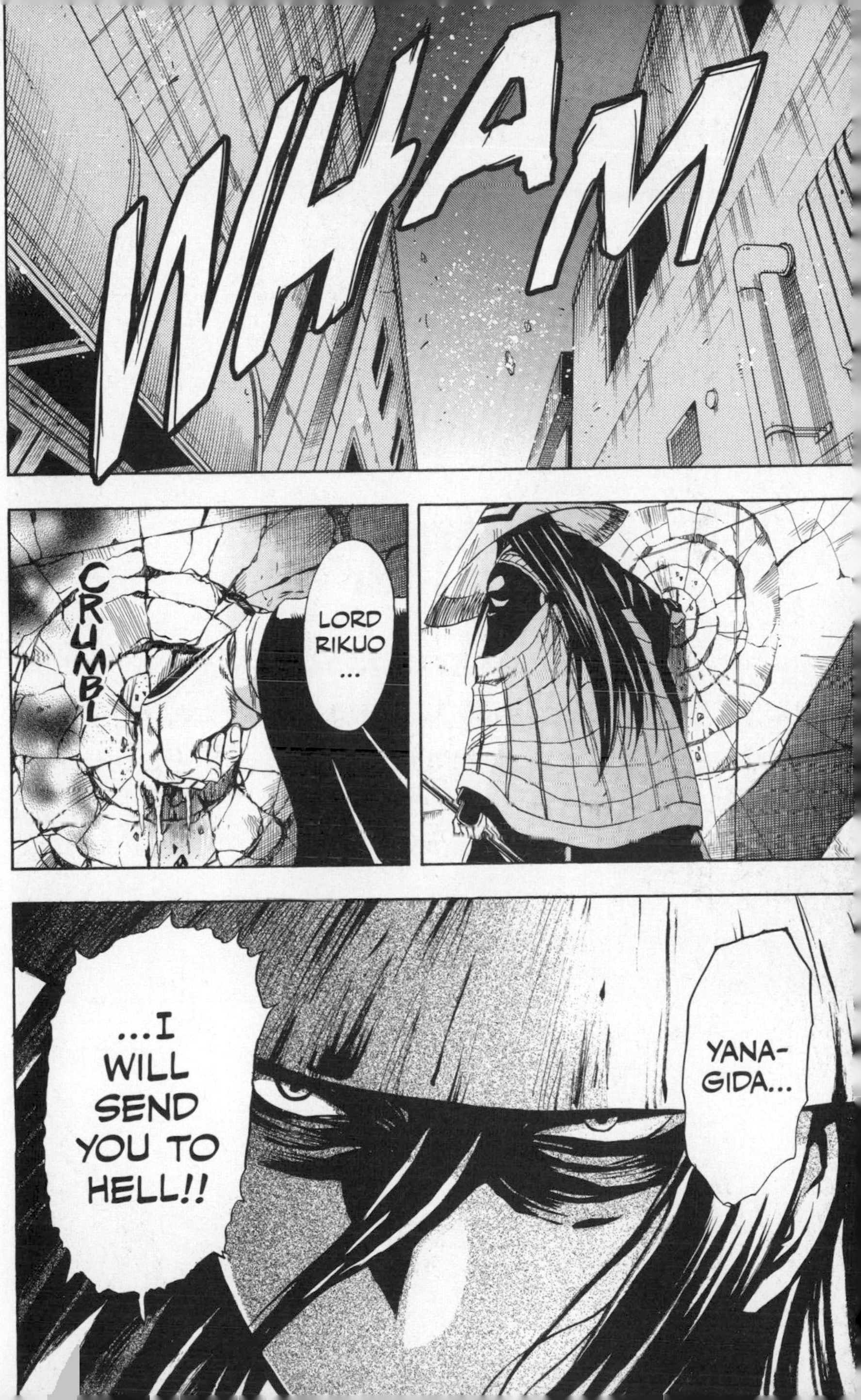
WHAM
LORD RIKUO ...
CRUMBL
YANA-GIDA...
...I WILL SEND YOU TO HELL!!

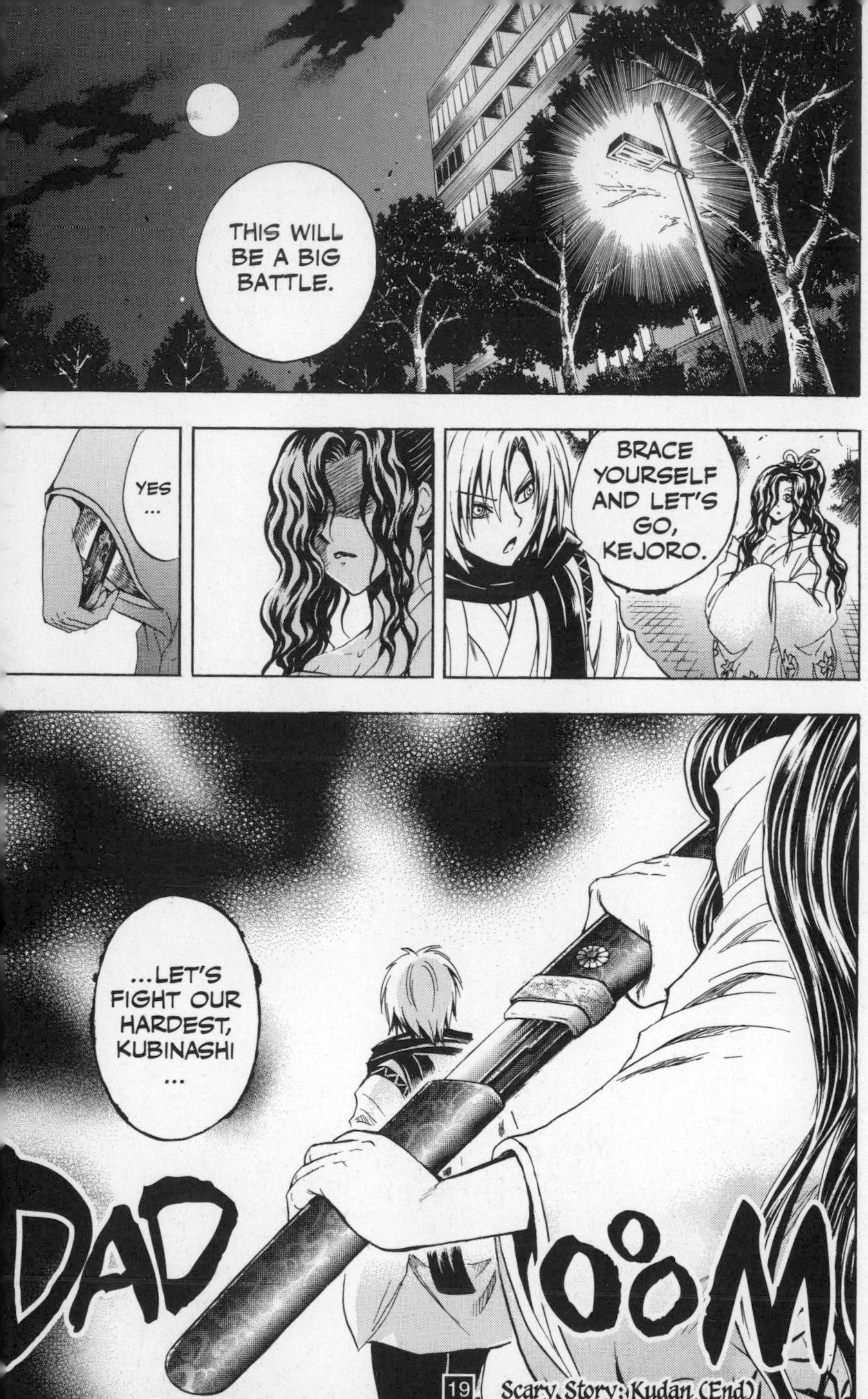
THIS WILL BE A BIG BATTLE.
BRACE YOURSELF AND LET'S GO, KEJORO.
YES ...
...LET'S FIGHT OUR HARDEST, KUBINASHI ...
DAD
OOOM

Scary Story: Kudan (End)

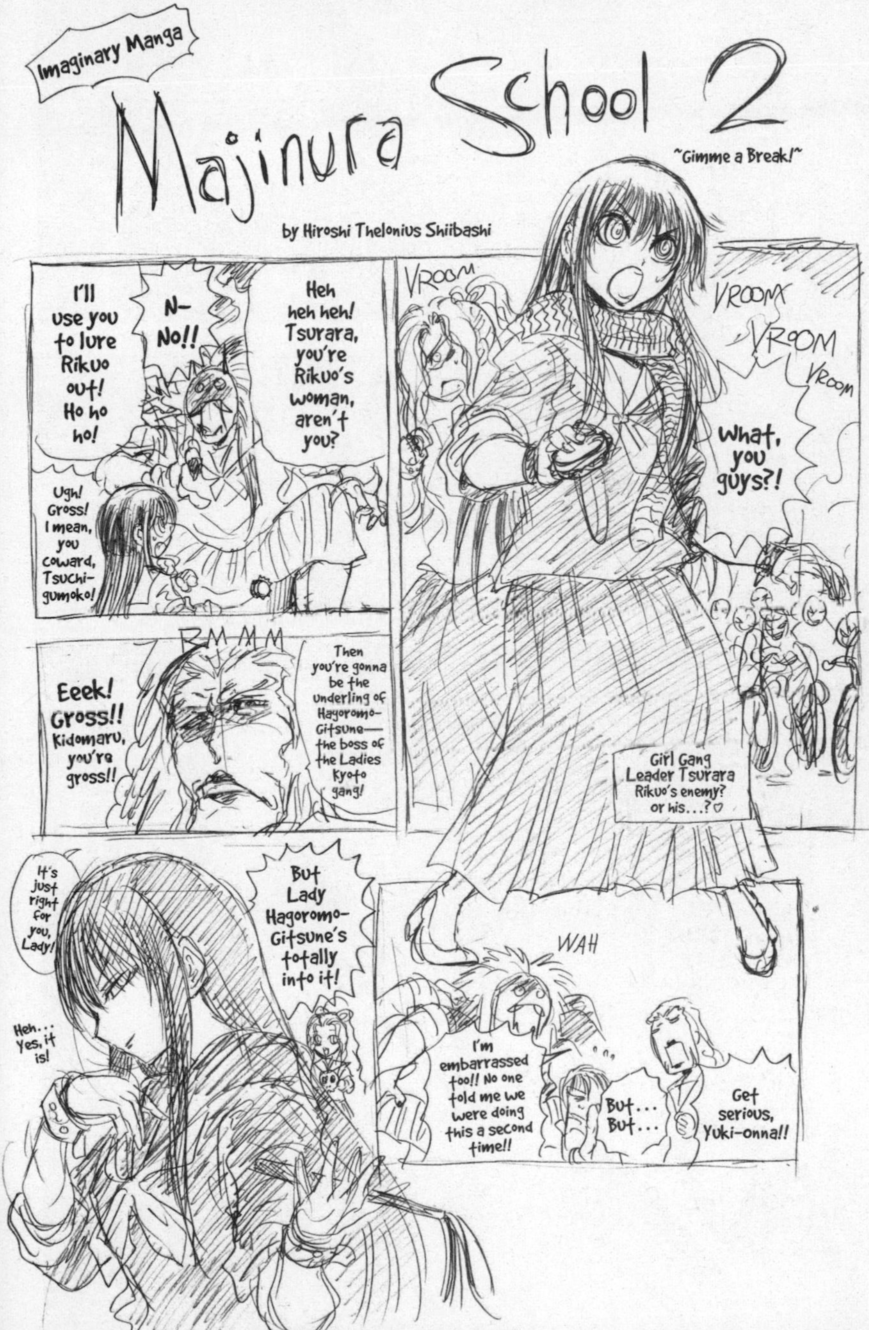
Imaginary Manga
Majinura School 2
~Gimme a Break!~
by Hiroshi Thelonius Shiibashi
VROOM
VROOM
Vroom
VROOM
What, you guys?!
Girl Gang Leader Tsurara Rikuo's enemy? or his...? ♡
Heh heh heh! Tsurara, you're Rikuo's woman, aren't you?
N- No!!
I'll use you to lure Rikuo out! Ho ho ho!
Ugh! Gross! I mean, you coward, Tsuchigumoko!
BMMM
Then you're gonna be the underling of Hagoromo-Gitsune—the boss of the Ladies Kyoto gang!
Eeek! Gross!! Kidomaru, you're gross!!
WAH
Get serious, Yuki-onna!!
But... But...
I'm embarrassed too!! No one told me we were doing this a second time!!
But Lady Hagoromo-Gitsune's totally into it!
It's just right for you, Lady!
Heh... Yes, it is!

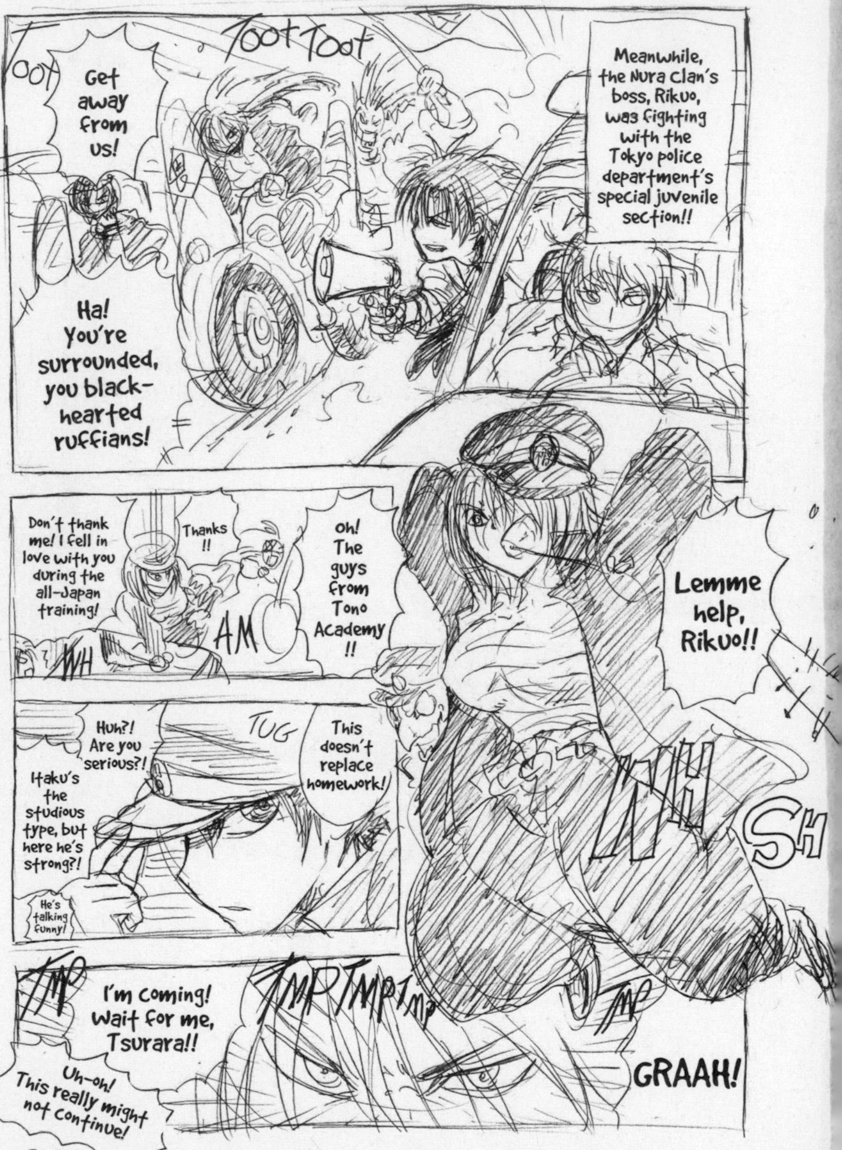

Meanwhile, the Nura Clan's boss, Rikuo, was fighting with the Tokyo police department's special juvenile section!!
TOOT TOOT
Get away from us!
TOOT
Ha! You're surrounded, you black-hearted ruffians!
Lemme help, Rikuo!!
WH
SH
Oh! The guys from Tono Academy!!
Thanks!!
Don't thank me! I fell in love with you during the all-Japan training!
AM
WH
This doesn't replace homework!
TUG
Huh?! Are you serious?!
Itaku's the studious type, but here he's strong?!
He's talking funny!
GRAAH!
TMP
TMP TMP TMP
I'm coming! Wait for me, Tsurara!!
TMP
Uh-oh! This really might not continue!
The End

IN THE NEXT VOLUME...
KUSOZU

Thanks to rumors, all of Tokyo is terrified of Rikuo and wants him dead! But Rikuo's got other problems too. In Shibuya, a yokai is turning human girls into monsters. And the yokai has a special spell in store for Rikuo when he tries to stop him.

AVAILABLE APRIL 2014!